D0331055

REDBOOK'S
WISE WOMAN'S DIET® COOKBOOK

REDBOOK'S
WISE WOMAN'S DIET® COOKBOOK

EDITED BY
Ruth Fairchild Pomeroy

NAL BOOKS
NEW AMERICAN LIBRARY
TIMES MIRROR
NEW YORK AND SCARBOROUGH, ONTARIO

Copyright © 1967, 1968, 1969, 1970, 1971, 1972, 1973, 1974, 1975, 1976, 1977, 1978, 1979, 1980, 1981, 1982, 1983 by The Hearst Corporation.

Wise Woman's Diet is a registered trademark of *Redbook* Magazine.

All rights reserved. For information address The New American Library, Inc.

Published simultaneously in Canada by The New American Library of Canada Limited.

NAL BOOKS TRADEMARK REG. U.S. PAT. OFF. AND FOREIGN COUNTRIES
REGISTERED TRADEMARK—MARCA REGISTRADA
HECHO EN HARRISONBURG, VA., U.S.A.

SIGNET, SIGNET CLASSICS, MENTOR, PLUME, MERIDIAN and NAL BOOKS are published *in the United States* by The New American Library, Inc., 1633 Broadway, New York, New York 10019, *in Canada* by The New American Library of Canada Limited, 81 Mack Avenue, Scarborough, Ontario M1L 1M8

Designed by Julian Hamer

Library of Congress Cataloging in Publication Data
Main entry under title:
Redbook's Wise woman's diet cookbook.
Includes index.
1. Low-calorie diet—Recipes.   I. Pomeroy, Ruth Fairchild.
II. Redbook.   III. Title: Wise woman's diet cookbook.
RM222.2.R433   1983   641.5′635   82-22467
ISBN 0-453-00436-9

First Printing, April, 1983

1   2   3   4   5   6   7   8   9

PRINTED IN THE UNITED STATES OF AMERICA

Acknowledgments

The Food and Nutrition Staff and the Editors of *Redbook* are grateful:

To Dr. George Christakis and his staff at the Nutrition Division of the Department of Health of the City of New York, who had the vision to develop a nutritionally balanced, calorie-restricted diet that catered to the tastes of eight different ethnic groups in New York and provided proof that if people could eat the foods they liked, dieting could be a pleasure. Their diet plan became *Redbook*'s first Wise Woman's Diet® in the January 1967 issue of the magazine. Dr. Christakis is today Chief of the Nutrition Division, Department of Epidemiology and Public Health at the University of Miami School of Medicine.

To Dr. Johanna Dwyer, director of the Frances Stern Nutrition Center, New England Medical Center Hospital, in Boston; Dr. Jules Hirsch, professor and senior physician to Rockefeller University Hospital in New York City; and Dr. Myron Winick, director of the Institute of Human Nutrition at Columbia University in New York City, our board of consultants since 1975 who have approved, enhanced, offered invaluable suggestions, updated and kept correct each development of *Redbook*'s Wise Woman's Diet.

And, indeed, to the *Redbook* readers who have participated in using the diet under observation, have written to say what they liked or didn't like about the diet, have made suggestions for ways the diet could better fit their life-styles; they have been our real taste-testers for the development and selection of the menus and recipes in this book.

Contents

Foreword

The most special letters we receive at *Redbook* are those from women who have discovered the Wise Woman's Diet. If you're wondering why this is *the* diet that works, one that is right for you, listen to what other women who had the same doubts have to say:

> *I would like to tell you that this Wise Woman's Diet is the best I've ever encountered. My husband and I started on the diet three weeks ago and I have lost 5½ pounds and he's lost a whopping 12!*
>
> Susan M. Tennison
> Manchaca, Texas

> *I am so delighted with the Wise Woman's Diet. It is so wonderful to have someone else plan the balanced meals and figure out the portions and determine the calories and have the scrumptious recipes easily available. With the Wise Woman's Diet I could diet forever.*
>
> Mrs. H. Rodenberg
> Lansing, Illinois

> *I am one of your biggest fans; one year ago I started on your Wise Woman's Diet and lost 20 pounds and have been able to keep it off! For six weeks or so I prepared almost all the diet dishes— some of them I liked so well that I still use them occasionally.*
>
> Mrs. Diana Sell
> Liberty Center, Indiana

If the diet works, does it involve cooking one meal for yourself and another for your family? Or does it mean being restricted to just a few foods and eating them until you're sick of them? Listen again:

> *My family and I have enjoyed tremendously the recipes in the Wise Woman's Diet. This is the first time we have dieted and eaten so well. My husband raved about the Basic Vinaigrette Dressing and I intend to serve the Skinny Tangerine Cheesecake to company—it is so delicious."*
>
> Jeane A. Swanton
> Holbrook, Massachusetts

With some reserve I started the Wise Woman's Diet and even followed some recipes to the letter that I felt I surely would not care for. They turned out to be good and I got so that I looked forward to seeing what tomorrow's menu would provide for me. My friend agreed with me when I served her one of my diet meals—she and her husband start their diets tomorrow!

Carla Wilks
Racine, Wisconsin

The Wise Woman's Diet doesn't require a radical change in eating habits. It requires some, of course, because you need to shed fattening old habits and develop new ones—ones that are going to help you lose weight and keep it off forever. The secret is in the portion sizes and cooking techniques. With the Wise Woman's Diet, you'll learn new ways to prepare favorite family recipes. Will the food taste good? Will it be difficult to prepare?

This diet, unlike others I have tried, satisfies my aesthetic interest in food and I have found that the energy I normally put into eating I am now putting into choosing and preparing the food.

Barbara Carnes
Fort Collins, Colorado

I have been truly impressed with how palatable the dishes are— and from a person who is very calorie-minded and fussy I want to say thanks!

Ms. Pamela G. Neilson
Arlington, Virginia

The Wise Woman's Diet helps you learn while you lose. You'll become a low-calorie cooking expert; you'll absorb valuable information about portions, calories and the foods you need for good nutrition. You'll be equipped to make valuable decisions about food for the rest of your life.

Though I rarely diet, I use my collection of Wise Woman's Diet recipes all the time, because I like the way the food tastes, because it's a healthy way to eat and because it's reassuring when I'm not dieting to know that what I'm eating is relatively low in calories.

Flora Davis
Princeton, New Jersey

I have wanted to write to tell you for some time now how much I enjoy and appreciate the Wise Woman's Diet. Although my husband and I are not "dieters" as such, these recipes are wonderfully enjoyable for us. They are simply delicious.

Kathy Gongaware
Delmont, Pennsylvania

There's one frequent question about the Wise Woman's Diet that we haven't been able to answer affirmatively—until now:

Have you ever published all the Wise Woman's Diets together in one volume? They would make a terrific cookbook.

> (Mrs.) Merrill Baylor
> Stroudsburg, Pennsylvania

The Wise Woman's Diet is by far the best and the easiest to stick with I have ever seen. I only wish you could compile all of these terrific recipes into one cookbook. I would be the first in line to buy it.

> Cheryl C. Smith
> Lexington, Kentucky

Please, please—won't you issue this wonderful, healthful diet plan in its entirety in book form?

> Mrs. Meredith Payne Schwirtz
> Kentfield, California

We hope that the great variety of foods in *Redbook*'s diet menus and recipes will surprise you and give you a new perspective on dieting. We also hope it will help you discover a new way of eating that will reward you with the confidence that you are in control of what you eat.

> ELIZABETH ALSTON
> Food and Nutrition Editor
> *Redbook* Magazine

Your Introduction to the Diet That Really Works

The diet you are about to meet in this book is one you'll be glad to know because it's filled with promises it can keep. On it you will lose weight, enjoy the foods you eat, never feel hungry, know you're eating all the right foods you need to feel better and look better and learn that this can be the end of any radical ups and downs in your weight.

If you've been an on-again, off-again dieter, never able to stay with a diet long enough to get to or keep your ideal weight, stop here and do three things: First, flip through this book, read a few of the menus and recipes and discover what experienced users of this diet have learned—that dieting doesn't have to be dull. If Baked Ziti, Barbecued Ribs, Roast Stuffed Capon, Apple Pie and Cream Puffs with Chocolate Sauce sound good to you, be assured they're all on this diet. Second, give up right now the idea that you were fated to be a little or a lot too fat for life; the alternative is to discover the lean-cooking techniques in these recipes, to be satisfied with reasonable servings of food and to enjoy eating to be slim. Third, read on; don't skip over the rest of this introduction. You'll learn a lot about yourself, your food habits and how painless it's really going to be to make this the last diet you'll ever need to use. And know that once you weigh what you want to weigh, you can keep the pounds off with the 1,800-calorie menus in Chapter 8 and the do-it-yourself instructions in Chapter 9.

How Much Will You Lose?

On this diet, designed for a safe, steady weight loss at 1,200 calories a day, most dieters will lose about 2 pounds a week. Your present weight, age, body type and activity all influence how much you will lose

1

and how fast. Big, heavy people will always have a more dramatic weight loss than smaller people or people who have just a little to lose. In fact, smaller people may need to shave calories down to 1,000 a day to lose weight. It's not a good idea to cut calories beyond that number and impossible to maintain a nutritionally balanced diet at fewer than 1,000 calories per day.

Because this is a nutritionally balanced diet you may stay on it for as long as it takes to reach your ideal weight. Though you probably wouldn't wish to, you could choose to have a different set of diet meals every day for 4½ months; that's how long it would take to sample each of the 124 1,200-calorie-day menus in this book.

When to Diet and When Not to

No one knows better than you when you need to diet. When last year's slacks won't button at the waist, when you always add a disguising jacket to a skirt and blouse outfit, when a tent-dress becomes your favorite, you need to get rid of some of the excess pounds. Looking better isn't the sole reason; feeling better physically and feeling better about yourself are equal rewards.

If you have more than 10 to 15 pounds to lose, check with your doctor before you begin; you may have health problems that need attention first or would dictate some food restrictions. Don't diet if you're pregnant or breast-feeding. When you're nourishing a growing fetus or an infant, your nutrient needs are different and you should work out your diet with your obstetrician. If you're in a stressful situation, it's best not to attempt to diet even though losing some weight may make you feel better. Try, until things are better, not to gain any more weight. Experiment, if you like, with the 1,800-calorie diets in Chapter 8.

Don't Start Tomorrow

Rushing into a diet can be a little like jumping into a pool before you know how to swim. Don't start a diet until you take stock of your eating habits and your ability to choose food wisely. Get a small notebook. Each morning when you get up, urinate, then weigh yourself on a good bathroom scale; record your weight in the notebook honestly, no wishful thinking.

Carry your notebook with you and write down everything you eat or drink (and how much) as soon as possible after eating. Rate portion sizes big, medium or small and don't forget to write down the snacks, if any. After a week of record-keeping, start consulting *Redbook's*

Up-to-Date Calorie Counter (page 319). At the end of each day estimate the number of calories you ate or drank.

How to Lose a Pound—or More

There's no magic to losing weight; the key is balancing the number of calories you eat with the number of calories you burn in the form of expended energy. A calorie is a measure of the energy a food will give; excess calories are stored in the body as fat amounting to added weight. Obviously, to lose weight you must eat fewer calories than you use each day to breathe, sleep, work, walk, play and digest your food.

Armed with the knowledge of what you've been eating, realize that to lose 1 pound you must take in 3,500 fewer calories a week—that's 500 less per day—than your body needs at its present weight to perform all the life processes. Therefore, if you eat 500 fewer calories each day you'll lose 1 pound in a week; 1,000 less, you'll lose 2 pounds. Realize that when you start to diet you'll probably lose more rapidly the first week because you'll lose some body fluid as well as fat. Then your weight loss will level off to the predicted rate, allowing for weekly fluctuations while your body adjusts to new eating patterns.

You and Your Family on a Diet

Because the meals on *Redbook*'s Wise Woman's Diet are nutritionally sound as well as appealing and satisfying, they can be shared by the family. Dieters don't have to feel conspicuous or deprived at mealtime toying with diet food while everyone else is enjoying a hearty meal. They simply trim their portions and enjoy the same food.

Men who want to lose weight should strive for a caloric intake of 1,600 calories a day to achieve a weight loss of about 2 pounds a week. If the man in your house is a serious dieter, share this introduction with him so he too can get a good idea where and how he's getting his excess calories. He can then increase portions of the 1,200-calorie diet to reach the 1,600 total.

Overweight children and teenagers do have special nutrient needs for proper growth. To manage their diets for weight control parents should consult a physician. However, the menus and recipes in this book can be safely enjoyed by all healthy persons of any age, providing they eat some of all of the foods included in any given day's menus, no matter whether they are eating diet-sized portions or larger portions. Skipping foods or their equivalent substitutes (see page 7) on the daily menus will upset the delicate balance of needed nutrients.

Set a Goal

Many dieters say, "I'd like to weigh what I weighed before I got married," or "I'd like to weigh what I weighed when I graduated from high school." Consult a good, recent height-weight chart to find the ideal weight range for your age and figure type. But be realistic; the ideal weight for you is the one at which you look and feel your best. Enter your present weight in the upper left-hand corner of a sheet of paper and your ideal weight in the lower left. Put it up in a conspicuous place—the refrigerator door will be a good reminder place—and record your losses on a downward curve. It looks more impressive than just recording figures.

It's Easier to Ease on Down

For some people, sticking to a 1,200-calorie diet overnight will be difficult. If you've been truly overeating, taking in far more calories than you need and steadily gaining weight, it may be easier, and more successful for you to start a gradual cutback to reach 1,200 calories a day. If your notebook says you've been eating 2,600 or more calories a day, try to cut back to about 2,000 calories a day for two days; plan the next two days at 1,800 calories. (The menus in Chapter 8 are calculated at that total.) For the next week allow yourself extras on the 1,200-diet menus to total 1,500 calories a day. Then aim for the 1,200-calorie diet. Your stomach won't shrink—that's a dieting misconception—but your appetite will adjust to fewer calories and less food. Even if it takes time, a slow weight loss is a good training period and you can be sure it will last much longer than a dramatic crash.

When You're Ready to Go

We recommend that you choose to start with Chapter 1, Eat the Foods You Love and Grow Thin. The menus and recipes there are great favorites that experienced dieters have said made them actually look forward to the meals, and they're all familiar foods that your family will enjoy sharing. Pick a week—there are four to choose from—and plan your shopping around those menus. If you must have such hazards as chocolate chip cookies or snack foods on hand for your family, set aside a special cupboard place for them that, for a while, will simply be off-limits for you.

How to Use Redbook's Wise Woman's Diet

Calorie counts appear in parentheses after each food listed on the menus. Whenever an asterisk appears before a menu item it indicates that a recipe follows. All of the menu serving portions are for one person—the dieter. Most menus are planned for three meals a day— breakfast, lunch and dinner; some weekends suggest a brunch and many menus include snack foods to eat any time. To make the diets as flexible as possible and suitable to your time and tastes,

You May:
- Switch meals around to suit yourself—eat lunch for dinner, dinner for breakfast.
- Save parts of meals for same-day snacks. Sometimes eating more frequently helps dieters.
- Redesign the menus to reduce your cooking time and please your personal taste, so long as the calorie total and food choices remain the same.
- Change the menus to take advantage of leftovers.
- Splurge occasionally, but stick as close as you can to diet portions.
- Season foods freely with herbs, horseradish, lemon juice, mustard, pepper, spices and vinegar. However, use salt and soy sauce sparingly; a high sodium (salt) intake can hamper your weight loss.
- Drink as much as you want of black coffee, clear tea, club soda, water. Go lightly on bouillon and consommé; they're low in calories but high in salt content.
- Tailor the diet to suit your tastes, but only by choosing from the Food Substitution List on page 7.

Alas, You May Not:
- Use milk in your coffee unless you subtract it from your daily milk allowance.
- Skip any of the major foods or snacks in the menus. They are there to give the needed nutrients.
- Add extra portions or foods not on the menu.
- Increase portion sizes.

HOW TO USE *REDBOOK*'S WISE WOMAN'S DIET RECIPES

In every recipe the diet serving allowance is stated at the end of the recipe. Also you will find either the yield (often stated in cups) or a suggested number of servings that allows for non-dieters eating larger portions. Only you can be the judge of how much nondieting members of your family will eat. It's a good idea to check recipe servings before you make up a recipe to be certain it will feed your family adequately. You may want to double some recipes.

If you're cooking for one or two, some recipes may need to be halved.

Recipe portions for dieters are usually given in cups or in normal portions such as 1 potato or apple or orange. Sometimes the diet serving is given as a portion (such as ¼) of the recipe when that is easier to use than a cup measure. The exception is in some preparations of meat, poultry and fish where the diet portion is necessarily stated in ounces because of the varying sizes of the cut of meat, the bird or the fish you may start with. Until you get used to knowing what 4 ounces of bone-in meat or 3 ounces of boneless looks like, it's best to get a small, inexpensive scale. Once you can visualize these common portions it isn't necessary to weigh in unless it's something you haven't judged before.

Leftovers may best be handled by freezing. If, for example, you have leftover New England Cod Chowder (Chapter 1, Menu 2), freeze one or more portions and use it to replace the salmon in Chapter 1, Menu 8. Look ahead to find a suitable spot for leftovers you plan to refrigerate; you know from experience they're a temptation to nibble.

HAVE A LITTLE FREEDOM

You are not expected to be a slave to the diet menus exactly as they appear in this book. If, for example, your family size is such that a meatloaf would last you to the point of boredom, make a simple broiled hamburger and munch the vegetable ingredients in the meatloaf separately. If you've rye bread on hand, don't feel compelled to go and buy a loaf of whole-wheat bread for one serving. You may substitute foods you prefer for those listed in the menus, but only if you choose a substitute from the same food group listed in the Food Substitution List, page 7, and choose it in a portion size that will keep the total calories for the day at or near 1,200.

Redbook's Wise Woman's Diet menus in Chapters 1, 2, 3, 4, 6 and 8 have been designed to provide a variety of foods and nutritional balance in each week's plan and we urge you to stick to a complete week's menus as far as possible. You may shift Thursday's meals to Monday, trade Friday's menus for Tuesday. You may even dip into another week's menus if they appeal to you. When you do that, it's preferable to substitute a chicken dinner for another chicken dinner, pasta for pasta, fish for fish, and use the alternate day's full menu.

Be prepared to enjoy this diet and be confident that you can weigh what you want to weigh always—in good form, good health and with a new appreciation of food that's good for you.

Redbook's
Food Substitution List

You may juggle diet menu items to suit your food preferences, but only if you choose a substitute from a like group of food in portions that will match as nearly as possible the calorie count listed on the diet menu.

Breads and Potatoes (includes cereals, rice, dried peas, beans and lentils and some vegetables)
½ bagel (76)
1 bran muffin (104)
1 slice bread
  Pumpernickel (79)
  Rye or whole wheat (61)
  White (68)
  1½-inch thick slice French bread (44)
½ English muffin (74)
1 corn tortilla (63)
1-ounce pita bread (80)
1 cup cooked cereal (100)
1 cup fortified ready-to-eat cereal (110)
1 cup cooked grits (125)
½ cup cooked dried beans, peas or lentils (106–115)
½ cup cooked corn (69)
½ cup cooked lima beans (95)
1 cup cooked pasta or noodles (192)
1 small potato (104)
½ cup cooked rice (93)
½ cup cooked sweet potatoes or yams (146)
1 cup unbuttered popcorn (23)
¼ cup Chinese noodles, from a can (55)
1 graham cracker (55)
2 rye wafers (45)

2 saltine crackers (24)
1 1½-ounce frozen waffle (120)

Fats
1 teaspoon butter or margarine (34)
1 ounce cream cheese (99)
1 tablespoon mayonnaise (100)
1 tablespoon vegetable oil (120)
1 tablespoon unsweetened whipped cream (26)

Milk (includes some cheeses)
1 cup skim milk or buttermilk (86)
1 ounce cheese
  American (106)
  Cheddar (113)
  Monterey Jack (106)
  Swiss (105)
  ½ cup 99%-fat-free cottage cheese (82)
½ cup unreconstituted evaporated skim milk (99)
⅓ cup instant nonfat dry milk (81)
½ cup plain low-fat yogurt (72)

Meat and Fish (includes dried beans, peas and lentils, cheese, eggs, poultry and peanut butter)
3 ounces cooked Canadian-style bacon (184)
½ cup cooked dried beans, peas or lentils (106–115)
3 ounces cooked lean beef sirloin, trimmed of visible fat (176)
3 ounces cooked chicken, without skin (115)
3 ounces cooked chicken livers (187)
1 ounce cheese
  American (106)
  Camembert (85)
  Cheddar (113)
  Monterey Jack (106)
  Mozzarella (80)
  Swiss (105)
  ½ cup 99%-fat-free cottage cheese (82)
2 ounces lean boiled ham (132)
3 ounces cooked lean lamb, trimmed of visible fat (158)
3 ounces cooked lean pork loin, trimmed of visible fat (216)
3 ounces cooked turkey, without skin (162)
3 ounces cooked lean veal loin, trimmed of visible fat (199)
1 large egg (82)
4 clams (56)
4 ounces cod, flounder, perch or sole, cooked (95)
3½ ounces canned salmon, drained (188)
3¼ ounces canned sardines, drained (174)
3½ ounces water-packed tuna (117)
1 tablespoon peanut butter (94)

Vegetables
½ cup alfalfa sprouts (19)
1 cup cooked cut asparagus spears (35)
1 cup bean sprouts (37)
1 cup cooked sliced beets (54)
1 cup cooked broccoli (40)
1 cup cooked brussels sprouts (56)
1 cup cooked shredded cabbage (29)
1 cup sliced carrots (48)
1 cup cooked cauliflower (28)
1 stalk celery (7)
1 cup chicory (14)
1 cup cooked collard greens (63)
1 cup sliced cucumber (16)
1 cup cooked eggplant (38)
1 cup cooked green beans (31)
½ cup cooked green peas (57)
1 green pepper (16)
1 cup cooked kale (43)
1 cup lettuce leaves (10)
1 cup mushrooms (20)
1 cup cooked mustard greens (32)
10 okra pods (31)
½ cup boiled onions (31)
1 large dill pickle (15)
10 radishes (10)
½ roasted red pepper, from a jar or can (23)
1 cup cooked spinach (41)
1 cup fresh spinach leaves (14)
1 cup cooked summer squash (25)
1 tomato (20)
1 cup tomato juice (46)
½ cup cooked winter squash (93)

Fruits
1 apple (61)
½ cup unsweetened applesauce (50)
3 apricots (55)
5 dried apricot halves (55)
½ banana (50)
½ cup blueberries (45)
¼ cantaloupe (41)
10 sweet cherries (47)
½ cup cranberry juice cocktail (82)
½ grapefruit (40)
½ cup grapefruit juice (51)
10 grapes (34)
1 guava (62)
1/10 honeydew (49)

¼ cup mandarin orange sections (23)
½ mango (55)
1 nectarine (88)
1 small orange (45)
½ cup orange juice (61)
½ papaya (59)
1 peach (58)
1 canned peach half with 1½ tablespoons syrup (59)
1 pear (90)
½ cup fresh pineapple (48)
½ cup unsweetened pineapple juice (68)
1 plum (32)
2 pitted prunes (52)
1 tablespoon raisins (26)
½ cup raspberries (35)
1 cup strawberries (55)
1 5 x 1-inch slice watermelon (55)

Nuts
10 whole almonds (60)
10 unshelled peanuts (105)
1 tablespoon peanut butter (94)
14 walnut halves (185)

NOTE: If you have on hand a particular cut of meat or a variety of fruit or vegetable not shown in this list of substitutions you can find the calorie count in *Redbook*'s Up-to-Date Calorie Counter starting on page 319. Also, packaged breads and cereals will have the caloric content printed on the box or wrapper.

CHAPTER ONE

Eat the Foods You Love and Grow Thin

There are any number of good reasons to start your diet with the menus and recipes in this chapter. It is planned for almost a month (twenty-eight days) of meals that followers of *Redbook*'s Wise Woman's Diet couldn't believe they could eat and still lose weight. Your family can't object to meals that include Fried Chicken, French Fries, Stuffed Pasta Shells, Blue Cheese Dressing, Chocolate Fondue, Eggs Benedict, Pot Roast in Wine and Strawberry Shortcake. And you'll prove to yourself that dieting doesn't have to be dull. You'll also prove in the month that you can lose about 10 pounds or more, painlessly.

The recipes in this chapter and throughout this book are designed to surprise you and make you a master of the cooking-lean technique of cutting calories without diminishing one whit the pleasures of eating.

BRUNCH

½ cup unsweetened frozen strawberries (27), mixed with ½ cup orange juice (61)
* Eggs Baked in Tomato Shells (136)
1 ounce cooked Canadian-style bacon (58) or boiled ham (61)
1 toasted English muffin (148), spread with 1½ teaspoons butter or margarine (51)
1 cup skim milk (86)

TO EAT ANY TIME

1 cup skim milk (86)
1 cup 4-grain multivitamin-and-iron-supplement cereal (110)

DINNER

* Oven-Fried Chicken (184)
1 cup cooked sliced carrots (48)
1 cup cooked green beans (31)
1 cloverleaf roll (83), spread with 1 teaspoon butter or margarine (34)
1 syrup-packed peach half, drained (54)

Eggs Baked in Tomato Shells

4 large tomatoes
4 large eggs
2 tablespoons dry bread crumbs
2 tablespoons grated Cheddar cheese

1 tablespoon chopped fresh parsley
¼ teaspoon salt
⅛ teaspoon black pepper

Heat oven to 425°F., or use a toaster oven. Cut a ¼-inch-thick slice from stem end of each tomato. Scoop out pulp with a teaspoon. (Pulp may be strained and added to soup or a glass of tomato juice.) Place tomatoes, cut side up, on a small baking pan and carefully crack an egg into each. Mix remaining ingredients in a small bowl and sprinkle over eggs. Bake about 15 minutes for soft-set eggs, up to 20 minutes for firm eggs. *Makes 4 servings.* For diet serving allow 1 stuffed tomato.

Per diet serving: 136 calories, 9 grams protein, 7 grams fat, 9 grams carbohydrate.

Oven-Fried Chicken

2½ to 3 pounds chicken legs and breasts (about 8 pieces), skin and visible fat removed
2 tablespoons butter or margarine
2 tablespoons lemon juice
1 teaspoon minced, peeled garlic
½ teaspoon salt
⅛ teaspoon black pepper
½ cup dry bread crumbs

Heat oven to 375°F. Rinse chicken and pat dry with paper towels. In a small skillet melt butter over moderate heat. Remove from heat; mix in lemon juice, garlic, salt and pepper. Place bread crumbs on a plate. Dip each piece of chicken in butter mixture to coat and roll in bread crumbs until coated evenly. Place on a lightly greased baking sheet and bake 50 minutes, until brown and crisp. *Makes 4 to 6 servings.* For diet serving allow ½ breast or 1 leg. Wrap and refrigerate 1 diet portion for lunch in Menu #2.

NOTE: Because this dish is such a favorite among dieters we've added microwave instructions that cut cooking time in half.

MICROWAVE INSTRUCTIONS: Melt butter in a 1½-quart casserole and coat chicken as directed above, substituting ¼ teaspoon garlic powder for the minced garlic. Place in a 3-quart oblong dish, with the meatiest pieces toward the outside of the dish. Cover with wax paper and cook 18 to 22 minutes on high, turning dish halfway around and removing wax paper after 10 minutes.

Per diet serving: 184 calories, 17 grams protein, 9 grams fat, 10 grams carbohydrate.

BREAKFAST

½ cup tomato juice (23)
1 bran muffin (103)
1 ounce Cheddar cheese (114)

LUNCH

Oven-Fried Chicken (reserved from
   Menu #1, 184)
Oriental Spinach: 1 cup cooked
  spinach (41), sprinkled with ½
   teaspoon sesame seeds (8) and a
   few drops of soy sauce
1 slice whole-wheat bread (61)
½ cup juice-packed pineapple
  chunks and 1 tablespoon of juice
  (48)

DINNER

* New England Cod Chowder (222)
1 slice pumpernickel bread (79),
  spread with 1 teaspoon butter or
  margarine (34)
* Broccoli–Tomato Salad (120)
16 unshelled roasted peanuts (168)

New England Cod Chowder

1 1-pound block frozen cod fillets
  or 1 pound fresh cod fillets
2 cups peeled potatoes cut in ¼-
  inch dice (about ¾ pound)

1 quart skim milk
1 to 1½ teaspoons salt
½ teaspoon dried thyme leaves

Remove fish from freezer and let stand 10 to 15 minutes at room temperature. Meanwhile, in a large saucepan bring potatoes and milk to a simmer over moderately high heat. Cover and cook 12 to 15 minutes, until potatoes are still slightly firm when pierced with a knife. Cut fish into 1-inch chunks. Add fish, salt and thyme to pan, and when simmering, cook 10 to 15 minutes longer, until fish is white and flaky and potatoes are tender. *Makes 8 cups.* For diet serving allow 2 cups.

Per diet serving: 222 calories, 28 grams protein, 2 grams fat, 25 grams carbohydrate.

Broccoli–Tomato Salad

2 cups water
1 bunch broccoli, stalks cut in 1-
  inch lengths and florets in 2-inch
  lengths (about 6 cups, cut up)
½ teaspoon salt
2 tablespoons vegetable oil

2 tablespoons cider vinegar
½ teaspoon salt
⅛ teaspoon black pepper
1½ cups cherry tomatoes, halved
  (about 6 ounces)

In a medium-sized saucepan bring water to a boil over moderately high heat. Add broccoli and ½ teaspoon salt; cover and cook 5 minutes, until crisp-tender. In a 2-quart serving bowl combine oil, vinegar, ½ teaspoon salt and the pepper. Drain broccoli well and toss in bowl with oil-and-vinegar mixture. Add cherry tomatoes and toss gently to mix. Serve warm or cold. *Makes 6 cups.* For diet serving allow 1½ cups.

Per diet serving: 120 calories, 6 grams protein, 7 grams fat, 9 grams carbohydrate.

Once and for All

"The single most important thing, in my estimation, about *Redbook's* Wise Woman's Diet is that it is a diet that a woman can follow on a long-term basis. The answer to the problem of overweight—to the degree that we do have an answer—is that one must change one's life-style permanently. It is not the kind of disorder that can be combatted by a single, radical effort. What's needed to maintain a desirable weight is a permanent alteration in the way one eats and how active one is."

—Jules Hirsch, M.D.
    Professor and Senior Physician,
      Rockefeller University Hospital,
      New York City
    Consultant to *Redbook's*
      Wise Woman's Diet

BREAKFAST

* Farina Crisp (114)
1 tablespoon raisins (26), mixed
   with ⅓ cup sweetened applesauce
   (77)
1 cup skim milk (86)

LUNCH

Sandwich Parisienne: 2 ounces
   boiled ham (122); 2 ½-inch-
   thick slices French bread (about
   2½ x 2 x ½ inches, 88), spread
   with 1 teaspoon Dijon-style
   mustard (4)
1 small orange (45)

DINNER

* Shrimp Egg Foo Young (373)
½ cup cooked white rice (93)
1 cup cooked green peas (114)
⅓ cup vanilla low-fat yogurt (65)

Farina Crisp

½ cup water
2 tablespoons quick-cooking, iron-
   enriched farina

1 teaspoon lightly salted butter or
   margarine

In a small saucepan bring water to a boil over moderately high heat; add farina, stirring constantly. Turn heat to moderate and cook 3 to 5 minutes, stirring frequently, until farina is very thick; remove from heat. In a small skillet melt butter over moderately high heat. Add farina, and using a large spatula, press into a 4-inch circle. Cook 3 to 5 minutes, until golden and crispy on bottom; turn and cook until other side is crisp. *Makes 1 diet serving.*

Per diet serving: 114 calories, 2 grams protein, 4 grams fat, 17 grams carbohydrate.

Shrimp Egg Foo Young

¾ cup chicken broth
2 teaspoons cornstarch
4 teaspoons soy sauce
4 large eggs
1 6-ounce package frozen tiny Alaska shrimp, thawed and drained

½ cup mung bean sprouts (fresh are best)
½ cup diced fresh mushrooms
2 tablespoons thin sliced scallion or green onion
½ teaspoon salt
3 teaspoons vegetable oil

In a small saucepan mix broth, cornstarch and soy sauce. When smooth, bring to a boil over moderately high heat, stirring constantly. Cook 1 to 2 minutes, until thick and clear; then keep sauce warm over low heat. In a medium-sized bowl beat eggs with a fork; fold in shrimp, bean sprouts, mushrooms, scallion and salt. In an 8-inch skillet heat 1 teaspoon of the oil over moderately high heat; add ½ cup of the egg-shrimp mixture and cook 1 minute. Turn and cook 1 to 2 minutes longer, until egg mixture is firm and golden on bottom. Remove to a dish and cover to keep warm. Make 3 more pancakes with remaining mixture, adding oil to pan as needed. Stack pancakes and pour sauce over them. *Makes 2 servings.* For diet serving allow ½ the egg foo young.

Per diet serving: 373 calories, 38 grams protein, 20 grams fat, 9 grams carbohydrate.

Go Take a Walk

"The optimal diet is one that brings into balance the amount of food consumed with the amount of energy expended. Reducing the number of calories is difficult, but it is probably easier than trying to shed pounds only by increasing one's level of physical activity. The best formula is to try to do some of both. Dieting means eliminating an activity, namely, eating; but exercise demands time, dedication and more disruption of one's lifestyle. Substitute danger times for eating with physical activity. Even walking will help out on both fronts."

—Johanna Dwyer, D.Sc.
Director Frances Stern Nutrition Center, New England Medical Center Hospital, Boston
Consultant to *Redbook*'s Wise Woman's Diet

BREAKFAST

½ grapefruit (40)
1 large egg, prepared any style,
 without butter or margarine (82)
1 slice whole-wheat bread, toasted
 (61), spread with 1 teaspoon
 butter or margarine (34)

LUNCH

Peanut Butter Sandwich: 2 tablespoons peanut butter (188); 2
 slices whole-wheat bread (122)
1 stalk celery (7)
½ medium-sized carrot, cut into
 strips (15)
1 green pepper, sliced (16)
1 cup skim milk (86)

DINNER

* Chicken Livers in Wine Sauce
 (248)
1 cup cooked broccoli (40)
½ cup cooked brown rice (116)
1 small apple (61)

TO EAT ANY TIME

1 cup skim milk (86)

Chicken Livers in Wine Sauce

1 pound chicken livers
2 tablespoons lightly salted butter
 or margarine
1 teaspoon minced, peeled garlic
1 cup sliced fresh mushrooms

½ cup dry white wine or chicken
 broth
1 tablespoon chopped fresh parsley
½ teaspoon salt
¼ teaspoon black pepper

Rinse livers, discard any bits of fat that cling to them and pat dry with paper towels. Cut each liver in half. In a medium-sized skillet melt butter over moderately high heat. Add garlic and cook 2 to 3 minutes, stirring constantly, until golden. Add livers and cook 3 minutes, stirring frequently. Add mushrooms and cook 3 to 5 minutes, until mushrooms are tender and livers are still pink in the middle. Remove to a plate and cover to keep warm. Add wine, parsley, salt and pepper to pan and cook over high heat, stirring frequently, until about ¼ cup liquid remains. Pour wine sauce over livers and mushrooms and serve. *Makes 4 servings.* For diet serving allow ¼ of the livers and sauce.

Per diet serving: 248 calories, 31 grams protein, 11 grams fat, 6 grams carbohydrate.

BREAKFAST

1 cup skim milk (86)
1 cup 4-grain multivitamin-and-iron-
supplement cereal (110)
½ sliced banana (50)

LUNCH

* Middle-Eastern Bread Salad (150)
1 ounce Cheddar cheese (114)
½ cup apricot nectar (72)

DINNER

3 ounces broiled beef sirloin steak,
trimmed of all visible fat (176)
* Oven French Fries (120)
Tossed Salad: 1½ cups torn romaine
lettuce leaves (15); 1 green pepper
ring (2); 1 red onion ring (3);
* Blue-Cheese Dressing (18)
10 red grapes (38)

TO EAT ANY TIME

1 slice whole-wheat bread (61),
spread with 1 tablespoon cream
cheese (49) or 1½ teaspoons
butter (51)
1 cup skim milk (86)

Middle-Eastern Bread Salad

2 cups chopped tomato (about 4
small tomatoes)
½ cup chopped, seeded cucumber
(about 1 small)
¼ cup chopped, peeled onion
2 tablespoons chopped fresh
parsley

1 tablespoon dried mint leaves
4 slices whole-wheat bread, toasted
and broken into pieces
2 tablespoons vegetable oil
2 tablespoons lemon juice
1 teaspoon salt
⅛ teaspoon black pepper

Combine tomato, cucumber, onion, parsley and mint in a small bowl
and top with bread pieces; cover and refrigerate until ready to serve.
Just before serving, add oil, lemon juice, salt and pepper. Toss gently
to mix. *Makes 4 cups.* For diet serving allow 1 cup.

Per diet serving: 150 calories, 4 grams protein, 8 grams fat, 18 grams carbohydrate.

Eat the Foods You Love and Grow Thin 19

Oven French Fries

3 baking potatoes, about 8 ounces   1 teaspoon vegetable oil
  each, peeled

Heat oven to 450°F. Slice potatoes into julienne strips and toss with
oil in a medium-sized bowl. Place strips in one layer on a baking sheet
or a jelly-roll pan. Bake 15 minutes; remove from oven, turn potatoes
with a metal spatula and bake 15 minutes longer, or until potatoes are
golden and crisp. *Makes 3 or 4 servings.* For diet serving allow ¼ of the
potatoes.

   NOTE: A toaster-oven may be used for one or two portions. Bake 25
minutes at 450°F.

Per diet serving: 120 calories, 3 grams protein, 1 gram fat, 24 grams carbohydrate.

Blue-Cheese Dressing

1 cup 99%-fat-free cottage cheese   1 tablespoon thin-sliced scallion or
3 tablespoons liquid skim milk   green onion (optional)
1 tablespoon lemon juice
1 ounce Roquefort or other blue
  cheese, crumbled

Put cottage cheese, milk and lemon juice in a blender. Cover and blend
20 seconds at low speed. Stop machine and scrape sides with a rubber
spatula. Cover and blend 20 seconds at medium speed, until creamy.
Scrape mixture into a small jar; fold in cheese and scallion. Tightly
covered, dressing keeps at least a week in the refrigerator. *Makes about
1 cup.* For diet serving allow 1 tablespoon. If desired, garnish with 1
sliced scallion before serving.

Per diet serving: 18 calories, 2 grams protein, 1 gram fat, 1 gram carbohydrate.

BREAKFAST

½ cup orange juice (61)
½ toasted English muffin (74),
   spread with 1 tablespoon peanut
   butter (94)

LUNCH

Grilled Cheese Sandwich: 2 ounces
   American cheese (212); 2 slices
   whole-wheat bread (122)
½ green pepper, sliced (8)
12 slices cucumber (8)
2 tablespoons raisins (52)

DINNER

* Country-Style Ribs (256)
1 cup steamed collard greens (60)
1 cloverleaf roll (83)
3 canned plums with 1½ tablespoons syrup (83)

TO EAT ANY TIME

1 cup skim milk (86)

Country Style Ribs

3 pounds pork loin country-style   1 teaspoon salt
   ribs   ¼ cup soy sauce
Water

With a sharp knife cut racks of ribs into individual ribs and remove any visible fat around meat. Place ribs in a Dutch oven; cover with water, add salt and bring to a boil over high heat. Reduce heat to moderate; cover pot and simmer 45 minutes, until ribs are tender when pierced with a fork. Heat oven to 450°F. Drain ribs (discard cooking liquid) and pat dry with paper towels. Arrange ribs on a foil-lined baking pan and brush with half the soy sauce; bake 15 minutes. Turn ribs; brush with the remaining sauce and bake 15 minutes longer, until ribs are brown and crisp. *Makes 6 servings.* For diet serving allow ⅙ of the ribs.

Per diet serving: 256 calories, 29 grams protein, 14 grams fat, 1 gram carbohydrate.

BREAKFAST
5 unsweetened cooked prunes (82)
1 slice whole-wheat bread, toasted
 (61), spread with 1 teaspoon
 butter or margarine (34)
1 cup skim milk (86)

LUNCH
½ cup orange juice (61)
Open-Face Chicken Sandwich:
 2 ounces cooked chicken without
 skin (93); 2 teaspoons mayonnaise
 (68); 1 iceberg lettuce leaf (3);
 ½ small tomato (10); 1 slice
 cracked-wheat bread (66)
1 small apple (61)

DINNER
* Stuffed Baked Shells with Tomato
 Sauce (341)
1 cup torn romaine lettuce leaves
 (10), with *Basic Vinaigrette
 Dressing (31)
1 syrup-packed peach half, drained
 (54)
4 whole almonds (24)

TO EAT ANY TIME
½ cup skim milk (43)
½ cup bran cereal with added
 thiamin and iron (69)

Stuffed Baked Shells with Tomato Sauce

½ cup chopped, peeled onion
½ teaspoon minced, peeled garlic
½ pound lean ground beef
1 15-ounce can tomato sauce
1 6-ounce can tomato paste
½ teaspoon salt
½ teaspoon dried oregano leaves
¼ teaspoon black pepper
1½ cups 99%-fat-free cottage
 cheese

1 large egg
¼ cup grated Parmesan cheese
2 tablespoons chopped fresh
 parsley
Few grains of ground nutmeg
4 ounces jumbo pasta shells,
 cooked according to package
 directions and drained (18
 shells)

Heat a large skillet or saucepan over moderate heat. Add onion, garlic and meat. Cook 5 minutes, stirring with a spoon to break up meat, until onion is soft and meat has lost its pink color. Pour off and discard any fat. Stir in tomato sauce, tomato paste, salt, oregano and pepper. Bring to a simmer; then turn heat to low and cook for about 15 minutes.

Meanwhile, in a medium-sized bowl mix cottage cheese, egg, Parmesan cheese, parsley and nutmeg. Heat oven to 350°F. Spread 2½ cups of the tomato sauce in an 11¾ x 7½ x 1¾ inch baking dish. Using a spoon, fill each cooked shell with the cheese mixture and top with a spoonful of remaining sauce. Arrange stuffed shells on tomato sauce. Bake 25 to 30 minutes, until hot and bubbly. *Makes 4 to 6 servings.* For diet serving allow 4 shells and about ⅔ cup of the sauce.

Per diet serving: 341 calories, 29 grams protein, 8 grams fat, 37 grams carbohydrate.

Basic Vinaigrette Dressing

¼ cup olive or vegetable oil ½ teaspoon salt
½ cup water ⅛ teaspoon black pepper
¼ cup red wine vinegar

Put all ingredients in a screw-top jar; cover and shake well to blend. Tightly covered, dressing will keep several days in refrigerator. *Makes 1 cup*. For diet serving allow 1 tablespoon.

Per diet serving: 31 calories, 0 grams protein, 3 grams fat, 0 grams carbohydrate.

Comes the Plateau

Most people can expect two periods of no weight loss—what are called plateaus—over a period of three months. But you can reach a plateau and still be losing as much fat as before. Your body is adjusting to your lowered caloric intake and using stored fat for energy though temporarily it doesn't show on your scale. Make sure you are really following your diet and are being honest about what you are eating. Also make sure you're not eating too much salt (and be aware that some foods have high sodium levels even if you don't add salt). Increase exercise and cut back on fluids. And relax; if the plateau doesn't last longer than a week, don't worry about it. If it does last longer, you could reduce daily caloric intake to 1,000 for a few days, never less than 1,000 calories and not more than 3 days.

BREAKFAST

½ cup unsweetened grapefruit juice
(51)
* Cinnamon French Toast (249),
with 1½ teaspoons maple syrup
(25)

DINNER

3 ounces lean roast leg of lamb,
trimmed of all visible fat (158)
½ cup cooked egg noodles (100)
Buttered Kale: ½ cup cooked kale
(22); 1 teaspoon butter or
margarine (34)
* Chocolate Fondue (29), with ½
sliced banana (50) and ½ sliced
small apple (30)

SUPPER

3 ounces canned salmon, drained
(188), with *Cool Cucumber
Sauce (61)
½ medium-sized carrot (15)
3 rye wafers (67)
⅓ cup fresh or unsweetened frozen
blueberries (30)
½ cup vanilla ice milk (90)

Cinnamon French Toast

1 large egg
¼ cup liquid skim milk
½ teaspoon vanilla extract
Few grains of salt

Few grains of ground cinnamon
2 slices white bread
1 teaspoon granulated sugar

Place egg, milk, vanilla, salt and cinnamon in a wide, shallow bowl or pie plate; beat well with a fork. Soak both sides of bread slices in egg mixture until most of it is absorbed. Place a nonstick skillet over moderate heat. Using a spatula or pancake turner, place bread slices side by side in skillet; pour any remaining egg mixture over them. Cook slices 2 to 3 minutes, until underside is lightly browned; turn and cook 2 to 3 minutes longer, until second side of bread is golden-yellow and egg is set. Serve sprinkled with the 1 teaspoon sugar. *Makes 1 diet serving.*

Per diet serving: 249 calories, 13 grams protein, 8 grams fat, 28 grams carbohydrate.

Chocolate Fondue

2 teaspoons cornstarch
1 cup water
¼ cup unsweetened cocoa
¼ cup granulated sugar

1 teaspoon vanilla extract
Few grains of salt
Cut-up fresh banana and apple

Mix cornstarch and water in a small saucepan. When smooth, add remaining ingredients except fruit and stir over moderately high heat until mixture boils 1 minute. Pour into fondue pot to keep warm, if desired. To eat, hold fresh fruit on a fork, dip into fondue—and enjoy. *Makes 1⅛ cups.* For diet serving allow 2 tablespoons fondue, ½ sliced banana and ½ sliced small apple. Nondieters may add cutup fresh pears and oranges if desired.

Per diet serving: 29 calories, 0 grams protein, 1 gram fat, 7 grams carbohydrate.

Cool Cucumber Sauce

⅓ cup plain low-fat yogurt
½ small cucumber, peeled and
   diced (about ¼ cup)

¼ teaspoon dried mint leaves or
   dillweed
⅛ teaspoon salt

Mix all ingredients in a small bowl. *Makes 1 diet serving.*

Per diet serving: 61 calories, 5 grams protein, 1 gram fat, 14 grams carbohydrate.

BREAKFAST

½ cup skim milk (43)
1 cup 4-grain multivitamin-and-iron-
supplement cereal (110)
½ cup sliced fresh or unsweetened
frozen strawberries (28)

LUNCH

* Cucumber and Cottage Cheese
Salad (98), on 2 slices rye bread
(122)
1 radish (1)
2 stalks celery (14)
½ green pepper, sliced (8)
2 purple plums (64)

DINNER

* Escarole Soup (38)
1 lean broiled pork chop, trimmed
of all visible fat (3 ounces cooked
meat, 216)
½ cup cooked whole-kernel corn
(70)
* Extra-Crisp Cabbage Salad (61)
1 slice whole-wheat bread (61),
spread with 1 teaspoon butter or
margarine (34)
* Peaches and "Cream" (62)

TO EAT ANY TIME

1 cup skim milk (86)
1 cup sweet cherries (82)

Cucumber and Cottage Cheese Salad

1 medium-sized cucumber, peeled,
seeded and diced (about 1 cup)
1 cup 99%-fat-free cottage cheese
1 tablespoon mayonnaise
1 tablespoon snipped chives
1 teaspoon lemon juice
¼ teaspoon salt
⅛ teaspoon black pepper
Few grains of ground red pepper
(optional)

Mix all ingredients in a small bowl. *Makes 2 cups salad.* For diet serving
allow ⅔ cup.

Per diet serving: 98 calories, 12 grams protein, 4 grams fat, 4 grams carbohydrate.

Escarole Soup

6 cups chicken broth
2 cups escarole leaves, torn into
2-inch pieces
¼ teaspoon black pepper

In a medium-sized saucepan bring broth to a boil over moderately high
heat. Stir in escarole and pepper, reduce heat to moderate and cook
5 to 7 minutes, until escarole is tender. *Makes 6 cups.* For diet serving
allow 1½ cups.

Per diet serving: 38 calories, 6 grams protein, 0 grams fat, 4 grams carbohydrate.

Extra-Crisp Cabbage Salad

5 cups fine-shredded green
  cabbage (about 1 pound)
15 ice cubes
½ cup cider vinegar

¼ cup water
2 tablespoons vegetable oil
½ to ¾ teaspoon salt
⅛ teaspoon black pepper

Place a third of the cabbage in a large bowl and top with 5 of the ice cubes. Repeat with remaining cabbage and ice, ending with ice. Cover tightly and refrigerate several hours or overnight. Before serving, remove any unmelted ice and drain all liquid from bowl. Combine remaining ingredients in a screw-top jar; shake well, pour over cabbage and toss. *Makes about 5 cups.* For diet serving allow ⅙ of the salad.

Per diet serving: 61 calories, 1 gram protein, 5 grams fat, 5 grams carbohydrate.

Peaches and "Cream"

½ cup evaporated skim milk,
  undiluted
1 teaspoon granulated sugar

½ teaspoon vanilla extract
4 fresh peaches, pitted and sliced

In a small bowl mix milk, sugar and vanilla. Makes ½ cup "cream." Put peach slices in 4 sherbet glasses; serve with "cream." *Makes 4 servings.* For diet serving allow 2 tablespoons "cream" and 1 sliced peach.

Per diet serving: 62 calories, 3 grams protein, 0 grams fat, 13 grams carbohydrate.

BREAKFAST

½ cup grapefruit juice (51)
* Double Cheese Toast (190)

LUNCH

1 slice whole-wheat bread (61),
  spread with 2 tablespoons peanut
  butter (188)
Fresh Vegetable Plate: ½ medium-
  sized carrot (15); 2 stalks celery
  (14); ½ green pepper, sliced (8)
15 sweet cherries (71)

DINNER

* Summer Squash Chowder (70)
* Shrimp and Poached Fish Salad
  (250)
1 teaspoon mayonnaise (34)
1 slice rye bread (61)
1 gingersnap cookie (29)

TO EAT ANY TIME

1 cup 4-grain multivitamin-and-iron-
  supplement cereal (110)
½ cup skim milk (43)

Double Cheese Toast

1 ounce sharp Cheddar cheese,
  diced fine
2 tablespoons 99%-fat-free cottage
  cheese

Few grains of salt
Few grains of black pepper
1 slice white bread, lightly **toasted**

Mix cheeses, salt and pepper in a small bowl. Spread on toast. Place on
a baking sheet in broiler 4 inches from heat source (or use a toaster-
oven) and broil about 3 minutes, until cheese is melted and lightly
browned. Serve at once. *Makes 1 diet serving.*

Per diet serving: 190 calories, 13 grams protein, 10 grams fat, 12 grams carbohydrate.

Summer Squash Chowder

1½ pounds summer squash, cut in
  ½-inch pieces (about 5 cups)
½ cup water
¼ teaspoon salt
½ cup evaporated skim milk,
  undiluted

2 tablespoons grated sharp
  Cheddar cheese (about ½
  ounce)

In a medium-sized covered saucepan bring squash, water and salt to a
simmer over moderate heat. Cook about 15 minutes, until squash is
tender. Add evaporated milk; cover and cook 5 minutes longer. Remove
from heat; add cheese and stir until melted. *Makes 4 cups chowder.* For
diet serving allow 1 cup.

Per diet serving: 70 calories, 5 grams protein, 1 gram fat, 9 grams carbohydrate.

Shrimp and Poached Fish Salad

1 1-pound block frozen cod or
flounder fillets, slightly thawed
Water
1 cup cider vinegar
1 carrot, peeled and cut in 4
pieces
1 onion, peeled and stuck with
3 cloves
1 sprig fresh parsley
1 2-inch bay leaf

4 or 5 peppercorns
½ teaspoon dried thyme leaves
¼ lemon
¼ cup freshly squeezed lemon
juice
1 6-ounce package frozen tiny
Alaska shrimp, thawed and
drained
¼ pound spinach leaves

Place fish in a large pot or skillet. Add enough water to barely cover fish and then remove fish to a plate. Add the vinegar, carrot, onion, parsley, bay leaf, peppercorns and thyme to water in pot. Cover and bring to a boil over moderately high heat; reduce heat to moderately low and simmer 20 minutes to make a well-flavored broth.

While broth simmers, rub the fish with lemon quarter, squeezing to release the juice. Place fish in hot broth, cover and simmer over moderately low heat for 12 to 15 minutes (5 to 7 minutes if fish is completely thawed); do not let water boil—just an occasional bubble should break the surface. Check fish for doneness; flesh should be white and opaque in the middle, not transparent. If not quite cooked, simmer 3 to 5 minutes longer. Remove cooked fish from pot and cool slightly. Flake fish into a bowl, removing any bones. Sprinkle with lemon juice and toss gently. Cover and chill several hours or overnight. Just before serving, toss shrimp with fish and serve on spinach leaves. *Makes 3 cups.* For diet serving allow ¾ cup fish mixture and 1 ounce (¼ of) spinach.

Per diet serving: 250 calories, 44 grams protein, 7 grams fat, 2 grams carbohydrate.

BREAKFAST

½ cup fresh or unsweetened frozen strawberries (28), mixed with ½ cup orange sections (39)
* Cottage Cinnamon Toast (127)

LUNCH

1 cup vegetable juice (41)
2 ounces part-skim mozzarella cheese (144)
2 ½-inch-thick slices French bread (about 2½ x 2 inches, 88)
Mushroom and Spinach Salad: 1 cup spinach leaves (14); ½ cup sliced fresh mushrooms (10); Basic Vinaigrette Dressing (recipe on page 23, 31)

DINNER

3 ounces lean broiled flank steak, trimmed of all visible fat (167)
* Ratatouille (66)
1 6-ounce baked potato (145)
* Blueberry Cheesecake (110)

TO EAT ANY TIME

1 cup skim milk (86)
1 slice rye or whole-wheat bread (61), spread with 1½ teaspoons butter or margarine (51)

Cottage Cinnamon Toast

1 slice whole-wheat bread, toasted
¼ cup pot cheese or 99%-fat-free cottage cheese
½ fresh peach, sliced
¼ teaspoon ground cinnamon
¼ teaspoon granulated sugar

Spread toast with pot cheese. Cover with peach slices and sprinkle with cinnamon and sugar. *Makes 1 diet serving.*

Per diet serving: 127 calories, 12 grams protein, 1 gram fat, 16 grams carbohydrate.

Ratatouille

1 tablespoon vegetable oil
½ cup chopped, peeled onion
1 teaspoon minced, peeled garlic
4 medium-sized tomatoes, chopped (about 1 pound)
1 medium-sized eggplant, about 1 pound, cut in ¼-inch slices
2 small zucchini squash, about ¼ pound each, cut in ¼-inch slices
1 large green pepper, seeded and cut into strips
3 tablespoons chopped fresh parsley
1 teaspoon dried basil leaves
1 teaspoon salt
½ teaspoon black pepper
½ teaspoon dried thyme leaves

In a Dutch oven or large saucepot heat oil over moderate heat. Add onion and garlic and cook 2 to 3 minutes, stirring often, until onion is light brown. Add remaining ingredients, cover and cook over low heat for 45 minutes, stirring every 8 to 10 minutes, until vegetables are tender and some liquid remains. Serve hot or cold. *Makes 6 cups.* For diet serving allow 1 cup.

Per diet serving: 66 calories, 2 grams protein, 3 grams fat, 9 grams carbohydrate.

Blueberry Cheesecake

1 tablespoon lightly salted butter
  or margarine
½ cup graham cracker crumbs
2 tablespoons cold water
2 tablespoons lemon juice
1 envelope unflavored gelatin
½ cup liquid skim milk

⅓ cup granulated sugar
Yolks of 2 large eggs
2 cups 99%-fat-free cottage cheese
1 tablespoon vanilla extract
Fresh or unsweetened frozen
  blueberries

In a small saucepan melt butter over moderate heat. Remove from heat, add graham cracker crumbs and mix until well coated. Press evenly over bottom and up sides of a 9-inch pie plate to within ½ inch of rim. Put water and lemon juice in blender; sprinkle with gelatin. Cover and blend 15 seconds at medium speed, until gelatin and liquid are mixed. In a small saucepan heat milk over moderate heat for 3 to 4 minutes, until tiny bubbles form around the edge of the pan. Pour into blender; cover and blend 10 seconds at low speed, until gelatin is completely dissolved. Scrape sides with a rubber spatula; cover and blend 20 seconds longer. Add sugar, egg yolks, cottage cheese and vanilla; cover and blend 1 minute at high speed, until smooth. Pour into prepared pie plate. Cover and chill in refrigerator at least 3 hours. Just before serving, garnish with blueberries. *Makes 8 to 10 servings.* For diet serving allow ⅒ of the cheesecake plus 1 tablespoon blueberries. Reserve 1 diet portion for a snack in Menu #12.

Per diet serving: 110 calories, 8 grams protein, 3 grams fat, 13 grams carbohydrate.

BREAKFAST

¼ cantaloupe (41), with ¼ cup
99%-fat-free cottage cheese (41)
4 Melba toast rounds (48), spread
with 2 teaspoons butter or
margarine (68)

LUNCH

3 ounces canned sardines, drained
(187); topped with 2 tablespoons
chopped, peeled onion (8)
1 slice pumpernickel bread (79)
10 red grapes (38)
½ cup skim milk (43)

DINNER

* Chicken Stir-Fry (268)
Buttered Rice: ½ cup cooked white
rice (93); 1 teaspoon butter or
margarine (34)
1 small tomato, sliced (20)
½ small cucumber, sliced (12)
¼ cup vanilla ice milk (45), served
with ½ cup mashed fresh or
unsweetened frozen strawberries
(28)

TO EAT ANY TIME

½ cup skim milk (43)
Blueberry Cheesecake (reserved from
Menu #11, 110)

Chicken Stir-Fry

2 whole chicken breasts, split,
boned and skinned (about 1
pound boneless)
¼ cup soy sauce
3 tablespoons dry sherry wine
1 teaspoon cornstarch
¼ teaspoon ground ginger
2 teaspoons vegetable oil
1 cup diagonally sliced celery

1 cup diced fresh mushrooms
(about 2½ ounces)
1 6-ounce package frozen Chinese
pea pods, thawed
1 6-ounce can bamboo shoots,
drained
½ cup sliced scallions or green
onions
1 teaspoon minced, peeled garlic
½ cup water

Cut chicken in ½-inch strips. In a large bowl combine soy sauce, sherry, cornstarch and ginger. Stir with a wire whisk until mixture is quite smooth. Add chicken and stir to coat. Cover bowl and refrigerate 20 minutes or up to 12 hours. Just before cooking, tip chicken into a colander or strainer set over a bowl; reserve liquid.

To cook: Heat a large, heavy skillet or wok over high heat until a few drops of water sizzle when dropped on the metal. Add the oil and tilt the pan gently in all directions until the oil coats the surface. When the oil is hot but not smoking, add the celery, mushrooms, pea pods, bamboo shoots, scallions and garlic and stir-fry 3 minutes, until hot. Remove vegetables to a bowl. Add drained chicken to skillet and stir-fry 4 minutes, until pieces are white and cooked through. Remove chicken to bowl with vegetables. Add soy sauce liquid and water to skillet and stir over moderate heat 3 to 5 minutes, until boiling and thickened. Add vegetables and chicken to skillet and cook about 2 minutes, stirring constantly, until hot. *Makes 6 cups.* For diet serving allow 1½ cups.

Per diet serving: 268 calories, 40 grams protein, 7 grams fat, 12 grams carbohydrate.

You'll Learn to Love Oven-Frying

Once you've tasted oven-fried fish or chicken, you won't *want* to go back to deep-fat frying. Oven-frying consists of dipping fish or chicken pieces in a small amount of butter or margarine that has been seasoned with lemon juice and/or mustard or garlic or paprika, coating with dry bread crumbs and baking. It produces a crisp, crunchy outside, moist inside and a wonderful-tasting piece of fish or chicken. You'll find many examples, and flavors, of this lighter frying technique in this book.

BREAKFAST

1¼ cups fortified high-protein cereal (110)
1 cup skim milk (86)
1 medium-size banana (101)
¾ cup orange juice (91)

LUNCH

* Cottage Cheese Summer Salad (158)
3 rye wafers (67)
2 plums (64)

DINNER

* Perfect Liver and Onions (229)
* New Potatoes Vinaigrette (132)
1 cup steamed green beans (31)
¼ small cantaloupe (41)

TO EAT ANY TIME

½ cup vanilla ice milk (90)

Cottage Cheese Summer Salad

½ cup creamed cottage cheese
1 small cucumber, peeled and diced
2 radishes, sliced thin

2 tablespoons minced scallion or green onion
¼ teaspoon salt
Few grains of black pepper

Combine ingredients in a small bowl. Salad can be made ahead, covered and refrigerated for 3 or 4 hours, in which case, peel, dice and add cucumber just before serving. *Makes 1 diet serving.*

Per diet serving: 158 calories, 18 grams protein, 5 grams fat, 10 grams carbohydrate.

Perfect Liver and Onions

1 tablespoon vegetable oil
4 medium-sized or 2 large sweet yellow onions, peeled, sliced thin and separated into rings
½ teaspoon salt

1 pound beef liver, cut into ½-to-¾-inch-thick slices
¼ teaspoon black pepper
Salt to taste

In a heavy, 12-inch skillet heat oil over moderately high heat. Add onions and the ½ teaspoon salt and toss in pan to coat with oil. Reduce heat to moderate and cook 5 minutes, stirring often, until onions are golden. Push onions to one side of pan. Sprinkle liver on both sides with pepper and add to skillet. Cook 3 minutes; turn and cook 3 minutes longer. Sprinkle liver with salt to taste and serve with onions. *Makes 4 servings.* For diet serving allow 3 ounces cooked liver and ¼ of the onions.

Per diet serving: 229 calories, 24 grams protein, 8 grams fat, 15 grams carbohydrate.

New Potatoes Vinaigrette

Water
1½ pounds unpeeled new potatoes
  (about 8 medium-sized),
  scrubbed and rinsed, or use
  small, frozen, whole potatoes

½ cup Basic Vinaigrette Dressing
  (recipe on page 23)
2 tablespoons chopped fresh
  parsley

Pour water to a depth of about 2 inches into a large saucepot and bring
to a boil over moderately high heat. Place potatoes in a steamer basket
and carefully lower basket into the saucepot. Reduce heat to moderate,
cover pan and steam 20 to 25 minutes, until potatoes are tender. Quickly
quarter the potatoes under cold running water and place in a mixing
bowl. Toss gently with dressing, sprinkle with parsley and serve. *Makes
4 cups.* For diet serving allow 1 cup.

Per diet serving: 132 calories, 3 grams protein, 2 grams fat, 26 grams carbohydrate.

If You Must Brown, Broil

Many traditional recipes for stews, pot roasts, chili and thick
soups call for browning the meat before going on with the rest
of the recipe. This process often calls for adding fat to the pan,
so you end up with that plus the fat that cooks out of the meat.
You can eliminate needless calories either by draining the browned
meat in a colander after browning and letting all unneeded fat
drain off or by briefly broiling the meat rather than browning
it in fat. Always broil on a rack over a broiler pan so fat drips
away from the meat. Remember that 1 tablespoon of oil has 120
calories. That's one-tenth of a 1,200-calorie diet.

BREAKFAST

½ mango (76)
1 slice whole-wheat bread, toasted
(61), spread with ¼ cup 99%-
fat-free cottage cheese (82) and
sprinkled with cinnamon

LUNCH

3 ounces broiled lean hamburger
(4 ounces before cooking, 186),
on 1 hamburger roll (119)
* "French Fried" Onion Rings (51)
1 large dill pickle (15)
1 cup skim milk (86)

DINNER

3 ounces roast lean pork loin,
trimmed of all visible fat (216;
wrap and reserve 3 ounces for
lunch in Menu #16)
1½ cups cooked broccoli (60)
1 cup cooked wax beans (30)
* Strawberry Shortcake (156)
¾ cup skim milk (65)

"French Fried" Onion Rings

Whites of 2 large eggs
½ teaspoon salt
⅛ teaspoon black pepper
⅓ cup unseasoned dry bread
crumbs

½ large sweet yellow onion,
peeled, sliced ¼ inch thick and
separated into rings

Heat oven to 450°F. Put egg whites, salt and pepper in a pie plate or
shallow baking dish and beat lightly with a fork just until broken up.
Put bread crumbs on wax paper or plate. Using tongs or a fork, dip
onion rings into egg white one at a time, turning to coat all over; then
dip in crumbs, turning to coat well. Put rings on an ungreased baking
sheet in a single layer and bake 10 minutes, until crisp and golden.
Makes 4 servings. For diet serving allow ¼ of recipe.

Per diet serving: 51 calories, 3 grams protein, 0 grams fat, 9 grams carbohydrate.

Strawberry Shortcake

2⅔ cups buttermilk baking mix
⅔ cup water
1 pint fresh or unsweetened frozen
  whole strawberries

1 teaspoon granulated sugar
Cream Chantilly (recipe below)

Heat oven to 425°F. Put baking mix and water in a medium-sized bowl and stir with a fork until just moist. Spread into an ungreased 8-inch round layer cake pan. Bake 15 to 20 minutes, until a cake tester inserted in center of cake comes out clean and top is golden-brown. Put pan on a wire cake rack to cool for 10 minutes. Turn out cake onto wire rack and let cool 15 minutes longer. Cake may be served warm or at room temperature. (It also may be made a day ahead, cooled completely, wrapped in a plastic bag and stored at room temperature.)

Just before serving, rinse fresh strawberries under cold running water and reserve 8 of the nicest berries for garnish. Hull remaining fresh berries; quarter hulled berries, put in a small bowl and sprinkle with sugar. Stir gently and let stand about 15 minutes. With a sharp knife cut shortcake in half horizontally and put bottom layer on a cake plate. Spread with about 1 cup of the Cream Chantilly and spoon on about 1 cup of the quartered strawberries. Cover with top half of cake; spread with remaining cream and top with remaining quartered strawberries. Garnish with reserved whole berries. *Makes 8 to 12 servings.* For diet serving allow 1/12 of the cake.

Per diet serving: 156 calories, 2 grams protein, 7 grams fat, 20 grams carbohydrate.

Cream Chantilly

White of 1 large egg
2 teaspoons granulated sugar

½ cup heavy cream

In a narrow, deep bowl (preferably stainless-steel) beat egg white with an electric beater at high speed until soft peaks form when white is lifted with a spatula. Add sugar, 1 teaspoon at a time, beating well after each addition. Stiff peaks now will hold when mixture is lifted. In another narrow, deep bowl whip cream until soft peaks form. Using a rubber spatula or large metal spoon, fold beaten egg white into whipped cream. *Makes about 2½ cups cream.*

Per 2 tablespoons (diet serving): 23 calories, 0 grams protein, 2 grams fat, 0 grams carbohydrate.

BREAKFAST

½ cup orange juice (61)
* Eggs Benedict (232)
½ cup sliced fresh or unsweetened
  frozen strawberries (27)

LUNCH

* Spinach Dip (50) with ½
  medium-sized carrot (15) and
  1 stalk celery (7), cut into strips
1 ounce Swiss cheese (107)
1 ounce Camembert cheese (85)
1 roasted red pepper from jar (23)
1 ½-inch-thick slice French bread
  (about 2½ x 2 inches, 44)
1 pear (90)

DINNER

3 ounces lean broiled sirloin steak,
  trimmed of all visible fat (176)
½ large baked potato (72)
Tomatoes Vinaigrette: ½ large
  ripe tomato, sliced thin (15)
  with Basic Vinaigrette Dressing
  (recipe on page 23, 31)
* Frozen Hot Chocolate (125)

TO EAT ANY TIME

4 dried apricot halves (44)

Eggs Benedict

¼ pound (4 slices) boiled ham
  or Canadian-style bacon
2 English muffins, split and
  toasted

4 large eggs, poached
Mock Hollandaise Sauce (recipe
  below)

Broil ham 5 to 7 inches from heat source, until lightly browned. Place muffin halves on plates; top each with a ham slice, a well-drained egg and the Mock Hollandaise Sauce. *Makes 3 or 4 servings.* For diet serving allow ¼ of the recipe, with 2 tablespoons sauce.

Per diet serving (including sauce): 232 calories, 25 grams protein, 11 grams fat, 16 grams carbohydrate.

Mock Hollandaise Sauce

Yolks of 2 large eggs
2 tablespoons all-purpose flour
¼ teaspoon salt
⅛ teaspoon white pepper

1 cup cold chicken broth
2 teaspoons lemon juice
1 tablespoon lightly salted butter
  or margarine

In a medium-sized bowl beat egg yolks with a wire whisk or fork until broken up. In the top of a double boiler beat flour, salt, pepper, broth and lemon juice until smooth. Place directly over moderately high heat and cook, stirring constantly, until mixture boils for 30 seconds. Slowly pour about ½ cup of the hot broth mixture into the egg yolks while beating constantly. Stir yolk mixture into broth mixture remaining in double boiler. Put over simmering, not boiling, water in bottom of double boiler and cook 2 to 4 minutes, stirring constantly, until thickened; do not boil. Remove from heat and stir in butter until melted; use immediately for Eggs Benedict. To reheat, warm sauce over simmering water in a double boiler. *Makes 1¼ cups sauce.* For diet serving allow 2 tablespoons sauce.

Per diet serving: 21 calories, 1 gram protein, 1 gram fat, 1 gram carbohydrate.

Spinach Dip

1 10-ounce package frozen chopped spinach, thawed and drained
2 tablespoons finely sliced scallion or green onion
1 8-ounce container plain low-fat yogurt
1 tablespoon mayonnaise
½ teaspoon salt
⅛ teaspoon white pepper

Mix all ingredients until well blended. *Makes 1½ cups dip.* For diet serving allow ¼ cup dip.

Per diet serving: 50 calories, 3 grams protein, 3 grams fat, 4 grams carbohydrate.

Frozen Hot Chocolate

¼ cup unsweetened cocoa
¼ cup granulated sugar
Few grains of salt
3 cups liquid skim milk
1 teaspoon vanilla extract

In a 2-quart saucepan mix cocoa, sugar, salt and milk and stir over moderate heat until cocoa is dissolved and mixture is smooth. Remove pan from heat and stir in vanilla; pour mixture into a 9-inch square baking pan and freeze several hours, or until firm. Before serving, remove from freezer and let soften about 20 minutes. Place half the mixture in a blender; cover and blend about 30 seconds, until thick and creamy. Pour into chilled cups or glasses. Repeat with remaining mixture. Serve immediately. *Makes 3 cups.* For diet serving allow ¾ cup.

Per diet serving: 125 calories, 7 grams protein, 1 gram fat, 24 grams carbohydrate.

BREAKFAST

* Berry–Buttermilk Shake (143)
½ toasted English muffin (74),
   spread with 1 teaspoon butter or
   margarine (34)

LUNCH

Open-Face Pork Sandwich: 3 ounces
   roast lean pork loin, trimmed of
   all visible fat (reserved from
   Menu #14, 216); 1 large lettuce
   leaf (2); 1 teaspoon mayonnaise
   (34); 1 slice rye bread (61)
½ medium-sized carrot, cut into
   strips (15)
½ green pepper, cut into strips (8)
2 fresh apricots (35)
1 cup skim milk (86)

DINNER

* Skewered Chicken Livers (274)
   with *Hot Bulgur (150)
½ papaya (59), served with lime
   wedge

Berry–Buttermilk Shake

1 cup whole fresh or unsweetened
   frozen strawberries

1 cup buttermilk
3 ice cubes

Put strawberries, buttermilk and ice cubes in a blender; cover and blend
at medium speed about 20 seconds, until smooth. *Makes 1 diet serving.*

Per diet serving: 145 calories, 10 grams protein, 1 gram fat, 25 grams carbohydrate.

Skewered Chicken Livers

½ cup soy sauce
¼ cup dry sherry wine (optional)
1 teaspoon minced, peeled garlic
1 teaspoon ground ginger or 2
   teaspoons grated fresh
   gingerroot
1 tablespoon vegetable oil
1 pound chicken livers

16 cherry tomatoes
1 small zucchini squash, cut into
   ½-inch-thick slices
12 small fresh mushrooms (about
   4 ounces)
Hot Bulgur (recipe on page 41)
4 scallion flowers (optional, see
   note)

In a small bowl mix soy sauce, sherry, garlic, ginger and oil until well
blended. Rinse livers under cold running water, discarding any bits of

fat that cling to them; pat dry with paper towels. Cut each liver in half. Thread livers and vegetables on four 12-inch skewers. Arrange skewers on a shallow, aluminum-foil-lined broiler pan and pour soy sauce mixture over them. Broil 4 inches from heat source for 10 minutes, turning once, until vegetables are tender and livers are browned on the outside and creamy-pink on the inside. Spread bulgur evenly on a large serving plate; arrange skewers on top and spoon pan juices over them. Garnish with scallion flowers and serve immediately. *Makes 3 or 4 servings.* For diet serving allow 1 skewer and ¼ cup pan juices.

NOTE: *To make scallion flowers,* wash 4 scallions or green onions; trim roots and tops to make a 3-inch-long piece of the white part. Hold one piece firmly in center and with a small, sharp knife cut five or six 1-inch-long slits down from each end. Cut remaining scallions the same way; then put into ice water for 5 minutes or longer. Ice water will cause them to fan out.

Per diet serving: 274 calories, 34 grams protein, 9 grams fat, 14 grams carbohydrate.

Hot Bulgur

In a medium-sized saucepan bring *1 cup water* to a boil. Stir in *1 cup bulgur wheat.* Remove pan from heat. Cover and let stand 20 to 30 minutes; bulgur will absorb water and swell. *Makes 2 cups hot bulgur.* For diet serving allow ½ cup.

Per diet serving: 150 calories, 5 grams protein, 1 gram fat, 32 grams carbohydrate.

Weighing In

On a slow and steady weight-loss diet, it's sometimes discouraging to weigh in every day. If it makes you happier, weigh in every third day, always in the morning, always after you urinate. One supportive suggestion: Get a piece of graph paper and plot your weight loss on it. Connect the dots each week. Trends often look far more encouraging than day-to-day results.

BREAKFAST

1 cup skim milk (86)
1 cup 4-grain multivitamin-and-iron-
   supplement cereal (110)
½ sliced banana (50)

LUNCH

1 cup canned vegetarian vegetable
   soup (78)
Chef's Tuna Salad: 1 cup torn
   lettuce leaves (10); 3 ounces
   canned water-packed tuna, drained
   (117); 1 ounce Swiss cheese, cut
   in julienne strips (107); ½ green
   pepper, sliced (8); Basic
   Vinaigrette Dressing (recipe on
   page 23, 31)
1 slice rye toast (61)
1 pear (90)

DINNER

* Linguini with Broccoli, Zucchini
   and Parmesan Cheese (208)
1 small tomato, sliced (20)
½ small cucumber, sliced (12)
¼ cantaloupe (41)

TO EAT ANY TIME

½ cup skim milk (43)
5 saltine crackers (60), spread with
   2 teaspoons peanut butter (62)

Linguini with Broccoli, Zucchini and Parmesan Cheese

4 ounces linguini (2 cups cooked)
1 tablespoon vegetable oil
1 teaspoon minced, peeled garlic
3 cups raw broccoli florets
3 cups ½-inch slices zucchini
   squash (about 12 ounces)

¼ cup grated Parmesan cheese
2 tablespoons skim milk
1 teaspoon dried basil leaves
Freshly ground black pepper

Cook linguini according to package directions for 8 minutes; drain and keep warm. Meanwhile, in a large skillet heat oil over moderate heat. Add garlic and cook 30 seconds. Add broccoli and cook 5 minutes, stirring constantly, until bright green. Add zucchini and toss with broccoli. Cover and cook vegetables 5 minutes longer, until heated but firm. Add linguini; remove skillet from heat and keep covered. In a small saucepan mix Parmesan cheese with milk and basil. Stir over moderate heat about 2 minutes, until cheese melts. Add to linguini and vegetables and toss gently to mix. Serve with pepper. *Makes 8 cups.* For diet serving allow 2 cups.

Per diet serving: 208 calories, 10 grams protein, 6 grams fat, 31 grams carbohydrate.

BREAKFAST

1 cup tomato juice (46)
¼ cup 99%-fat-free cottage cheese
  (82)
1 slice whole-wheat bread (61)
1/10 honeydew melon (49) with
  lime wedge

LUNCH

Open-Face Sardine Sandwich:
  1 3-ounce can sardines, drained
  (187); 2 slices red onion (6); 1
  slice rye bread (61)
1 stalk celery, cut in strips (7)
½ medium-sized carrot, sliced (15)
1 pear (90)

DINNER

* Pork Stroganoff (221)
½ cup cooked brown rice (116)
Buttered Beans: 1 cup cooked wax
  or green beans (31); 1 teaspoon
  butter or margarine (34)
6 seedless grapes (20)

TO EAT ANY TIME

1 nectarine (88)
1 cup skim milk (86)

Pork Stroganoff

1 tablespoon lightly salted butter
  or margarine
1 pound lean boneless pork
  shoulder, trimmed of all visible
  fat and cut into 3 x ¼-inch
  strips
¼ cup chopped, peeled onion

1 cup beef broth
¼ pound fresh mushrooms, sliced
  (about ¾ cup)
¾ cup plain low-fat yogurt
2 tablespoons chopped fresh
  parsley

In a large skillet melt butter over moderately high heat. Add pork and
cook 5 to 8 minutes, stirring constantly, until meat is well browned.
Stir in onion, beef broth and mushrooms. Cover pan and simmer 20 to
30 minutes, until meat is tender. Reduce heat to low. Stir in yogurt
and heat without boiling. Garnish with chopped parsley before serving.
Makes 4 servings. For diet serving allow ¼ of the meat and sauce.

Per diet serving: 221 calories, 21 grams protein, 12 grams fat, 6 grams carbohydrate.

BREAKFAST

1 cup whole fresh or unsweetened
frozen strawberries (55)
1 slice toasted raisin bread (66)
1 cup skim milk (86)

LUNCH

* Hot Bean and Garlic Soup (216)
½ cup creamed cottage cheese (109)
with ¼ cup raisins (104), 1
tablespoon chopped walnuts (49)
and ⅛ teaspoon ground nutmeg

DINNER

* Eggplant Pie (273)
2 cups torn romaine lettuce leaves
(20) with Basic Vinaigrette
Dressing (recipe on page 23, 31)
½ cup well-chilled juice-packed
crushed pineapple with 2 tablespoons of juice (48)
½ cup skim milk mixed with ½ cup
coffee and poured over ice (43)

TO EAT ANY TIME

½ cup 4-grain multivitamin-and-
iron-supplement cereal (55)
½ cup skim milk (43)

Hot Bean and Garlic Soup

1 20-ounce can white kidney beans
or chick-peas, drained and
rinsed
1 13¾-ounce can chicken broth

¼ cup fresh parsley sprigs, packed
tight to measure
1 large clove garlic, peeled
¼ teaspoon dried mint leaves

In a 2-quart saucepot heat beans and chicken broth over moderate
heat. When hot, pour into a blender; add remaining ingredients, cover
and blend at medium speed for 15 seconds, or until smooth. Pour soup
back into pot and heat to serving temperature. *Makes 3¼ cups.* For
diet serving allow 1½ cups.

Per diet serving: 216 calories, 15 grams protein, 1 gram fat, 38 grams carbohydrate.

Eggplant Pie

1 small eggplant (about 1 pound), peeled and cut into ¼-inch-thick slices
½ teaspoon salt
⅛ teaspoon black pepper
2 medium-sized ripe tomatoes, sliced
1 medium-sized green pepper, seeded and cut into rings
1 small onion, peeled and sliced thin

2 tablespoons olive or vegetable oil
1 teaspoon minced, peeled garlic
1 teaspoon dried oregano or basil leaves
4 ounces part-skim mozzarella cheese, sliced thin
½ cup Parmesan cheese, preferably freshly grated (2 ounces)

Arrange eggplant in one layer on a baking sheet; sprinkle with ¼ teaspoon of the salt and the pepper and broil 6 inches from heat source for 8 minutes, or until lightly browned. Heat oven to 375°F. Line a 10-inch pie plate with the eggplant slices, browned side down, overlapping in a circular pattern. Arrange alternating slices of tomato, pepper and onion over eggplant. Drizzle with oil and sprinkle with garlic, oregano and the remaining ¼ teaspoon of salt. Bake 25 minutes. Arrange mozzarella slices in one layer on top of pie; sprinkle with Parmesan cheese and bake 15 minutes longer, or until cheese is golden. Cut into wedges to serve. *Makes 4 servings.* For diet serving allow ¼ of the pie.

Per diet serving: 273 calories, 18 grams protein, 18 grams fat, 12 grams carbohydrate.

How Not to Be a Slave in the Kitchen

If cooking is not your favorite thing, look at ways to simplify the diet menus. The trick is to identify the main ingredients in a recipe as opposed to the ingredients that are there to add flavor and variety. For example, in Menus #20 and #21 on the following pages you can simply broil a piece of fish for Friday's dinner and serve it with a lemon wedge. Cook enough rice to have some leftover (unbuttered) to make Saturday's Summer Rice Salad easy. For Saturday brunch, nibble 6 pitted prunes just as they come from the box and pick up a spit-roasted chicken from a market for dinner.

BREAKFAST

1 cup corn flakes (110)
1 cup skim milk (86)
1 small peach (38)

LUNCH

¾ cup tomato juice (35)
Grilled Cheese Sandwich: 2 ounces
    American cheese (212); 2 slices
    whole-wheat bread (122); 1
    teaspoon butter or margarine (34)
1 large dill pickle (15)
½ green pepper, cut into strips (8)
½ cup diced fresh pineapple (40)

DINNER

* Crunchy Broiled Fish (252)
6 cooked asparagus spears (29)
1 cup cooked summer squash (25)
Buttered Rice: ½ cup cooked white
    rice (93); 1 teaspoon butter or
    margarine (34)
15 sweet cherries (71)

Crunchy Broiled Fish

1 1-pound block frozen flounder,
    perch or sole fillets
1½ tablespoons lightly salted
    butter or margarine, melted
¼ cup dry bread crumbs

2 tablespoons chopped fresh
    parsley
2 tablespoons lemon juice
¼ teaspoon salt
⅛ teaspoon black pepper

Put frozen block of fish on a rack in a broiler pan and brush with about 1 teaspoon of the butter. Broil about 5 inches from heat source for about 10 minutes; brush with butter and broil 10 minutes longer, until golden-brown on top and opaque in center. In a small bowl mix bread crumbs, parsley, lemon juice, salt and pepper. Spoon over fish and drizzle with remaining butter. Broil 2 to 3 minutes longer, until crumbs are browned. *Makes 4 servings.* For diet serving allow ¼ of the recipe.

Per diet serving: 252 calories, 35 grams protein, 11 grams fat, 5 grams carbohydrate.

BRUNCH

2 4-inch whole-wheat pancakes
  (made from whole-wheat pancake
  and waffle mix, 108); spread with
  ½ tablespoon margarine (51)
Lemon Topping: 1 tablespoon
  lemon juice mixed with 1 teaspoon sugar (15)
* Spiced Prunes (105)
½ cup plain low-fat yogurt (72)

TO EAT ANY TIME

1 cup skim milk (86)
½ small cantaloupe (82), with ½
  cup creamed cottage cheese (108)
4 unshelled roasted peanuts (42)

DINNER

* Crispy Mustard Chicken (209)
* Summer Rice Salad (228)
8 steamed asparagus spears (40)
1 cup whole fresh or unsweetened
  frozen strawberries (55)

Spiced Prunes

¾ pound prunes (about 30 large)
5 inches stick cinnamon

4 inches lemon peel, removed
  with a vegetable peeler
Water

Place prunes, cinnamon, lemon peel and enough water to just cover the prunes in a medium-sized saucepan. Bring to a boil over moderate heat, reduce heat to moderately low, cover pan and cook about 3 minutes, or until prunes are tender and plump. Cover and chill several hours. *Makes 4 or 5 servings.* For diet serving allow 6 prunes.

Per diet serving: 105 calories, 2 grams protein, 0 grams fat, 27 grams carbohydrate.

Crispy Mustard Chicken

4 pounds broiler-fryer chicken
  parts
6 tablespoons Dijon-style mustard
3 tablespoons minced scallion or
  green onion

½ teaspoon dried tarragon leaves
⅛ teaspoon black pepper
½ cup unseasoned dry bread
  crumbs

Rinse chicken parts and pat dry with paper towels. Arrange chicken, skin side down, on the rack of a broiler pan. Broil 5 inches from heat source for 10 minutes; turn and broil 10 minutes longer. Meanwhile, in a small bowl mix mustard, scallion, tarragon and pepper. Spread mustard mixture evenly over pieces of chicken and sprinkle with bread crumbs. Broil, skin side down, 10 minutes; turn and broil 5 minutes longer, or until browned and crisp. *Makes 4 to 6 servings.* For diet serving allow 4 ounces boneless cooked chicken. Wrap 1 diet serving and store in refrigerator for Monday lunch, Menu #23.

Per diet serving: 209 calories, 28 grams protein, 6 grams fat, 10 grams carbohydrate.

Summer Rice Salad

1 13¾-ounce can chicken broth
1 cup uncooked converted long-grain white rice
1 tablespoon olive or vegetable oil
3 tablespoons wine vinegar
½ teaspoon dried dillweed or 1 tablespoon snipped fresh dillweed

½ teaspoon dried basil leaves
½ teaspoon salt
¼ teaspoon black pepper
1 cup halved cherry tomatoes
1 cup sliced celery
1 cup sliced, peeled carrots

In a heavy, 2-quart saucepan bring broth to a boil over moderately high heat. Add rice, bring to a boil and then reduce heat to low, cover pan and cook 20 minutes, or until rice is tender and broth has been absorbed. Tip rice into a salad bowl; add oil, vinegar, dillweed, basil, salt and pepper; toss gently to mix. Cover and refrigerate 2 hours or longer to chill and blend flavors. Just before serving, add remaining ingredients and toss. *Makes 4½ cups.* For diet serving allow 1 cup.

Per diet serving: 228 calories, 5 grams protein, 4 grams fat, 44 grams carbohydrate.

BREAKFAST

1 medium-sized orange, sliced (71)
1 large soft-cooked egg (82)
1 slice white bread (68)

LUNCH

Bacon, Lettuce and Tomato
    Sandwich: 2 strips cooked bacon
    (86); ½ small sliced tomato
    (10); 1 leaf lettuce (1); 2 tea-
    spoons mayonnaise (67); 2 slices
    white bread (136)
2 medium-sized, canned, water-
    packed peach halves (48)

DINNER

* Pot Roast in Wine (255)
* German-Style Red Cabbage (39)
⅛ head iceberg lettuce (4¾ inches
    in diameter, 12), with * Piquant
    Salad Dressing (11)
* Baked Fruit Cup (75)

TO EAT ANY TIME

2 cups skim milk (172)
½ small grapefruit (40)
1 small carrot (30)

Pot Roast in Wine

1 3-pound beef eye round
¾ cup thinly sliced, peeled onion
1 large clove garlic, peeled and
    crushed
2 beef bouillon cubes, dissolved
    in 2 cups boiling water
½ cup Burgundy wine
2 bay leaves

½ teaspoon dried oregano leaves
¾ teaspoon salt
¼ teaspoon celery seeds
¼ teaspoon black pepper
12 small white onions, peeled
    (about ½ pound)
12 medium-sized whole
    mushrooms (about ½ pound)

Heat oven to 350°F. Place meat fat side down in an ovenproof Dutch oven over moderately high heat and brown quickly on all sides. Remove meat and pour off excess fat from Dutch oven. Reduce heat to moderate, add sliced onion and garlic to Dutch oven and cook until lightly browned. Return meat to Dutch oven, add bouillon, wine, bay leaves, oregano, salt, celery seeds and pepper. Bring to a boil. Cover and bake 2 hours. Add white onions and mushrooms; bake 30 minutes longer, until vegetables and meat are fork-tender. Remove meat to serving platter. Skim off fat from gravy; discard bay leaves. *Makes 4 servings with leftovers.* For diet serving allow 3 ounces cooked meat, ¼ cup gravy, 2 onions and 2 mushrooms. Gravy may be thickened for non-dieters. Wrap and reserve 2 ounces pot roast for Tuesday lunch, Menu #24.

Per diet serving: 255 calories, 30 grams protein, 7 grams fat, 16 grams carbohydrate.

German-Style Red Cabbage

6 cups shredded red cabbage
  (about 1½ pounds)
½ cup water
¼ cup cider vinegar

½ medium-sized apple, peeled
  and cubed
1 tablespoon granulated sugar
1 teaspoon salt

Place all ingredients in a saucepan over moderately high heat; cover and bring to a boil. Reduce heat to moderately low and cook 15 to 20 minutes, stirring occasionally, or until cabbage is crisp-tender. *Makes 4 servings.* For diet serving allow ½ cup.

Per diet serving: 39 calories, 1 gram protein, 0 grams fat, 9 grams carbohydrate.

Piquant Salad Dressing

½ cup tomato juice
1 tablespoon vegetable oil
¼ teaspoon minced, peeled garlic
½ teaspoon dried basil or oregano
  leaves
½ teaspoon salt

¼ teaspoon paprika
Few grains of black pepper
1 tablespoon cornstarch
⅓ cup water
¼ cup wine vinegar

In a small saucepan bring tomato juice, oil, garlic, dried herb, salt, paprika and pepper to a boil over moderately high heat. Mix cornstarch with water and stir into tomato juice mixture. Boil ½ minute, stirring constantly. Remove from heat and stir in vinegar. Chill. Dressing keeps well stored in a screw-top jar in refrigerator. Shake before using. *Makes about 1¼ cups.* For diet serving allow 1 tablespoon.

Per diet serving: 11 calories, 0 grams protein, 1 gram fat, 1 gram carbohydrate.

Baked Fruit Cup

2 medium-sized oranges
1 medium-sized apple
½ cup Emperor grapes, halved
  and seeded

¼ teaspoon curry powder
  (optional)
4 teaspoons flaked coconut

Cut oranges in half crosswise and remove sections with a sharp knife, leaving a shell. Reserve shells. Place orange sections in a bowl. Peel and core apple and chop coarsely; add to orange. Add grapes and curry powder and mix. Spoon fruits into the orange shells. Place 1 teaspoon coconut on each. Place filled shells in a shallow baking dish. (This much may be done ahead of time.) Just before serving, bake orange cups in a preheated 350°F. oven 20 minutes and serve slightly warm. *Makes 4 servings.* For diet serving allow 1 orange cup.

Per diet serving: 75 calories, 1 gram protein, 1 gram fat, 16 grams carbohydrate.

BREAKFAST

½ cup plain low-fat yogurt (72)
1 cup fresh or unsweetened frozen
  strawberries (55)
1 slice whole-wheat bread (61),
  spread with 1 teaspoon butter or
  margarine (34)

LUNCH

Crispy Mustard Chicken (reserved
  from Menu #21, 209)
Tossed Salad: 1 cup torn lettuce
  leaves (10); ½ carrot, sliced (15),
  5 radishes (4); ½ cup alfalfa
  sprouts (18); Blue-Cheese
  Dressing (recipe on page 20, 18)
½ cup juice-packed pineapple
  chunks with 2 tablespoons of
  juice (48)

DINNER

* Tomato–Cheese Casserole (322)
Broccoli Salad: 1 cup cooked
  broccoli (40); Basic Vinaigrette
  Dressing (recipe on page 23, 31)
1 ½-inch-thick slice French bread
  (about 2½ x 2 inches, 44)
10 seedless grapes (34)
1 cup skim milk (86)

TO EAT ANY TIME

6 unshelled roasted peanuts (63)
½ cup skim milk (43)

Tomato–Cheese Casserole

1 tablespoon lightly salted butter
  or margarine
1¼ cups diced, peeled onion
1 28-ounce can whole, peeled
  tomatoes, drained
12 saltine crackers, coarsely
  crumbled

4 ounces sharp Cheddar cheese,
  grated (about 1 cup)
4 large eggs
½ teaspoon salt
⅛ teaspoon black pepper
½ teaspoon dried basil leaves

In a 1½-quart rangetop-to-oven casserole melt butter over moderate heat. Add onion; increase heat slightly and cook 5 minutes, stirring often, until onion begins to brown. Add tomatoes and cook about 5 minutes longer, breaking them up with a spoon, until most of their liquid has evaporated. Take pot off heat and stir in crackers and cheese. In a mixing bowl beat eggs with remaining ingredients until foamy. Stir beaten eggs into tomato mixture. Place casserole in oven and turn on oven to 350°F. Bake 45 minutes, until the top is lightly browned. *Makes 4 servings.* For diet serving allow ¼ of the casserole.

NOTE: Tomato liquid may be used in a soup or sauce or as a beverage.

Per diet serving: 322 calories, 17 grams protein, 19 grams fat, 21 grams carbohydrate.

BREAKFAST

½ cup orange juice (61)
1 large egg (82), prepared any style
without butter or margarine
1 slice whole-wheat bread, toasted
(61), spread with 1 teaspoon
butter or margarine (34)
½ cup skim milk (43)

LUNCH

2 ounces pot roast (reserved from
Menu #22, 122)
4 spears asparagus (19)
2 teaspoons mayonnaise (66)
1 slice rye bread (61)
1 medium-sized peach (38)
½ cup skim milk (43)

DINNER

* Hamburger au Poivre (212)
1 cup watercress (7), with 5 radishes
(4)
1 cup steamed green beans seasoned
with sage (31)
½ cup mashed potatoes (61), with
1 teaspoon butter or margarine
(34)
½ cup frozen vanilla low-fat yogurt
(97)

TO EAT ANY TIME

1 cup skim milk (86)
10 seedless grapes (34)

Hamburger au Poivre

1 pound lean ground beef
4 teaspoons cracked or coarsely
ground black pepper
Salt
½ cup beef broth

1 tablespoon chopped fresh
parsley
1 teaspoon lemon juice
¼ teaspoon Worcestershire sauce
Few drops of Tabasco sauce
(optional)

Shape ground beef into four ½-inch-thick burgers; place on a small baking sheet. Press ½ teaspoon of the pepper into each side of the burgers. If possible, cover and refrigerate 30 minutes. Heat a large skillet over moderately high heat. When hot, sprinkle skillet with salt and add burgers. Cook 3 to 4 minutes, until well-browned on bottom; turn and cook 3 to 4 minutes longer for medium. (For well-done, cook about 2 minutes longer per side.) Meanwhile, mix remaining ingredients in a small saucepan and bring to a boil over moderate heat. Transfer burgers to a serving plate and top with the parsley sauce. *Makes 4 burgers and ½ cup sauce.* For diet serving allow 1 burger and 2 tablespoons sauce.

Per diet serving: 212 calories, 25 grams protein, 11 grams fat, 1 gram carbohydrate.

BREAKFAST

½ English muffin (74), spread
  with 2 teaspoons peanut butter
  (62)
1 large orange (78)
1 cup skim milk (86)

LUNCH

Tossed Salad: 1 cup torn lettuce
  leaves (10); 1 tomato, sliced (20);
  2 ounces Swiss cheese, slivered
  (214); *Herbed Vinaigrette
  Dressing (37)
1 4½ x ½-inch unsalted bread stick
  (19)
1 large dill pickle (15)
1 medium-sized peach (38)

DINNER

* Broiled Chicken Livers with Tart
  Soy Dip (182)
Buttered Rice: ½ cup cooked white
  rice (93); 1 teaspoon butter or
  margarine (34)
Buttered Broccoli: 1 cup cooked
  broccoli (40); 1 teaspoon butter
  or margarine (34)
2 fresh apricots or 2 dried apricot
  halves (36)

TO EAT ANY TIME

1 cup skim milk (86)
½ banana (50)

Herbed Vinaigrette Dressing

½ small onion, peeled
1 large clove garlic, peeled
2 tablespoons olive or vegetable
  oil
3 tablespoons wine vinegar
¼ cup water

¼ teaspoon salt
¼ teaspoon black pepper
1 teaspoon dried basil or oregano
  or tarragon leaves
¼ teaspoon granulated sugar

Place all ingredients in a blender; cover and blend at high speed about
10 seconds, or until smooth. Dressing can be stored in a screw-top jar
in the refrigerator. *Makes about ⅔ cup dressing.* For diet serving
allow 1 tablespoon.

Per diet serving: 37 calories, 0 grams protein, 3 grams fat, 1 gram carbohydrate.

Broiled Chicken Livers with Tart Soy Dip

1 pound chicken livers
2 teaspoons vegetable oil
1 teaspoon granulated sugar
¼ cup soy sauce

1½ tablespoons red wine vinegar
6 to 8 drops Tabasco sauce
¼ cup minced scallion or green
  onion

Rinse livers, discarding any bits of fat that cling to them, and pat dry
with paper towels. Line a broiler pan with aluminum foil; arrange

livers in pan and broil 4 inches from heat source for 4 minutes on each side. While livers cook, combine remaining ingredients in a small bowl; divide into 4 smaller bowls. *Makes 3 or 4 servings.* To serve, center a bowl of soy dip on each serving plate and surround with livers. For diet serving allow ¼ of recipe.

Per diet serving: 182 calories, 23 grams protein, 9 grams fat, 6 grams carbohydrate.

Know Thyself

"The dieter should try to identify her particular pitfall and then attack it on her own terms. One woman whose weakness was easily accessible snacks that she wolfed down without thinking found it helpful to stop buying them, and if others in the home did, to store them in an awkward-to-reach place. Another who absent-mindedly polished off the family's breakfast leftovers discovered that scraping all the leftovers onto one plate so they didn't look so appetizing prevented her nibbling while she scraped plates and loaded the dishwasher. A reformed smoker, who was overeating to replace the oral sensation cigarettes had given her as well as to keep her hands occupied, took up embroidery and chewing diet gum. If a dieter can isolate her particular weakness and try to control it for four or five days a week, she eventually can blot it out almost entirely."

—Johanna Dwyer, D.Sc.
Director, Frances Stern Nutrition Center, New England Medical Center, Boston
Consultant to *Redbook*'s Wise Woman's Diet

BREAKFAST

1 cup 4-grain multivitamin-and-iron-
supplement cereal (110)
1 cup skim milk (86)
1 medium-sized peach (38)

LUNCH

Tuna Sandwich: 3 ounces water-
packed tuna, drained (117); 2
teaspoons mayonnaise (68); 1
stalk celery, finely chopped (7);
2 slices whole-wheat bread (122)
1 cup skim milk (86)

DINNER

1½ cups chicken broth (33)
3 ounces lean pork chop, broiled
(151)
* Steamed Mixed Vegetables (76)
Buttered Baked Potato: 1 2½-inch-
round potato (about 3½ ounces,
104); 2 teaspoons butter or
margarine (68)
½ cup vanilla ice milk (90)
½ cup fresh or unsweetened frozen
raspberries (35)

Steamed Mixed Vegetables

Water
2 medium-sized carrots, peeled
and cut into ¼-inch diagonal
slices (1 cup)
2 cups raw cauliflower florets
2 small zucchini squash, cut into
¼-inch slices (2 cups)

2 small yellow squash, cut into
¼-inch slices (2 cups)
1 6-ounce package frozen Chinese
pea pods
½ teaspoon salt
¼ teaspoon black pepper

Fill a large saucepot or Dutch oven with water to a depth of 1 inch.
Put a steamer basket in pot, cover and bring to a boil over moderately
high heat. Layer vegetables in steamer basket in order given. Cover
and steam 10 to 12 minutes, until crisp-tender. Sprinkle with salt and
pepper. *Makes 3 or 4 servings.* For diet serving allow ¼ of recipe.

Per diet serving: 76 calories, 5 grams protein, 0 grams fat, 15 grams carbohydrate.

BREAKFAST

1 cup cooked iron-enriched farina
(100)
1 cup skim milk (86)
¼ cantaloupe (41)

LUNCH

1 cup tomato juice (46)
Cheese Sandwich: 2 ounces part-
skim mozzarella cheese (144);
1 roasted sweet red pepper (23);
2 ½-inch-thick slices French bread
(about 2½ x 2 inches, 88)
1 small zucchini squash, cut in
strips (22)
1 pear (90)

DINNER

* Basque-Style Cod (121)
Buttered Rice: ½ cup cooked brown
rice (116); 1 teaspoon butter or
margarine (34)
Buttered Kale: 1 cup cooked kale
(44); 1 teaspoon butter or
margarine (34)
1 cup cooked green beans with
lemon wedge (31)
20 sweet cherries (94)
1 cup skim milk (86)

Basque-Style Cod

1 1-pound block frozen cod fillets

Tomato Sauce:
1½ teaspoons olive or vegetable
oil
¼ cup chopped, peeled onion
¼ teaspoon minced, peeled garlic

2 medium-sized ripe tomatoes,
chopped (about 2 cups)
½ teaspoon salt
Few grains to ¼ teaspoon crushed
red pepper flakes
3 large pimiento-stuffed green
olives, sliced thin

Remove cod from package and let stand at room temperature while
you prepare tomato sauce. In a medium-sized skillet heat oil over moderate heat. Add onion and garlic and cook 2 to 3 minutes, stirring
frequently, until onion is translucent but not brown. Add tomatoes,
salt and red pepper. Simmer 5 minutes, stirring frequently, until sauce
is thickened. Cut frozen cod lengthwise into 2 pieces and then into 1-
inch cubes. Add cod to skillet; cover and simmer 10 minutes. Turn
fish over. Add sliced olives; cover and simmer 5 to 10 minutes more,
or until fish flakes easily. *Makes 3 or 4 servings.* For diet serving allow
¼ of the recipe.

Per diet serving: 121 calories, 21 grams protein, 3 grams fat, 3 grams carbohydrate.

BREAKFAST

½ cup fresh or unsweetened frozen
strawberries (28)
1 medium-sized poached egg (72),
served on 1 slice whole-wheat
bread, toasted (61)

LUNCH

* Vegetable Cottage Cheese (137)
2 leaves iceberg lettuce (2)
½ tomato (10)
1 medium-sized carrot, peeled and
cut into sticks (30)
1 slice whole-wheat bread (61)
1 medium-sized peach (38)

DINNER

* Oriental Beef and Vegetables
(421)
½ cup cooked rice (93)
1 cup mixed green salad (8), with
Piquant Salad Dressing (recipe
on page 50, 11)
½ cup juice-packed pineapple
chunks with 2 tablespoons of
juice (48)

TO EAT ANY TIME

1½ cups skim milk (129)
½ cup sweet cherries (41)

Vegetable Cottage Cheese

1 16-ounce container creamed
cottage cheese
2 tablespoons finely chopped
scallion or green onion
¼ cup chopped, seeded green
pepper

2 tablespoons chopped canned
pimiento
2 teaspoons prepared horseradish
¼ teaspoon salt

Thoroughly mix all ingredients in a bowl. Cover and chill. *Makes 3 or 4
servings.* For diet serving allow ½ cup cottage cheese mixture.

Per diet serving: 137 calories, 17 grams protein, 5 grams fat, 5 grams carbohydrate.

Oriental Beef and Vegetables

Instant meat tenderizer
1 1½-pound flank steak
2 teaspoons vegetable oil
2 medium-sized onions, peeled
and sliced
2 medium-sized green peppers,
seeded and cut into 1-inch
pieces
1 cup beef broth or bouillon
3 medium-sized tomatoes, peeled
and sliced

1 cup fresh bean sprouts
1 clove garlic, peeled and finely
chopped
½ teaspoon ground ginger
2 tablespoons soy sauce
2 tablespoons vinegar
2 teaspoons granulated sugar
2 teaspoons cornstarch
1 tablespoon water
2 cups cooked brown rice

Use meat tenderizer on the steak according to package directions; slice meat into ¼-inch thick slices. Heat oil in a large skillet over moderately high heat. Add meat and cook until lightly browned on both sides; remove slices as they are browned. When all the meat is browned, reduce heat to moderately low; add onions and green peppers to skillet and cook 5 minutes, stirring occasionally. Add beef broth, tomatoes, bean sprouts, garlic, ginger, soy sauce, vinegar and sugar; cook 5 minutes. Mix together cornstarch and water and stir into vegetable mixture in skillet; mix well. Add browned meat to skillet and heat about 5 minutes, stirring gently until sauce is slightly thickened. Serve mixture over rice. *Makes 3 or 4 servings.* For diet serving, allow 3 ounces meat, ¼ of the vegetables and ½ cup rice.

Per diet serving: 421 calories, 31 grams protein, 14 grams fat, 46 grams carbohydrate.

Have No Regrets

When *Redbook* editors have worked directly with groups of women following the Wise Woman's Diet, the dieters have been asked to keep a diet-diary recording of what they ate, when they ate, how they felt, if and when they cheated. Not one of them escaped moments of feeling absolutely starved and, the inevitable, having a binge day. Succumbing to an extra piece of pizza or not being able to stop eating the party hors d'oeuvres isn't the worst thing that could happen. The worst would be abandoning the will to keep on dieting. Reward yourself with a fresh start and forget the lapse.

CHAPTER TWO

Quick and Easy Diets for Busy Days

Rushed days, dieters say, are the dangerous ones. The temptation to eat whatever's in the refrigerator can scuttle your best intentions. The fourteen days of menus and recipes in this chapter were designed for just such days. There are few recipes to prepare each day; there are several carry-over food menus. The Chicken Barbecue made on Sunday is ready and waiting for Tuesday's dinner. There are several stir-fry dishes, one of the quickest and easiest ways to prepare food. Also, there are microwave instructions for many of the dishes in this chapter; they can save more minutes.

Use this chapter as planned, or dip into it when another diet menu has a dish that seems too complicated. When you do that, replace with the same foods—a fish dish for a fish dish, pork for pork—the balancing act never changes. It's best to use the whole day's menus as planned but not absolutely necessary so long as calorie count doesn't go over 1,200.

BREAKFAST

1 cup cooked iron-enriched farina
(100)
1 medium-sized egg (72), prepared
any style with 1 teaspoon butter
or margarine (34)
½ cup orange juice (61)
1 cup skim milk (86)

LUNCH

1½ cups chicken broth (33)
1 slice cheese pizza (⅛ of 14-inch
pie, 168)
¼ cantaloupe (41)

DINNER

* Beef Curry (227)
Parslied Rice: ½ cup cooked rice
(93); 1 tablespoon chopped
parsley; 1 teaspoon butter or
margarine (34)
Tossed Salad: 2 cups torn lettuce
leaves (20) with *Garlic
Vinaigrette Dressing (31)
* Creamy Tofu Pie (207)

Beef Curry

2 teaspoons vegetable oil
1 pound 10 ounces lean stew beef,
cut into 1½-inch cubes
2 cups sliced, peeled onions
2 tablespoons flour
1 tablespoon curry powder
1 13¾-ounce can beef broth
½ cup dry red wine

¼ cup light or dark seedless raisins
1½ teaspoons minced, peeled
garlic
½ teaspoon dried thyme leaves
1 bay leaf
½ teaspoon salt
⅛ teaspoon black pepper

In a large, heavy saucepot heat 1 teaspoon oil over moderately high heat. Add half the meat and brown on all sides; remove to a plate. Brown remaining meat. Add another 1 teaspoon oil to pot, stir in onions and cook 4 to 5 minutes, stirring occasionally, until translucent and golden. Stir in flour and curry powder and cook 30 seconds longer, stirring constantly. Add remaining ingredients and stir until blended. Bring to a boil, add beef and reduce heat to moderately low; cover pot and simmer about 1 hour and 10 minutes, stirring occasionally, until meat is tender. *Makes 4 cups.* For diet serving allow ⅙ of recipe.

MICROWAVE INSTRUCTIONS: Put beef in a 4-quart baking dish; omit oil. Cover and cook about 8 minutes on high, stirring after 4 minutes, until beef loses its pink color. Pour off all but about 1 tablespoon of accumulated juices. Add onions, sprinkle with flour, then stir in remaining ingredients. Cover and cook 10 minutes on high, stirring after 5 minutes. Uncover and cook 10 minutes longer, stirring after 5 minutes. Let stand 5 minutes before serving.

Per diet serving: 227 calories, 29 grams protein, 7 grams fat, 12 grams carbohydrate.

Garlic Vinaigrette Dressing

2 tablespoons vegetable oil
3 tablespoons wine vinegar
1 teaspoon dry mustard
¼ cup water

1 clove garlic, peeled and cut in
  half
¼ teaspoon salt
¼ teaspoon black pepper

Place all ingredients in a small screw-top jar; cover and shake vigorously. Dressing keeps well in refrigerator; shake again before using. Leave garlic in dressing but do not serve. *Makes about ½ cup.* For diet serving allow 1 tablespoon.

Per diet serving: 31 calories, 0 grams protein, 3 grams fat, 0 grams carbohydrate.

Creamy Tofu Pie

2 large eggs
1 pound 6 ounces tofu (soybean
  curd; see note below),
  preferably medium-firm texture
2 tablespoons fresh-squeezed
  lemon juice
½ cup granulated sugar
1 teaspoon vanilla extract

1 teaspoon freshly grated lemon
  peel
2 tablespoons lightly salted butter
  or margarine
¾ cup graham cracker crumbs
½ cup Golden Apricot Spread
  (recipe on page 64)

Put 1 egg and half the tofu and lemon juice into a blender or food processor; cover and blend 50 to 60 seconds, until smooth and creamy. Pour into a bowl; repeat with remaining egg, tofu and lemon juice. Stir in sugar, vanilla and lemon peel. Heat oven to 325°F. Melt butter in a small saucepan and stir in crumbs; press into bottom and up the sides of a 9-inch pie plate. Fill with tofu mixture. Bake 50 to 55 minutes, until a cake tester inserted in the middle comes out clean. Remove from oven and cool on a wire rack. Cover and chill 3 hours or longer. Before serving, pipe or spoon Golden Apricot Spread on top. *Makes 6 to 8 servings.* For diet serving allow ⅛ of pie.

Note: This creamy pie tastes very much like Italian cheesecake. But it's made with tofu—soybean curd—which is higher in protein and much lower in fat than cream cheese. Look for it packaged in plastic tubs in the fresh produce or refrigerator section of your market. Or find the square white cakes loose in water in an Oriental market.

Microwave Instructions: Prepare filling as directed above. In a 9-inch pie plate melt butter, stir in graham cracker crumbs and press into the bottom

Per diet serving: 207 calories, 9 grams protein, 8 grams fat, 28 grams carbohydrate.

and sides of plate to form crust. Add filling and cook 18 to 20 minutes on medium, giving dish a quarter turn every 5 minutes. Pie is done when outside edge is firm and center is just beginning to set. Cover and let stand 10 minutes. Chill to serve as directed on preceding page.

Is Sugar Really a Villain?

Sugar is one of the few foods that contain only carbohydrate; most foods are a combination of proteins, fats and carbohydrate. Dr. Myron Winick, one of *Redbook*'s Wise Woman's Diet consultants, had this to say about that question:

"Scientifically, sugar is a villain in only two ways. One has to do with teeth—sugar causes cavities. But the problem is not just the amount of sugar in the diet; it's the form of the sugar. If the sugar is consumed in a gooey, sticky form, like honey, it's even more cariogenic [cavity-causing].

"The other problem with sugar is that it's a sweet, pleasant but low-density source of calories. If you're dieting and limited to a certain number of calories a day, you're not going to feel full if you get a great number of calories from sugar. You will tend to eat more, and consequently it will be more difficult to diet."

At 17 calories a teaspoon, a little extra sugar here and there may not seem important. But if everything else remains the same and you add a teaspoon of sugar each day for a year that adds up to 6,205 calories or 1½ pounds on your scale, or 7 pounds in 5 years or 14 pounds in ten years. . . .

BREAKFAST

½ toasted English muffin (74),
spread with 2 teaspoons peanut
butter (63)
½ banana (50)
1 cup skim milk (86)

· LUNCH

Ham Sandwich: 2 ounces lean boiled
ham (122); 1 teaspoon mustard
(4); 1 lettuce leaf (1); 2 slices
rye bread (122)
1 large dill pickle (15)
1 pear (90)

DINNER

* Meatball Vegetable Soup (331)
1 small roll (1 ounce, 78), spread
with *Golden Apricot Spread
(10)
* Chocolate Pudding (110)

TO EAT ANY TIME

¼ cantaloupe (41)

Meatball Vegetable Soup

Meatballs:
1 pound lean ground beef
¼ cup uncooked iron-enriched
farina
¼ cup finely chopped, peeled
onion
½ teaspoon minced, peeled garlic
1 tablespoon chopped fresh
parsley
2 tablespoons grated Parmesan
cheese
¼ teaspoon salt

⅛ teaspoon black pepper
2 tablespoons tomato paste
1 large egg

Broth:
2 13¾-ounce cans beef broth
½ teaspoon salt
1 cup 1-inch slices celery
1 cup 1-inch slices peeled carrot
1 small onion, sliced and peeled
1 teaspoon dried basil leaves

Mix all meatball ingredients in a large bowl. In a large saucepan bring broth ingredients to a boil over moderately high heat. Form meat mixture into 12 balls, using 2 tablespoons for each. Add meatballs to boiling broth; cover pan, reduce heat to moderately low and simmer 45 minutes, until meatballs are cooked and vegetables are tender. *Makes 6 cups.* For diet serving allow ¼ of recipe.

MICROWAVE INSTRUCTIONS: Cut celery and carrots for broth in ½-inch pieces. Add to remaining broth ingredients in a 4-quart bowl; cover and cook about 15 to 20 minutes on high until vegetables are tender. Prepare meatballs as directed above and add to boiling broth. Cover and cook 5 minutes until meatballs are firm. Let stand, covered, 10 minutes before serving.

Per diet serving: 331 calories, 31 grams protein, 15 grams fat, 16 grams carbohydrate.

Golden Apricot Spread

1 11-ounce box dried apricots 1 cup water

In a small saucepan bring apricots and water to a simmer over moderately low heat; cover and cook 15 minutes, until apricots are tender. Put into a blender or food processor; cover and blend 40 to 50 seconds, until a smooth puree. Transfer to a pint container; cover and refrigerate. Spread keeps at least 3 weeks in the refrigerator; longer if frozen. *Makes 1¾ cups.* For diet serving allow 1 teaspoon.

MICROWAVE INSTRUCTIONS: Put apricots and water into a 1-quart baking dish or bowl. Cover and cook about 8 minutes on high, stirring every 2 minutes, until apricots are tender. Cover and let stand 5 minutes. Puree as directed above.

Per diet serving: 10 calories, 0 grams protein, 0 grams fat, 2 grams carbohydrate.

Chocolate Pudding

⅓ cup unsweetened cocoa 1 13-ounce can evaporated skim
¼ cup granulated sugar milk, undiluted
¼ teaspoon salt 1 large egg
  1½ teaspoons vanilla extract

Mix cocoa, sugar and salt in a heavy, medium-sized saucepan. Gradually whisk in milk and egg. When smooth, cook over low heat, stirring constantly, until mixture just begins to boil; to ensure a smooth pudding, this should take 15 to 20 minutes. Remove from heat and stir in vanilla. Pour into 6 individual serving dishes. Cover and chill several hours. Pudding thickens as it cools and keeps 3 to 4 days in the refrigerator. *Makes about 2 cups or 6 servings.* For diet serving allow ⅓ cup.

Per diet serving: 110 calories, 7 grams protein, 1 gram fat, 19 grams carbohydrate.

BREAKFAST

1 cup fresh or unsweetened frozen
  strawberries (55)
1 cup 4-grain multivitamin-and-iron
  supplement cereal (110)
1 cup skim milk (86)

LUNCH

* Garden Grill Open Sandwich
  (371)

DINNER

¾ cup chicken broth (16)
* Stir-Fried Liver with Peppers and
  Onions (286)
½ cup cooked rice (93)
1 tangerine (40)

TO EAT ANY TIME

Grapes in Yogurt: ½ cup sliced
  seedless green grapes (53), ½ cup
  plain low-fat yogurt (72), 1
  teaspoon brown sugar (17)

Garden Grill Open Sandwich

2 slices whole-wheat bread
2 1-ounce slices Muenster cheese
2 thin slices onion, separated into
  rings
3 fresh mushrooms, sliced thin

1 small green pepper, seeded and
  sliced thin
2 teaspoons wine vinegar
¼ teaspoon dried oregano leaves

Place bread on a small baking sheet and toast on one side under broiler or in a toaster-oven. Turn bread over and place 1 slice of cheese on each untoasted side. On each slice of cheese arrange half the onion rings, mushrooms and pepper slices; sprinkle with vinegar and oregano and broil 4 inches from heat source for 5 minutes, or until cheese is bubbly around the edges. *Makes 1 diet serving.*

Per diet serving: 371 calories, 24 grams protein, 17 grams fat, 37 grams carbohydrate.

Stir-Fried Liver with Peppers and Onions

1 pound beef or calves liver, sliced
  about ½-inch thick
2 tablespoons vegetable oil
2 teaspoons flour
¼ teaspoon black pepper
3 large sweet yellow onions (about
  1 pound), peeled and sliced
  ⅛-inch thick

3 medium-sized green peppers
  (about 1 pound), seeded and
  cut into ⅛-inch-wide strips
1½ teaspoons salt
4 teaspoons cider vinegar

Cut liver slices into ¼-inch-thick strips—about the size of a French fried potato. (Liver and vegetables may be cut up ahead of time, covered and refrigerated until needed.) In a large, heavy skillet heat 1 tablespoon of the oil over moderately high heat. Add liver, sprinkle with flour and pepper and cook 2 to 3 minutes, stirring once. When liver is just pink in the middle, remove to a serving platter and keep warm. Add remaining 1 tablespoon of oil to the skillet and add onions, peppers and salt; fry vegetables 1 minute, stirring constantly with 2 large spoons. Cover skillet, reduce heat to moderate and cook about 2 minutes, until vegetables are crisp-tender. Return liver to skillet, add vinegar and toss over high heat, using spoons, for about 1 minute to heat through and blend flavors. *Makes 4 to 6 servings.* For diet serving allow 3 ounces cooked liver and ¼ of the vegetables.

MICROWAVE INSTRUCTIONS: In a 3-quart baking dish mix liver strips, flour and pepper; omit oil. Cover and cook about 5 minutes, stirring every 2 minutes, until liver loses its pink color. Cover and let stand. Put onions, peppers and salt in a 3-quart baking dish; omit oil. Cover and cook 6 minutes on high, stirring every 3 minutes, until tender. Add vegetables to liver, stir in vinegar and cook 1 minute until heated through.

Per diet serving: 286 calories, 25 grams protein, 12 grams fat, 21 grams carbohydrate.

But Must I Eat Liver?

Many prospective dieters have shuddered at the obvious—that liver is on the Wise Woman's Diet menu once a week. The main reason—liver is a great source of iron, a mineral that's important for women of child-bearing years. Iron usually occurs only in small amounts in most foods, so it's especially important to eat wisely on 1,200 calories. And since liver is also an excellent source of vitamin A, thiamin and riboflavin it's an important food for people of all ages to learn to enjoy. We urge you to try chicken livers, the mildest of the lot, and delicious hot or cold. Cook them until they are still pink in the middle and they won't develop a bitter taste; at least try them in the Yakitori Skillet Dinner in Chapter 4, or Chicken Livers Provençal in Chapter 6, or Skewered Chicken Livers served with Hot Bulgur in Chapter 1.

BREAKFAST

½ cup orange juice (61)
1 medium-sized egg prepared any
   style (72)
1 toasted English muffin (148),
   spread with 1 tablespoon Golden
   Apricot Spread (recipe on page
   64, 30)
1 teaspoon butter or margarine (34);
   use to prepare egg or on muffin

LUNCH

Open-Face Ham Sandwich: 2 ounces
   boiled ham (122); 1 slice cracked-
   wheat bread (66)
1 ¾ x 6 inch slice raw green
   cabbage (24)
1 medium-sized carrot, peeled (30)
Yogurt Dip: ¼ cup plain low-fat
   yogurt (32); 1 teaspoon Dijon-
   style mustard (4)

DINNER

* Eggplant "Lasagna" (266)
Mixed Italian Salad: 1 cup torn
   romaine leaves (10); 1 small
   zucchini squash, sliced thin (22);
   1 roasted red pepper, chopped
   (23); 3 slices red onion (10);
   *White Wine Salad Dressing
   (36)
½ cup water-packed sweet cherries
   (add ¼ teaspoon almond extract,
   if desired, 59)

TO EAT ANY TIME

1½ cups skim milk (129)
4 large fresh mushrooms (20)

Eggplant "Lasagna"

1 large unpeeled eggplant (about
   2 pounds)
1 tablespoon olive oil
1½ cups chopped, peeled onion
1 teaspoon minced, peeled garlic
1 16-ounce can tomato sauce
1 teaspoon dried basil leaves
2 cups pot cheese or dry-curd
   cottage cheese
3 tablespoons water
½ teaspoon salt
¼ teaspoon black pepper
1 tablespoon dried parsley leaves
½ cup Parmesan cheese, preferably
   freshly grated

Wipe eggplant with a damp cloth and cut into ½-inch-thick slices.
Arrange one layer of slices on a baking sheet and broil 4 inches from
heat source for 20 minutes, turning slices once. Repeat with remaining
slices. Meanwhile, in a medium-sized skillet, heat oil over moderately
high heat; stir in onion and garlic and cook until onion is soft and
golden, about 5 minutes. Remove and set aside about ¼ cup of the
onion-garlic mixture. Add tomato sauce and basil to skillet, bring to
a boil, lower heat and let simmer about 5 minutes. In a medium-sized

mixing bowl place reserved onion mixture, pot cheese, water, salt, pepper and parsley; mix well.

Heat oven to 375°F. Spread a thin layer of the tomato sauce in the bottom of a 13½ x 8¾ x 1¾-inch baking pan. Arrange half the eggplant slices evenly over the sauce, spread with the pot cheese mixture and top with remaining eggplant in an even layer. Pour remaining tomato sauce over eggplant and sprinkle with Parmesan cheese. (Eggplant "Lasagna" may be prepared ahead to this point and covered and refrigerated until needed.) Bake 25 to 30 minutes, until cheese is melted and bubbly. (If pan is placed in the oven directly from the refrigerator, increase baking time by 15 to 20 minutes.) *Makes 4 to 6 servings.* For diet serving allow ⅙ of the "lasagna."

Per diet serving: 266 calories, 18 grams protein, 13 grams fat, 20 grams carbohydrate.

White Wine Salad Dressing

1 teaspoon minced, peeled garlic
½ teaspoon salt
¼ teaspoon black pepper
¼ cup lemon juice preferably freshly squeezed

2 tablespoons dry white wine or dry vermouth
2 tablespoons olive or vegetable oil

Place garlic and salt in a small bowl and mash with a fork or spoon. When smooth, add remaining ingredients and beat with a fork to mix well. Recipe may be doubled and dressing stored in a screw-top jar in the refrigerator. *Makes ½ cup.* For diet serving allow 1 tablespoon.

Per diet serving: 36 calories, 0 grams protein, 3 grams fat, 1 gram carbohydrate.

BREAKFAST

* Strawberry–Pear Shake (136)
1 slice whole-wheat bread (61),
  spread with 1 teaspoon butter or
  margarine (34)

LUNCH

Mexican Sandwich: 1 corn tortilla
  (65), filled with ½ cup 99%-fat-
  free cottage cheese (82) and
  topped with *Mexican Salsa (12)
1 medium-sized peach (38)

DINNER

Chicken and Rice Soup: 1½ cups
  chicken broth (33) with ¼ cup
  cooked rice (46)
2 large eggs, prepared any style
  (164), with 2 teaspoons butter
  or margarine (68)
Fresh Vegetable Salad: 1 cup
  zucchini slices (22); 1 cup yellow
  squash slices (25); ½ seeded
  green pepper, sliced (8); 1 stalk
  celery, sliced (7); Garlic
  Vinaigrette Dressing (recipe on
  page 23, 31)
1 small roll (1 ounce, 78)
2 plums (64)

TO EAT ANY TIME

5 dried, pitted prunes (130)
1 cup skim milk (86)

Strawberry–Pear Shake

1 cup fresh or unsweetened frozen
  strawberries
1 ripe pear, peeled, cored and cut
  into chunks

½ cup plain low-fat yogurt
½ cup liquid skim milk
1 teaspoon granulated sugar

Put all ingredients into a blender; cover and blend 40 to 50 seconds at
medium speed, until smooth and frothy. *Makes 2½ cups.* For diet
serving allow ½ of recipe.

Per diet serving: 136 calories, 6 grams protein, 2 grams fat, 26 grams carbohydrate.

Mexican Salsa

2 large tomatoes, peeled and
  chopped (about 2 cups; see
  note)
⅓ cup thin-sliced scallion or
  green onion
⅓ cup chopped fresh parsley

2 tablespoons chopped canned
  green chilies
1 teaspoon minced, peeled garlic
¾ teaspoon salt
¼ teaspoon dried oregano leaves

Put all ingredients in a medium-sized bowl and toss gently to mix. Cover and refrigerate until serving time. *Makes 2 cups salsa.* For diet serving allow ⅓ cup.

NOTE: To peel tomatoes, plunge into boiling water for 1 minute. Drain, rinse with cold water and peel.

Per diet serving: 12 calories, 1 gram protein, 0 grams fat, 3 grams carbohydrate.

It Tastes Better the Second Day

You've heard that said about soups, stews and ragouts for the reason that flavors seem to blend more harmoniously on standing. The cooking-lean reason for second-day goodness is that when you chill the stew, you can skim off any fat that has hardened on the surface before reheating. Every scooped-off tablespoon is a saving of 120 calories!

BREAKFAST

½ cup skim milk (43)
1 cup cooked iron-enriched farina
(100), topped with ¼ cup
chopped apple (15) and sprinkled
with cinnamon

LUNCH

Grilled Cheese Sandwich: 2 ounces
American cheese (210); 2 slices
whole-wheat bread (122); 1 teaspoon butter or margarine (34)
1 small zucchini squash, cut in
strips (22)
½ small cucumber, cut in spears
(12)
1/10 honeydew melon (49)

DINNER

* Broiled Fish Steaks (243)
½ cup steamed kale (22)
1 whole-wheat roll (61), spread with
1 teaspoon butter or margarine
(34)
Blueberry–Orange Cup: ½ cup
fresh or unsweetened frozen
blueberries (45), mixed with ½
cup orange juice (61) in a glass
½ cup skim milk (43)

TO EAT ANY TIME

1 ounce water-packed tuna, drained
(39), served on 2 lettuce leaves
(2), with 1½ teaspoons
mayonnaise (50)

Broiled Fish Steaks

2 tablespoons butter or margarine,
melted
2 tablespoons lemon juice
2 ½-inch-thick cod or halibut
steaks (about ¾ pounds each)

Salt
Black pepper
Paprika, if desired

Mix butter and lemon juice in a small pan. Place fish steaks in a broiler
pan without a rack and brush with half the lemon-butter. Sprinkle
lightly with salt, pepper and paprika. (Paprika gives an added golden
brown color to broiled fish.) Broil 3 to 5 inches from heat source for
3 minutes. Turn steaks, brush with remaining lemon-butter and broil
3 to 4 minutes longer, until fish is opaque in center. *Makes 4 servings.*
For diet serving allow ½ steak.

NOTE: If using frozen fish steaks, cook 6 to 7 inches from heat source
and double the cooking time.

MICROWAVE INSTRUCTIONS: In a 2-quart oblong baking dish melt butter
with lemon juice. Add fish and turn to coat with lemon-butter. Sprinkle with
seasonings. Cover and cook about 9 minutes on medium, rearranging steaks
after 6 minutes so that sides facing inside face outside. Fish is done when it
just begins to turn opaque. Cover and let stand 5 minutes. This fish is somewhat more like poached than broiled fish, but delicious.

Per diet serving: 243 calories, 32 grams protein, 12 grams fat, 0 grams carbohydrate.

BREAKFAST

1 cup 4-grain multivitamin-and-iron-
  supplement cereal (110)
½ banana (50)
1 cup skim milk (86)

LUNCH

Swiss Cheese Sandwich: 2 ounces
  Swiss cheese (214); 1 small
  tomato, sliced (20); 1 lettuce
  leaf (1); 1 teaspoon mayonnaise
  (34); 2 slices rye bread (122)
1 medium-sized peach (38)
1 cup skim milk (86)

DINNER

* Skillet Pork Chops with Apricot
  Sauce (248), garnished with 2
  dried apricot halves (18)
1 cup cooked broccoli (40)
1 slice whole-wheat bread (61),
  spread with 1 teaspoon butter or
  margarine (34)
½ cup diced fresh pineapple (40)

Skillet Pork Chops with Apricot Sauce

1 teaspoon lightly salted butter
  or margarine
1 teaspoon vegetable oil
4 loin pork chops, trimmed of
  separable fat (about 1 pound
  12 ounces)

½ cup water
¼ cup Golden Apricot Spread
  (recipe on page 64)
⅛ teaspoon salt
⅛ teaspoon black pepper
½ teaspoon granulated sugar

In a large skillet melt butter and oil over moderate heat; add pork and
cook 15 minutes on each side, until meat is no longer pink in middle.
Remove to a plate and keep warm. Add water, Golden Apricot Spread,
salt, pepper and sugar to pan; cook 1 minute, stirring up brown bits
on bottom of pan, until smooth. Pour sauce over the pork. *Makes 4
servings.* For diet serving allow ¼ of recipe.

Per diet serving: 248 calories, 23 grams protein, 13 grams fat, 8 grams carbohydrate.

BRUNCH

2 4-inch whole-wheat pancakes
(made from whole-wheat pancake
and waffle mix, 166)
* Orange Sauce (16)
1 medium-sized egg, prepared any
style without butter or margarine
(72)
2 dried prunes (33)
1 cup skim milk (86)

DINNER

* Chicken Barbecue (145)
1 ear corn, 5 x 1¾ inches (70),
steamed or broiled, served with
1 tablespoon butter or margarine
(100)
½ small tomato, sliced (10)
½ small cucumber, sliced (12)
1 cup cooked green beans (31),
served warm or cold with Garlic
Vinaigrette Dressing (recipe on
page 23, 31)
1 4 x 8 inch wedge watermelon
(111)

TO EAT ANY TIME

½ cup tomato juice (23)
2 ounces Cheddar cheese (228)
6 saltine crackers (74)

Orange Sauce

1 cup orange juice, preferably
fresh-squeezed

1½ teaspoons cornstarch

In a small saucepan mix orange juice with cornstarch until well blended. Cook 3 to 4 minutes over moderate heat, stirring constantly with a wire whisk, until mixture boils. Serve warm over whole-wheat pancakes. *Makes 1 cup.* For diet serving allow 2 tablespoons.

MICROWAVE INSTRUCTIONS: In a 2-cup measuring cup or a small bowl mix orange juice and cornstarch. Cover and cook about 3½ minutes on high, stirring once each minute, until boiling and thickened.

Per diet serving: 16 calories, 0 grams protein, 0 grams fat, 4 grams carbohydrate.

Chicken Barbecue

1 teaspoon minced, peeled garlic
1 teaspoon salt
1½ cups tomato juice
¼ cup cider or wine vinegar
3 tablespoons soy sauce
2 tablespoons Worcestershire
 sauce
1 tablespoon catsup
1 tablespoon lemon juice
⅛ teaspoon celery seed
1 3½-pound broiler-fryer chicken,
 cut up
2 additional chicken legs and
 thighs

On a board sprinkle the garlic with the salt and mash to a paste with the blade of a knife. In a small pan combine garlic mixture and remaining ingredients except chicken and bring to a simmer over moderate heat; cook about 10 minutes. Pour sauce into a large, shallow baking dish and cool slightly. Fold chicken wing tips under, add chicken to sauce and turn to coat. Cover and marinate 1 hour at room temperature or up to 12 hours in the refrigerator, turning chicken pieces several times.

Line a broiler pan with aluminum foil. Arrange chicken pieces in the broiler pan without a rack and baste with the sauce. Broil 7 inches from the heat for 12 minutes. Turn; baste and broil 10 minutes longer. If desired, remaining sauce may be placed in a small pan, simmered for 10 minutes and served with the chicken. *Makes 4 to 6 servings.* For diet serving allow ½ breast or 2 legs and 2 tablespoons sauce. Wrap and reserve 1 diet serving for dinner in Menu #10, and 2 ounces cooked chicken for lunch in Menu #13.

Timesaver tip: Omit marinade; broil chicken, brushing with soy sauce and lemon juice.

Microwave Instructions: Mix sauce ingredients in a small bowl; cover and cook on high 5 minutes. Arrange chicken in one layer in two 2-quart or one 3-quart oblong baking dish, having meatiest portions face the outside of the dish. Pour sauce over chicken and let marinate.

Cover chicken with wax paper to prevent spattering and cook on high about 20 minutes. Every 5 minutes spoon sauce over chicken and rearrange pieces so uncooked parts face outside of dish. Cook uncovered for last 5 minutes. Cover and let stand 10 minutes. This tastes more like a well-seasoned stewed chicken, still delicious.

Per diet serving: 145 calories, 27 grams protein, 3 grams fat, 4 grams carbohydrate.

BREAKFAST

1 small orange, sliced (45)
1 medium-sized egg (72), prepared
  any style with 1 teaspoon butter
  or margarine (34)
1 slice whole-wheat bread (61),
  spread with 1 teaspoon Golden
  Apricot Spread (recipe on page
  64, 10)

LUNCH

Sardine, Tomato and Watercress
  Sandwich: 2 ounces sardines,
  drained (125); 1 small sliced
  tomato (20); 10 sprigs watercress
  (7); 2 slices pumpernickel bread
  (158); 2 teaspoons butter (68)
1 small pear (90)

DINNER

* Swedish Meat Cakes (194)
1 cup raw cauliflower florets (27),
  with White Wine Salad Dressing
  (recipe on page 68, 36)
* Sweet and Sour Beets (37)
Yogurt Parfait: ½ cup water-packed
  sweet cherries (59); ½ cup plain
  low-fat yogurt (72)

TO EAT ANY TIME

1 cup skim milk (86)

Swedish Meat Cakes

¾ pound lean ground beef
½ cup creamed cottage cheese
1 small onion, peeled and minced

Scant ¼ teaspoon ground nutmeg
⅛ teaspoon black pepper
A light sprinkling of salt

In a large mixing bowl place ground beef, cottage cheese, onion, nutmeg and pepper and mix thoroughly with clean hands; shape mixture into 4 1-inch-thick cakes. Sprinkle salt evenly over the bottom of a heavy, 10-inch skillet. Place skillet over high heat until salt begins to brown lightly or when a few drops of water sprinkled into the pan skip across the salt. Add meat cakes to pan and pan-broil about 4 minutes on each side for medium-well-done cakes. *Makes 4 servings.* For diet serving allow 1 cake.

Per diet serving: 194 calories, 22 grams protein, 10 grams fat, 3 grams carbohydrate.

Sweet and Sour Beets

1 tablespoon honey
2 tablespoons cider vinegar
½ teaspoon salt

1 1-pound can julienne beets,
drained

In a small saucepan mix honey, vinegar and salt; add beets and toss gently. Cook over moderate heat just until hot, stirring constantly. Serve hot or cold. *Makes about 2 cups.* For diet serving allow ½ cup.

MICROWAVE INSTRUCTIONS: In a 1½-quart baking dish mix all ingredients as directed above. Cover and cook 2 minutes on high, stirring after 1 minute, until heated through.

Per diet serving: 37 calories, 1 gram protein, 0 grams fat, 9 grams carbohydrate.

Dressing Up Vegetables Without Inflating the Calories

The temptation when serving vegetables is to dress them with the habitual pat of butter, or cream sauce or even hollandaise sauce. Increase your repertoire of ways to serve vegetables at a lower calorie cost. Use ½ rather than 1 tablespoon of butter, melt it with 1 tablespoon lemon juice (4 calories) to pour over asparagus, green beans or spinach. Or add a dried or fresh chopped herb to the butter to toss with shredded cooked cabbage, steamed new potatoes or carrots. Make a cream sauce with ½ cup of low-fat yogurt (72 calories) warmed and tossed with crisp-cooked cauliflower. Have hollandaise sauce on broccoli but make it according to the low-calorie recipe used with Eggs Benedict, Chapter 1. Or braise vegetables in bouillon and they'll need no added dressing or salt.

BREAKFAST

1 cup tomato juice (46)
½ cup 99%-fat-free cottage cheese
  (82), sprinkled with cinnamon
1 slice whole-wheat bread (61)

LUNCH

3 ounces sardines, drained (187)
* Rice and Vegetable Salad (180)
1/10 honeydew melon (49)

DINNER

1 cup beef broth (34)
Chicken Barbecue (reserved from
  Menu #8, 145)
Buttered Rice: ½ cup cooked brown
  rice (116); 1 teaspoon butter or
  margarine (34)
* Russian Carrot Salad (79)
1 slice rye bread (61), spread with
  1 teaspoon butter or margarine
  (34)
½ cup fresh or unsweetened frozen
  raspberries (35)

TO EAT ANY TIME

½ cup skim milk (43)
10 thin pretzel sticks (12)

Rice and Vegetable Salad

1 cup uncooked converted long-
  grain white rice
¼ cup red wine vinegar
2 tablespoons vegetable oil
1 tablespoon water
½ teaspoon salt
⅛ teaspoon white pepper

1½ cups diced zucchini squash
½ cup sliced radishes
1 tablespoon chopped fresh
  dillweed
6 tablespoons plain low-fat yogurt
2 tablespoons thin-sliced scallion
  or green onion

Cook rice according to package directions. In a small bowl mix vinegar, oil, water, salt and pepper and toss with hot rice. Add zucchini, radishes and dill and toss to mix; cover and refrigerate until serving time. Just before serving, top with yogurt and scallion. *Makes about 6 cups.* For diet serving allow ⅙ of recipe.

Per diet serving: 180 calories, 4 grams protein, 5 grams fat, 28 grams carbohydrate.

Russian Carrot Salad

3 medium carrots, peeled, trimmed
and coarsely grated (about 2
cups)
½ tablespoon vegetable oil
1½ tablespoons cider vinegar
½ teaspoon salt

Few grains of black pepper
2 tablespoons chopped fresh
parsley
2 tablespoons thin-sliced scallion
or green onion

Put all ingredients in a bowl and toss to blend. *Makes 2 cups.* For diet
serving allow 1 cup.

Per diet serving: 79 calories, 1 gram protein, 3 grams fat, 12 grams carbohydrate.

Whose Diet Is It?

"At the present time physicians can give advice about diet and
exercise, monitor blood pressure and make sure people don't try
bizarre and dangerous ways of losing weight. But the daily practice
of the diet and the necessary determination are something only the
obese can provide for themselves. What doctors can do for the
obese is not lie to them, but rather to tell them that getting thin
involves a conscious decision and continuous work."

—Jules Hirsch, M.D.
Professor and Senior Physician,
Rockefeller University Hospital,
New York City
Consultant to *Redbook*'s
Wise Woman's Diet

BREAKFAST

1 cup 4-grain multivitamin-and-iron-supplement cereal (110)
½ cup fresh or unsweetened frozen blueberries (45)
1 cup skim milk (86)

LUNCH

* Creamy Lebanese Tuna Salad (235)
¾ cup fresh or unsweetened frozen strawberries (42)

DINNER

* Chicken Livers and Onions (195)
1 steamed potato (2½ inches in diameter, 104)
Buttered Broccoli: 1 cup cooked broccoli (40); 2 teaspoons butter or margarine (68)
Tossed Salad: 1 cup torn lettuce leaves (10); 1 small tomato, sliced (20); Garlic Vinaigrette Dressing (recipe on page 61, 31)
1/10 honeydew melon (49)

TO EAT ANY TIME

1 cup skim milk (86)
8 unshelled roasted peanuts (84)

Creamy Lebanese Tuna Salad

¼ cup plain low-fat yogurt
2 tablespoons minced scallion or green onion
1 tablespoon chopped fresh dillweed or 1 teaspoon dried dillweed
¼ teaspoon salt
⅛ teaspoon black pepper
⅓ cup diced, peeled cucumber
1 7-ounce can water-packed tuna, drained
2 1-ounce whole-wheat pita breads
1 cup spinach leaves

In a small bowl mix yogurt, scallion, dill, salt and pepper. Add cucumber and tuna and toss gently. Just before serving, line pitas with spinach and fill each with half the tuna mixture. *Makes 2 servings.* For diet serving allow 1 filled pita.

Per diet serving: 235 calories, 34 grams protein, 1 gram fat, 20 grams carbohydrate.

Chicken Livers and Onions

1 pound chicken livers
2 teaspoons vegetable oil
3 cups sliced, peeled onions

¼ teaspoon salt
Few grains of black pepper

Rinse livers; discard any bits of fat that cling to them and pat dry with paper towels. In a large skillet heat 1 teaspoon of the oil over moderate heat. Stir in onions; cover and cook 25 minutes, until tender. Remove to a plate. Add remaining 1 teaspoon oil, the livers, salt and pepper to skillet and cook 5 to 6 minutes, occasionally stirring gently, until livers are browned but still slightly pink in the center. Add onions and toss with livers to heat. *Makes 4 servings.* For diet serving allow ¼ of recipe.

MICROWAVE INSTRUCTIONS: Put onions in a 2-quart baking dish; omit oil. Cover and cook 5 minutes on high, stirring after 3 minutes, until tender. Add liver, salt and pepper and cook about 4 minutes until livers lose their pink color. Cover and let stand 5 minutes.

Per diet serving: 195 calories, 22 grams protein, 7 grams fat, 11 grams carbohydrate.

All Visible Fat Removed . . .

You'll see that direction in many of the recipes in this book for two reasons. First, a gram of fat has more than twice as many calories (9) as a gram of protein or carbohydrate (4 each). Since calorie-cutting is one big objective of this diet, removing and discarding all visible or separable fat from meats and poultry will help keep you lean.

Meats that have the fat and meat closely attached to bone, such as spareribs and lamb breast, can be de-fatted by a preliminary simmering in water for 45 minutes before baking or broiling. Three pounds of country-style pork loin spareribs will give up a surprising ⅓ cup of fat (750 calories).

BREAKFAST

1 cup cooked iron-enriched farina
(100)
6 dried pitted prunes (99)
1 cup skim milk (86)

LUNCH

Spinach Chef's Salad: 2 cups spinach
leaves (28); 1 ounce Swiss cheese
(105); 2 ounces lean boiled ham
(122); ½ cup mung bean sprouts
(18); ½ green pepper, sliced (8);
2 radishes (1); Basic Vinaigrette
Dressing (recipe on page 23, 31)
2 rye wafers (45)

DINNER

* Pork and Broccoli Stir-Fry (314)
½ cup cooked brown rice (116)
1½ cups cooked carrots (72)
1 small orange (45)

Pork and Broccoli Stir-Fry

⅓ cup water
2 tablespoons soy sauce
2 tablespoons dry sherry wine
1 to 2 teaspoons grated fresh
gingerroot or 1 teaspoon ground
ginger
1½ teaspoons cornstarch
½ teaspoon minced, peeled garlic

¼ teaspoon crushed red pepper
flakes
10 ounces lean boneless pork loin,
trimmed of separable fat and
cut into ¼ x 2-inch strips
1 tablespoon vegetable oil
4 cups raw broccoli florets

In a small bowl mix water, soy sauce, sherry, ginger, cornstarch, garlic
and red pepper flakes. Add pork; cover and refrigerate for 30 minutes.
Put pork mixture into a colander set over a bowl to drain; reserve
liquid. In a wok or 14- to 15-inch skillet heat oil over high heat; add
pork and stir-fry 2 to 3 minutes, until meat has lost its pink color. Add
broccoli and stir-fry 2 to 3 minutes longer, until broccoli is bright green
and crisp-tender. Add reserved soy sauce mixture and cook 40 to 50
seconds longer, until thickened. *Makes about 6 cups.* For diet serving
allow 3 cups.

MICROWAVE INSTRUCTIONS: Marinate pork and drain as directed above.
Put pork in a 4-quart baking dish; omit oil. Cover and cook on high 3
minutes, stirring once each minute. Add broccoli and cook 5 minutes longer,
stirring every 2 minutes, until crisp-tender. In a small bowl cook reserved
soy mixture about 2 minutes on high until thickened. Stir into pork and
broccoli and cook 1 minute longer until heated through.

Per diet serving: 314 calories, 25 grams protein, 18 grams fat, 11 grams carbohydrate.

BREAKFAST

1 cup plain low-fat yogurt (144),
  mixed with ½ cup unsweetened
  applesauce (50), and 3 tablespoons toasted wheat germ (81)
1 slice raisin bread (66), spread with
  1 teaspoon butter or margarine
  (34)

LUNCH

Chicken Sandwich: 2 ounces cooked
  chicken reserved from Menu #8,
  sliced (93); 2 lettuce leaves (2);
  1 teaspoon mayonnaise (34); 2
  slices cracked-wheat bread (132)
1 carrot, cut in sticks (30)
1 green pepper, cut in strips (16)
1 small apple (61)

DINNER

* Portuguese Baked Fish (151)
½ cup cooked rice (93)
1 cup cooked summer squash (25)
Romaine Salad: 2 cups torn romaine
  leaves (20); 3 thin slices red
  onion (10); White Wine Salad
  Dressing (recipe on page 68, 36)
1 tangerine (40)

TO EAT ANY TIME

1 cup skim milk (86)

Portuguese Baked Fish

1 pound frozen fish fillets, any
  variety, thawed
1 tablespoon olive oil
1 cup chopped, peeled onion
¾ teaspoon salt

1 7½-ounce jar roasted sweet red
  peppers, drained
¼ cup chopped fresh parsley
  (optional)

Heat oven to 425°F. Separate fish fillets, rinse in cold water and pat dry with paper towels. Spread oil over bottom of a shallow ovenproof baking dish and sprinkle with onion. Bake 10 minutes. Arrange fish fillets on top of onion and sprinkle with salt; scatter peppers evenly over fish. Bake 10 to 15 minutes, until fish is white and flakes easily with a fork. Sprinkle with parsley, if desired. *Makes 4 servings.* For diet serving allow ¼ of the fish and vegetables.

MICROWAVE INSTRUCTIONS: Put oil and onion in a 2-quart oblong baking dish; cover and cook on high 3 minutes until onion is translucent. Arrange fish on top of onion so that thickest portion of fillets face the outside of the dish. Sprinkle with salt and place peppers evenly over fish. Cover and cook 3 minutes until fish just begins to become opaque. Cover and let stand 5 minutes. Sprinkle with parsley, if desired.

Per diet serving: 151 calories, 21 grams protein, 4 grams fat, 7 grams carbohydrate.

BREAKFAST

½ cup plain low-fat yogurt (72)
½ cup fresh or unsweetened frozen
  strawberries (27)
1 slice whole-wheat bread (61),
  spread with 1 teaspoon butter or
  margarine (34)

LUNCH

Chef's Salad: 1 cup spinach leaves
  (14); 1 cup romaine lettuce leaves
  (10); 1 ounce Swiss cheese (107);
  1 ounce lean boiled ham (61);
  6 cherry tomatoes (20); 2
  tablespoons Garlic Vinaigrette
  Dressing (recipe on page 61, 62)
2 ½-inch-thick slices French bread
  (2½ x 2 inches, 88)
2 plums (64)

DINNER

* Lentil and Turnip-Green Soup
  (224)
1 small roll (1 ounce, 78), spread
  with 1 teaspoon butter or
  margarine (34)
1/10 honeydew melon (49)
1 cup skim milk (86)

TO EAT ANY TIME

1 cup skim milk (86)
1 large dill pickle (15)

Lentil and Turnip-Green Soup

1 teaspoon vegetable oil
1 cup chopped, peeled onions
1 teaspoon minced, peeled garlic
2 tablespoons chopped fresh
  parsley
4 cups water
1 cup dried lentils, rinsed and
  drained

2 teaspoons beef-flavor instant
  bouillon granules
1 10-ounce package frozen turnip
  greens
⅛ teaspoon black pepper
¼ cup grated Parmesan cheese

In a large saucepan heat oil over moderately high heat. Add onions, garlic and parsley and cook 3 to 4 minutes, stirring occasionally, until onions are translucent. Add water, lentils and bouillon granules and bring to a boil. Reduce heat to moderately low, cover pan and simmer 45 minutes, until lentils are tender. Add greens and pepper; cover pan and cook 10 to 15 minutes longer, stirring occasionally, until greens are tender. Serve with cheese. *Makes 5 cups.* For diet serving allow 1¼ cups.

MICROWAVE INSTRUCTIONS: Put onion, garlic and parsley (omit oil) in a 4-quart bowl; cover and cook 2 minutes on high. Add water, lentils and bouillon; cover and cook 15 minutes, stirring every 5 minutes, until lentils are soft. Add turnip greens and pepper and cook 10 minutes longer, stirring every 3 minutes to break up greens. Add ½ to 1 cup more water if soup seems too thick. Cover and let stand 5 minutes. Serve with cheese.

Per diet serving: 224 calories, 16 grams protein, 3 grams fat, 35 grams carbohydrate.

Your Own Reward System

One experienced dieter told *Redbook* that she kept a coffee cup on top of the refrigerator and every time she opened the refrigerator door with a nibbling intent and closed it without indulging, she dropped a quarter in the cup. At the end of each day her husband matched her quarter collection in kind, and when the Reward Kitty was large enough, they used it to buy a most-wanted record or tape. Of the reward system, Dr. Johanna Dwyer says:

"When a woman embarks on a diet, she decides the terms of the contract with herself and arranges her own reward system. If she realizes her weaknesses, creates rewards for her strengths and learns to tell which is which, she'll bypass—or at least survive—the dangerous times of dieting and emerge thinner and prouder for it."

CHAPTER THREE

Save Pennies While You Shed Pounds

Even though you know you'll be saving money on the impulse-buying snacks that used to find their way into your shopping cart, there are still times when any food budget needs a little extra paring down. These fourteen days of budget-conscious menus were developed to help you resist the most expensive cuts of meat, and instead to use good buys like turkey drumsticks, stewing beef, frankfurters, and the less expensive vegetables such as cabbage and turnips. These menus are planned, too, to save your time and energy. There are six optional freeze-ahead dinners where by preparing double portions you can make one preparation time equal two meals. It's a myth that you can't count calories comfortably on a budget.

BREAKFAST

3 4-inch buckwheat pancakes (made from buckwheat pancake and waffle mix, 162)
1 small banana (63), mashed with ¼ cup plain low-fat yogurt (38)

LUNCH

Ham and Cheese Open-Face Sandwich: 1 slice bread (68); 1 slice boiled ham (1 ounce, 61); 1 slice American cheese (105); ½ tomato, sliced (10)
½ green pepper, sliced (8)
1 tangerine (40)

DINNER

¾ cup tomato juice (34) with 1 slice lemon (1)
* Tarragon Baked Cornish Game Hens (196)
* Braised Peas and Lettuce (58)
Spinach–Mushroom Salad: 2 cups spinach leaves (28); 2 mushrooms, sliced (14); Garlic Vinaigrette Dressing (recipe on page 61, 31)
* Hot Spiced Fruit (100)

TO EAT ANY TIME

1 cup skim milk (86)
1 stalk celery (7), stuffed with 1 tablespoon peanut butter (94)

Tarragon Baked Cornish Game Hens

2 1½-pound Cornish game hens, thawed if frozen
¼ cup dry white wine
2 tablespoons lemon juice
2 teaspoons vegetable oil

¼ teaspoon minced, peeled garlic
2 teaspoons dried tarragon leaves
1 teaspoon salt
¼ teaspoon black pepper

Remove giblets from Cornish hens; reserve for use in soup stock. Rinse hens and pat dry with paper towels. Cut each hen in half lengthwise with shears or a sharp knife. In a 12-x-9-x-2-inch baking pan mix wine, lemon juice, oil, garlic, tarragon leaves, salt and pepper. Turn hens in marinade to coat thoroughly and let stand with cut sides down. Cover and chill 1 hour. Heat oven to 350°F. Turn hens over. Bake, uncovered, 30 minutes. Turn hens again; baste with pan juices. Bake 30 minutes more, basting every 10 to 15 minutes. To complete browning, broil hens 6 inches from heat source for 2 to 3 minutes. Transfer hens to heated serving dish. Cover to keep warm. Skim off and discard fat from pan juices. Serve pan juices with hens. *Makes 4 servings.* For diet serving allow ½ Cornish hen and ¼ of pan juices.

To freeze: Prepare double recipe. Place 4 hen halves in a plastic freezer container and add half the pan drippings. Seal and freeze.

To reheat: Heat oven to 350°F. Remove frozen hens from plastic

container and place in a baking pan. (No need to thaw.) Cover with aluminum foil. Bake 35 to 40 minutes, or until hot.

Per diet serving: 196 calories, 25 grams protein, 10 grams fat, 2 grams carbohydrate.

Braised Peas and Lettuce

¼ cup water
½ teaspoon salt
6 dark-green iceberg lettuce leaves,
    cut into ½-inch-wide strips

1 10-ounce package frozen green
    peas
¼ cup chopped fresh parsley

Put water, salt and half the lettuce strips in a 2-quart saucepan. Add frozen peas, parsley and remaining lettuce. Cover and cook about 15 minutes over moderate heat, until peas are cooked. *Makes 4 servings.* For diet serving allow ¼ of the peas and lettuce mixture.

Per diet serving: 58 calories, 4 grams protein, 0 grams fat, 11 grams carbohydrate.

Hot Spiced Fruit

1 8-ounce can juice-packed sliced
    pineapple, drained (see note)
1 8¾-ounce can unpeeled apricot
    halves (about 8 halves),
    drained, each half cut in 2

3 tablespoons water
¼ teaspoon ground cinnamon
¼ teaspoon ground cloves
1 teaspoon butter or margarine,
    cut in tiny pieces

Heat oven to 350°F. Arrange drained pineapple and apricots in an 8- or 9-inch pie plate. Mix water with cinnamon and cloves. Pour over fruit. Dot with butter. Bake 15 to 20 minutes, basting fruit with the liquid 2 or 3 times. Serve warm. *Makes 3 or 4 servings.* For diet serving allow ¼ of the fruit and syrup.

NOTE: Chill juice and use as a beverage; ¼ cup has 62 calories.

For diet serving: 100 calories, 1 gram protein, 1 gram fat, 24 grams carbohydrate.

BREAKFAST

½ medium grapefruit (40)
½ cup cooked iron-enriched farina
  (50)
1 cup skim milk (86)

LUNCH

Liverwurst Sandwich: 2 slices rye
  bread (122); 2 ½-inch-thick
  slices liverwurst (244)
3 cherry tomatoes (6)
1 stalk celery (7)
1 small apple (61)

DINNER

* Savory Braised Beef (297)
Mixed Green Salad: 2 cups mixed
  salad greens (20); 4 sliced radishes
  (4); 12 slices cucumber (8);
  *Buttermilk–Herb Salad Dressing
  (7)
* Orange Ambrosia (68)

TO EAT ANY TIME

1 cup skim milk (86)
1 medium banana (101)

Savory Braised Beef

1 tablespoon vegetable oil
1½ pounds boneless beef chuck,
  cut into 2-inch pieces and
  trimmed of all visible fat
1½ cups water
¾ cup sliced, peeled onion
1 cooking apple, peeled, cored and
  thinly sliced

1½ teaspoons salt
Few grains of black pepper
7 small new potatoes, peeled
4 2-inch wedges of cabbage
1 14½-ounce can sliced tomatoes
1 tablespoon cornstarch
1 tablespoon water

Heat oil in a Dutch oven over moderately high heat, add meat and
lightly brown on all sides. Add the 1½ cups water and the onion,
apple, salt and pepper; cover and cook over moderately low heat for 1
hour and 15 minutes. Add potatoes and cook, covered, 10 minutes
more. Arrange cabbage wedges over meat and cook, covered, 30 minutes longer or until vegetables and meat are tender. Pour tomatoes
over meat and heat 5 minutes. Remove cabbage, potatoes and meat
to serving platter. In a small bowl mix cornstarch with the 1 tablespoon
water and stir into meat juices; boil 1 minute or until sauce is thickened.
Makes 3 or 4 servings. For diet serving allow 3 ounces of cooked meat,
¼ of the gravy, 1 potato and 1 cabbage wedge.

Per diet serving: 297 calories, 28 grams protein, 11 grams fat, 21 grams carbohydrate.

Buttermilk–Herb Salad Dressing

1 cup buttermilk
1 tablespoon prepared mustard
1 teaspoon instant minced onion
2 teaspoons finely chopped fresh
  parsley or 1 teaspoon dried
  parsley flakes

⅛ teaspoon dried dillweed
⅛ to ¼ teaspoon salt
Few grains of pepper

Combine all ingredients in a small screw-top jar and shake to blend well. Chill several hours. Shake well before serving. Can be stored, tightly covered, in refrigerator about 1 week. *Makes 1 cup.* For diet serving allow 1 tablespoon.

Per diet serving: 7 calories, 1 gram protein, 0 grams fat, 1 gram carbohydrate.

Orange Ambrosia

1 cup orange sections (about 3
  small oranges)
1 small banana, sliced

½ cup juice-packed pineapple
  chunks, drained (see note)
¼ cup flaked coconut

Combine all ingredients. Mix and chill until serving time. *Makes 4 servings.* For diet serving allow ⅓ cup.

NOTE: Chill juice and use as a beverage; ¼ cup has 62 calories.

Per diet serving: 68 calories, 1 gram protein, 1 gram fat, 17 grams carbohydrate.

BREAKFAST

½ cup orange juice (61)
1 cup 4-grain multivitamin-and-iron-
  supplement cereal (110)
1 cup skim milk (86)
½ banana (50)

LUNCH

Tossed Tuna Salad: 3 cups torn
  lettuce leaves (30); 3 ounces
  water-packed tuna, drained (117);
  1 roasted sweet red pepper from
  a jar, sliced (15); 3 slices red
  onion (9); Basic Vinaigrette
  Dressing (recipe on page 23, 31)
1 slice whole-wheat bread (61)
1 cup tomato juice (46)

DINNER

1 4-ounce lean ground lamb patty,
  broiled (232)
Cherry Tomato Salad: 1 cup sliced
  cherry tomatoes (40); Basic
  Vinaigrette Dressing (recipe on
  page 23, 31)
* Hot Lentil Salad (162)
* Oranges in Red Wine (113)

Hot Lentil Salad

1 cup dried lentils, rinsed and
  drained
3 cups water
¼ teaspoon minced, peeled garlic
1 teaspoon salt
¼ teaspoon black pepper
1 tablespoon lemon juice

2 tablespoons red wine vinegar
1 tablespoon olive or vegetable oil
1 teaspoon dried mint leaves or
  2 teaspoons fresh leaves,
  chopped
½ cup diced, peeled red onion
¼ cup chopped fresh parsley

In a heavy, 2-quart saucepot bring lentils and water to a boil over high heat. Reduce heat to low, cover pot and simmer 30 minutes. Remove pot from heat and let stand, covered, 10 minutes. Meanwhile, in a bowl mash the garlic with the salt until smooth. Stir in remaining ingredients. Add hot lentils and toss gently with a fork to blend. *Makes about 2½ cups.* For diet serving allow ½ cup. Chill remaining salad and serve 1 diet portion cold for lunch in Menu #4.

Per diet serving: 162 calories, 10 grams protein, 3 grams fat, 24 grams carbohydrate.

Oranges in Red Wine

3 tablespoons granulated sugar
1 cup water
1 cup dry red wine
2 whole cloves
1 1-inch stick cinnamon

3 lemon slices
½ teaspoon vanilla extract
4 navel oranges, peeled and left
   whole

In a medium-sized saucepan bring sugar and water to a boil over high heat. When sugar is dissolved, add remaining ingredients except vanilla and oranges and return to boiling. Reduce heat to moderately low and simmer 15 minutes. Add vanilla. Strain syrup over oranges in a serving bowl. Chill. *Makes 3 or 4 servings.* For diet serving allow 1 orange and ¼ of the syrup.

Per diet serving: 113 calories, 2 grams protein, 0 grams fat, 27 grams carbohydrate.

Low-Cost Substitutes

Cost, in this case, is calories. There are several little ways you can cut calories; not any will add up to a lot in one meal, but over a period of a week or a month or a lifetime they're worth doing.

Flour vs. cornstarch. These thickeners are about the same calorically, but cornstarch has twice the thickening power of flour. Give it preference in gravies, sauces, puddings to use half as much thickener.

Cocoa vs. chocolate. Almost fat-free, cocoa is lower in calories than chocolate. Try it in Cream Puffs with Chocolate Sauce, Chapter 5.

Thin-sliced bread vs. regular-sliced. White breads can range from 41 calories per thin slice to 74 per thick slice. If you habitually choose the thin slice, you can count the difference.

BREAKFAST

½ medium-sized grapefruit (40)
1 large soft-boiled egg (82)
1 cloverleaf roll (83)
1 teaspoon butter or margarine (34)
   to use on egg or roll

LUNCH

½ cup Hot Lentil Salad, served
   cold (reserved from Menu #3,
   162)
¼ head iceberg lettuce (14), with
   ½ green pepper, sliced (8)
1 ounce Muenster cheese (92)
3 whole-grain rye wafers (67)
1 pear (90)

DINNER

* Chicken Livers with Green Herbs
   (250)
* Deviled Celery Salad (52)
½ cup cooked brown rice (116)
1 syrup-packed peach half with 2½
   tablespoons syrup (85) and 1½
   tablespoons dry sherry wine (18)

Chicken Livers with Green Herbs

½ pound chicken livers
2 teaspoons vegetable oil
1 teaspoon butter or margarine
½ teaspoon salt
⅛ teaspoon black pepper
¼ teaspoon minced, peeled garlic

2 tablespoons minced scallion or
   green onion
2 tablespoons chopped fresh
   parsley
2 tablespoons dry white wine

Rinse livers, discarding any bits of fat that cling to them, and pat dry with paper towels. Heat oil and butter in a medium-sized skillet over high heat. When butter foam subsides, add livers, sprinkle with salt and pepper and cook 2 minutes, stirring constantly. Add garlic, scallion and half the parsley and cook 1 minute. Add the wine and cook 1 minute longer, stirring constantly. Sprinkle with remaining parsley. *Makes 2 servings.* For diet serving allow ½ the liver.

Per diet serving: 250 calories, 30 grams protein, 12 grams fat, 5 grams carbohydrate.

Deviled Celery Salad

2 teaspoons Dijon-style mustard
2 teaspoons lemon juice
2 teaspoons vegetable oil
2 tablespoons water

¼ teaspoon salt
⅛ teaspoon black pepper
3 cups thin-sliced celery

In a bowl mix mustard, lemon juice, oil, water, salt and pepper. Add celery and toss. *Makes 3 cups.* For diet serving allow 1 cup.

Per diet serving: 52 calories, 1 gram protein, 3 grams fat, 5 grams carbohydrate.

Saving Pennies

Eggs are sold by the dozen but sized by weight. As a general rule, if there is less than a seven-cent price difference between one size and the next smaller size, you'll get more for your money by buying the larger size, but 1 large egg has 82 calories and 1 medium egg 72.

Cereals you cook yourself are nearly always less expensive than ready-to-eat cereals. Read cereal labels carefully. They will tell you what percentage of the United States Recommended Daily Allowance (U.S. RDA) of vitamins and minerals one serving provides.

With vegetables, it's the cost per serving that counts. A pound of fresh peas yields two ½-cup servings; a 10-ounce package of frozen yields three; a 16-ounce can, four. Never discard the liquid from canned vegetables; it contains a substantial proportion of the vitamins and minerals. Add it to soups or, if an appropriate flavor, to tomato juice to make a vegetable juice cocktail.

BREAKFAST

1 cup 4-grain multivitamin-and-iron-
supplement cereal (110)
¾ cup skim milk (65)
½ cup sliced fresh or unsweetened
frozen peaches (32)

LUNCH

Sardines on Rye: 2 ounces drained
sardines, including skin and bones
(124); 1 slice rye bread (61),
with 1 teaspoon butter or
margarine (34)
Cottage Cheese Salad: ½ cup
cottage cheese (82); 4 sliced green
pimiento-stuffed olives (26); 1
cup torn lettuce leaves (10)
1 large plum (50)

DINNER

1 cup hot beef broth with lemon
slice (23)
* Ham and Rice Salad (405)
8 spears steamed fresh or frozen
asparagus (20)
* Pineapple Frappé (68)

TO EAT ANY TIME

1 cup skim milk (86)

Ham and Rice Salad

1 cup uncooked converted long-
grain white rice
2 cups chicken broth
2 tablespoons vegetable oil
4 tablespoons wine vinegar
½ teaspoon Dijon-style mustard
¾ teaspoon salt
¼ teaspoon black pepper
2 tablespoons chopped fresh
dillweed or 1 tablespoon dried
dillweed

¼ teaspoon dried basil leaves
2 tablespoons chopped scallion or
green onion
1 cup diced, peeled carrots
2 medium-sized tomatoes, sliced
10 ounces fully cooked ham,
trimmed of all fat and cut into
short, thin strips (about 2 cups)

Cook rice in chicken broth according to package directions until tender
but still slightly firm. In a large serving bowl mix the oil, vinegar,
mustard, salt, pepper, dill and basil. Add hot, cooked rice and toss to
mix. Cover and refrigerate 1 hour or longer. Just before serving add remaining ingredients and toss; taste, add a little more vinegar if desired.
Makes about 6 cups, or 3 to 4 servings. For diet serving allow ¼ of the
salad.

Per diet serving: 405 calories, 18 grams protein, 16 grams fat, 47 grams carbohydrate.

Pineapple Frappé

½ cup unsweetened pineapple
  juice

3 ice cubes
Fresh mint sprig (optional)

Put pineapple juice and ice cubes in an electric blender; cover and blend a few seconds on high speed until ice cubes are just crushed. Pour into a tall glass and garnish with mint, if desired. *Makes 1 diet serving.*

Per diet serving: 68 calories, 0 grams protein, 0 grams fat, 17 grams carbohydrate.

A Label-Reader Be

It takes a little extra time in the supermarket to stop to read labels, but think of it as time not spent hovering longingly at the cookie display. These are some of the most important bits of information on foods that nutrition labels reveal: the calories per serving, the grams of protein, fat and carbohydrate per serving, the percentage of the United States Recommended Daily Allowance (U.S. RDA) of vitamins and minerals. Labels will tell you whether a fruit is water-packed, juice-packed or packed in heavy syrup, whether fish is packed in water or oil. You can discern the caloric difference between a plain frozen vegetable and one packed in a fancy sauce. Choose, of course, the water-packs. At the cereal shelf, choose carefully to meet your needs; all cereals have nutritional labeling. What you choose when you shop is what will end up being your diet at home.

BREAKFAST

Breakfast Open-Face Sandwich: 1
English muffin (148), topped
with 1 ounce Cheddar cheese
(114) and broiled 2 minutes
1 cup tomato juice (46)

LUNCH

1 3-ounce broiled lean hamburger
(4 ounces before cooking, 186),
spread with 1 teaspoon catsup
(5), on 1 hamburger roll (119)
1 pear (90)
1 cup skim milk (86)

DINNER

Appetizer Consommé: 1 cup
cooked kale (44), stirred into
1½ cups hot chicken broth (33)
* Fish with Pureed Vegetable Sauce
(142)
1 cup sliced red cabbage (28), with
Basic Vinaigrette Dressing (recipe
on page 23, 31)
1 slice whole-wheat bread (61)

TO EAT ANY TIME

½ cup orange juice (61)

Fish with Pureed Vegetable Sauce

3 cups water
1 small onion, peeled and
quartered
3 carrots, peeled and cut into
1-inch chunks
1 stalk celery, cut into ¾-inch
chunks
¼ cup chopped scallion or green
onion

2 to 3 tablespoons lemon juice
1 teaspoon salt
1 bay leaf
4 sprigs parsley
¼ teaspoon dried thyme leaves
1 pound fresh sole or flounder
fillets
Yolk of 1 large egg
1 teaspoon Dijon-style mustard

Put a 10-ounce custard cup or empty tuna can upside down in a large
saucepot or Dutch oven at least 10 inches in diameter. Add water and
bring to a boil over moderately high heat. Add onion, carrots, celery,
scallion, lemon juice, salt, bay leaf, parsley and thyme. Fold fish fillets
into thirds and arrange them on an 8-inch plate; put plate on top of
custard cup. Bring vegetables and liquid to a boil and cover pot; reduce
heat to moderately low and cook 15 to 20 minutes, until vegetables are
tender and fish is opaque in thickest part. Remove plate of fish and
keep warm.

Put about 1 cup of the hot liquid, some of the vegetables, the egg
yolk and mustard into a blender; cover and blend 40 seconds on low
speed, until smooth. Pour into a bowl; blend remaining liquid and
vegetables. Stir sauce to mix. Arrange fish on serving plates or platter
and spoon sauce over. *Makes 4 servings.* For diet serving allow ¼ of
the fish and sauce.

Per diet serving: 142 calories, 22 grams protein, 3 grams fat, 7 grams carbohydrate.

BREAKFAST

1 small orange, sliced (45)
1 cup cooked oatmeal (132), with
  2 tablespoons seedless raisins (52)
1 cup skim milk (86)

LUNCH

Cottage Cheese Platter: ½ cup
  creamed cottage cheese (119), on
  1 lettuce leaf (1), with ½ small
  tomato, sliced (10), 1 small carrot,
  cut into sticks (15), and 6 slices
  cucumber (4)
1 slice white bread (68)
3 medium-sized water-packed
  apricot halves (32)

DINNER

* Roast Turkey Drumsticks (220)
* Turnip–Onion Casserole (37)
1 cloverleaf roll (83)
* Marinated Green Bean Salad (40)
* Pears Poached in Red Wine (54)

TO EAT ANY TIME

1 cup skim milk (86)
1 tangerine (40)
5 dried pitted prunes (82)

Roast Turkey Drumsticks

1 tablespoon vegetable oil
1 3¼- to 3¾-pound package
  frozen turkey drumsticks,
  thawed (3 drumsticks; see
  note)
¼ teaspoon crumbled dried
  rosemary leaves

¼ teaspoon dried thyme leaves
½ teaspoon salt
⅛ teaspoon black pepper
½ cup dry red wine
¼ cup chopped, peeled onion
½ cup chicken broth or bouillon

Heat oven to 350°F. Heat oil in a skillet over moderately high heat. Add turkey drumsticks and brown on all sides. Place drumsticks in a shallow baking dish. Mix rosemary, thyme, salt and pepper; sprinkle over drumsticks. In a small bowl mix wine, onion and broth and pour into baking dish. Roast drumsticks for 45 minutes, basting occasionally with wine mixture. Reduce heat to 325°F.; cover drumsticks with a lid or with foil and roast 1 to 1¼ hours longer or until tender. To serve, slice meat from bone. *Makes 4 servings.* For diet serving allow 3 ounces cooked turkey without skin and ¼ of the sauce.

NOTE: Use fresh turkey drumsticks if available.

Per diet serving: 220 calories, 6 grams protein, 11 grams fat, 1 gram carbohydrate.

Turnip–Onion Casserole

Vegetable oil to grease casserole
1⅓ pounds yellow turnip
  (rutabaga)
2 cups thinly sliced, peeled onion

Salt and black pepper
1 chicken bouillon cube
⅓ cup boiling water
1 tablespoon butter or margarine

Heat oven to 350°F. Lightly oil a 2-quart ovenproof casserole. Pare turnip, cut in half and then across into thin slices. Measure 5 cups sliced turnip. Arrange alternate layers of turnip and onion in greased casserole. Sprinkle each layer with salt and pepper. Dissolve bouillon cube in boiling water and pour over vegetables. Dot vegetables with butter. Cover casserole and bake along with turkey drumsticks for 45 minutes at 350°F. and then 1¼ to 1½ hours at 325°F. *Makes 4 or 5 servings.* For diet serving allow ⅕ of the casserole.

NOTE: If preparing turnip casserole by itself, bake it at 325°F. for 2 to 2¼ hours.

Per diet serving: 37 calories, 1 gram protein, 1 gram fat, 6 grams carbohydrate.

Marinated Green Bean Salad

1 9-ounce package frozen French-
  style green beans
½ medium-sized onion, peeled
  and thinly sliced

¼ cup bottled low-calorie Italian
  salad dressing
¼ cup water
8 Boston lettuce leaves

Cook beans according to package directions; drain, cool and place in a shallow dish. Arrange onion on top of beans. Mix salad dressing and water together and pour over vegetables. Cover vegetables and chill 2 to 3 hours in refrigerator. Serve on lettuce. *Makes 4 servings.* For diet serving allow 2 lettuce leaves and ¼ of the vegetables.

Per diet serving: 40 calories, 2 grams protein, 1 gram fat, 6 grams carbohydrate.

Pears Poached in Red Wine

⅓ cup water
2 tablespoons red wine
1 3-inch cinnamon stick
1 teaspoon granulated sugar
1 slice lemon

Few grains of ground nutmeg
Few grains of salt
2 ripe pears, peeled, halved and
  cored

In a medium-sized saucepan bring the water, wine, cinnamon, sugar, lemon, nutmeg and salt to a boil over moderate heat. Add pears; cover and simmer 15 to 20 minutes, until pears are just tender. Discard cinnamon stick. Chill pears in syrup several hours. *Makes 3 or 4 servings.* For diet serving allow ½ pear and ¼ of the syrup. Reserve 1 diet serving for dinner dessert in Menu #8.

Per diet serving: 54 calories, 0 grams protein, 0 grams fat, 14 grams carbohydrate.

What Are You Paying for Calories or the Lack of Them?

The dairy counter, especially, has such an array of choices, butter versus whipped butter; cream cheeses versus whipped creamed cheese and imitation cream cheeses; plain yogurts, low-fat yogurts and fruit-flavored yogurts; margarine and diet margarines; whole milk and skim milk and low-fat milk. It pays to check the labels and make decisions about what you'll use. Check the cost of canned dietetic foods against regular packs. And then watch for new products; they're continually appearing on the market. Weigh cost against the calories carefully.

BREAKFAST

½ pink grapefruit, plain or broiled (40)
* Egg in a Nest (145)
1 cup skim milk (86)

LUNCH

Liverwurst Sandwich: 1 slice rye bread (61); 2 ounces liverwurst (150); 1 slice red onion (3)
3 cherry tomatoes (5)
½ medium-sized carrot, cut into strips (15)
1 stalk celery, cut into strips (7)
¼ cup creamed cottage cheese (60)

DINNER

* Deviled Beef Brisket (300)
½ cup steamed broccoli (20)
½ cup cooked egg noodles (100)
* Dilled Cabbage–Carrot Slaw (39)
Pears Poached in Red Wine (reserved from Menu #7, 54)

TO EAT ANY TIME

* Chocolate–Banana Shake (124)

Egg in a Nest

1 slice white bread, toasted
1 large egg, yolk and white separated

Few grains of salt
Few grains of black pepper

Heat oven to 350°F. or use a toaster-oven. Put toast on a baking sheet. In a small, deep bowl beat egg white with an electric or rotary beater until stiff peaks hold when beater is lifted. Swirl beaten egg white over toast, making a well in the center. Drop egg yolk in well; sprinkle with salt and pepper. Bake 15 to 20 minutes, or until egg white is golden brown. *Makes 1 diet serving.*

Per diet serving: 145 calories, 9 grams protein, 7 grams fat, 13 grams carbohydrate.

Deviled Beef Brisket

1¼ pounds boneless beef brisket
1 small onion, peeled and quartered
¼ teaspoon minced, peeled garlic
1 small bay leaf
2 to 3 cups water

1 tablespoon dark corn syrup
1 tablespoon bottled steak sauce
2 teaspoons Dijon-style mustard
1 teaspoon cornstarch
½ teaspoon salt

Put the beef, onion, garlic and bay leaf into a medium-sized skillet. Add enough water to just cover the meat. Cover skillet and bring to a boil over moderately high heat. Reduce heat to moderately low and simmer 1½ to 2 hours, until meat is tender. Heat oven to 350°F. Remove beef from liquid in skillet and place in a small roasting pan; reserve liquid. Combine corn syrup, steak sauce, mustard, cornstarch, salt and 1 cup of reserved liquid from brisket. Pour over beef. Bake 30 minutes, basting 2 or 3 times. Remove beef from pan and cut into very thin slices. Arrange slices on serving platter and pour pan gravy over them. *Makes 3 or 4 servings.* For diet serving allow ¼ of the meat and gravy. Wrap and reserve 3 ounces of brisket for lunch in Menu #9.

To freeze: Prepare double recipe and put half the beef slices and gravy in a plastic freezer container. Seal and freeze.

To reheat: Place plastic container of beef in the refrigerator to thaw. Put thawed meat in a medium-sized skillet and heat over moderate heat about 15 minutes, until hot.

Per diet serving: 300 calories, 26 grams protein, 18 grams fat, 6 grams carbohydrate.

Dilled Cabbage–Carrot Slaw

½ small onion, peeled and grated
¾ cup plain low-fat yogurt
½ tablespoon mayonnaise
½ teaspoon salt

¼ teaspoon dried dillweed
3 cups shredded cabbage
1½ small carrots, peeled and
coarsely grated

In a medium-sized bowl mix onion, yogurt, mayonnaise, salt and dillweed; add cabbage and carrots and toss to mix. *Makes 3 cups.* For diet serving allow ½ cup.

Per diet serving: 39 calories, 2 grams protein, 1 gram fat, 5 grams carbohydrate.

Chocolate–Banana Shake

½ cup liquid skim milk
½ small ripe banana

2 teaspoons chocolate-flavored
drink mix
2 or 3 ice cubes

Put all ingredients in a blender. Cover and blend 20 to 30 seconds at medium speed, until smooth and frothy. *Makes 1 diet serving.*

Per diet serving: 124 calories, 5 grams protein, 0 grams fat, 26 grams carbohydrate.

BREAKFAST

½ cup vegetable juice cocktail (27),
  with ½ teaspoon Worcestershire
  sauce (2) and 1 lemon wedge (1)
1 cup cooked iron-enriched farina
  (100), with 1 teaspoon butter or
  margarine (34) and 2 teaspoons
  honey or brown sugar (34)
½ cup skim milk (43)

LUNCH

Open-Face Beef Brisket Sandwich:
  1 slice rye bread (61), spread with
  1 teaspoon prepared mustard (4);
  3 ounces beef brisket (reserved
  from Menu #8, 235) or 2½
  ounces sliced roast beef (246); 2
  leaves lettuce (2); 2 radishes (2)

DINNER

* Tuna–Noodle Florentine (320)
1 cup cooked green beans (31)
* Orange–Red Onion Salad (43)
  with Piquant Salad Dressing
  (recipe on page 50, 11)
½ cup vanilla low-fat yogurt (97)
¼ cup fresh or unsweetened frozen
  strawberries (14)

TO EAT ANY TIME

1 cup skim milk (86)
4 vanilla wafers (56)

Tuna–Noodle Florentine

1 10-ounce package frozen
  chopped spinach
4 ounces medium egg noodles
  (about 2 cups), cooked
1 7-ounce can and 1 3-ounce can
  water-packed tuna, drained and
  flaked

1 tablespoon butter or margarine
2 tablespoons flour
½ teaspoon salt
1½ cups liquid skim milk
¼ cup grated Parmesan cheese
2 tablespoons chopped fresh
  parsley (optional)

Cook spinach according to package directions. Drain well, pressing out as much liquid as possible. Spread evenly over bottom of a 10-x-6-x-1¾-inch baking dish. Cover with a layer of cooked noodles and top with flaked tuna. Heat oven to 350°F. In medium-sized saucepan melt butter over moderate heat. Stir in flour and salt. Remove pan from heat and cool 1 minute. Whisk in milk ¼ cup at a time. When mixture is smooth, return to heat and cook, stirring or whisking constantly, until thickened and boiling. Spoon sauce over tuna in baking dish. Sprinkle with cheese. Bake 25 to 30 minutes, or until hot and bubbly. If desired, sprinkle with parsley. *Makes 3 or 4 servings.* For diet serving allow ¼ of tuna-noodle mixture.

To freeze: Prepare double recipe in 2 separate baking dishes. Cover one dish with aluminum foil and freeze.

To reheat: Thaw at room temperature for 1 hour. Heat oven to 350°F. Bake 30 to 35 minutes, until hot and bubbly.

Per diet serving: 320 calories, 33 grams protein, 7 grams fat, 29 grams carbohydrate.

Orange–Red Onion Salad

4 large lettuce leaves
2 large navel oranges, peeled and
 sliced crosswise into 8 slices

1 small red onion, peeled and
 sliced into rings
4 tablespoons Piquant Salad
 Dressing (recipe on page 50)

Arrange lettuce leaves, orange slices and onion rings on 4 individual plates. Spoon 1 tablespoon salad dressing over each serving. *Makes 4 servings.* For diet serving allow 1 plate.

Per diet serving: 54 calories, 1 gram protein, 1 gram fat, 11 grams carbohydrate.

Seeing the Light

The fastest-growing area in the food industry is "light" foods. These are products designed to appeal to people watching their weight. "Light" may be applied to products low in caffeine, low in sodium (salt) or, more and more frequently, to products that have fewer calories than their traditional counterparts. Look for reduced fat (and sometimes reduced sodium) cheeses, "light" macaroni, "light" beer and wines, imitation mayonnaise, reduced calorie spreads without the use of artificial sweeteners and milder (less salt) soy sauce.

BREAKFAST

½ cup creamed cottage cheese (119), mixed with ½ cup plain low-fat yogurt (72)
½ cup fresh or unsweetened frozen strawberries (27)
1 slice raisin bread, toasted (66)

LUNCH

* Quick Clam–Vegetable Chowder (140)
1 slice whole-wheat bread (61)
2 ½-inch-thick slices liverwurst (122)
1 cup salad greens (10), tossed with Basic Vinaigrette Dressing (recipe on page 23, 31)

DINNER

* Frank and Applekraut Casserole (255)
1 slice rye bread (61)
Fresh Vegetable Relish Tray: ½ carrot, sliced (15); 1 stalk celery, sliced (7); ¼ green pepper, sliced (4); 1 radish (1)
½ cup vanilla ice milk (90) with 3 syrup-packed unpeeled apricot halves and 1¾ tablespoons syrup (73)

TO EAT ANY TIME

½ cup skim milk (43)

Quick Clam–Vegetable Chowder

1 8-ounce bottle clam juice
1 10½-ounce can minced clams, drained and liquid reserved
1 large potato, peeled and cut into ½-inch cubes (about 1 cup)
6 scallions or green onions, sliced
2 small carrots, peeled and coarsely grated (about 1 cup)
¼ teaspoon dried thyme leaves
¼ to ½ teaspoon salt
¾ cup instant nonfat dry milk
1 cup water

Pour clam juice and liquid from the minced clams into a medium-sized saucepan; add potatoes and bring to a simmer over moderate heat. Cook about 10 minutes, until potatoes are almost tender. Reduce heat to moderately low; add scallions, carrots, thyme and salt to saucepan and cook 10 minutes longer. Mix dry milk and water; add to pan with drained minced clams and heat soup just to boiling point. *Makes 4 servings.* For diet serving allow 1 cup.

NOTE: Chowder may be prepared the day before and stored in covered container in refrigerator. To carry for lunch, reheat and pack in a wide-necked, insulated container.

Per diet serving: 140 calories, 13 grams protein, 1 gram fat, 19 grams carbohydrate.

Frank and Applekraut Casserole

1 teaspoon butter or margarine
1 medium-sized onion, peeled and
  sliced thin
2 small tart cooking apples, such
  as Pippins, peeled, cored and
  diced

1 16-ounce can sauerkraut
2 teaspoons caraway seeds
4 2-ounce frankfurters, slashed
  diagonally 6 times

Heat oven to 350°F. In a medium-sized saucepan melt butter over
moderate heat. Add onion and cook 3 to 5 minutes, stirring frequently,
until lightly browned. Add apples and cook 2 to 3 minutes, stirring
constantly. Add sauerkraut and caraway seeds; toss gently to mix well.
Transfer mixture to a 1½-quart casserole dish. Place frankfurters on
top. Bake 30 minutes, until sauerkraut mixture is hot and frankfurters
are browned. *Makes 3 or 4 servings.* For diet serving allow ¼ of sauerkraut mixture and one frankfurter.

To freeze: Prepare double recipe of sauerkraut mixture and place half
of it in a plastic freezer container. Seal and freeze.

To reheat: Put plastic container of sauerkraut mixture in refrigerator
to thaw. Heat oven to 350°F. Place thawed mixture in a 1½-quart
casserole dish. Add frankfurters and bake 35 minutes, or until hot.

Per diet serving: 255 calories, 9 grams protein, 17 grams fat, 18 grams carbohydrate.

BREAKFAST

* Yogurt Breakfast Nog (165)

LUNCH

Sardine Salad Plate: 3 ounces sardines with skin and bones, drained (187), with 2 scallions or green onions (14); 2 slices tomato (8); 2 lettuce leaves (2); ½ medium-sized carrot, cut into strips (15); and 1 small stalk celery, cut into strips (5)
1 slice rye bread (61)

DINNER

* Vegetable–Beef Roulades (274)
½ cup cooked egg noodles (100), sprinkled with ¼ teaspoon finely chopped walnuts (13)
* Baked Dilled Tomatoes (50)
* Orange Freeze (142)

TO EAT ANY TIME

¾ cup skim milk (65)
1¼ cups fortified high-protein cereal (107)

Yogurt Breakfast Nog

1 cup plain low-fat yogurt
1 egg
½ cup syrup-packed sliced peaches, drained

2 tablespoons wheat germ
1 tablespoon honey
Few grains of ground nutmeg

Put yogurt, egg, peaches, wheat germ and honey into a blender. Cover and blend 10 seconds at medium speed, until smooth. Pour into glasses. Sprinkle with nutmeg. *Makes about 1½ cups, or 2 servings.* For diet serving allow ¾ cup.

Per diet serving: 165 calories, 10 grams protein, 5 grams fat, 20 grams carbohydrate.

Vegetable–Beef Roulades

2 cups water
2 medium-sized carrots, peeled, each cut into 8 pieces, 3½ x ¼ inches
1 pound lean ground beef
1 egg
3 tablespoons chopped, peeled onion
2 tablespoons wheat germ

2 tablespoons catsup
2 teaspoons Worcestershire sauce
1½ teaspoons prepared horseradish
1 teaspoon salt
¼ teaspoon black pepper
1 8-ounce can whole green beans, drained

Bring water to a boil in a small saucepan. Add carrots and cook 3 to 5 minutes, until crisp-tender; drain. In a medium-sized bowl thoroughly combine the beef, egg, onion, wheat germ, catsup, Worcestershire sauce, horseradish, salt and pepper. Divide meat mixture into 4 equal parts. On a piece of wax paper pat one piece of meat into a 4½-x-6-inch rectangle. Beginning at one narrow end, lay 4 carrot sticks and ¼ of the green beans alternately across meat; roll up meat jelly-roll style. Press meat together at ends of roll and at seam to enclose vegetables completely. Repeat with remaining 3 portions of meat. Place rolls in a 10-x-6-x-1¾-inch baking dish. Cover with aluminum foil. (At this point rolls may be refrigerated until baking time.) Heat oven to 350°F. Bake meat rolls, covered, for 30 minutes. Uncover and bake 10 to 15 minutes longer, until browned. *Makes 3 or 4 servings.* For diet serving allow 1 meat roll.

To freeze: Prepare double recipe. After baking, wrap 4 rolls securely in aluminum foil and freeze.

To reheat: Heat oven to 350°F. Place frozen meat rolls, in aluminum foil, on baking sheet. Bake 25 to 35 minutes, or until hot.

Per diet serving: 274 calories, 28 grams protein, 13 grams fat, 10 grams carbohydrate.

Baked Dilled Tomatoes

4 tomatoes, about 6 ounces each
Few grains of salt
Few grains of black pepper
2 tablespoons unseasoned dry
   bread crumbs

1 teaspoon dried dillweed or
   snipped fresh dillweed
1½ teaspoons butter or margarine,
   cut in tiny pieces

Heat oven to 350°F. Cut out and discard tomato cores. Cut a thin slice from the top of each tomato; discard. Cut edge of tomato in zigzag pattern, if desired. Place tomatoes, cut side up, in a baking dish about 8 inches square. Sprinkle with salt, pepper, bread crumbs and dill. Dot with butter. Bake 20 to 25 minutes, until fork-tender. *Makes 3 or 4 servings.* For diet serving allow 1 tomato.

Per diet serving: 50 calories, 1 gram protein, 2 grams fat, 7 grams carbohydrate.

Orange Freeze

1 6-ounce can frozen orange juice
  concentrate, thawed, undiluted
1 cup liquid skim milk
¼ cup water

¼ cup instant nonfat milk (in
  dry form)
1 tablespoon lemon juice
2 tablespoons confectioners' sugar
Mint sprigs (optional)

Mix orange juice concentrate and skim milk in a small bowl. In another small bowl mix water and dry milk; beat with a rotary or electric beater at medium speed until soft peaks hold when beater is lifted. Add lemon juice and continue beating until stiff peaks hold. Beat in confectioners' sugar. Fold into orange mixture. Freeze 1 to 2 hours, until ice crystals form around edges and on top. Mix thoroughly with a fork. Smooth surface with a rubber spatula. Cover with aluminum foil. Freeze until firm, 2 hours or longer. If desired, serve garnished with mint sprigs. *Makes 4 servings.* For diet serving allow ¼ of the mixture.

Per diet serving: 142 calories, 5 grams protein, 0 grams fat, 31 grams carbohydrate.

Dependable Nibbles

When the urge to eat is too strong to resist, have a safety formula or two tucked in the back of your mind—some combinations of low-calorie foods that are particularly satisfying to you. A few that can satisfy a hunger pang at a cost of less than 50 calories:

A hot cup of tea (no cream or sugar) with a 2½-inch square graham cracker . . . 29 calories; a cup of black coffee with two 1¾-inch vanilla wafers sandwiched with a teaspoon of whipped topping . . . 42 calories; a cup of hot bouillon, made with a cube, and three plain Melba toast rounds . . . 32 calories; a glass of club soda and 10 small pretzel sticks . . . 12 calories; a glass of iced tea with lemon (no sugar) with 1 cup of popped corn (no butter) . . . 42 calories.

BREAKFAST

1 medium-sized orange (45)
¾ cup wheat-bran cereal (96)
1 cup skim milk (86)

LUNCH

Ham Roll-Ups: 2 ounces sliced,
  boiled ham (122), wrapped
  around 2 dill pickle spears (6)
1 slice whole-wheat bread (61),
  spread with 1 teaspoon *Herbed
  Butter (17) or ½ teaspoon plain
  butter or margarine (17)
¼ cup creamed cottage cheese (60),
  with 1 tablespoon wheat germ
  (28) and 1 teaspoon honey (21)

DINNER

* Steaming Onion Soup (58)
* Quick Shrimp Creole (138)
¾ cup cooked brown rice (174)
1 wedge of lettuce (⅛ head, 9),
  served with 1 tablespoon bottled
  low-calorie dressing (7)
* Orange–Rhubarb Dessert (129)

TO EAT ANY TIME

1 ounce Cheddar cheese (114)
4 whole-wheat crackers (36)

Herbed Butter

½ cup butter or margarine, at
  room temperature
¼ cup liquid skim milk

3 tablespoons chopped fresh
  parsley
1 teaspoon dried basil leaves
1 teaspoon dried chervil leaves

In a small, deep bowl beat butter with an electric beater or wire whisk until very smooth. Beat in milk about 1 teaspoon at a time, scraping sides of bowl occasionally. When all milk is added, beat in parsley, basil and chervil. Pack into crock or jar, cover and store in refrigerator. Use as a low-calorie butter-substitute. Let stand at room temperature 30 minutes before serving. *Makes about 1 cup.* For diet serving allow 1 teaspoon.

Per diet serving: 17 calories, 0 grams protein, 2 grams fat, 0 grams carbohydrate.

Steaming Onion Soup

1½ teaspoons vegetable oil
1 medium-sized onion, peeled and
  sliced thin

2 13¾-ounce cans beef broth
1 teaspoon Worcestershire sauce

In a medium-sized saucepan heat oil over moderately high heat. Add onion and cook 3 to 5 minutes, stirring frequently, until deep golden brown. Add beef broth and Worcestershire sauce. Heat just to boiling. *Makes about 4 cups.* For diet serving allow ¼ of soup, about 1 cup.

Per diet serving: 58 calories, 5 grams protein, 1 gram fat, 7 grams carbohydrate.

Quick Shrimp Creole

2 teaspoons olive or vegetable oil
½ cup sliced celery
½ cup sliced, seeded green pepper
¼ cup chopped, peeled onion
¼ teaspoon minced, peeled garlic
1 16-ounce can stewed tomatoes
½ teaspoon salt
¼ teaspoon pepper
¼ teaspoon dried basil leaves, crushed
1 12-ounce package frozen shelled, deveined medium-sized shrimp, cooked according to package directions

In a medium-sized skillet heat oil over moderate heat. Add celery, green pepper, onion and garlic and cook 5 to 7 minutes, stirring often, until tender. Add stewed tomatoes, salt, pepper and basil leaves. Heat thoroughly, stirring constantly. Add shrimp and heat through. *Makes 3 or 4 servings.* For diet serving allow ¼ of the shrimp mixture.

To freeze: Prepare double recipe. Place half the shrimp mixture in a plastic freezer container. Seal and freeze.

To reheat: Put plastic container of shrimp creole in refrigerator to thaw. Place thawed shrimp mixture in a medium-sized skillet or saucepan and heat over moderately low heat, stirring 2 or 3 times, until hot.

Per diet serving: 138 calories, 22 grams protein, 1 gram fat, 10 grams carbohydrate.

Orange–Rhubarb Dessert

1 16-ounce package frozen rhubarb, thawed
⅓ cup orange juice
2 teaspoons freshly grated orange peel
½ cup granulated sugar

Combine rhubarb, orange juice, orange peel and sugar in a medium-sized saucepan. Cook over moderately low heat for 10 to 15 minutes, stirring occasionally, until mixture is thick and rhubarb is very soft. Serve warm or cold. *Makes 4 servings.* For diet serving allow ¼ of rhubarb mixture, about ½ cup.

Per diet serving: 128 calories, 1 gram protein, 0 grams fat, 31 grams carbohydrate.

BREAKFAST

¾ cup fresh or unsweetened frozen
  strawberries (41)
1 cup creamed cottage cheese (217)
1 slice pumpernickel bread (79)

LUNCH

Antipasto Hero: 1 hard roll (156)
  filled with 1 small sliced tomato
  (20); 1 ounce sliced part-skim
  mozzarella cheese (72); 1 slice red
  onion (3); 1 tablespoon Basic
  Vinaigrette Dressing (recipe on
  page 23, 31), to sprinkle over
  vegetables and cheese

DINNER

* Magic Rice (306)
* Chinese Cabbage and Cucumber
  Salad (34)
½ cup fresh or unsweetened frozen
  blueberries (45)

TO EAT ANY TIME

1 cup skim milk (86)
1 cup 4-grain multivitamin-and-iron-
  supplement cereal (110)

Magic Rice

Rice:
1¾ cups water
¼ cup soy sauce
1 cup uncooked converted long-
  grain white rice

Egg Pancakes:
4 large eggs
2 teaspoons vegetable oil

Vegetables:
½ cup diced, drained canned
  water chestnuts
½ cup thin-sliced scallions or
  green onions
2 sweet red peppers, seeded and
  diced

In a 2-quart saucepan bring water and soy sauce to a boil over moderately high heat; stir in rice, reduce heat to low, cover pan and simmer 20 to 25 minutes, until rice is tender and liquid is absorbed. Meanwhile, make the egg pancakes. Beat the eggs in a small bowl. In a heavy, 10-inch skillet heat 1 teaspoon of the oil over moderately high heat (when a drop of water skips across the bottom of the pan, it's ready). Pour ¼ cup of the egg mixture into the skillet to make a thin coat on the bottom. Cook 20 to 30 seconds, until "pancake" is set. Working quickly, lift edge of pancake, grasp with fingers and turn over. Cook 20 seconds longer, until underside is lightly browned; turn onto a plate to cool. Repeat with remaining egg mixture, using remaining teaspoon of oil when necessary. Stack pancakes and with a very sharp knife slice into thin slivers.

To serve, stir water chestnuts into hot, cooked rice and arrange on a shallow serving platter. Arrange egg slivers, scallions and peppers in bands over the rice. Serve some of the cold egg slivers and vegetables with the hot rice. *Makes 3 or 4 servings.* For diet serving allow ¼ of the recipe.

Per diet serving: 306 calories, 11 grams protein, 8 grams fat, 46 grams carbohydrate.

Chinese Cabbage and Cucumber Salad

¼ cup white vinegar
1 tablespoon water
½ teaspoon salt
½ teaspoon granulated sugar

1 pound Chinese cabbage, cut into 1-inch pieces (about 4 cups)
2 medium-sized cucumbers, peeled and sliced
1 carrot, peeled

Mix vinegar, water, salt and sugar in a salad bowl. Add the cabbage and cucumbers. Working over the bowl and using a vegetable peeler, slice the carrot into long, thin strips. Toss salad and serve. *Makes 3 or 4 servings.* For diet serving allow ¼ of the salad.

Per diet serving: 34 calories, 2 grams protein, 0 grams fat, 8 grams carbohydrate.

BREAKFAST

2 4-inch whole-wheat pancakes
(made from whole-wheat pancake
and waffle mix, 166), topped with
½ cup unsweetened applesauce
(50), heated and sprinkled with
nutmeg

LUNCH

* Beef and Barley Soup (186)
1 slice pumpernickel bread (79)
1 ounce Jarlsberg cheese (115)
5 dried apricots (55)
½ cup skim milk (43)

DINNER

* Chicken Marsala (161)
½ cup cooked egg noodles (100)
Romaine Salad: 2 cups sliced
romaine (20); 5 sliced pitted ripe
olives (30); 1 slice red onion (3);
Basic Vinaigrette Dressing
(recipe on page 23, 31)
½ cup seedless green grapes (54)

TO EAT ANY TIME

½ cup skim milk (43)
¾ cup bran flakes with added
thiamin and iron (70)

Beef and Barley Soup

1 pound beef soup bones
½ pound soup meat or chuck
roast, cut into 1-inch cubes
¾ cup chopped, peeled onion
1 cup sliced, peeled carrots
1 cup sliced celery
1 bay leaf
2 sprigs fresh parsley

1 teaspoon salt
¼ teaspoon ground pepper
4½ cups water
1 16-ounce can tomatoes
½ cup uncooked pearl barley
1½ tablespoons chopped fresh
parsley

In a heavy, 4- to 6-quart pot put the bones, meat, onion, ½ cup of the carrots, ½ cup of the celery, the bay leaf, parsley sprigs, salt, pepper and water. Bring to a boil over moderately high heat. Reduce heat to low; cover and simmer for about 2½ hours. Lift out bones and when cool enough to handle, remove any meat from them. Put meat back in soup; discard bones. With a metal spoon skim off any fat from surface of soup. Add tomatoes, barley and the remaining ½ cup carrots and celery. Partly cover the pot and cook 45 minutes to 1 hour, until vegetables and barley are tender. Just before serving, stir in the chopped parsley. *Makes 5½ cups soup, or 4 to 5 servings.* For diet serving allow 1 cup.

Per diet serving: 186 calories, 13 grams protein, 3 grams fat, 27 grams carbohydrate.

Chicken Marsala

1 pound boneless, skinless chicken
  breasts (4 half breasts)
2 tablespoons flour
1 tablespoon lightly salted butter
  or margarine

½ teaspoon salt
¼ teaspoon black pepper
¼ cup sweet Marsala or sherry
  wine

Rinse chicken breasts and pat dry with paper towels. Place chicken breasts between 2 sheets of wax paper on a board and pound with a meat mallet or rolling pin until thin. Sprinkle both sides of chicken with flour. In a large, heavy skillet melt butter over moderately high heat; add chicken breasts and brown 2 minutes on each side. Turn heat to low, sprinkle chicken with salt and pepper and add wine. Cover pan and simmer 3 to 5 minutes. *Makes 3 or 4 servings.* For diet serving allow ¼ of the chicken.

Per diet serving: 161 calories, 23 grams protein, 5 grams fat, 1 gram carbohydrate.

Beware the Restaurant's Diet Plates

Two of the most common diet offerings in restaurants are the Lo-Calorie Hamburger Plate and the Fresh Fruit Plate. In the hamburger offering, the bun (119 calories) is eliminated and usually replaced by a scoop of creamed cottage cheese (½ cup = 109 calories), a meager saving of 10 calories unless you eat the two slices of tomato that garnish the plate reducing the calorie saving to about 8. The Fresh Fruit Salad Plate can be even more deceiving. First discern how much of it is fresh. Or is it syrup-packed and hence sugar-coated? Usually it bears a dollop of cottage cheese (little harm), but the "garnish" is a healthy portion of fruit gelatin cubes (about 10 calories per 1-inch cube).

CHAPTER FOUR

Diets for Brown-Bag Lunches-to-Go

Lunch-to-go implies that you're running a home and a job and can't possibly spend a lot of time in the kitchen except, perhaps, on weekends. The easy-does-it weekday dinners in these fourteen days of diet menus were designed to respect an already-full work day. There are good sandwiches—the easiest brown-bag filler— for some lunches, but there are some more rewarding lunches like Sardine and Potatoes Vinaigrette, Shrimp Salad and Take-Along Antipasto that can beat the humdrum lunch routine and still keep you on your diet, and perhaps even engender a little envy among co-workers.

BREAKFAST

½ cup orange juice (61)
1 cup cooked iron-enriched farina
(100)
1 cup skim milk (86)

LUNCH

Open-Face Cheddar Cheese
Sandwich: 2 ounces Cheddar
cheese (228); 1 slice cracked-
wheat bread (66)
4 cherry tomatoes (7)
2 medium-size dill pickles (3½
inches long, 15)
4 dried apricot halves (44)

DINNER

* Pineapple–Watercress Soup (91)
1 lean broiled pork chop, trimmed
of all visible fat (3 ounces cooked
meat, 227)
1 cup cooked green beans (31)
1 cup torn romaine lettuce leaves
(10), tossed with *Parslied
Vinaigrette Dressing (31)
½ cup unsweetened applesauce (50)

TO EAT ANY TIME

½ cup skim milk (43)
10 unshelled roasted peanuts (105)

Pineapple–Watercress Soup

3 cups canned unsweetened
pineapple juice, well chilled

1½ cups chopped watercress

Place juice and watercress in a blender. Cover and blend at high
speed 30 to 40 seconds, until cress is liquefied and soup is dark green.
Makes about 4½ cups. For diet serving allow 1 cup.

Per diet serving: 91 calories, 0 grams protein, 0 grams fat, 23 grams carbohydrate.

Parslied Vinaigrette Dressing

¼ cup water
2 tablespoons vegetable oil
2 tablespoons red wine vinegar
1 tablespoon lemon juice

2 teaspoons chopped fresh parsley
¼ teaspoon salt
¼ teaspoon black pepper

Put all ingredients into a screw-top jar; cover and shake until well
blended. Dressing will keep several days in refrigerator. *Makes about
½ cup.* For diet serving allow 1 tablespoon.

Per diet serving: 31 calories, 0 grams protein, 3 grams fat, 0 grams carbohydrate.

BREAKFAST

* Peach Ambrosia (305)
1 slice raisin bread, toasted (66)

LUNCH

* Sardines with Potatoes Vinaigrette
  to Go (286)
1 crisp flat bread wafer (20)
1 cup skim milk mixed with ¼ cup
  coffee and poured over ice (86),
  carried in a thermos bottle

DINNER

* Cuban Marinated Steak (224)
1 medium-sized ear yellow sweet
  corn, boiled (70)
Mushroom Salad: 4 ounces raw
  mushrooms, sliced (32); 2 slices
  red onion (6); 2 leaves lettuce
  (2); tossed with Parslied Vinaigrette Dressing (recipe on page
  116, 31)
1 small orange, sliced (45)

TO EAT ANY TIME

¾ cup tomato juice (34)

Peach Ambrosia

1 cup plain low-fat yogurt
¼ cup instant nonfat dry milk
½ cup syrup-packed peach slices,
  drained

1 teaspoon honey
6 ice cubes

Place all ingredients in a blender; cover and blend at medium speed 15 seconds. Stop machine and push mixture down. Cover and blend 15 seconds longer, or until smooth. *Makes 1 diet serving.*

Per diet serving: 305 calories, 15 grams protein, 4 grams fat, 53 grams carbohydrate.

Sardines with Potatoes Vinaigrette to Go

1 medium unpeeled potato,
  steamed or boiled
2 tablespoons Parslied Vinaigrette
  Dressing (recipe on page 116)
1 tablespoon chopped fresh
  parsley

1 teaspoon thin-sliced scallion or
  green onion
2 ounces (4 to 6) drained sardines
2 lettuce leaves

Peel potato as soon as it is cool enough to handle and cut into slices ¼-inch thick. Place warm slices in a plastic container and spoon Vinaigrette Dressing over them. Sprinkle with the chopped parsley and scallion. Cover and refrigerate overnight. Pack sardines and lettuce separately. To serve, arrange potatoes on lettuce, top with sardines and pour any dressing left in the container over all. *Makes 1 diet serving.*

Per diet serving: 286 calories, 17 grams protein, 13 grams fat, 24 grams carbohydrate.

Cuban Marinated Steak

1 cup red wine vinegar
⅓ cup orange juice
4 drops Tabasco sauce
¼ teaspoon black pepper
½ cup finely chopped, peeled
   onion

4 large cloves garlic, peeled and
   minced
2 tablespoons vegetable oil
2 pounds top round steak, cut 2
   inches thick
2 tablespoons chopped fresh
   parsley (optional)

In a large, shallow dish combine vinegar, orange juice, Tabasco, pepper, onion, garlic and 1 tablespoon of the oil. With a sharp knife lightly score a diagonal pattern on the top of the steak. Place meat in marinade and marinate in refrigerator 3 to 5 hours, turning meat occasionally. Place steak in broiler pan without a rack. Brush meat with some of the remaining oil and broil 5 inches from heat source 12 to 14 minutes on each side, brushing occasionally with oil. If desired, heat some of the marinade in a small saucepan, add the parsley and serve with the steak. *Makes 8 servings.* For diet serving allow 3 ounces cooked meat and 1 tablespoon marinade.

NOTE: Leftover cooked meat can be wrapped and stored in the refrigerator or freezer. Use it for lunches or another main dish.

Per diet serving: 224 calories, 24 grams protein, 13 grams fat, 1 gram carbohydrate.

Safety First

A hot soup or leftover stew is great on wintertime lunch-to-go menus, but be sure you have a good insulated container that will keep it hot. Pour hot water in the container to warm it five to ten minutes before you are ready to pack the hot food. Foods should stay really hot—140°F. or above—to prevent growth of bacteria.

BREAKFAST

1 cup 4-grain multivitamin-and-iron-
   supplement cereal (110)
½ banana (50)
1 cup skim milk (86)
½ cup orange juice (61)

LUNCH

Tuna Sandwich: 2 ounces water-
   packed tuna, drained (78); 2
   teaspoons mayonnaise (68); 1
   stalk celery, chopped (7); 2 slices
   whole-wheat bread (122); 2 leaves
   lettuce (2; see note below)
1 syrup-packed peach half with 1½
   tablespoons syrup (59)

DINNER

1 cup beef broth (30)
* Tomatoes Stuffed with Chick-Peas
   and Mozzarella (302)
Tossed Salad: 2 cups torn lettuce
   leaves (20); Parslied Vinaigrette
   Dressing (recipe on page 116, 31)
½ cup strawberry-flavored gelatin
   (80)
1 cup skim milk (86)

NOTE: Put a lettuce leaf between each slice of the bread and the filling
to keep salad from soaking into bread.

Tomatoes Stuffed with Chick-Peas and Mozzarella

4 large ripe tomatoes (about 2
   pounds)
¼ teaspoon black pepper
½ teaspoon salt
⅔ cup quick-cooking iron-
   enriched farina
½ cup chicken broth
2 tablespoons red wine vinegar

1 tablespoon vegetable oil
1 teaspoon dried basil leaves
¼ teaspoon salt
¾ cup chopped, seeded green
   pepper
1 cup drained, canned chick-peas
4 ounces part-skim mozzarella
   cheese, cut into ½-inch cubes

Using a small, sharp knife, remove and discard cores from tomatoes.
Scoop pulp and seeds out of tomatoes, being careful not to break
through outer skin; put pulp into a blender. Add the pepper and ½
teaspoon salt; cover and blend 30 seconds at medium speed until
pureed. Heat oven to 350°F. Mix farina, chicken broth and ¾ cup of
the tomato puree. Spoon evenly into four 5- to 6-inch-diameter baking
dishes. Add vinegar, oil, basil and ¼ teaspoon salt to tomato puree
remaining in blender. Cover and blend 5 seconds. Put remaining tomato
puree, peppers, chick-peas and cheese into a bowl, toss to mix and
spoon evenly into tomato shells. Put stuffed tomatoes in baking dishes
with farina and bake 30 minutes, or until tomatoes are cooked. *Makes
4 servings.* For diet serving allow 1 stuffed tomato and ¼ of farina
mixture.

Per diet serving: 302 calories, 16 grams protein, 9 grams fat, 41 grams carbohydrate.

BREAKFAST

* Dried Beef on Toast (165)
1 cup tomato juice (46)

LUNCH

* Russian Cottage Salad (224)
  with *Relatively Russian Dressing
  (86)

DINNER

* Yakitori Skillet Dinner (395)
¼ medium-sized cantaloupe (41)
⅓ cup green grapes (32)
½ cup vanilla low-fat yogurt (97)

TO EAT ANY TIME

1 cup skim milk (86)
1 crisp rye wafer (21)

Dried Beef on Toast

1 ounce dried beef (4 large
  pieces), soaked a few seconds
  in hot water and drained
1 slice cracked-wheat bread,
  toasted

1 teaspoon butter or margarine
1 teaspoon prepared mustard
1 leaf Boston lettuce

Heat beef for a few seconds in a small skillet, broiler or toaster-oven. Spread toast with butter and mustard, cut in half and sandwich with beef and lettuce. *Makes 1 diet serving.*

Per diet serving: 165 calories, 13 grams protein, 7 grams fat, 14 grams carbohydrate.

Russian Cottage Salad

1 slice pumpernickel bread
1 cup torn romaine leaves
½ cup creamed cottage cheese
6 cucumber slices

⅓ cup grated carrot
⅓ cup Relatively Russian Dressing
  (recipe below)

Pack all ingredients separately. At lunchtime, put the pumpernickel on a plate, top with romaine leaves (they'll overflow bread); put cottage cheese on romaine, arrange cucumbers and grated carrot on top. Pour dressing over salad and eat with a knife and fork. *Makes 1 diet serving.*

Per diet serving (with dressing): 310 calories, 26 grams protein, 7 grams fat, 37 grams carbohydrate.

Relatively Russian Dressing

½ cup buttermilk
3 tablespoons chili sauce
3 tablespoons creamed cottage
  cheese
½ teaspoon salt

½ teaspoon lemon juice
2 tablespoons chopped sweet
  pickle
1 tablespoon thin-sliced scallion
  or green onion

Place all ingredients except pickle and scallion in a blender; cover and blend at high speed until well blended and thickened. Stir in pickle and scallion. Tightly covered, dressing keeps 4 days in refrigerator. *Makes about ⅔ cup.* For diet serving allow ⅓ cup.

Per diet serving: 86 calories, 6 grams protein, 1 gram fat, 13 grams carbohydrate.

Yakitori Skillet Dinner

1 pound chicken livers
¼ cup soy sauce
1 tablespoon dry sherry wine or
  water
¼ teaspoon ground ginger
1 large clove garlic, peeled and
  cracked open
6 ounces skinless, boneless chicken
  breast, cut in 1-inch squares

3 tablespoons vegetable oil
6 ounces fresh mushrooms (about
  7 medium), sliced ¼-inch thick
1 6-ounce package frozen Chinese
  pea pods, slightly thawed
2 tablespoons water
8 ounces vermicelli, cooked according to package directions

Rinse livers; discard any bits of fat that cling to them and pat dry with paper towels. Cut livers in half. In a small bowl combine soy sauce, wine, ginger and garlic; add chicken pieces and toss to coat them. Heat 2 tablespoons of the oil in a large, heavy skillet over moderately high heat; add about half the livers and cook about 3 minutes, turning to brown both sides. Remove livers to a plate and repeat with remaining livers, removing them from skillet when they are done. Add remaining oil, drained chicken breast and mushrooms to skillet and cook about 3 minutes, stirring constantly. Return livers to skillet with reserved chicken marinade and cook about 3 minutes, stirring frequently. Add pea pods and cook about 3 minutes, until pods are crisp-tender.

Remove meats and vegetables to a large heated platter. Stir the 2 tablespoons water into the juices in the skillet; add the hot, drained vermicelli and stir gently about 1 minute. Add the meat and vegetables and toss gently with the vermicelli. *Makes 6 servings.* For diet serving allow ⅙ of the meat, vegetable and vermicelli mixture.

Per diet serving: 395 calories, 36 grams protein, 12 grams fat, 35 grams carbohydrate.

BREAKFAST

1 medium egg prepared any style
    without butter or margarine (72)
1 slice whole-wheat bread (61)
¾ cup skim milk (65)
1 small orange, sliced (45)

LUNCH

¾ cup tomato juice (34)
1 slice pumpernickel bread (79)
1 ½-inch-thick slice Braunschweiger
    (64)
* Take-Along Antipasto (40)

DINNER

1 cup beef bouillon (30)
* Grandma's Sole (354)
1 cup torn spinach leaves (14),
    tossed with Parslied Vinaigrette
    Dressing (recipe on page 116, 31)
½ sliced pear (45)
1 ounce Gruyere cheese (115)

TO EAT ANY TIME

½ cup skim milk (43)
1 cup 4-grain multivitamin-and-iron-
    supplement cereal (110)

Take-Along Antipasto

3 cups water
10 small fresh mushrooms
1 medium-sized green pepper,
    cored, seeded and cut into strips

2 medium-sized carrots, peeled
    and cut into strips
1 cup raw cauliflower florets
1 cup bottled low-calorie Italian
    dressing

In a medium-sized saucepan bring water to a boil. Add mushrooms and cook 1 to 2 minutes, until tender. With a slotted spoon remove mushrooms from boiling water and put in a medium-sized bowl. Add green pepper strips to water; cook 2 to 3 minutes, until crisp-tender. Remove and add to mushrooms. Add carrots and cauliflower to water; cook 3 to 4 minutes, until crisp-tender. Remove and add to bowl. Add Italian dressing to vegetables and toss to mix. Cover and chill 12 hours or longer. Before packing, drain vegetables well. Reserve drained dressing for use on salads. Marinated vegetables keep well for several days in refrigerator. *Makes 4 servings.* For diet serving allow ¼ of vegetables.

Per diet serving: 40 calories, 2 grams protein, 0 grams fat, 7 grams carbohydrate.

Grandma's Sole

1 tablespoon butter or margarine,
  cut in tiny pieces
1 medium-sized onion, peeled and
  sliced thin
2 medium-sized potatoes, peeled
  and sliced thin

1 1-pound block frozen sole or
  flounder fillets
½ teaspoon salt
¼ teaspoon black pepper
1 8-ounce can stewed tomatoes
2 tablespoons chopped fresh
  parsley (optional)

Heat oven to 375°F. Use a little of the butter to grease a 12-x-8-x-2-inch baking dish. Arrange onion and potatoes in dish; place fish in center of dish on the vegetables. Sprinkle with salt and pepper, pour tomatoes over all and dot with remaining butter. Cover with foil and bake in center of oven 1 hour. Baste fish with pan juices and sprinkle with parsley. *Makes 2 servings.* For diet serving allow ½ the fish and vegetables.

Per diet serving: 354 calories, 42 grams protein, 8 grams fat, 28 grams carbohydrate.

Take a Break

When you're on a diet—even if you're not—it's important to take a real break and enjoy your lunch hour. Keep a pretty plate and a knife, fork and spoon at work. Enjoy what you eat, then take a walk, visit with a friend, close your door and do a few light exercises. Lunchtime shouldn't be just a time for the eating alarm to be satisfied.

BREAKFAST

½ cup low-fat vanilla yogurt (97)
½ cup fresh or unsweetened frozen
  strawberries (27)
1 slice whole-wheat bread (61),
  spread with 1 teaspoon butter or
  margarine (34)

LUNCH

Grilled Cheese Sandwich (see note):
  1 ounce Swiss cheese (107); ½
  small tomato, sliced (10); 1
  teaspoon butter or margarine
  (34); 2 slices whole-wheat bread
  (122)
1 small apple (61)

DINNER

1 cup vegetable-juice cocktail (41)
* Sherried Chicken Livers (285)
1 cup cooked green beans (31)
1 ½-inch-thick slice French bread
  (about 2½ x 2 inches, 44)
* Pineapple Chunks with Pineapple
  Ice (98)

TO EAT ANY TIME

½ cup popped popcorn (20)
1 cup skim milk (86)
5 unshelled roasted peanuts (52)

NOTE: If Saturday is a lunch-to-carry day for you, make a plain cheese sandwich of the Grilled Cheese Sandwich ingredients. If you prefer, use 1 teaspoon mayonnaise and a little mustard instead of 1 teaspoon butter.

Sherried Chicken Livers

1 pound chicken livers
2 tablespoons flour
¼ teaspoon salt
⅛ teaspoon pepper
1 tablespoon butter or margarine
¼ cup finely chopped, peeled
  onion

1 4-ounce can mushroom stems
  and pieces, undrained
⅓ cup dry sherry wine
⅛ teaspoon dried thyme leaves
2 tablespoons chopped fresh
  parsley

Rinse livers, discard any bits of fat that cling to them and pat dry with paper towels. Cut each liver in half. Mix flour, salt and pepper together and sprinkle over livers. In a medium-sized skillet melt ½ the butter over moderately low heat. Add onions and cook until tender but not brown. Remove onions from skillet. Add chicken livers and remaining butter and cook over moderately high heat 5 to 8 minutes until livers are lightly browned but still pink in the middle. Add onion, mushrooms, sherry and thyme. Cook, stirring occasionally, until sauce bubbles and mushrooms are hot. Serve garnished with chopped parsley. *Makes 4 servings.* For diet serving allow ¼ of the livers and sauce.

Per diet serving: 285 calories, 26 grams protein, 13 grams fat, 9 grams carbohydrate.

Pineapple Chunks with Pineapple Ice

2 20-ounce cans juice-packed   1 cup skim milk
  pineapple chunks   ½ teaspoon vanilla extract

Drain pineapple juice into a medium-sized metal bowl; cover chunks and refrigerate until serving time. Mix milk and vanilla with pineapple juice; freeze 1 hour, until ice crystals form around edge. Beat smooth with an electric mixer. Freeze 1 hour longer and beat again. Return to freezer and freeze 5 to 6 hours longer, until solid. Remove ice from freezer 10 minutes before serving to soften. Scoop ice into stemmed glasses and top with reserved pineapple chunks. Refreeze any leftover ice; will keep a week in an airtight container. *Makes 3 cups ice.* For diet serving allow ⅛ of recipe, a rounded ⅓ cup.

Per diet serving: 98 calories, 2 grams protein, 1 gram fat, 23 grams carbohydrate.

Eating-Out Strategy

You can't always live in the safe cocoons of your own brown-bag lunch or your home-prepared food. If possible, avoid eating out for the first week you're on the diet. So much is beyond your control: how the food has been prepared, what's available on the menu. And then, of course, there's always the temptation of something that sounds simply too marvelous to resist. Some rules of thumb: Choose lean broiled fish, chicken, meats (hold the gravy or sauces); choose plain tuna rather than tuna salad; avoid mixture dishes like eggplant parmigiana or boeuf bourguignon or coq au vin that may be loaded with preparation-calories you can't see.

BREAKFAST

* Steamed Eggs with Salmon (179)
2 crisp rye wafers (45)

LUNCH

Danish Fruit Soup: ¾ cup plain yogurt (94) and 1 tablespoon sour cream (25), spooned over ½ cup sweetened frozen raspberries, partially defrosted (123) and ⅓ cup fresh or unsweetened frozen blueberries, partially defrosted (28); topped with 2 tablespoons crunchy nutlike cereal nuggets (55)

DINNER

* Beef Barbecue (232)
* Dilled Squash Compote (45)
Tomato and Watercress Salad: 3 slices of a large tomato (24); 3 watercress sprigs (1); salt, black pepper and minced fresh basil leaves
2 ¼-inch slices French bread (2½ x 2 inches, 44)
1/10 honeydew melon (49) with lime wedge (2)

TO EAT ANY TIME

1 cup skim milk (86)
½ cup 4-grain multivitamin-and-iron-supplement cereal (54)
1 ounce Swiss cheese (107)

Steamed Eggs with Salmon

½ cup plus 2 tablespoons water
5 large eggs
⅛ teaspoon salt
Black pepper

1 7¾-ounce can of salmon, drained and flaked
1 tablespoon minced scallion or green onion

In a 10-inch skillet bring water to a boil over moderately high heat. Beat eggs in a bowl with salt and pepper, pour into skillet and reduce heat to moderate. Cook about 2 minutes, stirring constantly with a large spoon or pancake turner and scraping large pieces of set egg from bottom of skillet. When almost all liquid is gone, stir in salmon and scallion. Continue stirring and cook a few seconds longer, until all liquid is absorbed. Serve immediately. *Makes 4 servings.* For diet serving allow ¼ of recipe.

Per diet serving: 179 calories, 18 grams protein, 11 grams fat, 1 gram carbohydrate.

Beef Barbecue

1½ cups tomato juice
2 tablespoons Worcestershire
   sauce
3 tablespoons soy sauce
¼ cup cider or wine vinegar
2 large cloves garlic, peeled and
   minced

1 teaspoon salt
1 tablespoon lemon juice
⅛ teaspoon celery seed
1 tablespoon catsup
1 2-pound shoulder or round steak
   for London broil (about 1½
   inches thick)

In a small pan mix all ingredients except meat and bring to a boil over moderate heat. Simmer sauce 10 minutes and then let cool. Pour sauce into a medium-sized, flat baking dish; add meat, cover and marinate in refrigerator 8 to 12 hours, turning meat several times. Heat broiler, remove meat from marinade and place on a rack in a broiler pan. Broil 4 to 5 inches from the heat source, allowing 7 to 10 minutes per side for medium-well-done; 5 to 7 minutes for rare; 12 to 15 minutes for well-done. Pour remaining marinade into a small pan and bring to a boil; simmer about 10 minutes. When meat is cooked, leave it in a warm place for 5 to 7 minutes before cutting in thin slices. Serve sauce separately. *Makes 6 to 8 servings.* For diet serving allow 3 ounces meat and 2 tablespoons sauce. Wrap 2 ounces of meat and save 1 tablespoon sauce for lunch in Menu #8.

Per diet serving: 232 calories, 24 grams protein, 13 grams fat, 3 grams carbohydrate.

Dilled Squash Compote

Water
3 medium-sized yellow squash
   (about 1 pound), sliced in
   ¾-inch rounds (3 cups)
4 small zucchini squash (about
   ¾ pound), sliced in ¼-inch
   rounds (2½ cups)

1 tablespoon vegetable oil
1 tablespoon vinegar
1 tablespoon water
¾ teaspoon salt
1 teaspoon dried dillweed

Fill a large saucepot or Dutch oven with water to a depth of about 1 inch and bring to a boil over high heat. Put squash in a steamer basket or large colander in the pot; reduce heat to moderate, cover and steam about 10 minutes, until squash is crisp-tender. Remove to a chilled bowl and toss gently with remaining ingredients. Chill at least 1 hour. Stir gently before serving. *Makes 4 to 6 servings.* For diet serving allow ⅔ cup.

Per diet serving: 45 calories, 2 grams protein, 2 grams fat, 5 grams carbohydrate.

BREAKFAST

* Strawberry Frost (164)
1 slice raisin bread, toasted (66),
   spread with ½ teaspoon butter or
   margarine (17)

LUNCH

Open-Face Barbecue Sandwich: 1
   slice white bread or toast (68);
   1 large leaf soft lettuce (3); 1
   tablespoon barbecue sauce from
   Menu #7 (6); 2 ounces beef,
   reserved from Menu #7 (147)
½ cup skim milk (43)

DINNER

* Green Vegetable Soup (206)
* Noodles with Cottage Cheese and
   Dill (350)
1 fresh or juice-packed canned peach
   half (23), with *Raspberry Sauce
   (15)

TO EAT ANY TIME

½ cup skim milk (43)
½ cup 4-grain multivitamin-and-
   iron-supplement cereal (55)

Strawberry Frost

1 cup liquid skim milk
½ cup unsweetened frozen
   strawberries, partially thawed
2 tablespoons instant nonfat dry
   milk

1 teaspoon sugar
1 teaspoon vanilla extract

Put all ingredients in a blender; cover and blend at medium speed about
30 seconds until thick and smooth. *Makes 1 diet serving.*

Per diet serving: 164 calories, 13 grams protein, 1 gram fat, 26 grams carbohydrate.

Green Vegetable Soup

1 tablespoon vegetable oil
¼ cup minced, peeled onion
2 10¾-ounce cans condensed
   chicken broth
2 cups water
½ teaspoon salt
10 fresh or frozen asparagus spears,
   cut in 2-inch pieces

½ pound skinless, boneless
   chicken breast, cut in ½-x-
   2-inch strips
1⅓ cups sliced zucchini squash,
   cut about ¼ inch thick
2 pounds fresh green peas, shelled;
   or 2 cups frozen green peas
4 cups shredded iceberg lettuce,
   packed tightly to measure

In a large saucepot or Dutch oven heat oil over moderate heat. Add
onion and cook, stirring frequently, just until onion is soft. Add broth,

water and salt and bring to a boil. Add remaining ingredients and cook 8 to 10 minutes, until peas are tender and asparagus is crisp-tender. *Makes about 10 cups.* For diet serving allow 2½ cups.

Per diet serving: 206 calories, 20 grams protein, 8 grams fat, 16 grams carbohydrate.

Noodles with Cottage Cheese and Dill

8 ounces medium egg noodles
2 cups creamed cottage cheese

2 tablespoons chopped fresh dillweed or 1 tablespoon dried dillweed
⅛ teaspoon black pepper

Cook noodles according to package directions; drain. Return hot, drained noodles to pot they were cooked in. Add cottage cheese, dill and pepper and toss gently with a large spoon to mix. Serve immediately. *Makes about 5 cups.* For diet serving allow 1 cup.

Per diet serving: 350 calories, 24 grams protein, 8 grams fat, 44 grams carbohydrate.

Raspberry Sauce

2 tablespoons water

1 10-ounce package frozen quick-thaw raspberries

Put water and berries in a blender. Break up berries with a rubber spatula. Cover and blend until smooth. Strain to remove seeds. *Makes about 1 cup.* For diet serving allow 1 tablespoon.

NOTE: If you have raspberries left from Menu #7 lunch (page 126), you may puree them in the same way and chill in refrigerator or freezer.

Per diet serving: 15 calories, 0 grams protein, 0 grams fat, 4 grams carbohydrate.

BREAKFAST

1 cup 4-grain multivitamin-and-iron-
supplement cereal (110)
1 cup skim milk (86)
½ cup fresh or unsweetened frozen
strawberries (55)

LUNCH

* Lentil, Mint and Garlic Salad
(328)
½ green pepper, cut in strips (8)
1 small carrot, peeled and cut in
strips (20)
1 cup skim milk (86)

DINNER

* Pasta with Fresh Zucchini Sauce
(268)
2 cups mixed salad greens (20),
tossed with 2 tablespoons Parslied
Vinaigrette Dressing (recipe on
page 116, 62)
* Creamy Peach Pudding (72)

TO EAT ANY TIME

½ cup 99%-fat-free cottage cheese
(82)

Lentil, Mint and Garlic Salad

2 cups water
¾ teaspoon salt
1½ cups dried lentils, rinsed and
drained
¼ cup lemon juice

2 tablespoons vegetable oil
1 teaspoon minced, peeled garlic
1½ teaspoons dried mint leaves
¼ teaspoon salt
¼ teaspoon black pepper

In a heavy, 2-quart saucepot bring water and the ¾ teaspoon salt to a
boil over moderately high heat. Add lentils, bring to a boil and then
reduce heat to low, cover pot and simmer 25 to 30 minutes, or until
lentils are just tender. Remove pan from heat and let stand covered
for 10 minutes. Meanwhile, combine remaining ingredients in a
medium-sized bowl. Add hot lentils, and toss gently. Cover and refrigerate 2 hours or longer to blend flavors. Covered tightly, mixture
will keep several days in the refrigerator. To carry, pack diet serving of
salad in a plastic container (wrap pepper and carrot strips from menu
separately). *Makes 4 cups.* For diet serving allow 1 cup.

Per diet serving: 328 calories, 18 grams protein, 7 grams fat, 48 grams carbohydrate.

Pasta with Fresh Zucchini Sauce

2 teaspoons vegetable oil
1 teaspoon minced, peeled garlic
½ pound fresh mushrooms, sliced
  ¼-inch thick
¾ pound small zucchini squash,
  halved lengthwise and cut in
  ¼-inch-thick slices

1 teaspoon dried basil leaves
1 15-ounce can tomato sauce
¼ cup water
¾ teaspoon salt
½ pound spaghetti or vermicelli
½ cup Parmesan cheese,
  preferably freshly grated

In a large skillet heat oil over moderate heat. Add garlic and mushrooms and cook, stirring frequently, until mushrooms are slightly softened. Add zucchini and cook 1 or 2 minutes, stirring frequently, until crisp-tender. Stir in basil and tomato sauce. Pour the ¼ cup of water into the tomato sauce can, swirl around and add to the skillet; stir in the salt. Cook just until sauce is well heated. Meanwhile, cook pasta according to package directions; drain. Serve hot, cooked pasta covered with sauce and sprinkled with Parmesan cheese. *Makes 4 cups sauce and 4 cups pasta.* For diet serving allow 1 cup cooked pasta, ⅔ cup of the sauce and 2 tablespoons grated Parmesan cheese.

Per diet serving: 268 calories, 11 grams protein, 7 grams fat, 42 grams carbohydrate.

Creamy Peach Pudding

1 cup diced fresh peaches or
  water-packed peach slices,
  drained
½ cup creamed cottage cheese

½ cup plain low-fat yogurt
1 tablespoon honey
½ teaspoon vanilla extract

Arrange fruit in the bottom of a shallow, 1-quart glass serving dish. Place remaining ingredients in a blender; cover and blend at medium speed 10 seconds, or until smooth and creamy. Pour sauce over fruit and stir gently to mix; cover and refrigerate 3 hours or overnight. *Makes 2 cups.* For diet serving allow ½ cup.

Per diet serving: 72 calories, 6 grams protein, 1 gram fat, 11 grams carbohydrate.

BREAKFAST

1 cup 4-grain multivitamin-and-iron-
 supplement cereal (110)
½ cup skim milk (43)
1 medium-sized banana (101)

LUNCH

Liverwurst Open-Face Sandwich:
 1 slice rye bread (61), spread with
 1 teaspoon prepared mustard (4);
2 ½-inch-thick slices liverwurst
 (122); 1 thin slice onion (2); 2
 small pickles (11); 2 slices hard-
 cooked egg (20)
1 cup skim milk (86)
1 cup sweet cherries (82)

DINNER

* Broiled Fish and Herbed Crumbs
 (167)
* Green Beans with Tomato Sauce
 (49)
Buttered New Potatoes: 2 boiled
 small new potatoes (104), with
 1 teaspoon butter or margarine
 (34), coarse salt and freshly
 ground pepper
½ cup chocolate ice milk (95)
1 glass iced coffee with 3 tablespoons
 skim milk (17), or hot coffee if
 preferred

TO EAT ANY TIME

1 cup skim milk (86)

Broiled Fish with Herbed Crumbs

3 tablespoons butter or margarine
2 tablespoons vegetable oil
2 tablespoons lemon juice
1-pound block frozen flounder
 fillets, thawed enough to
 separate

½ cup soft, fresh bread crumbs
1 teaspoon dried basil leaves
½ teaspoon fennel seed
 (optional)
¼ teaspoon black pepper

Melt butter in a small pan over low heat, remove from heat and stir
in oil and lemon juice. Separate the fillets and brush with 1½ tablespoons of butter mixture. Put crumbs, basil, fennel and pepper in a
blender; cover and blend 10 seconds at high speed. Combine crumb
mixture with remaining butter mixture and pat evenly on top of the
fillets. Put fillets on a rack in a broiler pan and broil about 5 inches
from the heat source for about 4 minutes, until crumbs are browned
and fish is cooked. *Makes 3 or 4 servings.* For diet serving allow ¼ of
the fish.

Per diet serving: 154 calories, 19 grams protein, 8 grams fat, 2 grams carbohydrate.

Green Beans with Tomato Sauce

1 tablespoon vegetable oil
1 large garlic clove, peeled
1 16-ounce can whole tomatoes,
  undrained
2 tablespoons chopped fresh
  parsley

½ teaspoon dried oregano leaves
¼ teaspoon salt
2 tablespoons tomato paste
Water
¾ pound fresh whole young green
  beans or 1 10-ounce package
  frozen whole green beans

In a small skillet heat oil over moderate heat; add garlic and cook until lightly browned. Add tomatoes, parsley, oregano and salt and break up tomatoes with a spoon. Stir in the tomato paste and simmer uncovered 15 minutes. Fill a large saucepot or Dutch oven with water to a depth of 1 inch and bring to a boil over high heat. Trim tips off fresh beans; leave small, firm beans whole; break larger ones into 1½-inch pieces. Put beans in a steamer basket or colander in the pot; cover, reduce heat to moderately high and steam 7 to 10 minutes, until just tender. Discard garlic clove and serve tomato sauce over the steamed beans. *Makes 4 to 6 servings.* For diet serving allow 12 whole beans and 2 tablespoons sauce.

Per calorie serving: 49 calories, 2 grams protein, 3 grams fat, 6 grams carbohydrate.

Desk-Drawer Drinks

Dieting and work don't always go together; a frustrating bout with a job problem can suggest a candy-bar reward. Desk-drawer drinks can be your solution. If you've a water cooler where you work, keep a jar of unsweetened instant tea on hand to stir up and quell your need for food. If boiling water is available, you've got it made. Tea bags, instant coffee, bouillon cubes, even some herb teas will give you a soothing break.

BREAKFAST

½ cup fresh or unsweetened frozen
strawberries (55)
1 cup creamed cottage cheese (239)
1 slice raisin bread, toasted (66)

LUNCH

* Antipasto Salad Sandwich (277)

DINNER

2 medium eggs, scrambled (144)
with 1 teaspoon butter or
margarine (34)
* Stir-Fried Vegetables (68)
½ cup cooked rice (93)
½ cup fresh or unsweetened frozen
blueberries (45)

TO EAT ANY TIME

¾ cup skim milk (65)
1 cup 4-grain multivitamin-and-iron-
supplement cereal (110)

Antipasto Salad Sandwich

2 tablespoons Basic Vinaigrette
    Dressing (recipe on page 23)
¼ teaspoon Dijon-style mustard
¼ teaspoon dried basil leaves
⅛ teaspoon minced, peeled garlic
½ small tomato, sliced
2 slices green pepper

2 slices sweet red pepper
2 pitted ripe olives, sliced
1 slice red onion
1 2-ounce Kaiser or crusty
    sandwich roll
1 tablespoon grated Parmesan
    cheese

The night before or early in the morning, mix the vinaigrette dressing, mustard, basil and garlic in a small bowl. Add the vegetables and toss lightly. Cover and refrigerate. When ready to pack lunch, halve and slightly hollow out the roll. Arrange tomato slices on the bottom half of roll and top with remaining vegetables. Sprinkle with Parmesan cheese and pour any remaining dressing over salad. Replace top of roll. Press roll firmly, wrap tightly and place under a heavy book when you get to work. *Makes 1 diet serving.*

Per diet serving: 277 calories, 8 grams protein, 10 grams fat, 36 grams carbohydrate.

Stir-Fried Vegetables

2 teaspoons vegetable oil
1 pound Chinese cabbage, cut
  into 1-inch pieces (about 4
  cups)
1 carrot, peeled and thinly sliced
½ cup thin-sliced scallion or
  green onion

2 sweet red peppers, seeded and
  cut into thin strips
¼ teaspoon salt
½ teaspoon black pepper
1 teaspoon sugar
¼ cup soy sauce

In a large skillet, heat the vegetable oil over moderately high heat. Add the cabbage and carrots and cook 2 minutes, tossing continuously with two spoons. Add the scallions and peppers and cook 1 minute more or until all vegetables are crisp-tender. Add salt, pepper, sugar and soy sauce and toss to blend in seasonings. Serve immediately. *Makes 4 servings.* For diet serving allow ¼ of the vegetables.

Per diet serving: 68 calories, 3 grams protein, 3 grams fat, 10 grams carbohydrate.

Wrapping It Up

Although all of the lunches-to-go in this chapter are designed to keep for four hours without refrigeration, it's wise to exercise some precaution with handling of all foods. Prepare food with clean hands and utensils, wrap them in clean wrappings or plastic containers. Avoid storing lunch where it will be exposed to high temperature or strong sunlight. A neat "refrigeration" trick: Freeze a small can of vegetable or tomato juice and pack it with a salad lunch. It'll keep the food cool and by lunchtime it will be defrosted to drink.

BREAKFAST

1 large hard-cooked egg (82)
1 slice cracked-wheat bread, toasted
  (66)
1 cup skim milk (86)

LUNCH

* Shrimp Salad (224)
2 crisp rye wafers (45)
1 cup tomato juice (46)

DINNER

* Beef and Mushroom Broil (328)
1 small ear cooked corn on the cob
  (70), with 1 teaspoon butter or
  margarine (34), salt and pepper
1 cup braised mustard greens or
  mixed mustard and turnip greens
  (35)
* Citrus Salad (77)

TO EAT ANY TIME

1 cup skim milk (86)
6 radishes (6)
½ green pepper (8)

Shrimp Salad

1 cup zucchini squash slices
About ¼ cup water
2 ounces frozen tiny Alaska shrimp
  (⅓ of a 6-ounce package)

2 teaspoons mayonnaise
2 teaspoons lemon juice

In a small skillet cook zucchini slices in water over moderately high heat until they are just crisp-tender, 3 to 5 minutes. Drain and plunge them into cold water to cool. Put cooled zucchini and shrimp into a plastic bag or container. Blend mayonnaise and lemon juice and put it into a separate container. At lunchtime, arrange zucchini slices on a plate, place shrimp in center and top with mayonnaise mixture. *Makes 1 diet serving.*

NOTE: Wrap and refrigerate remaining shrimp to use for another lunch or dinner. Shrimp will keep 2 or 3 days.

Per diet serving: 224 calories, 29 grams protein, 9 grams fat, 7 grams carbohydrate.

Beef and Mushroom Broil

1¼ pounds lean ground beef
12 medium-sized fresh mushrooms
(about ½ pound)
Black pepper

1 tablespoon plus 1 teaspoon
soy sauce
1 tablespoon vegetable oil
2 firm ripe tomatoes, ½ pound
each, halved

Heat broiler. Divide ground beef into 4 equal portions. Wipe mushrooms with a damp cloth or paper towel and trim a thin sliver from each stem. Remove stems, chop them coarsely and press some into the middle of each portion of meat; wrap meat around mushroom pieces and flatten each portion into ¾-inch-thick burgers. Put burgers in a broiler pan without a rack and sprinkle with pepper; spread tops of burgers with half the soy sauce. Broil 2 to 3 inches from heat source for 4 to 5 minutes. Rub mushroom caps with oil. Turn burgers, sprinkle with pepper and remaining soy sauce and arrange tomato halves and mushroom caps around them. Broil 4 to 5 minutes longer for medium-well-done meat. *Makes 4 servings.* For diet serving allow 1 burger, a tomato half and 3 mushrooms.

Per diet serving: 328 calories, 32 grams protein, 18 grams fat, 8 grams carbohydrate.

Citrus Salad

2 grapefruits

2 oranges, peeled and segmented

Halve grapefruits; loosen flesh with a grapefruit knife or spoon and remove membrane. Over a small bowl, cut orange segments and grapefruit flesh into small pieces, toss and fill the grapefruit shells with this mixture. Cover and chill until serving time. *Makes 4 servings.* For diet serving allow 1 filled grapefruit half.

Per diet serving: 77 calories, 1 gram protein, 0 grams fat, 20 grams carbohydrate.

BREAKFAST

½ grapefruit (40)
1 cup 4-grain multivitamin-and-iron-
   supplement cereal (110)
½ cup skim milk (43)

LUNCH

½ cup canned green pea soup
   prepared with water (65)
Open-Face Ham Sandwich: 2 ounces
   boiled ham (122); 1 teaspoon
   mayonnaise (34); 1 teaspoon
   mustard (4); 1 slice whole-wheat
   bread (61)
1 medium-sized carrot, cut in strips
   (30)
1 green pepper, sliced (16)
4 dried pitted prunes (66)

DINNER

* Crispy Salad Tortillas (410)
1 small apple (61)

TO EAT ANY TIME

Hot Cocoa: 1 cup skim milk (86);
   1 tablespoon unsweetened cocoa
   (14); 2 teaspoons sugar (31);
   ground cinnamon

Crispy Salad Tortillas

1 large tomato, diced
1 small red onion, peeled and
   diced
5 pimiento-stuffed olives, sliced
½ teaspoon salt
2 to 3 drops Tabasco sauce
1 tablespoon vegetable oil
2 tablespoons lime juice or red
   wine vinegar

4 frozen corn tortillas, thawed
   according to package directions
1 8¾-ounce can red kidney beans,
   rinsed and drained
1 cup shredded iceberg lettuce
1 ounce coarsely grated sharp
   Cheddar cheese (about ¼ cup)

Heat oven to 350°F. In a large bowl combine the tomato, onion, olives, salt, Tabasco, oil and lime juice and toss to blend. Let stand 10 minutes. Place the 4 tortillas on a baking sheet and heat in oven 10 minutes. Tip bowl of vegetables slightly so that juices in bottom run to one side of bowl. With the back of a spoon mash about half the beans into the dressing to thicken. Fold in remaining beans. To serve, place a tortilla on a plate and top with about ½ cup of the salad, some shredded lettuce and cheese. Fold over firmly and eat like a sandwich. *Makes 2 servings.* For diet serving allow 2 tortillas, 1 cup of the salad and ½ the lettuce and cheese.

Per diet serving: 410 calories, 16 grams protein, 14 grams fat, 57 grams carbohydrate.

BREAKFAST

* Swiss-Cheese Pancakes (211)
  with ½ cup unsweetened applesauce (50)

LUNCH

Salmon Salad Sandwich: 2 ounces
  drained canned salmon (125);
  2 teaspoons mayonnaise (67);
  ½ cucumber, sliced (15); 1 slice
  rye bread, toasted (61)
* Icy Chocolate Milk Shake (117)

DINNER

* One-Pot Autumn Dinner (397)
2 cups romaine lettuce (20), tossed
  with Basic Vinaigrette Dressing
  (recipe on page 23, 31)
* Spoon Pears (113)

Swiss-Cheese Pancakes

1 egg
1½ slices whole-wheat bread
½ cup grated Swiss cheese
2 tablespoons liquid skim milk

¼ teaspoon baking powder
⅛ teaspoon salt
1 teaspoon vegetable oil

Place all ingredients except oil in a blender; cover and blend at high speed 30 seconds to make a thick, smooth batter. In a medium-sized, nonstick or well-seasoned heavy skillet heat ½ teaspoon of the oil over moderate heat. Drop the batter by tablespoonfuls into the skillet, using the back of a spoon to spread each pancake slightly. Cook 1 to 1½ minutes, turning once, until pancakes are evenly browned. Repeat with remaining batter and oil. *Makes 8 pancakes.* For diet serving allow 4 pancakes.

Per diet serving: 211 calories, 13 grams protein, 14 grams fat, 10 grams carbohydrate.

Icy Chocolate Milk Shake

1 cup liquid skim milk
1 tablespoon cocoa

1 teaspoon granulated sugar
3 ice cubes

Put all ingredients in a blender. Cover and blend until smooth and foamy. *Makes 1 diet serving.*

Per diet serving: 117 calories, 10 grams protein, 1 gram fat, 18 grams carbohydrate.

One-Pot Autumn Dinner

Soup Base:
3 quarts water
1 10½-ounce can condensed beef
  broth
2 to 3 pounds boneless beef
  chuck shoulder
2 pounds beef bones, cracked
1 8-ounce can stewed tomatoes
2 onions, peeled, and each stuck
  with 2 whole cloves

2 carrots, peeled and halved
2 stalks celery, halved
1 clove garlic, flattened and
  peeled
¼ cup fresh parsley sprigs, packed
  tight to measure
1 tablespoon salt
8 peppercorns

In an 8- or 10-quart saucepot bring all ingredients to a boil over high heat. Cover pot, reduce heat to low and simmer 2 to 3 hours, until meat is tender. Remove meat and reserve. Discard beef bones, onions, carrots and celery. Wrap and refrigerate or freeze half the meat for luncheon sandwiches. Keep remaining meat warm.

To Finish Soup:
2 carrots, peeled and sliced
4 white turnips, peeled and diced

½ pound green beans, rinsed and
  cut into 1-inch lengths
2 onions, peeled and sliced
¼ pound medium egg noodles

Bring soup broth to a boil over high heat. Add remaining ingredients and cook 10 minutes, until noodles are tender. *Makes 4 servings.* For diet serving place in large soup plates 3 ounces meat, ¼ of the vegetables, ½ cup noodles, and as much broth as desired.

Per diet serving: 397 calories, 43 grams protein, 7 grams fat, 40 grams carbohydrate.

Spoon Pears

4 medium-sized firm pears, peeled,
  cored and cut into chunks
¼ cup water
1 tablespoon lemon juice

1 slice lemon
1 tablespoon granulated sugar
1 3-inch cinnamon stick

Place all ingredients in a small saucepot and bring to a boil over high heat, stirring occasionally. Reduce heat to low, cover and cook 20 to 25 minutes, until pears begin to soften but still hold their shape. Uncover pot, increase heat to high and boil 2 minutes, until pan juices form a syrupy glaze. Transfer pears to a serving bowl, cover and refrigerate an hour or longer. *Makes 2 cups.* Serve warm or cold. For diet serving allow ½ cup.

Per diet serving: 113 calories, 1 gram protein, 0 grams fat, 28 grams carbohydrate.

CHAPTER FIVE

Entertaining While You Diet: Menus Company Can Share

The old idea of laying out a groaning board is, fortunately, passé. Serving food that is perfectly prepared and beautifully presented is more to be admired today. La Cuisine Minceur, or "slim cooking," a popular movement generally credited to French chef Michel Guérard, has become a more gracious way to entertain and, of course, to diet. The menus and recipes in this chapter are good examples of that trend. Several of them are recipes from Michel Guérard, who, with his wife, is owner of the restaurants Les Près et Les Sources d'Eugénie in Southern France. André Soltner, chef-owner of Lutece, considered by many to be New York City's top French restaurant, Jovan Trboyevic, owner of the famous Le Perroquet restaurant in Chicago, Christiana Sutor, a creative food writer, and Irena Chalmers, president of Irena Chalmers Cookbooks, Inc., have all contributed their expertise to recipes in this chapter. Dine well.

NOTE: The menus in this chapter are not designed to be used on successive days. They are planned around special dinners for special occasions; however, each day's menu is nutritionally balanced. When you plan to entertain while dieting, follow the full day's menus given with the company dinner you select.

BREAKFAST

½ grapefruit (40)
1 teaspoon sugar (15)
* Waffle-with-the-Works (197)

LUNCH

* Liptauer Cheese Salad (142; see
    note)
1 cup shredded red cabbage (22)
1 slice rye bread (61)
1 cup tomato juice (46)
3 tablespoons seedless raisins (78)

DINNER

* Sliced Steak with Wine Sauce
    (179)
1 baked potato (2½ x 4½ inches,
    145)
* Tomatoes Provençale (57)
Tossed Salad: 4 large leaves escarole
    (5); 10 sliced radishes (10); 1
    teaspoon vegetable oil (40);
    1 tablespoon lemon juice (4)
1 syrup-packed peach half with
    1 tablespoon syrup (59) and 2
    tablespoons dry red wine (12)

TO EAT ANY TIME

1 cup skim milk (86)

NOTE: If desired, save ½ of the Liptauer Cheese Salad diet serving to eat as an appetizer before dinner.

Waffle-with-the-Works

1 frozen waffle
¼ cup unsweetened applesauce
Few grains of salt

1 ounce grated sharp Cheddar
    cheese (about ¼ cup)

Heat oven to 400°F. or use toaster-oven. Place waffle on a sheet of foil on a baking sheet or the toaster-oven baking tray and heat in oven 7 minutes. Spread applesauce evenly over waffle; sprinkle with salt and cheese and return to oven for 5 minutes, until cheese is hot and bubbly. *Makes 1 diet serving.*

Per diet serving: 197 calories, 8 grams protein, 11 grams fat, 15 grams carbohydrate.

Liptauer Cheese Salad

1 cup creamed cottage cheese
1 tablespoon minced scallion or
    green onion
1 small green pepper, seeded and
    diced (½ cup)

2 tablespoons diced roasted sweet
    red pepper or pimiento
⅛ teaspoon salt
Few grains of white pepper
¼ teaspoon caraway seeds

Mix all ingredients in a small bowl. *Makes just over 1 cup.* Tightly covered, leftover salad can be stored in the refrigerator for 2 days. For diet serving allow ½ the salad.

Per diet serving: 142 calories, 17 grams protein, 5 grams fat, 7 grams carbohydrate.

Sliced Steak with Wine Sauce

2 tablespoons butter or margarine
⅔ cup chopped fresh mushrooms
½ cup chopped scallion or green
    onion
1 cup dry red wine

1 10½-ounce can beef gravy
2½ pounds top round steak, cut
    2 inches thick
2 tablespoons lemon juice,
    preferably freshly squeezed

In a heavy skillet melt the butter over moderate heat. Add mushrooms and scallion and cook, stirring occasionally until vegetables are lightly browned. Add wine and turn heat to low. Simmer 5 to 8 minutes until liquid is reduced to about half. Add beef gravy and stir until smooth. Keep sauce hot over very low heat.

Put steak on a broiling pan with a rack and place it in the oven about 3 inches from heat. Broil about 8 minutes on one side. Turn steak and broil about 5 minutes more for medium-rare. Remove steak to a cutting board and slice diagonally into thin slices. Stir lemon juice into sauce and bring it quickly to a boil. Serve sauce separately. *Makes 6 to 8 servings.* For diet serving allow 3 ounces of steak and 1 tablespoon of sauce.

Per diet serving: 179 calories, 28 grams protein, 5 grams fat, 2 grams carbohydrate.

Tomatoes Provençale

8 medium tomatoes
½ teaspoon salt
¼ teaspoon black pepper
½ cup finely chopped fresh
    parsley

2 teaspoons minced, peeled garlic
½ cup dry bread crumbs
1 tablespoon butter or margarine,
    cut in tiny pieces

Heat oven to 350°F. Cut out and discard tomato cores. Cut tomatoes in half and place cut sides up on a large shallow baking pan. Sprinkle halves with salt and pepper. Mix parsley and garlic and spread on tomato halves. Sprinkle bread crumbs over parsley. Dot with butter. Bake 20 to 25 minutes, until tomatoes are fork-tender but still hold their shape. *Makes 8 servings.* For diet serving allow 2 tomato halves.

Per diet serving: 57 calories, 2 grams protein, 1 gram fat, 11 grams carbohydrate.

BREAKFAST

½ cup orange juice (61)
1 cup 4-grain multivitamin-and-iron-
  supplement cereal (110)
¾ cup skim milk (65)
1 slice white bread, toasted (68),
  spread with 1 teaspoon butter or
  margarine (34)

LUNCH

* Asparagus and Tuna Salad (230)
1 slice whole-wheat bread, toasted
  (61)
1 cup tomato juice (46)

DINNER

1 cup chicken broth (from Poached
  Chicken recipe, below, 66)
* Michel Guérard's Chicken
  Poached in Apple Cider (297)
1 ½-inch-thick slice French bread
  (about 2½ x 2 inches, 44), spread
  with 2 teaspoons butter or
  margarine (68)
½ grapefruit (40), sprinkled with
  1 teaspoon brown sugar (17) and
  broiled

Asparagus and Tuna Salad

1 3-ounce can water-packed tuna,
  drained
1 8-ounce can asparagus spears,
  tips or pieces, drained

1 roasted sweet red pepper or
  pimiento, slivered
¼ teaspoon dried basil leaves
Lemon wedges

Place tuna in the center of a serving plate. Arrange asparagus in a circular pattern around tuna and top with pepper slivers in a crisscross pattern. Sprinkle with basil; serve with lemon. *Makes 1 diet serving.*

Per diet serving: 230 calories, 30 grams protein, 8 grams fat, 10 grams carbohydrate.

Michel Guérard's Chicken Poached in Apple Cider

1 3- to 3¼-pound broiler-fryer
  chicken
2 carrots, peeled and cut into
  thirds
2 small white turnips, peeled and
  quartered
2 medium-sized onions, peeled
  and quartered
1 teaspoon salt
2 cups apple cider

3 cups water
2 medium-sized zucchini squash,
  washed and cut into 1-inch-thick
  rounds
2 firm apples, such as Golden
  Delicious, peeled, cored and
  quartered
1 teaspoon finely grated lemon
  peel

Rinse chicken and place in a Dutch oven or large saucepot with carrots, turnips, onions, salt, cider and water. Cover and bring to a boil over high heat. Reduce heat to moderately low and simmer 40 minutes. Add zucchini and apples to pot, cover and cook 5 minutes longer, until zucchini and apples are crisp-tender. With a slotted spoon remove zucchini from pot and keep warm. Transfer apples to a blender; add 2 cups of the cooking liquid and the lemon peel, cover and blend at medium speed until smooth. Pour mixture into a small saucepan and bring to a boil over high heat. Boil 5 to 7 minutes, until the consistency of a rich sauce. Keep sauce warm. Remove chicken to a plate; remove skin and use poultry scissors to cut chicken into 6 serving pieces. Arrange chicken on a serving platter, discard onions and surround chicken with the remaining cooked vegetables. Serve sauce on the side. Reserve remaining broth to serve as a first course for dinner. *Makes 4 to 6 servings.* For diet serving allow ⅙ of the chicken and ¼ of the vegetables and sauce.

Per diet serving: 297 calories, 31 grams protein, 8 grams fat, 26 grams carbohydrate.

But What Will My Guests Think?

Your secret when you're entertaining is portion-control. Expect that guests will, if they choose, eat their fill of the superb roast beef or stuffed capon or mashed potatoes. But keep an eagle eye on the size of your own portions. Assume your guests are enjoying themselves so much they won't notice your smaller plate. One experienced dieter volunteered, "I served that Blueberry Cheesecake [Chapter 1] to a bunch of my girlfriends for a dessert and coffee and they loved it. And I thought, 'Great, it was good for them.'" If it eases your hostess's soul, put out extras like hot rolls and butter—for guests only.

BREAKFAST

1 medium-sized orange (78)
1 large poached egg (82)
1 slice white bread, toasted (68),
spread with 1 teaspoon butter or
margarine (34)

LUNCH

Ham and Bean Salad: 1 cup canned
white beans, drained (210); 1
ounce boiled ham, slivered (66);
2 slices onion (6); ¼ head lettuce,
shredded (18); 1 teaspoon
vegetable oil (40); 1 tablespoon
wine vinegar
1 pear (90)

DINNER

* André Soltner's Sole au Vin
  Blanc (179)
1 unpeeled medium-sized steamed
  or boiled potato (104)
1 cup cooked spinach (41)
* André Soltner's Simple Baked
  Apple (109)

TO EAT ANY TIME

¾ cup skim milk (65)
1 saltine cracker (12)

André Soltner's Sole au Vin Blanc

1 tablespoon butter
1 medium-sized onion, peeled and
  sliced thin
1 pound fresh fillets of sole or
  1 1-pound block frozen sole
  fillets, thawed
¼ teaspoon salt
⅛ teaspoon white pepper

1 large ripe tomato, peeled, seeded
  and cut into eighths or 1 8-ounce
  can whole peeled tomatoes,
  drained
¼ cup parsley sprigs, packed
  tight to measure
2 tablespoons dry white wine
2 tablespoons water

Heat oven to 400°F. In a shallow 12-x-7-inch rangetop-to-oven baking dish melt butter over low heat; add onion and cook 5 minutes, stirring often, until onion is soft but not browned. Remove onion to a plate. Arrange fillets in dish, overlapping them slightly, and sprinkle with salt and pepper. Spoon onions evenly over fillets, arrange tomato and parsley sprigs on top and pour the wine and water over fish. Press a sheet of wax paper gently but firmly over fillets. Bring to a simmer over high heat. As soon as liquid begins to simmer, transfer dish to center of oven and bake 10 to 12 minutes, until fish is white in the center. Carefully transfer fillets and vegetables to a serving platter, leaving cooking liquid in dish. Place dish over high heat and boil liquid 2 to 3 minutes to reduce slightly. Pour over fish and serve. *Makes 3 servings.* For diet serving allow ⅓ of the fish and vegetables.

Per diet serving: 179 calories, 27 grams protein, 5 grams fat, 6 grams carbohydrate.

André Soltner's Simple Baked Apple

4 small baking apples, such as
Rome Beauty, cored

4 teaspoons butter
4 teaspoons sugar

With a vegetable peeler remove an inch-wide strip from around the middle of each apple. Arrange apples in a small baking dish and fill cavities with butter and sugar. Place dish in oven and turn on oven to 350°F. Bake about 40 minutes, basting apples 2 or 3 times with pan juices, until apples are almost tender but still hold their shape. *Makes 4 servings.* For diet serving allow 1 baked apple.

Per diet serving: 109 calories, 0 grams protein, 4 grams fat, 18 grams carbohydrate.

Whipped Cream?

Heavy cream isn't totally a no-no; you'll find it as an ingredient in the Chantilly Cream that's sandwiched between layers and spread on top of our Strawberry Shortcake, Chapter 1. But very much heavy cream at 821 calories per cup could easily ruin a 1,200-calorie diet.

When a recipe calls for *liquid* heavy cream, try using evaporated skim milk for only 198 calories per cup. When you think *whipped* cream would taste great on a dessert, opt for frozen whipped topping at 10 calories per tablespoon. You'll find it deliciously used to fill the Cream Puffs with Chocolate Sauce, Chapter 5.

BREAKFAST

1 cup tomato juice (46)
1 large egg, prepared any style (82), with 1 teaspoon butter or margarine (34)
1 slice white bread, toasted (68)

LUNCH

Nut Salad Sandwich: 2 tablespoons peanut butter (188); 1 medium-sized carrot, grated (15); 1 stalk celery, sliced (7); 2 slices raisin bread (122)
1 medium-sized apple (77)

DINNER

* Jovan Trboyevic's Boeuf à la Ficelle (148)
1 medium unpeeled, steamed or boiled potato (104)
6 large leaves lettuce (12), with *Jovan Trboyevic's Special Vinaigrette Dressing (63)
1 pear (90)

TO EAT ANY TIME

½ cup liquid skim milk (43)
2 whole-grain rye wafers (45)
½ ounce Swiss cheese (54)

Jovan Trboyevic's Boeuf à la Ficelle
(Rare Poached Beef with Horseradish Sauce)

1 2½- to 3-pound piece top round steak, trimmed of all visible fat
1 10½-ounce can condensed beef broth
Water
1 cup creamed cottage cheese

4 teaspoons prepared white horseradish
2 teaspoons Dijon-style mustard
6 tablespoons beef broth from pot
¼ teaspoon salt
Coarse salt

If desired, tie meat with white twine for easier handling. Place meat and broth in a Dutch oven or large saucepot and add water to barely cover meat. Remove meat, cover pot and bring broth to a boil over high heat. Carefully lower meat into boiling broth, and when liquid returns to boiling, cover pot, reduce heat to moderately low and simmer for exactly 15 minutes per pound, turning meat halfway through cooking time. Lift cooked meat onto a warm platter and let stand 5 minutes in a warm place before carving.

While meat rests, prepare sauce: Place cottage cheese, horseradish, mustard, warm beef broth and the ¼ teaspoon of salt in a blender; cover and blend at medium speed 40 seconds, until smooth. Scrape into a serving bowl. (*Makes 1 cup sauce.*) Remove twine from meat if used, slice meat very thin and serve with coarse salt and the horseradish sauce. *Makes 8 to 10 servings.* For diet serving allow 3 ounces of cooked meat and 2 tablespoons of the sauce.

NOTE: This dish gets its name from the ficelle (white string) with which it can be tied. Originally the meat was suspended in the broth by string from a skewer laid across the top of the pot.

Per diet serving: 148 calories, 23 grams protein, 5 grams fat, 1 gram carbohydrate.

Jovan Trboyevic's Special Vinaigrette Dressing

¼ teaspoon minced, peeled garlic
½ teaspoon salt
2 tablespoons sherry vinegar or
   red wine vinegar
3 tablespoons water
2 tablespoons olive or vegetable oil

2 tablespoons chopped fresh
   parsley
1 tablespoon capers, rinsed,
   drained and chopped
⅛ teaspoon salt

In a small bowl mash garlic and the ½ teaspoon salt to a paste with the back of a spoon. Add the vinegar and stir to dissolve salt. Stir in remaining ingredients. *Makes ½ cup.* For diet serving allow 2 tablespoons.

Per diet serving: 63 calories, 0 grams protein, 7 grams fat, 0 grams carbohydrate.

BREAKFAST

1¼ cups 4-grain multivitamin-and-
iron-supplement cereal (110)
¾ cup skim milk (65)
½ medium grapefruit (40)

LUNCH

3 ounces canned salmon, drained
(188); 1 large leaf lettuce (2)
1 slice white bread, toasted (68)
½ cup skim milk (43)

DINNER

* Senegalese Soup (87)
* Beef Ragout (401)
½ cup cooked rice (93)
Lettuce Raft: about 1/6 medium
head iceberg lettuce (18), with
Piquant Salad Dressing (recipe
on page 50, 11)
* Bananas and Oranges Flambé (79)

Senegalese Soup

1 10¾-ounce can condensed
cream of chicken soup
1⅓ cups liquid skim milk
1 tablespoon lemon juice

½ teaspoon curry powder
1 teaspoon chopped chives
(optional)

In a small saucepan mix soup, skim milk, lemon juice and curry powder.
Heat over moderate heat, stirring occasionally. Pour into soup mugs
and sprinkle with chives. Serve hot or cold. *Makes about 2¼ cups.* For
diet serving allow ¼ of the soup.

Per diet serving: 87 calories, 4 grams protein, 4 grams fat, 9 grams carbohydrate.

Beef Ragout

1 tablespoon vegetable oil
1 pound beef top round, cut into
1-inch cubes, all visible fat
removed
2 tablespoons tomato paste
2 tablespoons flour
2 cups beef broth
10 small white onions, peeled
1 bay leaf

2 tablespoons chopped fresh
parsley
½ teaspoon salt
¼ teaspoon black pepper
¼ pound fresh mushrooms,
quartered (about ¾ cup)
2 medium-sized carrots, peeled
and cut into 2-inch lengths

In a medium-sized saucepan heat oil over moderately high heat. Add
meat cubes and brown well on all sides. Remove meat from pan and
keep warm. Stir tomato paste and flour into pan drippings. Gradually
add beef broth, stirring constantly, until smooth and boiling. Add

onions, bay leaf, parsley, salt, pepper and beef cubes. Mix well. Cover pan, reduce heat to moderately low and simmer 1¼ hours. Add mushrooms and carrots. Cook 20 to 30 minutes longer, until carrots are tender. *Makes 4 servings.* For diet serving allow ¼ of the ragout.

Per diet serving: 401 calories, 37 grams protein, 21 grams fat, 13 grams carbohydrate.

Bananas and Oranges Flambé

2 small bananas, peeled and cut
   in half lengthwise
1 navel orange, peeled and cut
   crosswise into 8 slices

1½ tablespoons butter or
   margarine
1 teaspoon brown sugar, packed
   to measure
2 tablespoons dark or light rum

Heat oven to 325°F. Arrange bananas in a 10-x-6-x-1¼-inch baking dish. Top with orange slices. Dot with butter and sprinkle with sugar. Bake 15 minutes. Heat rum in a small saucepan. Ignite with a match and pour, flaming, over fruit. *Makes 4 servings.* For diet serving allow ¼ of the fruit and syrup.

Per diet serving: 79 calories, 1 gram protein, 4 grams fat, 10 grams carbohydrate.

But What Will My Hostess Think?

Being entertained is far more difficult than entertaining, especially if your hostess has prepared her most elaborate pasta casserole or her elegant moussaka. If she's a true friend and you've warned her that you're dieting, she won't do that to you. But if she's the boss's wife, it's best to just out and say, "I *am* on a diet; it looks delicious but I'd like a small portion, please." Treat whatever it is as a necessary lapse and don't be thrown by it. Go right back to your diet the next day.

BREAKFAST

* Old-Fashioned Oat–Buttermilk
  Pancakes (125)
3 tablespoons unsweetened applesauce (18)
1 slice ham (1 ounce, 66)
¾ cup skim milk (65)

LUNCH

3 ounces water-packed tuna, drained
  (117), with 1 lemon wedge (1)
1 slice whole-wheat bread (61)
1 medium-sized carrot, cut in
  julienne strips (30)
1 cup skim milk (86)
1 small banana (63)

DINNER

* Chicken à l'Orange (280)
½ cup cooked brown rice (116)
½ cup sliced beets (27)
3 large romaine lettuce leaves (15),
  served with 1 tablespoon Jovan
  Trboyevic's Special Vinaigrette
  Dressing (recipe on page 149, 32)
* Brandied Coffee Jelly (104)

Old-Fashioned Oat–Buttermilk Pancakes

1 cup old-fashioned rolled oats
1 cup buttermilk
1 egg
¼ cup flour
1 tablespoon granulated sugar

½ teaspoon baking powder
½ teaspoon baking soda
⅛ teaspoon ground cinnamon
1 tablespoon butter or margarine,
  melted

Mix oats and buttermilk in a small bowl; cover and refrigerate overnight. Add egg, flour, sugar, baking powder, baking soda and cinnamon.
Mix thoroughly. Stir in butter. Heat a lightly greased griddle over
moderately high heat. Drop 2 tablespoons batter onto griddle for each
pancake. Cook until undersides are brown. Turn and brown other
side. *Makes 12 pancakes.* For diet serving allow 2 pancakes.

Per diet serving: 125 calories, 5 grams protein, 4 grams fat, 18 grams carbohydrate.

Chicken à l'Orange

2 whole chicken breasts, about
  1¼ pounds, skinned and split
¼ cup flour
½ teaspoon salt
Few grains of black pepper
1 tablespoon butter or margarine
1 cup water

½ cup orange juice
1 chicken-flavored bouillon cube
¼ teaspoon ground ginger
2 teaspoons cornstarch
1 tablespoon water
1 navel orange, peeled and cut
  crosswise into 8 slices

Rinse chicken breasts and pat dry with paper towels. In a plastic bag mix flour, salt and pepper. Add 1 piece of chicken to bag. Shake until well coated with flour; remove from bag. Repeat with remaining breasts. In a heavy, medium-sized skillet melt butter over moderate heat. Add chicken breasts and brown for about 4 minutes on each side, turning once. Add the 1 cup water, the orange juice, bouillon cube and ginger. Cover and simmer over low heat 30 minutes, until chicken breasts are tender. Move chicken to one side of skillet. Mix cornstarch with the 1 tablespoon water and stir into liquid in pan. Cook for about 1 minute, stirring constantly, until thickened and boiling. Add orange slices and heat gently. *Makes 4 servings.* For diet serving allow ½ chicken breast and ¼ of the orange slices and sauce.

Per diet serving: 280 calories, 32 grams protein, 9 grams fat, 15 grams carbohydrate.

Brandied Coffee Jelly

1 envelope unflavored gelatin
¼ cup sugar
⅛ teaspoon salt

1¾ cups strong coffee
1 tablespoon brandy
½ cup frozen whipped topping

In a small saucepan combine gelatin, sugar and salt. Stir in coffee. Place over low heat and stir until gelatin is completely dissolved. Stir in brandy. Pour into a 9-x-5-x-2¾-inch loaf pan and cool about 30 minutes. Chill until firm. Cut into ½-inch cubes and serve in sherbet glasses. Spoon 2 tablespoons whipped topping over each serving. *Serves 4.* For diet serving allow ¼ of the jelly and 2 tablespoons whipped topping.

Per diet serving: 104 calories, 2 grams protein, 2 grams fat, 15 grams carbohydrate.

BREAKFAST

1 medium egg (72) scrambled with
¼ cup diced, drained canned
tomatoes (16) and 1 teaspoon
butter or margarine (34)
2 broiled little link sausages (150)
1 slice whole-wheat bread, toasted
(61)
Citrus Compote: ½ small orange,
peeled and sectioned (22); ½
grapefruit, peeled and sectioned
(40)

LUNCH

3 ounces canned salmon, drained
(188), with *Minted Cucumber
Sauce (49)
10 seedless green grapes (34)

DINNER

* Mongolian Hot Pot (289)
1 ½-inch-thick slice French bread
(2½ x 2 inches, 44)
* Tangerine-Buttermilk Sherbet
(139)

TO EAT ANY TIME

½ cup skim milk (43)
½ cup tomato juice (23)

Minted Cucumber Sauce

⅓ cup plain low-fat yogurt
½ small cucumber, peeled and
diced

¼ teaspoon dried mint leaves
⅛ teaspoon salt

Mix all ingredients in a small bowl. Serve with canned salmon. *Makes
1 diet serving.*

Per diet serving: 49 calories, 3 grams protein, 1 gram fat, 6 grams carbohydrate.

Mongolian Hot Pot

2 13¾-ounce cans chicken broth
1 10½-ounce can condensed beef
broth, diluted according to
directions on can
¼ teaspoon ground ginger
¼ teaspoon monosodium
glutamate (optional)
¼ pound uncooked medium egg
noodles (about 3 cups)
½ pound flank steak, trimmed of
all fat and cut into ¼-x-2-x-
1-inch slices (about 1½ cups)

½ pound boneless, skinless
chicken breast, cut into 1-inch
chunks (about 1 cup)
4 cups washed fresh spinach
leaves
¼ pound fresh mushrooms, sliced
thin
1 small onion, peeled, sliced thin
and separated into rings
1 lemon, quartered (optional)

In a large saucepot or Dutch oven place chicken broth, diluted beef broth, ginger and, if used, monosodium glutamate; bring to a boil over high heat. Add noodles and boil uncovered 5 minutes. Add beef and chicken and boil 1 minute, stirring often. Add spinach, mushrooms and onion and boil 1 minute longer. Ladle into soup bowls and serve with lemon wedges. *Makes 4 servings.* For diet serving allow ¼ of the hot pot.

Per diet serving: 289 calories, 32 grams protein, 6 grams fat, 25 grams carbohydrate.

Tangerine-Buttermilk Sherbet

1 6-ounce can tangerine juice   2 cups buttermilk
   concentrate, undiluted

Place the concentrate and half the buttermilk in a blender; cover and blend at high speed 30 seconds, until smooth. Add remaining buttermilk and blend a few seconds at low speed. Pour into four 8-ounce paper cups, or custard cups; cover and freeze several hours, until firm. Remove from freezer about 20 minutes before serving to soften slightly. *Makes 4 servings.* For diet serving allow 1 sherbet cup.

Per diet serving: 139 calories, 5 grams protein, 1 gram fat, 28 grams carbohydrate.

BREAKFAST

½ grapefruit (40)
1 cup iron-enriched farina (100),
    topped with 1 teaspoon butter or
    margarine (34), and 1 teaspoon
    brown sugar (17)
1 cup skim milk (86)

LUNCH

* Roman Toasted Cheese (178)
4 dried pitted prunes (66)

DINNER

½ cup beef consommé over ice (15)
* Roast Stuffed Capon (404)
* Whipped Cauliflower (35)
6 frozen asparagus spears, cooked
    (18)
1 small tomato, sliced (20), with
    *Low-Calorie Mayonnaise (20)
* Christiana Sutor's Stewed Pears
    with Raspberry Sauce (131)

TO EAT ANY TIME

½ cup skim milk (43)

Roman Toasted Cheese

1 1-ounce slice Muenster cheese
1 slice white bread, lightly toasted
½ small roasted sweet red pepper
    or pimiento, slivered

Few grains of salt
Dried oregano leaves

Place cheese on toast, top with slivered pepper and sprinkle lightly with salt. Place on a sheet of foil and broil 4 inches from heat source (or use toaster-oven) for about 3 minutes, until cheese is bubbly and lightly browned. Remove from broiler and sprinkle with oregano just before serving. *Makes 1 diet serving.*

Per diet serving: 178 calories, 10 grams protein, 9 grams fat, 15 grams carbohydrate.

Roast Stuffed Capon

1 6- to 7-pound capon, with
    giblets (see note)
Salt
4 slices white bread, torn into
    small pieces
¾ cup finely chopped peeled
    onion
1 cup coarsely chopped celery

2 tablespoons finely chopped
    fresh parsley
1 large carrot, peeled and coarsely
    shredded (about 1 cup)
½ teaspoon salt
Few grains black pepper
¼ cup chicken broth or water

Wash capon well; drain and pat dry with paper towels. Finely chop or grind the gizzard, heart and liver. Sprinkle capon lightly with salt, inside and out. Heat oven to 325°F. In a medium bowl, mix bread, chopped giblets, onion, celery, parsley, carrot, the ½ teaspoon salt and pepper together. Moisten with chicken broth. Stuff capon lightly with the stuffing. Insert skewers at body openings; lace with string and tie legs together. Fasten neck skin to the back with a skewer. Fold wing tips under back. Place capon on a rack in a shallow roasting pan, breast up. Roast, uncovered, 2 to 2¾ hours, basting occasionally with drippings from the roasting pan. Capon is done when drumstick-thigh joint will move easily and meat on drumstick is soft when pressed with fingers. *Makes 4 servings, with leftovers* for luncheon sandwiches or another main dish. For diet serving allow 5 ounces meat without skin and ¼ cup of dressing.

NOTE: If roasting chicken is more easily available, use it instead of capon. Remove any extra fat from cavity before stuffing.

Per diet serving: 404 calories, 53 grams protein, 16 grams fat, 9 grams carbohydrate.

Whipped Cauliflower

1 large head cauliflower (about 2 pounds), trimmed of all outer leaves
Water
½ teaspoon salt
⅛ teaspoon white pepper
½ cup liquid skim milk

Cut cauliflower into very small florets and stems into 1-inch pieces. Place in a steamer basket or colander and rinse under cold water. Fill a Dutch oven or large saucepot with water to a depth of 1 inch and bring to a boil over high heat. Place container of cauliflower in pot, cover and steam 10 minutes, until cauliflower is very tender when pierced with a fork. Lift out cauliflower and discard cooking water. Put salt, pepper, 2 tablespoons of the milk and ¼ of the cauliflower in a blender; cover and blend at high speed until cauliflower is smooth, stopping machine often to push down contents. Put pureed cauliflower back in saucepot. Puree remaining cauliflower with milk in 2 or 3 batches. Mix pureed cauliflower in saucepot and then cover and heat for a few minutes over low heat. *Makes about 4 cups.* For diet serving allow 1 cup.

Per diet serving: 35 calories, 3 grams protein, 0 grams fat, 6 grams carbohydrate.

Low-Calorie Mayonnaise

1 egg
1 tablespoon vegetable oil
1 teaspoon Dijon mustard
1 tablespoon lemon juice

2 tablespoons plain low-fat yogurt
1 cup low-fat cottage cheese
Few grains of salt
Few grains of white pepper

Place egg in a blender, cover and blend for 10 seconds. Add oil. Cover and blend for 10 seconds. Add the mustard, lemon juice, yogurt and cottage cheese and blend for 30 seconds until mixture is smooth. Season to taste with salt and pepper. Store in a covered jar in the refrigerator. Dressing will keep for 1 week. *Makes 1¼ cups.* For diet serving allow 1 tablespoon.

Per diet serving: 20 calories, 2 grams protein, 2 grams fat, 1 gram carbohydrate.

Christiana Sutor's Steamed Pears with Raspberry Sauce

Water
6 large, not-too-ripe Bartlett or
    Anjou pears
Peel of 1 large orange, removed
    with a vegetable peeler

3 tablespoons lemon juice,
    preferably fresh-squeezed
1 8-ounce container frozen
    raspberries, thawed
6 mint leaves

Put water in a 4- to 6-quart saucepot or Dutch oven to measure 1½ inches deep. Put a custard cup upside down in center of pot and balance a plate on the cup. Cover pot and bring water to a boil over high heat. Meanwhile, peel pears, leaving stems intact; scoop out and discard cores from blossom end. Put a 1-inch-long strip of orange peel inside each cored pear; dip pears in lemon juice to prevent browning. Stand pears on plate inside pot and cover; reduce heat to moderate and steam 10 to 25 minutes, until pears are tender when pierced with a small, sharp knife. (Cooking time depends on ripeness of pears.) When done, uncover and let stand until cool enough to handle. Pears may be served warm or chilled. If to be chilled, cover with clear plastic wrap to delay browning. Pears will retain color 3 to 4 hours refrigerated.

Using a large wooden spoon, press raspberries through a strainer; discard seeds. Shortly before serving, pour raspberry puree onto a large, rimmed serving plate. Stand pears in puree. Poke a hole in each pear with a wooden pick and insert stem of mint leaf. *Makes 6 servings.* For diet serving allow 1 pear and 1 tablespoon of the sauce.

Per serving: 131 calories, 2 grams protein, 1 gram fat, 31 grams carbohydrate.

BREAKFAST

½ cup orange juice (61)
* Creamy Cheese Baked Egg (171)
1 slice whole-wheat bread (61)
½ cup skim milk (43)

LUNCH

* Chunky Clam Stew (154)
1 corn muffin (130)
1 syrup-packed peach half, with
 1½ tablespoons syrup (59)

DINNER

* Perfect Roast Beef (161)
* Sautéed Mushrooms (66)
½ large baked potato (72)
Tossed Salad: 1 cup torn lettuce
 leaves (10); 1 small tomato (20);
 1 tablespoon Jovan Trboyevic's
 Special Vinaigrette Dressing
 (recipe on page 149, 32)
* Cream Puffs with Chocolate
 Sauce (165)

Creamy Cheese Baked Egg

1 tablespoon plain low-fat yogurt
1 tablespoon sour cream
1 large egg

½ ounce Cheddar cheese, grated
 (2 tablespoons)

Heat oven to 400°F. or use a toaster-oven. In a small bowl mix yogurt and sour cream. Spray an 8-ounce custard cup with vegetable cookware spray. Break egg into prepared cup, top with yogurt mixture and sprinkle with cheese. Bake 10 to 12 minutes in regular oven or 8 to 9 minutes in a toaster-oven, until egg is set and cheese has melted. *Makes 1 diet serving.*

Per diet serving: 171 calories, 11 grams protein, 13 grams fat, 2 grams carbohydrate.

Chunky Clam Stew

2 8-ounce cans chopped clams,
 drained and liquid reserved
2 onions, peeled and diced
4 stalks celery, diced
3 carrots, peeled and diced
1 medium-sized potato, peeled
 and diced

1 16-ounce can whole peeled
 tomatoes
1 8-ounce bottle clam juice
2 3-inch strips lemon peel
¼ teaspoon dried thyme leaves
½ teaspoon dried basil leaves
¼ teaspoon salt
⅛ teaspoon black pepper

In a large saucepot or Dutch oven place the clam liquid and all remaining ingredients except the clams. Bring to a boil over high heat and then reduce heat to moderately low and simmer 20 minutes. Taste for seasoning, adding more thyme, basil, salt and pepper if desired.

Add clams and cook 5 minutes longer. Discard lemon peel before serving. *Makes 6 cups.* For diet serving allow 1½ cups.

Per diet serving: 154 calories, 13 grams protein, 1 gram fat, 24 grams carbohydrate.

Perfect Roast Beef

1 4-pound top round beef roast   Cracked or coarsely ground
                                        black pepper

Heat oven to 500°F. Sprinkle meat all over with the pepper and place, fat side up, on a rack in a roasting pan. Roast meat, allowing 7 minutes per pound for rare, 8 minutes for medium-rare. Turn off heat and leave roast in oven 2 hours longer *without opening oven door.* Serve warm or cover and chill several hours in refrigerator. *Makes 10 to 12 servings.* For diet serving allow 3 ounces, or 3 thin slices.

Per diet serving: 161 calories, 27 grams protein, 5 grams fat, 0 grams carbohydrate.

Sautéed Mushrooms

8 teaspoons butter or margarine   Salt and black pepper (optional)
1 pound fresh mushrooms, sliced

In a medium-sized skillet melt butter over moderate heat. Add mushrooms and cook, stirring occasionally, about 5 minutes until mushrooms are soft and some liquid cooks out of them. Sprinkle with salt and pepper if desired. *Makes 8 servings.* For diet serving allow ⅛ of the mushrooms.

Per diet serving: 66 calories, 2 grams protein, 6 grams fat, 3 grams carbohydrate.

Cream Puffs with Chocolate Sauce

1 cup water
4 tablespoons lightly salted butter
  or margarine
1 teaspoon granulated sugar
¼ teaspoon salt

1 cup all-purpose flour
4 large eggs
1¼ cups frozen whipped topping,
  thawed
Chocolate Sauce (recipe below)

In a heavy, medium-sized saucepan heat water, butter, sugar and salt over moderately high heat until butter melts and mixture comes to a rolling boil. Reduce heat to low. Remove pan from heat, and while stirring liquid with a wooden spoon, add the flour all at once. Put pan back over heat and stir mixture vigorously for about 1 minute, until it leaves sides of pan and clings to spoon. Remove from heat. Let cool 4 to 6 minutes. Add eggs, one at a time, beating well after each addition. Dough will be smooth and glossy. Heat oven to 425°F. Scrape ¼-cups of dough 2 inches apart onto greased baking sheets. Moisten fingers and smooth surface of dough. Bake 15 minutes, until puffs are light golden brown; reduce heat to 375°F. and bake 15 minutes longer, until cream puffs are puffed and golden-brown. Turn off oven and remove baking sheet. Using a sharp, pointed knife, make a horizontal slit in the side of each cream puff. Return to oven for about 15 minutes, leaving door ajar, to dry insides of puffs. Remove from oven and transfer cream puffs to wire cake racks to cool. (Cream puffs now may be frozen in an airtight container. Before filling, thaw, place on a baking sheet and bake 5 to 10 minutes at 350°F.)

Up to 2 hours before serving, fill each cream puff with about 2 tablespoons of the whipped topping and refrigerate. Just before serving, top with Chocolate Sauce. *Makes 11 cream puffs.* For diet serving allow 1 filled cream puff and 2 tablespoons chocolate sauce.

Per diet serving (including sauce): 165 calories, 3 grams protein, 9 grams fat, 18 grams carbohydrate.

Chocolate Sauce

2 teaspoons cornstarch
1 cup water
¼ cup unsweetened cocoa

¼ cup granulated sugar
1½ teaspoons vanilla extract
Few grains of salt

Mix cornstarch and water in a small saucepan. When smooth, add remaining ingredients and stir over moderately high heat until mixture boils 1 minute. Remove from heat and cool. Sauce keeps well stored in an airtight container in the refrigerator; it also may be frozen. *Makes 1⅛ cups.* For diet serving allow 2 tablespoons.

Per diet serving: 29 calories, 0 grams protein, 1 gram fat, 7 grams carbohydrate.

BREAKFAST

1 cup 4-grain multivitamin-and-iron-
   supplement cereal (110)
¾ cup skim milk (65)
1 syrup-packed peach half, drained
   (54)
1½ tablespoons seedless raisins (39)

LUNCH

2 ounces lean boiled beef (132)
1 slice rye bread (61)
⅔ cup coleslaw (79)
1 large dill pickle (15)
1 small apple (61)

DINNER

* Broiled Cod with Garlic Sauce
   (239)
Tossed Salad: 2 cups torn romaine
   lettuce (20); ½ medium-sized
   cucumber, peeled and diced (15);
   2 pitted ripe olives (12); 1
   teaspoon vegetable oil (40); 1
   tablespoon lemon juice (4)
* Michel Guérard's Orange à
   l'Orange (76)

TO EAT ANY TIME

1 cup skim milk (86)
¾ cup grape juice (88)

Broiled Cod with Garlic Sauce

1 1-pound block frozen cod fillets,
   partially thawed
1 tablespoon flour
1 tablespoon olive oil
1 teaspoon coarsely chopped,
   peeled garlic

½ teaspoon salt
1 tablespoon olive oil
1 egg
1 tablespoon lemon juice,
   preferably freshly squeezed

Line a broiler pan with foil. Dry block of fish with paper towels. Spread flour evenly over fish with fingers. Place fish on prepared broiler pan and brush with 1 tablespoon oil. Broil 5 inches from heat for 15 minutes. Meanwhile, mash garlic to a paste with the salt and add it with the remaining ingredients to a blender; cover and blend at medium speed 10 seconds, until smooth. Pour half the garlic sauce over fish and broil 2½ minutes. Pour remaining sauce over fish, baste with pan drippings and broil 2 minutes longer, until a light-golden crust forms. *Makes 3 servings*. For diet serving allow ⅓ of the fish.

Per diet serving: 239 calories, 30 grams protein, 12 grams fat, 2 grams carbohydrate.

Michel Guérard's Orange à l'Orange

6 small seedless oranges, scrubbed
and rinsed
2 tablespoons sugar
Water

1 cup fresh or unsweetened frozen,
partially thawed strawberries
1 kumquat or peeled kiwi, cut into
6 slices; or 6 seedless green
grapes (for garnish)

With a vegetable peeler remove the peel from the oranges in long strips. With a sharp knife cut peel into very fine slivers. Put peel and sugar in a saucepan, cover with water and bring to a boil over moderately high heat; reduce heat to moderate and simmer 2 minutes. Drain peel. Meanwhile, remove white pith from oranges and cut them into sections with a serrated knife. Hull fresh strawberries. Puree berries in a blender and spoon onto 6 small serving plates. On each plate arrange orange sections like a pinwheel and place a slice of kumquat or kiwi or a grape in the center. Sprinkle orange-peel slivers over top. *Makes 6 servings.* For diet serving allow 1 orange dessert plate.

Per diet serving: 76 calories, 1 gram protein, 0 grams fat, 18 grams carbohydrate.

Alcohol—the Burning Question

All wines and liquors contain calories, so if you do enjoy an occasional glass of wine or other alcoholic beverage, you may lose weight more slowly.

Gin, rum, vodka and whiskey contain 97 to 110 calories per 1½ fluid ounces; 12 fluid ounces of beer, 150 calories; 3½ fluid ounces of dry wine, 87; sweet wine, about 141.

Good alternate party drinks for dieters: wine spritzer (white wine topped with club soda) and—for no calories at all—club soda au naturel or the now-fashionable mineral water. Both are good with a wedge of lime.

BREAKFAST

¾ cup 99%-fat-free cottage cheese
 (123)
½ cup orange juice (61)

LUNCH

Roast Beef Sandwich: 3 ounces lean
 roast beef (161); 1 lettuce leaf
 (1); 2 teaspoons mayonnaise (68);
 2 slices whole-wheat bread (122)
¼ cantaloupe (41)

DINNER

* Chicken Breasts with Creamy
 Mustard Sauce (196)
Buttered Noodles: ½ cup cooked
 noodles (100); 1 teaspoon butter
 or margarine (34)
Buttered Beans: 1 cup cooked green
 beans (31); 1 teaspoon butter or
 margarine (34)
* Snow Pudding (120)

TO EAT ANY TIME

1¼ cups skim milk (109)

Chicken Breasts with Creamy Mustard Sauce

1 teaspoon butter or margarine
1 teaspoon vegetable oil
2 whole boned, skinned chicken
 breasts, cut in half (about 1
 pound 4 ounces)

½ cup plain low-fat yogurt
2 tablespoons Dijon-style mustard

In a large skillet heat butter and oil over moderately high heat. When butter is melted, add chicken breasts and cook 3 to 4 minutes on each side, until no longer pink in center. Remove to a plate and keep warm. Quickly add yogurt to skillet and stir to incorporate brown bits from bottom of pan. Add mustard and stir 30 to 40 seconds, until heated. Add chicken and cook 30 seconds longer, spooning sauce over breasts. *Makes 4 servings.* For diet serving allow ¼ of recipe.

Per diet serving: 196 calories, 34 grams protein, 5 grams fat, 2 grams carbohydrate.

Snow Pudding

1 envelope unflavored gelatin
½ cup granulated sugar
1¼ cups hot water
¼ cup freshly squeezed lemon
  juice
1 teaspoon freshly grated lemon
  peel

Few grains of salt
2 egg whites
2 tablespoons granulated sugar
1 cup thinly sliced fresh or canned
  peaches
Fresh mint sprigs
Custard Sauce (recipe below)

In a medium saucepan combine gelatin and the ½ cup sugar. Add hot water and place over low heat. Stir until gelatin is dissolved. Remove from heat and stir in lemon juice, lemon peel and salt. Chill until the consistency of unbeaten egg white. In a medium bowl beat egg whites until soft peaks form. Gradually add the 2 tablespoons sugar and continue beating until peaks are stiff and glossy. Fold beaten egg whites into thickened gelatin mixture. Pour into a 3½-cup mold and chill until firm. Unmold pudding and garnish with peach slices and mint. Serve with Custard Sauce (recipe below) spooned over each serving. *Serves 8.* For diet serving allow ⅛ of the pudding and peaches and 3 tablespoons of custard sauce.

Per diet serving (including sauce): 120 calories, 4 grams protein, 1 gram fat, 22 grams carbohydrate.

Custard Sauce

1½ cups liquid skim milk
2 egg yolks
2 tablespoons granulated sugar

⅛ teaspoon salt
¾ teaspoon vanilla extract

Heat milk in a saucepan over low heat until bubbles appear around the edges. In a small bowl beat egg yolks with a fork; blend in sugar and salt. Gradually stir about 1 cup of the hot milk into egg yolk mixture; return to saucepan. Cook over low heat, stirring constantly, until mixture coats a metal spoon. Cool and add vanilla. Chill until serving time. *Makes 1½ cups.* For diet serving allow 3 tablespoons.

Per diet serving: 42 calories, 2 grams protein, 1 gram fat, 5 grams carbohydrate.

BREAKFAST

1 medium-sized egg (72), prepared any style without butter or margarine

1 slice cracked-wheat bread (66), spread with ½ teaspoon butter or margarine (17)

1 cup tomato juice (46)

LUNCH

Spinach–Mushroom Salad: 3 cups torn spinach leaves (42); ½ cup fresh mushrooms, sliced (10); Jovan Trboyevic's Special Vinaigrette Dressing (recipe on page 149, 63)

1 ounce Swiss cheese (107)

2 crisp rye wafers (45)

1 tablespoon raisins (26)

DINNER

* Crudités with Low-Calorie Dip (46)

* Irena Chalmers's Quick Pepper Lamb (296)

½ cup cooked mashed turnip (20)

1 cup cooked green beans (31)

½ cup cooked noodles (50)

* Lemon Meringue Pie (197)

TO EAT ANY TIME

¾ cup skim milk (65)

Crudités with Low-Calorie Dip

1 cup pot cheese
¾ cup buttermilk
Few grains salt
⅛ teaspoon dried dillweed
Celery sticks, cut from 8 stalks celery

Carrot sticks, cut from 4 peeled carrots
2 cups raw cauliflower florets

Put pot cheese, buttermilk, salt and dillweed in a blender and blend on high speed until smooth. Refrigerate in a covered container until serving time. Prepare celery and carrot sticks and cauliflower florets and store in a plastic bag in refrigerator until serving time. *Makes 1⅔ cups of dip, or 8 servings.* For diet serving allow ⅛ of the vegetables and 2 tablespoons of dip. Non-dieters may add other vegetables such as zucchini sticks, broccoli florets, or raw mushrooms.

Per diet serving: 46 calories, 4 grams protein, 0 grams fat, 7 grams carbohydrate.

Irena Chalmers's Quick Pepper Lamb

1 6-pound leg of lamb, boned,
   butterflied and trimmed of
   excess fat
2 tablespoons vegetable oil

3 tablespoons Dijon-style mustard
3 tablespoons cracked black
   peppercorns

Brush both sides of lamb with oil and spread with mustard. Press peppercorns into mustard. Put lamb on oiled rack of a broiler pan and broil 4 to 5 inches from heat source for 15 minutes. Turn and broil 10 minutes longer for medium-rare. Remove from broiler and let stand 10 minutes before slicing. *Makes 6 to 8 servings.* For diet serving allow 4 ounces, 3 thin slices of the lamb.

Per diet serving: 296 calories, 38 grams protein, 15 grams fat, 0 grams carbohydrate.

Lemon Meringue Pie

Low-Fat Pie Shell (recipe on
   page 168), baked
3 tablespoons cornstarch
1 envelope unflavored gelatin
½ cup granulated sugar
1¾ cups water
3 large eggs, yolks and whites
   separated
2 tablespoons granulated sugar

1 teaspoon freshly grated lemon
   peel
¼ cup lemon juice, preferably
   fresh-squeezed
⅛ teaspoon cream of tartar
Few grains of salt
2 tablespoons granulated sugar

Prepare Low-Fat Pie Shell. While it cools prepare filling. In a medium-sized, heavy saucepan mix cornstarch, gelatin and the ½ cup sugar; stir in water. Bring to a boil over low heat, stirring constantly with a wooden spoon; let boil 1 minute and remove from heat. In a small bowl beat egg yolks with 2 tablespoons sugar. Stir yolks constantly while you gradually add about ¼ cup of the hot cornstarch mixture. Gradually stir yolk mixture into remaining cornstarch mixture in pan. Cook 1 to 2 minutes over low heat, stirring constantly until thick. Remove from heat and stir in lemon peel and juice; cool. Pour mixture into pie shell. In a large bowl beat egg whites with an electric mixer at high speed until foamy; beat in cream of tartar and salt. When soft peaks hold when whites are lifted with a spatula, add the remaining 2 tablespoons sugar and beat until stiff peaks hold when whites are lifted. Spread meringue over top of pie to edges. Broil 5 inches from heat source for 1 to 2 minutes, until golden-brown. Serve pie warm or refrigerate (loosely covered) up to 2 days. *Makes 8 to 10 servings.* For diet serving allow ⅒ of the pie.

Per diet serving: 197 calories, 4 grams protein, 5 grams fat, 33 grams carbohydrate.

Low-Fat Pie Shell

1½ cups all purpose flour
1 tablespoon granulated sugar

3 tablespoons lightly salted butter
or margarine, cut in pieces
6 tablespoons ice water

Mix flour and sugar in a medium-sized bowl; add butter and cut in with a pastry blender or two knives until butter is in pieces the size of oatmeal. Sprinkle water over mixture and continue working until it clumps together. Using hands, form dough into a ball and knead once or twice on a lightly floured surface; wrap in plastic wrap and let stand 30 minutes. Heat oven to 400°F. Press dough over bottom and up sides of a 9-inch pie plate. Line with a piece of wax paper and fill to a depth of ½ inch with dried beans or rice (see note). Bake 20 minutes, until lightly browned. Remove beans and wax paper. Cool pie shell before filling. Makes 1 crisp pie shell (980 calories).

NOTE: Wax paper and dried beans or rice prevent crust from puffing while baking. The beans or rice may be used over and over again for this purpose.

The Home-to-the-In-Laws Crisis

If going home to his or your parents for dinner frequently is part of your life-style, you may be in for a great deal more dieting difficulty than you'll encounter anywhere else. Not to eat any of his mother's famous chocolate cake, not to be part of the big-family-gathering camaraderie of second helpings, refusing the second glass of wine not only takes courage on your part but it may make it inevitable that you'll have to gird yourself for some animosity or scorn or laughter or all three. Solicit as many sympathetic feelings as you can before the event and remember, it's *your* waistline, no one else's. Let *them* eat cake.

CHAPTER SIX

As American As,
Yes, Apple Pie

Hamburgers, hot dogs, pizza and pasta may not all be American in origin, but fast-food eating places have made them an integral part of American eating habits. You can have them all on this twenty-one-day diet, but be prepared for what the dieticians call portion-control. If pizza has been a nonstop food for you, maybe it's best to skip it until your appetite is satisfied with one or two slices. Dr. Winick, one of *Redbook*'s diet consultants, once wrote, "I can't think of a single food that is so prohibitively caloric that it can't be eaten occasionally. Of course, many people have a particular food obsession that must be recognized, because for them, trying to eat 'just one' cookie or sparerib or whatever is like falling out of a skyscraper window and expecting to drop only one floor."

The menus in this chapter were planned to appeal to most families' tastes and to be enjoyed by dieters and non-dieters. If you don't use these menus on consecutive days skip around, but always substitute a fish dinner for a fish dinner, chicken for chicken, beef for beef and so on. It's always safest to follow a full day's menus for assured nutritional balance.

BREAKFAST

1 medium-sized orange (78)
* Breakfast Bread Pudding (201)

LUNCH

1 cup clear beef bouillon, made with
a bouillon cube (5)
3 saltine crackers (36)
Tuna Sandwich: 2 ounces water-
packed tuna (78); 1½ teaspoons
mayonnaise (51); 2 leaves
romaine lettuce (2); 2 slices
whole-wheat bread (122)
½ medium-sized carrot (15)
½ green pepper (8)

DINNER

* Pork Loin Roast Teriyaki (270)
Buttered Peas and Mushrooms: 1
cup cooked green peas (114),
mixed with ½ cup sliced mushrooms (10) which have been
cooked in 1 teaspoon butter or
margarine (34)
2 cups torn lettuce leaves (20), with
*Garlic Blue-Cheese Dressing
(18)
½ cup juice-packed pineapple
chunks and 1 tablespoon of the
juice (48)

TO EAT ANY TIME

1 cup skim milk (86)

Breakfast Bread Pudding

8 slices white bread, cubed
3 large eggs
3 cups liquid skim milk
¼ cup granulated sugar

2 teaspoons vanilla extract
¼ teaspoon ground nutmeg
⅛ teaspoon ground cinnamon
¼ teaspoon salt

Place bread in an even layer in the bottom of a 10-x-6-x-1¾-inch baking
dish. In a medium-sized bowl beat eggs with remaining ingredients and
pour over bread. Put dish in a larger pan and fill larger pan with hot
water to a depth of 1 inch. Put in oven and turn on oven to 325°F.;
bake 1 hour, until pudding is firm to the touch. Then, if desired, turn
oven to broil; place dish 6 inches from heat source for 2 minutes, until
golden brown on top. *Makes 6 servings.* For diet serving allow ⅙ of
the pudding. Reserve 1 diet portion for dessert in Menu #2.

Per diet serving: 201 calories, 10 grams protein, 4 grams fat, 31 grams carbohydrate.

Pork Loin Roast Teriyaki

1 4½-pound pork loin roast,
  backbone removed
1 clove garlic, peeled and cut in
  half

½ cup soy sauce
½ cup dry sherry wine
1 tablespoon grated fresh
  gingerroot (see note)

Rub the meat with the halved clove of garlic. Mix the soy sauce, sherry and ginger in a large, shallow dish or pan; add the halved garlic clove and the meat. Marinate for 3 to 5 hours in the refrigerator, turning meat 3 or 4 times. Heat oven to 375°F. Line the bottom of a shallow roasting pan with foil; remove meat from marinade and place it on a rack in the pan. Roast 2½ to 3 hours, or until a meat thermometer inserted in the thickest part of the meat registers 185°F. During the first 2 hours of cooking, baste meat several times with some of the marinade. *Makes 6 servings.* For diet serving allow 4 ounces of cooked meat. Wrap and reserve 3 ounces cooked meat for lunch in Menu #2.

NOTE: Fresh gingerroot is available in most supermarkets. Wrap and store in freezer and grate as needed without thawing.

Per diet serving: 270 calories, 33 grams protein, 16 grams fat, 0 grams carbohydrate.

Garlic Blue-Cheese Dressing

1 cup 99%-fat-free cottage cheese
3 tablespoons liquid skim milk
1 tablespoon lemon juice

1 teaspoon finely minced, peeled
  garlic
1 ounce Roquefort or other blue
  cheese, crumbled

Put cottage cheese, milk, lemon juice and garlic in a blender. Cover and blend 20 seconds at low speed. Stop machine and scrape sides with a rubber spatula. Cover and blend 20 seconds at medium speed, until creamy. Scrape mixture into a small jar; fold in cheese. Tightly covered, dressing keeps at least a week in the refrigerator. *Makes about 1 cup.* For diet serving allow 1 tablespoon.

Per diet serving: 18 calories, 2 grams protein, 1 gram fat, 1 gram carbohydrate.

BREAKFAST

1 cup skim milk (86)
* Skinny Granola (188), sprinkled
  with 1 tablespoon raisins (26)

LUNCH

Pork Sandwich: 3 ounces Roast Pork
  Loin Teriyaki (reserved from
  Menu #1, 203); 1 teaspoon
  mayonnaise (34); 2 slices rye
  bread (122)
1 small apple (61)

DINNER

* Crisp Baked Chicken (179)
Buttered Broccoli: ¾ cup cooked
  broccoli (30); 1 teaspoon butter
  or margarine (34)
Breakfast Bread Pudding (reserved
  from Menu #1, 201)

TO EAT ANY TIME

½ cup skim mik (43)

Skinny Granola

¼ cup honey
¼ cup hot water

1 teaspoon almond extract
4 cups rolled oats

Heat oven to 250°F. In a large mixing bowl mix honey, water and almond extract. Add oats; using hands, mix oats with liquids until thoroughly combined. Tip oat mixture out onto a baking sheet and spread to a depth of about ½ inch. Bake 1 hour, until golden brown, stirring once after 30 minutes. Let cool completely before storing in an airtight container. *Makes 4 cups.* For diet serving allow ½ cup. Reserve 1 diet portion for a snack in Menu #4.

Per diet serving: 188 calories, 6 grams protein, 3 grams fat, 36 grams carbohydrate.

Crisp Baked Chicken

1 2½- to 3-pound broiler-fryer
  chicken, cut in half
6 tablespoons Low-Calorie Sour
  Cream (recipe on page 173)
2 tablespoons freshly squeezed
  lemon juice
½ teaspoon crushed dried
  rosemary leaves

¼ teaspoon salt
⅛ teaspoon black pepper
4 teaspoons packaged cereal
  crumbs
⅛ teaspoon paprika
1 tablespoon minced, fresh parsley

Heat oven to 375°F. Wash and dry chicken. Blend Low-Calorie Sour Cream, lemon juice, rosemary, salt and pepper. Spread half the sour cream mixture over chicken and arrange in a shallow baking dish; bake uncovered 50 minutes, or until fork-tender. Brush the chicken with remaining sour cream mixture. Sprinkle with crumbs and paprika; continue to bake 10 minutes longer. Garnish with parsley. *Makes 4 servings.* For diet serving allow 4 ounces cooked chicken with topping. Wrap 1 diet serving and store in refrigerator for lunch in Menu #3.

Per diet serving: 179 calories, 28 grams protein, 5 grams fat, 4 grams carbohydrate.

Low-Calorie Sour Cream

1 8-ounce container pot cheese or   ¾ cup buttermilk
  dry curd cottage cheese   Few grains salt

Put cheese, buttermilk and salt in a blender. Blend at high speed until smooth and creamy. Once during blending, stop blender and scrape down sides of the container with a rubber spatula. Refrigerate in a covered container. Mixture will keep for several days. *Makes about 1½ cups.* To use as a dressing for fruit or greens, allow 1 tablespoon for a diet serving.

Per diet serving: 10 calories, 2 grams protein, 0 grams fat, 1 gram carbohydrate.

BREAKFAST

1 medium-sized tangerine (40)
1 cup skim milk (86)
1 cup 4-grain multivitamin-and-iron-
supplement cereal (110)

LUNCH

1 cup clear chicken broth (22)
Crisp Baked Chicken (reserved from
Menu #2, 179)
2 rye wafers (45), spread with
1 teaspoon butter or margarine
(34)
1 pear (90)

DINNER

1 cup tomato juice (46)
* Aware Burgers on a Bun (324)
Tossed Salad: 1 cup torn lettuce
leaves (10); 1 cup torn fresh
spinach leaves (14); Herbed
Vinaigrette Dressing (recipe on
page 53, 37)
* Skinny Tangerine Cheesecake
(122)

TO EAT ANY TIME

½ cup skim milk (43)
5 thin pretzel sticks (6)

Aware Burgers on a Bun

1½ cups finely chopped fresh
mushrooms (about ⅓ pound)
¾ cup finely diced, seeded green
pepper
¼ cup finely diced, peeled carrot
¾ cup minced, peeled onion

1½ pounds lean ground beef
2½ teaspoons soy sauce
6 hamburger buns, toasted
Chicory leaves and cherry
tomatoes (optional)

Put mushrooms, green pepper, carrot, onion, beef and soy sauce into
a bowl. Mix gently with hands. Shape into six 1-inch-thick burgers.
Heat a heavy, 10-inch skillet over high heat (when a drop of water
skips across bottom of skillet, it's ready); place burgers in skillet so
that they do not touch. Cook 3 minutes on each side for medium-rare,
turning only once. Put hamburgers into buns. If desired, arrange on a
platter and garnish with chicory leaves and cherry tomatoes. *Makes 6
servings.* For diet serving allow 1 burger with 1 bun.

Per diet serving: 324 calories, 27 grams protein, 12 grams fat, 25 grams carbohydrate.

Skinny Tangerine Cheesecake

1 tablespoon butter or margarine
½ cup graham cracker crumbs
2 tablespoons cold water
2 tablespoons freshly squeezed
   lemon juice
1 envelope unflavored gelatin
½ cup skim milk

⅓ cup granulated sugar
Yolks of 2 large eggs
2 cups 99%-fat-free cottage cheese
1 tablespoon vanilla extract
2 cups tangerine sections or 2
   6½-ounce cans mandarin orange
   sections, drained

In a small saucepan melt butter over moderate heat. Remove from heat; add graham cracker crumbs and mix until well coated. Press evenly over bottom of a 9-inch springform pan. Put water and lemon juice in a blender; sprinkle with gelatin. Cover and blend 15 seconds at medium speed, until gelatin and liquid are mixed. In a small saucepan heat milk over moderate heat for 3 to 4 minutes, until tiny bubbles form around the edge of the pan. Pour into blender; cover and blend 10 seconds at low speed, until gelatin is completely dissolved. Scrape sides with a rubber spatula; cover and blend 20 seconds longer. Add sugar, egg yolks, cottage cheese and vanilla; cover and blend 1 minute at high speed, until smooth. Pour into prepared pan. Cover and chill at least 3 hours in refrigerator. Run a knife around the outer edge of the cheesecake to loosen and remove sides of pan. Garnish cheesecake with tangerine sections. *Makes 8 to 10 servings.* For diet serving allow ⅟₁₀ of the cheesecake plus 5 tangerine sections. Reserve 1 diet portion for dessert in Menu #5. Cheesecake keeps well in the refrigerator.

NOTE: Cheesecake may be prepared in a 9-inch pie plate. Press crumbs over bottom and up sides to within ½ inch of the rim.

Per diet serving: 122 calories, 8 grams protein, 3 grams fat, 16 grams carbohydrate.

BREAKFAST

½ cup grapefruit juice (51)
1 cup iron-enriched farina, sprinkled
  with cinnamon (100)
½ cup skim milk (43)

LUNCH

Sandwich Italiano: 2 ounces part-
  skim mozzarella cheese (144);
  1 roasted sweet red pepper (23);
  2 leaves romaine lettuce (2); 1
  slice (about 3 x 2 x ½ inches)
  Italian bread (28)
10 whole almonds (85)

DINNER

* Seasoup (282)
¾ cup torn lettuce leaves (8), with
  Herbed Vinaigrette Dressing
  (recipe on page 53, 37)
* Winter Fruits with Creamy
  Orange Dressing (150)

TO EAT ANY TIME

Skinny Granola (reserved from
  Menu #2, 188)
¾ cup skim milk (65)

Seasoup

1 tablespoon olive oil
1 cup chopped, peeled onion
1 teaspoon minced, peeled garlic
1 8-ounce can tomatoes, drained
  and liquid reserved
1 8-ounce bottle clam juice
1 8-ounce can chopped clams,
  drained and liquid reserved

1 2-inch piece orange peel,
  removed with a vegetable peeler
¼ teaspoon dried thyme leaves
⅛ teaspoon black pepper
½ cup chopped fresh parsley
1 pound frozen cod or haddock
  fillets, thawed and cut into
  2-inch chunks

In a medium-sized saucepan heat oil over moderately high heat; stir in onion and cook until soft, about 5 minutes. Add garlic and drained tomatoes and cook about 5 minutes longer, breaking up tomatoes with a spoon. Add clam juice, reserved liquid from tomatoes and clams, the orange peel, thyme, pepper and ¼ cup of the parsley. Bring mixture to a boil, then lower heat to moderate and simmer 15 minutes. Increase heat, and when mixture is boiling, add clams and fish; cook 5 minutes longer, until fish is white and flakes easily. Sprinkle soup with remaining ¼ cup parsley. *Makes 3 or 4 servings.* For diet serving allow ¼ of the soup.

Per diet serving: 282 calories, 40 grams protein, 10 grams fat, 8 grams carbohydrate.

Winter Fruits with Creamy Orange Dressing

1 cup plain low-fat yogurt
¼ cup frozen orange juice
   concentrate, undiluted
1 crisp sweet apple, such as
   McIntosh, cored and sliced

1 orange, peeled and sectioned
1 banana, sliced
4 pitted prunes, diced

Mix yogurt and orange concentrate in a small bowl. Arrange fruits on 4 plates; serve with orange dressing. *Makes 4 servings.* For diet serving allow ¼ of the fruit and dressing.

Per diet serving: 150 calories, 4 grams protein, 1 gram fat, 33 grams carbohydrate.

The Case of the "Fattening Foods"

Would-be dieters often say, "But I never eat 'fattening foods.'" If we are told that the ideal is to eat a variety of foods, which ones are "fattening" and why? We asked Dr. Myron Winick, one of *Redbook*'s Wise Woman's Diet consultants, and he explained it this way:

"Body fat can be made from any of the three food sources— fats, carbohydrates and protein. Fats and carbohydrates can be used by the body in two ways; they are converted to energy or they are stored, usually as body fat. But protein has a third possible use, building tissues. So if you take in more calories than you need, and those extra calories are in potato chips, they very likely will turn into body fat. If the excess calories are in fillet of flounder, however, they may go to building tissue. That is why potato chips —primarily fat and carbohydrates—are more 'fattening' than flounder, which is primarily protein. Of course, if you eat too much more of the flounder, that too will be converted to fat."

BREAKFAST

1 medium-sized orange, sliced (78)
1 large egg, soft-cooked (82)
1 slice whole-wheat bread (61)

LUNCH

3 ounces lean broiled hamburger
  (210), on 1 hamburger roll (119)
½ tomato, sliced (10)
1 cup mixed green salad (10), with
  Herbed Vinaigrette Dressing
  (recipe on page 53, 37)
¼ cantaloupe (41)

DINNER

* Braised Liver and Vegetables
  (212)
½ cup mashed potatoes (68)
1 cup steamed green beans (31)
3 large romaine lettuce leaves (3),
  with *Low-Calorie Tomato Salad
  Dressing (12)
½ cup fresh or unsweetened frozen
  blueberries (45)

TO EAT ANY TIME

2 cups skim milk (172)

Braised Liver and Vegetables

1 cup beef broth or bouillon
1 cup coarsely chopped, peeled
  onion
1 medium-sized carrot, peeled
  and diced
1 stalk celery, chopped

1½ pounds beef liver, sliced
  ½-inch thick
¼ cup dry red wine
1 bay leaf
¼ teaspoon salt
Few grains black pepper

Heat ¼ cup of the beef broth in a skillet over moderately low heat; add the onion and cook until tender, stirring occasionally. Add the remaining ¾ cup beef broth, carrot and celery to the skillet; cover and cook 15 minutes or until vegetables are almost tender. Add liver, wine, bay leaf, salt and pepper to skillet; cover and cook 15 to 20 minutes or until liver is tender, turning occasionally. Remove liver to a warm platter. Pour vegetable mixture into the container of a blender. Blend at high speed until smooth. Serve sauce over liver. *Makes 4 servings.* For diet serving, allow 3 ounces of liver and 7 tablespoons of the sauce.

Per diet serving: 212 calories, 26 grams protein, 5 grams fat, 13 grams carbohydrate.

Low-Calorie Tomato Salad Dressing

1½ cups tomato juice
3 tablespoons wine vinegar
2 tablespoons vegetable oil
1 clove garlic, peeled

½ teaspoon dried basil leaves
⅛ teaspoon dried oregano leaves
¼ teaspoon salt
1 teaspoon granulated sugar

Place all ingredients in a jar with a tight-fitting lid; cover and shake well. Chill several hours. Shake before using. *Makes about 1¾ cups.* For diet serving allow 1 tablespoon.

Per diet serving: 12 calories, 0 grams protein, 1 gram fat, 1 gram carbohydrate.

When "Choice" Is Not Better

Check the grades of beef in your supermarket. *Good* grade has less fat marbled through it than *Choice* grade; *Choice* has less than *Prime*. Get to know which cuts are leaner. Beef round, for example, contains much less fat than beef tenderloin; ground round contains less fat than ground chuck. Pork shoulder, leg or loin has less fat than spareribs.

BREAKFAST

1 cup cooked iron-enriched farina
   (100)
1 cup skim milk (86)
¼ cantaloupe (41)

LUNCH

1 cup tomato juice (46)
Ham Sandwich: 2 ounces lean boiled
   ham (122); 2 large lettuce leaves
   (2); 1 teaspoon mustard (4); 1
   teaspoon butter or margarine
   (34); 2 slices rye bread (122)
Vegetable Relish Plate: 8 thin slices
   cucumber (4); 1 stalk celery (7);
   2 radishes (1)

DINNER

* Chicken Garden Pot (257)
1 slice whole-wheat bread (61),
   spread with 1 teaspoon butter or
   margarine (34)
1 cup skim milk (86)
* Chocolate Angel Food Cake (62)

TO EAT ANY TIME

1 ounce Camembert cheese (85)
1 ½-inch-thick slice French bread
   (about 2½ x 2 inches, 44)

Chicken Garden Pot

2 teaspoons vegetable oil
½ cup chopped, peeled onion
1 teaspoon minced, peeled garlic
2½ cups chopped fresh tomatoes
   (about 1 pound)
1 medium-sized eggplant (about
   1 pound), cut into ¼-inch slices
2 small zucchini squash (about ½
   pound), cut into ¼-inch slices

3 pounds chicken thighs,
   drumsticks and breasts, skin
   removed
1 large green pepper, seeded and
   cut into strips
3 tablespoons chopped fresh
   parsley
1 teaspoon dried basil leaves
1 teaspoon salt
½ teaspoon black pepper
½ teaspoon dried thyme leaves

In a large saucepot or Dutch oven heat oil over moderate heat. Add onion and garlic and cook 2 to 3 minutes, stirring occasionally, until onion is light brown. Add remaining ingredients; cover pot and cook over low heat for 20 minutes. Uncover pot and cook 25 to 30 minutes longer, stirring occasionally, until vegetables are tender and chicken is cooked through. *Makes 4 to 6 servings.* For diet serving allow 1¼ cups vegetables plus ½ chicken breast or 1 drumstick and 1 thigh.

Per diet serving: 257 calories, 35 grams protein, 6 grams fat, 16 grams carbohydrate.

Chocolate Angel Food Cake

⅓ cup unsweetened cocoa
⅓ cup water
½ teaspoon vanilla extract
Whites of 4 large eggs (see note)
Few grains of salt

⅓ cup granulated sugar
¼ cup flour
2 teaspoons baking powder
8 pecan or walnut halves
(optional)

Heat oven to 350°F. In a small saucepan cook cocoa and water over low heat for about 1 minute, stirring constantly, until mixture is thick and has just begun to boil. Remove from heat and stir in vanilla. In a large, deep, narrow bowl (preferably metal) beat egg whites and salt with an electric mixer or rotary beater until foamy. Add sugar, 1 tablespoon at a time, beating well after each addition. Soft peaks now will hold when whites are lifted with a spatula. Quickly add cocoa mixture and beat 20 to 30 seconds longer, until just blended. Sift flour and baking powder together over egg white mixture, ¼ at a time, folding in with a rubber spatula after each addition. Scrape batter into an ungreased 8-inch round layer cake pan. Bake 20 to 25 minutes, until cake begins to pull away from sides of pan.

Remove pan from oven and place, upside down, on a wire cake rack to cool for 20 minutes. Run a knife around edge of cake to loosen from pan and carefully turn out onto wire rack. Cool completely before serving. Just before serving, arrange pecan halves on top of cake. *Makes 6 to 8 servings.* For diet serving allow ⅛ of cake. Cake keeps well in refrigerator or freezer. Wrap and reserve 1 diet serving for dinner in Menu #8.

NOTE: Cover and refrigerate egg yolks and reserve for use in French Toast, Menu #7.

Per diet serving: 62 calories, 3 grams protein, 1 gram fat, 13 grams carbohydrate.

BREAKFAST

* French Toast (140), with 1½
  teaspoons maple syrup (25)
1 small peach, sliced (38), mixed
  with ½ cup fresh or unsweetened
  frozen blueberries (45)

LUNCH

Peanut Butter Sandwich: 1½
  tablespoons peanut butter (141);
  1 tablespoon raisins (26); 2 slices
  whole-wheat bread (122)
½ green pepper, sliced (8)
1 cup skim milk (86)

DINNER

* Baked Ziti (294)
Spinach Salad: 1 cup fresh spinach
  leaves (14); ½ cup sliced fresh
  mushrooms (10); Parslied Vinaigrette Dressing (recipe on page
  116, 31)
* Phyllo Apple Pie (165)

TO EAT ANY TIME

½ cup orange juice (61)

French Toast

Yolks of 4 large eggs or 2 whole
  large eggs
¼ cup liquid skim milk

1 teaspoon ground cinnamon
4 slices white bread
1 teaspoon butter or margarine

In a large pie plate or baking pan beat egg yolks, milk and cinnamon with a fork until well mixed. Add bread and soak 10 minutes, turning once, until egg mixture is absorbed. In a large skillet melt butter over moderate heat. Add bread; cook 5 to 7 minutes, turning once, until browned. *Makes 4 slices.* For diet serving allow 1 slice.

Per diet serving: 140 calories, 9 grams protein, 7 grams fat, 12 grams carbohydrate.

Baked Ziti

1 pound lean ground beef
1 cup chopped, peeled onion
8 cups chopped fresh tomatoes
  (about 3 pounds)
1 teaspoon dried basil leaves
1½ teaspoons salt
¼ teaspoon pepper

8 ounces ziti, cooked according to
  package directions and drained
4 ounces part-skim mozzarella
  cheese, cut into ½-inch cubes
2 tablespoons Parmesan cheese,
  preferably freshly grated

In a large, heavy saucepot or Dutch oven cook ground beef and onions 10 minutes over moderately high heat, stirring occasionally to break up beef. When meat is brown and onions are soft, drain and discard fat in pot; add tomatoes, basil, salt and pepper. Cook 30 minutes, stirring occasionally, until sauce is thickened and flavors are blended. (Sauce may be made 1 to 2 days ahead and refrigerated.) Heat oven to 350°F. Mix ziti and tomato sauce in a 2½-quart baking dish; stir in mozzarella; sprinkle with Parmesan. Cover and bake 15 minutes; uncover and bake 15 minutes longer, until hot. *Makes 6 to 8 servings.* For diet serving allow ⅛ of recipe.

Per diet serving: 294 calories, 21 grams protein, 10 grams fat, 31 grams carbohydrate.

Phyllo Apple Pie

¼ cup granulated sugar
1 tablespoon cornstarch
1 teaspoon ground cinnamon
⅛ teaspoon ground cloves
3 pounds firm eating apples, such as Granny Smith, peeled, cored and cut into eighths (about 8 cups)

2 tablespoons lemon juice
8 sheets (¼ pound) phyllo dough (see note)
2 tablespoons lightly salted butter or margarine, melted

Heat oven to 325°F. In a small bowl mix sugar, cornstarch, cinnamon and cloves. In a large bowl toss apples with lemon juice; add sugar mixture and stir to coat. In a 9½-inch deep-dish pie plate put 1 sheet of phyllo dough so that edges hang over the side; brush dough inside pie plate with about ½ teaspoon of the butter. Put another sheet of phyllo dough across the first and brush it with more of the butter. Repeat layers once more, brushing each sheet of phyllo with about ½ teaspoon of the butter. Spoon apple mixture into pie plate. Cover with the remaining 4 sheets of phyllo, brushing each with some of the remaining butter. Form excess phyllo dough into an edge by rolling it under, toward the pie plate rim. If dough is dry and cracks, moisten with wet fingertips. With a sharp knife make 3 slits in top of pie. Bake 40 to 45 minutes, until top of pie is golden-brown. *Makes 6 to 8 servings.* For diet serving allow ⅛ of pie.

NOTE: Phyllo (or filo) dough, which can be found in the refrigerator or freezer section of most supermarkets, also is known as strudel leaves.

Per diet serving: 165 calories, 2 grams fat, 3 grams protein, 34 grams carbohydrate.

BRUNCH

½ cup orange juice (61)
* Scrambled Eggs with Green
Pepper (277)
2 ounces cooked Canadian-style
bacon (116)
1 slice whole-wheat bread (61),
spread with 1 teaspoon butter or
margarine (34)
1 cup skim milk (86)

DINNER

* Barbecued Ribs (248)
* Creamy Potato Salad (182)
1 dill pickle (15)
Tomato and Cucumber Salad: 1
tomato, sliced (20); ½ cucumber,
sliced (8); Parslied Vinaigrette
Dressing (recipe on page 116, 31)
Chocolate Angel Food Cake
(reserved from Menu #6, 62)

Scrambled Eggs with Green Pepper

4 large eggs
¼ cup liquid skim milk
½ cup chopped, seeded green
pepper

¼ teaspoon salt
⅛ teaspoon black pepper
1 teaspoon butter or margarine

In a medium-sized bowl whisk eggs, milk, green pepper, salt and pepper until foamy. In a large skillet melt butter over moderately high heat. Add egg mixture and cook 4 to 5 minutes, stirring occasionally, until eggs are set and no longer runny. *Makes 2 servings.* For diet serving, allow ½ of the recipe.

Per diet serving: 277 calories, 13 grams protein, 22 grams fat, 6 grams carbohydrate.

Barbecued Ribs

3 pounds pork loin country-style
ribs
Water
2 teaspoons salt
1 teaspoon minced, peeled garlic
1½ cups tomato juice

2 tablespoons Worcestershire
sauce
3 tablespoons soy sauce
¼ cup cider or wine vinegar
1 tablespoon lemon juice
⅛ teaspoon celery seed
1 tablespoon catsup

With a sharp knife cut racks of ribs into individual ribs and remove any visible fat around meat. Place ribs in a Dutch oven and cover with water; add 1 teaspoon of the salt and bring to a boil over high heat. Reduce heat to moderate; cover pot and simmer 45 minutes, until meat is tender when pierced with a fork. On a board sprinkle the garlic with the remaining teaspoon of salt and mash to a paste using the blade of a knife. In a small pan combine garlic mixture and remaining ingredients and bring to a simmer over moderate heat; cook about 10 minutes. Pour sauce into a large, shallow baking dish and cool slightly. Drain ribs (discard cooking liquid), add to sauce and turn to coat. Cover and marinate 1 hour at room temperature or overnight in the refrigerator, turning ribs several times.

Line a broiler pan with aluminum foil. Arrange ribs in broiler pan without a rack and baste with the sauce. Broil 7 inches from heat source for 8 minutes. Turn, baste and broil 10 minutes longer. If desired, remaining sauce may be placed in a small pan, simmered for 10 minutes and served with the ribs. *Makes 4 to 6 servings.* For diet serving allow ⅙ of the ribs.

Per diet serving: 248 calories, 29 grams protein, 14 grams fat, 1 gram carbohydrate.

Creamy Potato Salad

2 pounds all-purpose potatoes, well scrubbed
1½ teaspoons salt
Water
¼ cup plain low-fat yogurt
¼ cup mayonnaise
1 teaspoon lemon juice
⅛ teaspoon black pepper
½ cup chopped, seeded green pepper
¼ cup chopped, peeled onion

Put potatoes and 1 teaspoon of the salt in a large saucepan; add water to cover. Cover pot and bring to a boil over high heat; reduce heat to moderate and simmer 20 to 25 minutes, until potatoes are just tender when pierced with a fork. Drain potatoes and rinse with cold water; peel and discard skins. Let stand at room temperature 45 minutes, until just warm. Meanwhile, in a large bowl mix the remaining ½ teaspoon salt with the yogurt, mayonnaise, lemon juice, pepper, green pepper and onion. Cut potatoes into ¾-inch pieces; add to yogurt mixture and toss gently but thoroughly. Cover and refrigerate up to 48 hours. *Makes about 6 cups salad.* For diet serving allow 1 cup.

Per diet serving: 182 calories, 4 grams protein, 8 grams fat, 25 grams carbohydrate.

BREAKFAST

½ cup orange juice (61)
1 heated frozen waffle (about
   4½ x 3¾ x ½ inches, 86), with
   1 tablespoon maple or maple-
   flavored syrup (50)

LUNCH

Peanut Butter Sandwich: 1½
   tablespoons peanut butter (141);
   2 slices whole-wheat bread (122)
½ green pepper (8)
1 cup skim milk (86)

DINNER

* Cheddar–Tomato Custard (245)
1 cup cooked green beans with pearl
   onions (42)
1 slice rye bread (61)
* Blueberry Crunch (128)

TO EAT ANY TIME

¾ cup skim milk (65)
1 cup 4-grain multivitamin-and-iron-
   supplement cereal (110)

Cheddar–Tomato Custard

2 16-ounce cans whole peeled
   tomatoes
6 ounces sharp Cheddar cheese,
   grated (1½ cups)
6 large eggs
1½ cups skim milk

½ teaspoon salt
½ teaspoon ground nutmeg
¼ teaspoon black pepper
1 14½-ounce can sliced baby
   tomatoes, drained

Heat oven to 350°F. Pour whole tomatoes into a strainer set over a bowl and press tomatoes with the back of a spoon to extract all excess liquid. Divide tomato pulp equally into six 10-ounce custard cups or individual baking dishes and sprinkle with cheese. Put eggs, milk, salt, nutmeg and pepper into a medium-sized bowl and beat with a rotary beater until frothy; pour egg mixture into custard cups. Arrange 2 or 3 tomato slices on top of each custard. Bake 30 minutes, until custard is set and a knife inserted 1 inch from edge comes out clean. *Makes 6 servings.* For diet serving allow 1 custard cup.

Per diet serving: 245 calories, 17 grams protein, 15 grams fat, 10 grams carbohydrate.

Blueberry Crunch

⅓ cup crunchy nutlike cereal
  nuggets
¼ teaspoon ground cinnamon
1 tablespoon granulated sugar
2 tablespoons lightly salted butter
  or margarine, at room
  temperature

1 9-ounce carton unsweetened
  frozen blueberries or 2 cups
  fresh blueberries
½ teaspoon granulated sugar
1 teaspoon freshly grated lemon
  peel

Heat oven to 450°F. or use a toaster-oven. Mix cereal, cinnamon and 1 tablespoon sugar in a small bowl. Using two knives or a pastry blender, cut butter into cereal mixture until evenly distributed and crumbly. Spread blueberries in an 8-inch pie plate or in 4 small custard cups; sprinkle with remaining ½ teaspoon of the sugar, the grated lemon peel and then the cereal mixture. Bake until brown on top. *Makes 3 or 4 servings.* For diet serving allow ¼ of pie or 1 custard cup.

NOTE: Blueberry Crunch also makes a good quick breakfast with a glass of skim milk or an eat-anytime snack, as calories allow.

Per diet serving: 128 calories, 1 gram protein, 6 grams fat, 18 grams carbohydrate.

The Once-a-Month Diet Crisis

Because many women who had dieted reported a real sweet craving or an insatiable hunger before menstruation, *Redbook* editors consulted Dr. Johanna Dwyer who, with her colleague Joanne De-Cristofaro, had studied several hundred women to see what appetite changes they reported prior to and during menses. They found little support for the sweet craving during the premenstrual period, but 25% of the women reported that they ate more than usual. Dr. Dwyer's advice:

"If you're following *Redbook*'s Wise Woman's Diet, before your menstrual period you can adjust the diet to accommodate your needs. Borrow from the next day, when you know you won't be quite so ravenous. And then, too, remember that just because you're premenstrual doesn't mean you have no willpower."

BREAKFAST

* Fruit Salad Shake (259)
1 ½-inch-thick slice French bread, 2½ x 2 inches (44), spread with 1 tablespoon peanut butter (95)

LUNCH

Sliced Egg Sandwich: 1 large hard-cooked egg, sliced (82); ½ roasted sweet red pepper from a jar (12); 2 lettuce leaves (4); 1 slice rye bread (61)
1 cup tomato juice (46)

DINNER

* Asparagus Bisque (82)
* Caraway Chicken (279)
Crunchy Vegetable Salad: 2 cups sliced raw cauliflower florets (46); 5 large pitted green olives (23); 3 slices red onion (11); Basic Vinaigrette Dressing (recipe on page 23, 31)
1 tangerine (39)

TO EAT ANY TIME

1 cup skim milk (86)

Fruit Salad Shake

1 cup buttermilk or skim milk
¼ cup frozen orange juice concentrate, undiluted
1 tablespoon honey
⅓ cup instant nonfat dry milk

1 cup fresh or unsweetened frozen strawberries
1 medium-sized ripe banana, quartered
1 cup ice cubes

Place all ingredients in a blender; cover and blend at high speed 1 minute, until shake is smooth. *Makes 3½ cups.* For diet serving allow 1¾ cups.

Per diet serving: 259 calories, 11 grams protein, 0 grams fat, 55 grams carbohydrate.

Asparagus Bisque

1 14½-ounce can cut asparagus spears
1 cup liquid skim milk

1 .21-ounce packet instant onion or chicken-flavored broth

Place all ingredients in a blender. Cover and blend at high speed 30 seconds, until smooth. Transfer to a small saucepan and bring to a boil, stirring often. *Makes 3 cups.* For diet serving allow 1½ cups.

Per diet serving: 82 calories, 8 grams protein, 1 gram fat, 12 grams carbohydrate.

Caraway Chicken

1 pound boneless, skinless chicken breasts (4 half breasts)
¼ cup dry white wine
1 tablespoon vegetable oil
½ teaspoon salt
⅛ teaspoon black pepper

¼ cup minced scallion or green onion
1 1-ounce slice Muenster cheese with caraway seeds, halved (see note)

Place chicken breasts, smooth side down, between 2 large sheets of wax paper. Using a mallet or the bottom of a heavy skillet, pound breasts to flatten to ¼-inch thickness. In a wide, shallow bowl mix the wine, oil, salt, pepper and half the scallion and then add the chicken breasts. Marinate 15 minutes, turning pieces once. Arrange chicken, smooth side down, in a broiler pan and baste with some of the marinade. Broil 5 inches from heat source for 5 minutes. Turn chicken and baste with remaining marinade. Top 2 of the half-breasts with a piece of cheese, sprinkle with the remaining scallions and broil 5 minutes longer, until cheese is bubbly and lightly browned. *Makes 2 servings of Caraway Chicken.* For diet serving allow 1 half breast with cheese. Wrap and refrigerate the one serving of plain chicken breast for lunch in Menu #11. Freeze the second serving for another lunch.

NOTE: If you can't find Muenster cheese with caraway seeds, use a plain Muenster slice and sprinkle 4 caraway seeds on each half breast.

Per diet serving: 279 calories, 39 grams protein, 12 grams fat, 1 gram carbohydrate.

BREAKFAST

1 cup 4-grain multivitamin-and-iron-
  supplement cereal (110)
1 cup skim milk (86)
1 cup fresh or unsweetened frozen
  strawberries (55)

LUNCH

Cold Chicken (reserved from Menu
  #10, 229)
1 tablespoon mayonnaise (102),
  blended with 1 tablespoon
  prepared mustard (12)
½ medium-sized carrot (15)
1 green pepper, sliced (16)
2 whole-grain rye wafers (45)

DINNER

* Little-Meat Chili (283)
Chili Garnishes: ¼ cup plain low-
  fat yogurt (31); ½ large hard-
  cooked egg, chopped (41); ¼
  cup chopped onion (16)
* Icy Buttermilk Cukes (61)
* Hot Pink Grapefruit (100)

Little-Meat Chili

1 tablespoon vegetable oil
2 cups diced, peeled onion
1 tablespoon minced, peeled garlic
1 pound ground beef round
4 to 6 teaspoons chili powder

1½ teaspoons salt
1 2-pound-3-ounce can Italian
  plum tomatoes, with the liquid
2 16-ounce cans red kidney beans,
  rinsed and drained

In a large saucepot or Dutch oven heat oil over moderately high heat.
Add onion and garlic and cook 5 minutes, stirring often, until onion is
soft. Add meat and cook 2 minutes, breaking up meat with a spoon,
until it begins to lose its red color. Add remaining ingredients and bring
to a boil, stirring often. Reduce heat to low and simmer 30 minutes,
stirring occasionally to prevent sticking. *Makes 5 to 7 servings.* For diet
serving allow 1 cup.

Per diet serving: 283 calories, 22 grams protein, 9 grams fat, 29 grams carbohydrate.

Icy Buttermilk Cukes

2 large cucumbers, scrubbed and
  sliced very thin
1 large red onion, peeled, sliced
  thin and separated into rings
1 tablespoon salt
Cold water

1 cup buttermilk or plain low-fat
  yogurt
2 tablespoons white vinegar
2 teaspoons sugar
¼ teaspoon black pepper

Place cucumbers and onion rings in a large bowl, sprinkle with the tablespoon salt and add enough cold water to cover vegetables. Refrigerate 30 minutes. Combine remaining ingredients in a screw-top jar, cover jar and shake dressing to blend. Thoroughly drain vegetables, toss with the dressing, cover salad and refrigerate 2 hours or longer. *Makes 3 or 4 servings.* For diet serving allow ¼ of the salad.

Per diet serving: 61 calories, 4 grams protein, 0 grams fat, 12 grams carbohydrate.

Hot Pink Grapefruit

1 large pink grapefruit, peeled   2 tablespoons rum
    and sectioned   1 tablespoon brown sugar

Arrange grapefruit sections in a spiral in a small, shallow baking dish; sprinkle with rum and brown sugar. Broil 3 inches from heat source for 10 minutes, until sugar is melted and bubbly. *Makes 2 servings.* For diet serving allow ½ grapefruit.

Per diet serving: 100 calories, 1 gram protein, 0 grams fat, 24 grams carbohydrate.

What About a Bedtime Snack?

If a snack before bedtime will make you rest more comfortably, by all means have it. Save some portion of the day's menu to eat then. It's a weight control myth that eating before bedtime puts on pounds. Calories do. You gain weight only when the number of calories consumed during the day exceeds the number of calories expended during the day.

BREAKFAST

6 unsweetened cooked prunes (164)
1 cup plain low-fat yogurt (144)
Cinnamon Toast: 1 slice whole-wheat bread (61); 1 teaspoon butter or margarine (34); ground cinnamon to taste

LUNCH

1 cup canned cream of asparagus soup, prepared with skim milk (80)
Swiss Cheese and Onion Open-Face Sandwich: 1 ounce Swiss cheese (107); 2 slices onion (6); 1 slice rye bread (61)

DINNER

* Chicken Livers Provençal (196)
½ cup cooked rice cooked in beef broth, if desired (93)
½ medium-sized cucumber, peeled and sliced (10); 1 teaspoon vegetable oil (40); 1 teaspoon wine vinegar
* Steamed Pears with Ginger (108)

TO EAT ANY TIME

¾ cup skim milk (65)
3 *Juicy Jellies (39)

Chicken Livers Provençal

1 pound chicken livers
2 teaspoons butter
2 teaspoons vegetable oil
2 tablespoons minced, peeled shallots or scallion or green onion

1 large ripe tomato, peeled, seeded and cut into ½-inch pieces (1 cup)
½ teaspoon minced, peeled garlic
½ teaspoon salt
⅛ teaspoon black pepper
¼ cup chopped fresh parsley

Rinse livers, discarding any bits of fat that cling to them; pat dry with paper towels. In a medium-sized, heavy skillet heat butter and oil over moderately high heat. When skillet is very hot and butter foam subsides, add livers. Cook 2 minutes, gently tossing the livers so that they brown evenly. Add shallots and cook 1 minute, stirring constantly. Add tomato and cook 1 minute, stirring often; sprinkle with garlic, salt and pepper and cook 1 minute longer, gently stirring the mixture. Stir in parsley and serve. *Makes 3 or 4 servings.* For diet serving allow ¼ of the livers and sauce.

Per diet serving: 196 calories, 23 grams protein, 9 grams fat, 6 grams carbohydrate.

Steamed Pears with Ginger

4 firm ripe Bartlett or Anjou pears
1 teaspoon lemon or lime juice
4 dime-sized slices of peeled fresh
   gingerroot or ¼ teaspoon
   ground ginger

2 teaspoon granulated sugar
Water

Cut a thin slice from the bottom of each pear if necessary, so that it will stand upright. Slice pear at stem end, about 1½ inches from top; scoop out core with a teaspoon. Put lemon juice, ginger and sugar into pear cavities. Stand pears in a steamer basket (see note). Fill a saucepot or Dutch oven with water to a depth of 1 inch; cover and bring to a boil over high heat. Carefully lower steamer basket into pot; cover and steam 8 to 10 minutes, until pears are almost tender. Serve warm. *Makes 4 servings.* For diet serving allow 1 pear.

NOTE: If you don't have a steamer basket, put each pear in a ramekin or custard cup. Put a wire cake rack in the bottom of the saucepot and fill pot with water to a depth of ¼ inch. When water boils, arrange dishes of pears on rack, cover and steam.

Per diet serving: 108 calories, 0 grams protein, 0 grams fat, 27 grams carbohydrate.

Juicy Jellies

3½ packages unflavored gelatin
   (3½ tablespoons gelatin)
1¼ cups cold water

1 6-ounce can frozen grape juice
   concentrate, undiluted and
   thawed

Sprinkle gelatin over water in a medium-sized saucepan. Stir over moderately low heat about 5 minutes, until gelatin is dissolved. Remove from heat and stir in juice concentrate. Pour into an 8-inch square baking pan, cover and refrigerate 2 hours or longer, until firm. Cut into 36 *squares.* For 1 diet serving allow 3 squares.

NOTE: Jellies also may be made with orange juice concentrate. In the diet menus, 9 jelly squares may replace 1 cup of juice. Keep leftover jellies refrigerated.

Per diet serving: 39 calories, 2 grams protein, 0 grams fat, 8 grams carbohydrate.

BREAKFAST

* Apricot Ambrosia (170)
1 slice whole-wheat bread, toasted,
  sprinkled with cinnamon (61)

LUNCH

No-Bun Cheeseburger: 2 ounces
  broiled lean hamburger (140); 1
  ounce American cheese (106);
  2 teaspoons catsup (10)
10 oven-heated frozen French fries
  (111)
¾ cup skim milk (65)

DINNER

* New Orleans Baked Fish (270)
½ cup cooked kale (22)
⅔ cup cooked brown rice (77)

TO EAT ANY TIME

15 unshelled roasted peanuts (166)

Apricot Ambrosia

1 cup plain low-fat yogurt
¼ cup instant nonfat dry milk
½ cup syrup-packed apricot
  halves, drained

1 teaspoon honey
6 ice cubes

Place all ingredients in a blender; cover and blend 15 seconds at medium speed. Stop machine and push mixture down. Cover and blend 15 seconds longer. *Makes 2 diet servings.* Recipe may be halved.

Per diet serving: 170 calories, 10 grams protein, 2 grams fat, 28 grams carbohydrate.

New Orleans Baked Fish

1 1-pound block frozen flounder
or sole fillets
1 large onion, peeled and sliced
into thin rings
1 large green pepper, seeded and
cut in strips
1 16-ounce can whole peeled
tomatoes, drained

6 thin slices lemon
1 teaspoon minced, peeled garlic
⅓ cup chopped fresh parsley
½ teaspoon salt
⅛ to ¼ teaspoon black pepper
¼ teaspoon dried thyme leaves

Heat oven to 375°F. Remove fish from freezer and let stand at room temperature 10 minutes. Cut into 4 equal pieces and arrange in the bottom of an 11¾-x-7½-x-1¾-inch baking dish. Arrange onion rings, pepper strips, tomatoes and lemon slices on top of fish; sprinkle with garlic, parsley, salt, pepper and thyme. Cover tightly with aluminum foil and bake 50 to 55 minutes, until fish is white and opaque in the thickest part. *Makes 3 or 4 servings.* For diet serving allow ¼ of the fish and vegetables.

NOTE: Use tomato liquid in a salad dressing or as a beverage.

Per diet serving: 270 calories, 36 grams protein, 10 grams fat, 8 grams carbohydrate.

Eat and Enjoy

When you eat, sit down, relax, eat and enjoy each mouthful. Don't talk on the phone, read a book or watch television at the same time. You can lose track of what you've eaten and end up feeling you haven't eaten at all. Also, you can find the distraction habit-forming; you'll end up feeling hungry every time you talk on the phone, read or watch television.

Concentrate on savoring your food. Eat slowly, in peaceful, pleasant surroundings. Concentrate and remember what eating-without-knowing-it can do to you.

BRUNCH
* Hot Tomato–Cheese Rolls (319)
* Raspberry Rhubarb (133)

DINNER
1 grilled frankfurter (176)
* Brown-Baked Potatoes (132)
½ cup sauerkraut (21)
½ cup raw cauliflower florets (12)
and 4 radishes (2), with ¼ cup
*Swiss Sour Cream (72) as a dip
1 4-x-8-inch wedge watermelon (53)

TO EAT ANY TIME
* Peachy Buttermilk Shake (160)
¾ cup skim milk (65)
½ cup 4-grain multivitamin-and-
iron-supplement cereal (55)

Hot Tomato–Cheese Rolls

2 large ripe tomatoes, diced
(about 2 cups)
8 ounces sharp Cheddar cheese,
diced (about 2 cups)

¼ teaspoon salt
⅛ teaspoon black pepper
6 hard, round crusty rolls, about
5 inches in diameter

In a small bowl mix the tomatoes, cheese, salt and pepper. Heat oven to 350°F. With a sharp knife cut a circular plug about 2 inches in diameter in the top of each roll; scoop out the soft inside of each roll. Fill each roll with ½ cup of the tomato-cheese mixture and replace plug. Wrap each roll in a square of foil, pressing roll down firmly so it holds together. Place wrapped rolls on a baking sheet and bake 20 minutes; loosen foil around rolls and bake 5 minutes longer, until just crisp. *Makes 6 rolls.* For diet serving allow 1 roll.

NOTE: Insides of rolls may be toasted and whirred in blender to make bread crumbs.

Per diet serving: 319 calories, 15 grams protein, 14 grams fat, 34 grams carbohydrate.

Raspberry Rhubarb

½ cup raspberry preserves
1½ pounds fresh rhubarb,
trimmed and cut into 1-inch
pieces (about 5 cups)

Spread preserves in the bottom of a heavy 2-quart saucepan and cover with rhubarb. Cover pot and cook over low heat about 30 minutes, until rhubarb is tender, stirring 2 or 3 times. Transfer to a serving dish, cover and refrigerate several hours or overnight. *Makes about 4 cups, or 4 servings.* For diet serving allow 1 cup.

Per diet serving: 133 calories, 1 gram protein, 0 grams fat, 33 grams carbohydrate.

Brown-Baked Potatoes

4 to 6 medium-sized baking   ½ teaspoon salt
  potatoes, scrubbed   ⅛ teaspoon black pepper
1 tablespoon vegetable oil

Heat oven to 400°F. Dry potatoes with paper towels. Halve each potato lengthwise and place cut side up on a baking sheet. Brush with oil, sprinkle with salt and pepper and bake 1 hour, until potatoes are tender and tops are browned and crisp. *Makes 4 to 6 servings.* For diet serving allow 2 halves.

Per diet serving: 132 calories, 3 grams protein, 4 grams fat, 21 grams carbohydrate.

Swiss Sour Cream

1 cup creamed cottage cheese   ¼ cup liquid skim milk
2 tablespoons lemon juice

Place ingredients in a blender; cover and blend at low speed about 30 seconds, or until very smooth. Transfer to a bowl, cover and refrigerate several hours before serving. Covered tightly, mixture will keep 4 or 5 days in the refrigerator. *Makes 1 cup.* For diet serving allow 1 tablespoon.

Per diet serving: 18 calories, 2 grams protein, 0 grams fat, 1 gram carbohydrate.

Peachy Buttermilk Shake

2 fresh peaches, pitted and   1 cup buttermilk or skim milk
  quartered   3 ice cubes

Place peach quarters, buttermilk and ice cubes in a blender; cover and blend at medium speed about 30 seconds, until smooth. *Makes 1 diet serving.*

Per diet serving: 160 calories, 11 grams protein, 0 grams fat, 31 grams carbohydrate.

As American as, Yes, Apple Pie   197

BRUNCH

* Stirred Eggs (160)
2 ounces Canadian-style bacon,
  broiled (116)
1 slice whole-wheat bread, toasted
  (61), spread with 1 teaspoon
  butter or margarine (34)
½ cup orange juice (61)

DINNER

* Italian Baked Chicken (150)
1 cup steamed diced zucchini (25)
½ cup cooked enriched egg noodles
  (100)
¾ cup seedless green grapes (79),
  with ¼ cup Swiss Sour Cream
  (recipe on page 197, 72)

TO EAT ANY TIME

2 *Davis Cups (160)
1 cup skim milk (86)
½ cup prune juice (98)

Stirred Eggs

¼ cup water
2 eggs, lightly beaten

Few grains of salt
Few grains of black pepper

In an 8-inch skillet bring water to a boil over moderately high heat. Beat eggs with salt and pepper, add to skillet, reduce heat to moderate and cook about 1 minute, stirring constantly, until eggs are fluffy and all of the water has been absorbed. *Makes 1 diet serving.*

Per diet serving: 160 calories, 12 grams protein, 12 grams fat, 0 grams carbohydrate.

Italian Baked Chicken

3½ pounds broiler-fryer chicken
  parts, skin removed
½ teaspoon salt
1 teaspoon dried oregano leaves
1 1-pound can whole peeled
  tomatoes, drained and diced

½ cup diced, peeled onion
1 teaspoon minced, peeled garlic
¼ cup Parmesan cheese,
  preferably freshly grated
  (1 ounce)

Line a broiler pan with foil. Rinse chicken and pat dry with paper towels. Place chicken in broiler pan and broil 5 inches from heat source for 10 minutes; turn and broil 10 minutes longer. Turn oven heat to 350°F. Place chicken in a 13-x-9-inch baking pan. Sprinkle chicken with salt and oregano and arrange tomatoes, onion, garlic and cheese evenly on top. Bake 30 minutes. *Makes 4 servings.* For diet serving allow 4 ounces cooked chicken.

Per diet serving: 150 calories, 18 grams protein, 6 grams fat, 6 grams carbohydrate.

Davis Cups

2 tablespoons honey
2 tablespoons water
¼ cup chunk-style peanut butter
2 teaspoons vanilla extract

1 egg
4¼ cups fortified high-protein cereal

Heat oven to 350°F. Place paper baking cups in each section of a 12-muffin tin. In a small saucepan heat honey, water and peanut butter over moderately low heat, stirring until blended; remove from heat and stir in vanilla. Beat egg in a large mixing bowl, add honey mixture and cereal and mix gently with clean hands until cereal is evenly coated. Pack about ¼ cup of cereal mixture into each baking cup. Bake 15 to 20 minutes, or until golden brown. *Makes 12 "cups."* For diet serving allow 2 "cups."

NOTE: Wrap extra cups well. They will keep in the refrigerator for 1 to 2 weeks. Use them for a snack or a quick breakfast, as calories permit.

Per diet serving: 160 calories, 7 grams protein, 6 grams fat, 19 grams carbohydrate.

BREAKFAST

* Apricot Cottage Cheese (111)
1 slice white bread (68)
½ cup orange juice (61)

LUNCH

3 ounces broiled lean hamburger
   (4 ounces before cooking, 210),
   with 1 teaspoon catsup (5)
1 large dill pickle (15)
½ medium-sized carrot, cut in strips
   (15)
1 small tomato, sliced (20)
1 slice pumpernickel bread (79)
1 nectarine (88)
1 cup skim milk (86)

DINNER

* Pan-Broiled Pork Chops (151)
* Braised Cabbage and Apples (70)
1 boiled potato (2½-inch diameter,
   104), with 1 teaspoon butter or
   margarine (34)
4 dried apricot halves (44)

TO EAT ANY TIME

½ cup fresh raspberries (35)
5 thin pretzel sticks (6)

Apricot Cottage Cheese

1 cup 99%-fat-free cottage cheese
1 tablespoon apricot preserves

1 teaspoon unsweetened cocoa

Mix cottage cheese and preserves in a small bowl. Sprinkle with cocoa just before serving. Eat with a spoon. *Makes 1 cup.* For diet serving allow ½ cup.

Per diet serving: 111 calories, 14 grams protein, 1 gram fat, 11 grams carbohydrate.

Pan-Broiled Pork Chops

4 pork loin chops (about 2
   pounds), trimmed of excess fat
½ cup water
2 tablespoons chopped fresh
   parsley

½ teaspoon dried rosemary
   leaves, crumbled
¼ teaspoon salt
⅛ teaspoon black pepper
4 thin slices apple, cored
   (optional)

Heat a 10- to 12-inch skillet over moderately high heat for 30 seconds. Add pork chops and cook 20 minutes, turning once, until chops are browned on both sides and thoroughly cooked. Remove to a plate; cover and keep warm. Drain and discard fat in pan but leave the brown bits. Add water, parsley, rosemary, salt and pepper to skillet; cook over moderately high heat 1 to 2 minutes, stirring constantly to dissolve brown bits. When about ¼ cup liquid remains, strain it over the meat. Garnish with apple slices. *Makes 4 servings*. For diet serving allow 1 chop.

Per diet serving: 151 calories, 17 grams protein, 9 grams fat, 0 grams carbohydrate.

Braised Cabbage and Apples

¼ cup water
6 cups finely shredded cabbage
(1 pound)
2 tablespoons cider vinegar
½ teaspoon salt

2 medium-sized cooking apples
(such as Rome Beauty or
McIntosh), cored and sliced
½ teaspoon granulated sugar

In a large saucepot or skillet (preferably not aluminum) bring water to a boil over moderately high heat; add cabbage, vinegar and salt and stir to mix. Cover pot and cook over moderately low heat for 20 to 25 minutes, until cabbage is wilted and tender. Add apples and sugar to pot and cook 5 minutes longer, stirring occasionally, until apples are tender. *Makes 3 or 4 servings*. For diet serving allow 1¼ cups.

Per diet serving: 70 calories, 2 grams protein, 1 gram fat, 17 grams carbohydrate.

BREAKFAST

* Strawberry Shake (156)
1 slice whole-wheat bread (61),
   spread with ½ teaspoon butter or
   margarine (17)

LUNCH

Burger on Whole-Wheat: 2½
   ounces lean, cooked hamburger
   (175); 2 teaspoons catsup (10);
   2 slices whole-wheat bread (122)
2 plums (64)
1 cup skim milk (86)

DINNER

1 cup beef broth (31)
* Spanish Tuna Salad (274)
1 cloverleaf roll (83), spread with
   1 teaspoon butter or margarine
   (34)
* Coffee Cloud (56)
½ cup skim milk (43)

Strawberry Shake

1 cup liquid skim milk
1 cup fresh or unsweetened
   frozen strawberries

½ teaspoon vanilla extract
1 teaspoon granulated sugar

Place all ingredients in a blender; cover and blend at high speed until smooth. Pour into a tall glass and garnish with a fresh berry if you wish. *Makes 1 diet serving.*

Per diet serving: 156 calories, 9 grams protein, 1 gram fat, 28 grams carbohydrate.

Spanish Tuna Salad

2 tablespoons olive oil
3 tablespoons red wine vinegar
½ teaspoon salt
¼ teaspoon black pepper
1 13-ounce can solid-packed
   tuna, drained
1 20-ounce can cannellini beans,
   drained and rinsed

1 7½-ounce jar or can roasted
   red sweet peppers or pimientos,
   drained and chopped
½ cup chopped, peeled sweet
   onion
Fresh parsley sprigs

In a small bowl mix oil, vinegar, salt and pepper. Arrange remaining ingredients on a platter. Just before serving, pour dressing over salad and toss. *Makes about 5 cups.* For diet serving allow ¼ of salad.

Per diet serving: 274 calories, 32 grams protein, 8 grams fat, 19 grams carbohydrate.

Coffee Cloud

1 envelope unflavored gelatin
1 tablespoon instant-coffee
   granules
¼ cup granulated sugar
Few grains of nutmeg

1 cup liquid skim milk
1 teaspoon vanilla extract
Whites of 2 large eggs, at room
   temperature

In a small saucepan mix gelatin, coffee, sugar and nutmeg. Stir in milk. Heat over moderately low heat, stirring constantly, until gelatin and coffee are dissolved. Remove from heat. Stir in vanilla. Chill 20 to 30 minutes, until slightly thickened. In a small, deep bowl beat egg whites with an electric or rotary beater until stiff peaks hold when beater is lifted. Whisk egg white clinging to beaters into coffee mixture; then fold in remaining egg white. Pour mixture into a 3-cup mold (see note). Chill at least 4 hours, until very firm.

To unmold: Dip mold into warm, not hot, water. Shake gently to loosen dessert. Place inverted serving plate on top of mold. Hold plate and mold together firmly and turn them over. Gently lift off mold. *Makes 6 servings.* For diet serving allow ½ cup.

NOTE: Instead of using a mold, dessert may be poured into 6 individual serving dishes.

Per diet serving: 56 calories, 4 grams protein, 0 grams fat, 10 grams carbohydrate.

BREAKFAST

½ cup orange juice (61)
* Breakfast Blintz (139)

LUNCH

2 ounces Cheddar cheese (228)
2 ½-inch slices French bread (2 x 2½ inches, 88)
4 radishes (2)
1 small apple (61)

DINNER

* Chicken Livers Teriyaki (160)
½ cup cooked rice (93)
* Zucchini and Carrot Salad (41)
* Pineapple Ice (65)

TO EAT ANY TIME

2 cups skim milk (172)
¾ cup 4-grain multivitamin-and-iron-supplement cereal (83)

Breakfast Blintz

1 slice white bread
¼ cup creamed cottage cheese
¼ teaspoon granulated sugar

¼ teaspoon vanilla extract
Few grains of ground cinnamon

Heat oven to 350°F. or use a toaster-oven. Flatten bread with a rolling pin. Mix remaining ingredients and spread diagonally across bread slice; bring opposite corners together and secure with a toothpick. Place on a square of aluminum foil and bake 15 to 20 minutes, until bread is golden. *Makes 1 diet serving.*

Per diet serving: 139 calories, 10 grams protein, 4 grams fat, 16 grams carbohydrate.

Chicken Livers Teriyaki

1 pound chicken livers
¼ cup soy sauce
¼ cup dry sherry wine
½ teaspoon minced, peeled garlic

1 teaspoon minced, peeled gingerroot or ½ teaspoon ground ginger

Rinse livers, discarding any bits of fat that cling to them; pat dry with paper towels. In a medium-sized bowl place the soy sauce, sherry, garlic and ginger; stir to mix and then stir in the chicken livers. Let livers marinate 15 minutes or cover and refrigerate several hours. Line a broiler pan with foil; arrange livers with marinade in pan and broil 4 inches from heat source for 10 minutes, turning once. Serve livers hot and pour pan juices over them. *Makes 3 or 4 servings.* For diet serving allow ¼ of the cooked livers.

Per diet serving: 160 calories, 22 grams protein, 4 grams fat, 5 grams carbohydrate.

Zucchini and Carrot Salad

1 tablespoon soy sauce
2 tablespoons freshly squeezed
  lemon juice
¼ teaspoon ground ginger
¼ teaspoon salt
1 teaspoon granulated sugar

3 medium-sized zucchini squash
  (about 1 pound), scrubbed
  and sliced thin
3 medium-sized carrots, peeled
  and coarsely shredded

In a salad bowl combine the soy sauce, lemon juice, ginger, salt and sugar. Add zucchini and carrots, toss gently and serve. *Makes 4½ cups.* For diet serving allow 1¼ cups.

NOTE: This salad is best when dressed just before serving.

Per diet serving: 41 calories, 2 grams protein, 0 grams fat, 9 grams carbohydrate.

Pineapple Ice

1 20-ounce can juice-packed
  pineapple

Place contents of can in a blender; cover and blend at high speed to a smooth puree. Pour mixture into a 9-inch square metal baking pan; cover and freeze 1 to 2 hours, until mixture is frozen 1 inch from edge of pan. Beat mixture smooth with a fork. Cover and freeze several hours until firm. Remove ice from freezer 10 minutes before serving to soften slightly. *Makes 2½ cups.* For diet serving allow ½ cup. Leftover ice may be stored in an airtight container in freezer for 1 week.

Per diet serving: 65 calories, 0 grams protein, 0 grams fat, 17 grams carbohydrate.

BREAKFAST

* Breakfast "Caviar" (96)
½ cup creamed cottage cheese
 (130)
3 whole-grain rye wafers (68)
Hot Orange Tea: hot tea mixed
 with ½ cup orange juice (61)
 and sprinkled with cinnamon

LUNCH

Sardines on Whole-Wheat: 2 ounces
 sardines, drained (124); ½
 tomato, sliced (10); 2 large leaves
 lettuce (5); 3 slices red onion
 (11); 1 tablespoon wine vinegar;
 few leaves of basil; 2 slices whole-
 wheat bread, toasted (122)
½ pear (45)

DINNER

* Farmer's Meat Loaf (260)
1 small baked potato (90)
Beet and Escarole Salad: ½ cup
 diced beets (28); 4 large leaves
 escarole (20); Basic Vinaigrette
 Dressing (recipe on page 23, 31)
* Hot Baked Jelly Apples (99)

Breakfast "Caviar"

½ pound dried, pitted prunes
 (1¼ cups)
1 cup water

2 teaspoons freshly squeezed
 lemon juice

In a small saucepan bring prunes and water to a boil over high heat. Reduce heat to moderately low and simmer uncovered for 1 hour, until prunes have absorbed most of the water. Transfer to a blender and add lemon juice. Cover and blend at medium speed 20 seconds, until smooth. *Makes 1⅛ cups.* Cover and store in refrigerator. For diet serving allow 3 tablespoons.

Per diet serving: 96 calories, 1 gram protein, 0 grams fat, 25 grams carbohydrate.

Farmer's Meat Loaf

¼ pound fresh mushrooms,
  chopped fine (1¼ cups)
1 large green pepper, seeded and
  diced fine (1 cup)
1 large carrot, peeled and diced
  (½ cup)

1½ cups minced, peeled onion
1½ pounds lean ground beef
1 cup plain low-fat yogurt
6 teaspoons soy sauce

Heat oven to 375°F. Mix vegetables in a large bowl. Add meat and, with
hands or two large spoons, work meat and vegetables together. Add
yogurt and all but 1 teaspoon of the soy sauce and mix thoroughly.
Turn out into a shallow baking pan and shape into an oval loaf about
11 x 6 inches. Bake 50 minutes. Combine remaining teaspoon of the
soy sauce with a few spoonfuls of the pan juices and brush over meat
loaf. Bake 10 minutes longer. *Makes 4 to 6 servings.* For diet serving
allow ⅙ of the loaf.

Per diet serving: 260 calories, 27 grams protein, 12 grams fat, 11 grams carbohydrate.

Hot Baked Jelly Apples

4 small Golden Delicious apples
8 teaspoons apricot preserves

Water

Heat oven to 375°F. With a vegetable peeler or apple corer, core each
apple. Peel an inch-wide strip from the circumference of each apple. Fill
the cavity of each apple with 2 teaspoons of the preserves. Place apples
in an 8-inch square baking dish and fill dish with water to a depth of
1 inch. Cover with foil and bake 30 minutes. Uncover and bake 20 to 30
minutes longer. Serve warm or cold. *Makes 4 servings.* For diet serving
allow 1 apple.

Per diet serving: 99 calories, 0 grams protein, 0 grams fat, 25 grams carbohydrate.

BREAKFAST

1 snack-sized bagel or ½ regular
   bagel (76), spread with ½ ounce
   cream cheese (50)
1 cup tomato juice (46)

LUNCH

* California Chicken Salad (222)
1 cup fresh spinach leaves (14)
1 slice whole-wheat bread (61),
   spread with 1 teaspoon butter or
   margarine (34)
½ cup vanilla low-fat yogurt (97)

DINNER

* Pita Pizza (336)
1 cup torn lettuce leaves (10), with
   Basic Vinaigrette Dressing
   (recipe on page 23, 31)
⅒ honeydew melon (49)

TO EAT ANY TIME

1 cup skim milk (86)
1 slice rye bread (61), spread with
   1 teaspoon butter or margarine
   (34)

California Chicken Salad

2 cups shredded, skinless, cooked
   chicken meat (¾ pound)
⅓ cup sliced cucumber
⅓ cup alfalfa sprouts
1 hard-cooked egg, peeled and
   chopped

2 tablespoons freshly squeezed
   lemon juice
4½ teaspoons vegetable oil
1½ teaspoons water
1½ teaspoons soy sauce
½ teaspoon Dijon-style mustard
⅛ teaspoon black pepper

In a medium-sized bowl mix chicken, cucumber, sprouts and egg; cover
tightly and refrigerate until serving time. In a small screw-top jar or
bowl mix remaining ingredients until well blended. Just before serving,
shake or whisk lemon juice dressing, pour over chicken and toss to
coat. *Makes 3 cups chicken salad.* For diet serving allow ¾ cup.

Per diet serving: 222 calories, 30 grams protein, 11 grams fat, 2 grams carbohydrate.

Pita Pizza

4 1-ounce pita breads
½ cup pizza sauce, from a can or jar
½ teaspoon dried oregano leaves
4 ounces grated mozzarella cheese
4 teaspoons grated Parmesan cheese
4 thin slices seeded green pepper
4 thin slices fresh mushroom (optional)

Heat oven to 400°F. (see note). Put pita breads bottom side up on a baking sheet. Spread each with 2 tablespoons pizza sauce and sprinkle with oregano. Top with mozzarella, Parmesan, green pepper and mushroom slices. Bake 10 minutes, until cheeses have melted. *Makes 4 "pizzas."* For diet serving allow 2 pizzas.

NOTE: Pita Pizzas may also be baked two at a time in a toaster-oven. Reduce cooking time to 5 minutes.

Per diet serving: 336 calories, 24 grams protein, 10 grams fat, 35 grams carbohydrate.

Being Prepared for a Hunger Attack

A crisis like the baby's crying all night or your boss's behaving as though nothing you said or did was right can bring on a hunger attack. Be prepared with an assortment of low-calorie foods like green peppers, green beans, celery, lettuce, cucumber, zucchini sticks. They're all good for munching on viciously and sometimes the munch is a greater need to satisfy than the hunger. Little rewards like raisins (26 calories per tablespoon) or pretzel sticks (12 calories for 10 sticks) will also ease the pang.

BREAKFAST

Fresh Fruit Compote: ½ orange, peeled and sectioned (32); ½ banana, sliced (50)
1 medium-sized egg, scrambled without fat (72)
2 *Melba Muffins (60), spread with 1 teaspoon butter or margarine (34)

LUNCH

½ cup creamed cottage cheese (130), mixed with 1 medium-sized carrot, diced (15) and ½ green pepper, diced (8)
4 radishes (5)
2 slices whole-wheat bread, toasted (122)
1½ cups tomato juice (69)

DINNER

* Steak with Red Peppers and Onions (307)
* Baked "French Fries" (65)
All-You-Want Salad: 1 cup chicory or escarole (10); 1 cup fresh spinach leaves (14); ¼ sweet onion, sliced (11); 5 cherry tomatoes (20); with Basic Vinaigrette Dressing (recipe on page 23, 31)
* Irish Coffee Mousse (141)

Melba Muffins

With a serrated knife, cut 1 *English muffin* horizontally into *4 thin slices*. (If muffins are very soft, freeze 30 minutes to firm before slicing.) Toast the slices. For diet serving allow 2 slices.

Per diet serving: 60 calories, 2 grams protein, 0 grams fat, 13 grams carbohydrate.

Steak with Red Peppers and Onions

1 1-pound bone-in sirloin steak, about 1 inch thick
1 tablespoon vegetable oil
½ pound sweet yellow onions, peeled and sliced (about 2 cups)

¼ teaspoon salt
1 large sweet red pepper, seeded and cut into 1½-inch-wide strips
1 tablespoon red wine vinegar
Coarse salt

Trim all fat from outer edges of meat. In a large skillet heat oil over moderate heat. Add onions and the ¼ teaspoon salt and cook 5 minutes, stirring often. Add pepper strips and vinegar, increase heat to moderately high and cook 5 minutes longer, stirring often, until onions begin to brown. Transfer vegetables to a serving platter, cover and keep warm.

Wipe skillet. Lightly sprinkle bottom of skillet with coarse salt and place over high heat. When a drop of water dropped in pan skips across the bottom, it's ready. Place steak in pan and cook 5 minutes per side for medium, 4 minutes per side for medium-rare. (Pan will smoke heavily.) Remove meat and let stand 5 minutes to retain juices. To serve, slice steak thinly and arrange over vegetables; pour meat juices over all. *Makes 2 servings.* For diet serving allow ½ the vegetables and 3 ounces cooked meat.

Per diet serving: 307 calories, 30 grams protein, 14 grams fat, 16 grams carbohydrate.

Baked "French Fries"

Heat oven to 400°F. Peel 2 *small all-purpose potatoes* and cut into *½-inch-thick strips*. Place on a cookie sheet and bake 20 to 25 minutes, until lightly browned. Sprinkle with coarse salt before serving. *Makes 2 diet servings*; recipe may be halved.

Per diet serving: 65 calories, 2 grams protein, 0 grams fat, 15 grams carbohydrate.

Irish Coffee Mousse

1 envelope unflavored gelatin	Cold water
1 tablespoon instant espresso coffee granules	⅔ cup instant nonfat dry milk
¼ cup boiling water	2 tablespoons granulated sugar
1 tablespoon Irish whiskey, or water	Few grains of salt
	½ teaspoon vanilla extract
	1 cup ice cubes

Put gelatin and coffee in the bottom of a blender; add boiling water, cover and blend at low speed 10 seconds, until gelatin and coffee dissolve. Place whiskey in a 1-cup measuring cup and fill with cold water to ½ cup. Add whiskey-water, nonfat dry milk, sugar, salt and vanilla to blender; cover and blend at medium speed 10 seconds. Add ice, cover and blend at high speed 30 seconds, until most of the ice has melted. Uncover blender and let mousse stand 5 minutes to set before spooning out. *Makes 2 servings.* For diet serving allow ½ the mousse.

Per diet serving: 141 calories, 11 grams protein, 0 grams fat, 24 grams carbohydrate.

CHAPTER SEVEN

The World of Food: International Favorites

If you've browsed over or eaten many of the foods in this book, you'll know that a great many cooking styles and flavors have been used to provide a variety of tastes. Yet, some dieters have told *Redbook* they long for ethnic foods they learned to love as a child. In the twenty-one diet menus in this chapter we've decalorized many of the suggested favorites. Warning, don't expect your grandmother (Italian, Jewish, Spanish, German, whatever) to pronounce these recipes "authentic." But if you don't tell her these are updated to be less caloric, she just might enjoy your results. They will at least satisfy your longings within caloric limits because they have been faithfully adapted to their original taste.

The recipes in this chapter are not designed for use on successive days, although the menus for each day are nutritionally balanced. To fit these menus into a dieting program you should substitute like dinner foods in your diet week: pasta on a pasta day, fish on a fish day and so on. It's best to use the full day's menus given with whichever dinner you select.

BREAKFAST

1 medium-sized apple (78)
½ English muffin (76), spread
  with 1 tablespoon peanut butter
  (94)

LUNCH

Open-Face Sardine Sandwich:
  *Sardine Spread (116); 1 slice
  pumpernickel bread (79)
Tossed Salad: 1 cup torn lettuce
  (10); ¼ cup sliced cucumber (4);
  Basic Vinaigrette Dressing
  (recipe on page 23, 31)

DINNER

* Gazpacho (90)
* Enchiladas (324)
* Mexican Orange and Onion Salad
  (79)
* Baked Custard (80)

TO EAT ANY TIME

1 oatmeal cookie (59)
1 cup skim milk (86)

Sardine Spread

1 3¾-ounce can boneless, skinless
  sardines, drained
3 tablespoons 99%-fat-free cottage
  cheese
1 tablespoon finely chopped,
  peeled red onion

1 tablespoon liquid skim milk
1 tablespoon lemon juice
⅛ teaspoon black pepper
Few grains of salt

Using a fork, mix all ingredients in a small bowl until sardines are in
small pieces and mixture is well blended. *Makes about ⅓ cup.* For diet
serving allow ½ recipe.

Per diet serving: 116 calories, 14 grams protein, 5 grams fat, 1 gram carbohydrate.

Gazpacho

¼ cup unseasoned dry bread
  crumbs
2 pimientos, from can or jar,
  drained and chopped
2 tablespoons olive oil
2 tablespoons water
1 teaspoon salt
1 teaspoon minced, peeled garlic

5 large tomatoes, chopped (about
  2 pounds)
2 tablespoons red wine vinegar
2 cups tomato juice, chilled
1 green pepper, seeded and diced
1 small cucumber, diced
½ cup thin-sliced scallions or
  green onions

Put the bread crumbs, pimientos, olive oil, water, salt and garlic into a blender. Cover and blend about 30 seconds at medium speed, until well blended. If mixture is very dry, add 1 tablespoon more water. Put mixture into a small bowl, cover and refrigerate. Rinse blender container and add tomatoes; cover and blend about 30 seconds at medium speed, until pureed. (There should be about 3 cups tomato puree.) Pour tomatoes into a strainer placed over a large bowl. Using the back of a wooden spoon, press tomato puree through strainer; discard seed residue. Add the bread crumb paste and vinegar to the tomato liquid and mix with a wire whisk until well blended and smooth. Stir in tomato juice. Serve at once or cover and chill. Serve green pepper, cucumber and scallions in small bowls for each person to sprinkle on soup. *Makes 4½ cups soup.* For diet serving allow ¾ cup soup with ⅙ of the vegetables.

Per diet serving: 90 calories, 2 grams protein, 5 grams fat, 11 grams carbohydrate.

Enchiladas

4 corn tortillas, thawed if frozen
1 pound lean ground beef
1 7½-ounce can taco sauce, 2
  tablespoons reserved
1 tablespoon canned chopped
  green chilies
⅛ teaspoon ground cumin seed
2 tablespoons water
1 ounce Cheddar cheese, grated
  (about ¼ cup)
¼ medium avocado, cut into 4
  slices

In a heavy ungreased skillet over moderately high heat warm the tortillas, 1 or 2 at a time so they aren't overlapping. Heat, turning frequently, until they are soft and pliable, about 30 to 60 seconds. Transfer tortillas to a tightly covered ovenproof dish and keep warm in a 200°F. oven while making filling. In a large skillet brown meat over moderate heat. Drain and discard fat from skillet. Add taco sauce (reserve 2 tablespoons to use later), chilies and cumin to meat. Cook over moderate heat about 5 minutes, stirring frequently, until liquid is evaporated. In a cup mix the reserved 2 tablespoons of taco sauce with 2 tablespoons of water. Coat a shallow baking pan with the sauce mixture. Remove tortillas from oven; turn oven up to 350°F. Spoon ½ cup of the hot meat filling on one half of each tortilla; fold other half over. Arrange in baking dish and sprinkle with grated cheese. Bake about 10 to 15 minutes, just until cheese is melted. Garnish with avocado slices. *Makes 2 servings.* For diet serving allow 2 enchiladas, each garnished with 1 slice of avocado.

Per diet serving: 324 calories, 21 grams protein, 10 grams fat, 32 grams carbohydrate.

Mexican Orange and Onion Salad

2 tablespoons water
1 tablespoon vegetable oil
1 tablespoon lime juice
1½ teaspoons wine vinegar
⅛ teaspoon minced, peeled garlic
¼ teaspoon salt
Few drops Tabasco sauce

2 large navel oranges, peeled and
  sliced thin
1 small red onion, peeled and
  sliced thin
3 small ripe black olives, sliced
  thin
5 radishes, sliced thin
4 romaine lettuce leaves

In a small screw-top jar combine water, oil, lime juice, vinegar, garlic, salt and Tabasco. Cover and shake well. Arrange oranges, onion, olives and radishes on lettuce in a salad bowl. Just before serving, shake dressing and pour over salad. Toss gently. *Makes 3 or 4 servings*. For diet serving allow ¼ of the salad.

Per diet serving: 79 calories, 1 gram protein, 4 grams fat, 11 grams carbohydrate.

Baked Custard

2 large eggs
3 tablespoons granulated sugar
Few grains of salt

½ teaspoon vanilla extract
2 cups liquid skim milk
Ground nutmeg

Heat oven to 350°F. In a small bowl beat eggs, sugar, salt and vanilla until well blended. Stir in milk. Divide into six 6-ounce custard cups. Place cups in a 2-inch-deep baking pan; add water to the baking pan to a depth of ½ inch. Bake 40 minutes, or until a knife inserted in the custard comes out clean. Remove from oven and remove custards from water. Chill thoroughly. Sprinkle with nutmeg before serving. Custard keeps well for 3 or 4 days covered in the refrigerator. *Makes 6 servings*. For diet serving allow 1 custard.

NOTE: Custard may also be cooked on top of the stove. Pour water into a large pan to a depth of ½ inch, add filled custard cups, cover and cook over low heat about 1 hour, until a knife inserted in the custard comes out clean.

Per diet serving: 80 calories, 5 grams protein, 2 grams fat, 12 grams carbohydrate.

BREAKFAST

1 cup 4-grain multivitamin-and-iron-
    supplement cereal (110)
½ banana (50)
1 cup skim milk (86)

LUNCH

1 cup tomato juice (46)
Tuna–Bean Salad: 1 3-ounce can
    water-packed tuna, drained (117);
    ½ cup cooked kidney beans
    (109); Basic Vinaigrette Dressing
    (recipe on page 23, 31)
1 large dill pickle (15)
1 slice whole-wheat bread (61)

DINNER

* Chili–Beef Tacos (231)
Relish Plate: 1 stalk celery (7);
    1 Jalapeno pepper (23); ½ large
    carrot (15)
½ cup vanilla low-fat yogurt (97)
5 whole almonds (30)

TO EAT ANY TIME

6 saltine crackers (72), spread
    with 1 tablespoon peanut butter
    (94)

Chili–Beef Tacos

Filling:
1½ pounds lean ground beef
½ cup chopped, peeled onion
2 teaspoons minced, peeled garlic
2 teaspoons chili powder
2 teaspoons dried oregano leaves
¾ teaspoon salt
½ teaspoon ground cinnamon
½ teaspoon crushed red pepper
    flakes
½ teaspoon ground cumin
1 cup beef broth

2 tablespoons tomato paste
2 tablespoons wine vinegar

To Finish:
6 taco shells
¼ head lettuce, shredded
1 large tomato, chopped
4 thin-sliced scallions or green
    onions
1 ounce sharp Cheddar cheese,
    coarsely grated (¼ cup)

Filling: Heat a 14- to 15-inch skillet over moderately high heat for 30 seconds; add beef and cook 5 to 7 minutes, stirring occasionally and breaking up large pieces with a spoon, until meat has lost its pink color. Remove from heat and tip meat into a colander to drain; discard fat. Return meat to pan; add onions and garlic and cook 3 to 4 minutes, stirring occasionally, until onions are soft and translucent. Add remaining filling ingredients and cook about 10 minutes over high heat, stirring frequently, until liquid is absorbed.

To finish: Fill each taco shell with some lettuce and tomato, ¾ cup of the meat mixture and ¼ of the chopped scallions and grated cheese. *Makes 6 tacos.* For diet serving allow 1 taco.

Per diet serving: 231 calories, 25 grams protein, 6 grams fat, 18 grams carbohydrate.

BREAKFAST

½ medium grapefruit (40)
1 cup 4-grain multivitamin-and-iron-
    supplement cereal (110)
1½ tablespoons raisins (39)
1 cup skim milk (86)

LUNCH

Tuna Salad: 3 ounces water-packed
    tuna, drained (117); 1 stalk
    celery (7); 1 teaspoon minced
    onion (2); Basic Vinaigrette
    Dressing (recipe on page 23, 31)
8 canned or cooked fresh asparagus
    spears, chilled (24)
2 saltine crackers (24)

DINNER

* Nachos (417)
Iced Orange Drink: 1 cup orange
    juice (122), served in a tall glass
    over 4 ice cubes

TO EAT ANY TIME

1 cup skim milk (86)
1 pear (90)

Nachos

2 20-ounce cans red kidney beans,
    drained
1 4-ounce can chopped green
    chilies, drained
6 ounces sharp Cheddar cheese,
    diced (about 1½ cups)
1 teaspoon dried oregano leaves
½ cup Low-Calorie Sour Cream
    (recipe on page 173)

1 large tomato, diced (about
    1 cup)
1 medium-sized sweet yellow
    onion, peeled and diced
    (about 1 cup)
1 6-ounce bag tortilla chips
1 head iceberg lettuce, cut into
    8 wedges

Heat oven to 400°F. In a shallow baking dish about 8 to 10 inches in
diameter, mix beans, chilies, cheese and oregano. Bake 10 minutes, until
cheese melts. Spoon Low-Calorie Sour Cream into center of dish.
Arrange tomato and onion in a circular fashion around the cream. Serve
from dish using chips and lettuce as scoopers. *Makes 6 servings.* For
diet serving allow ⅙ of the dish.

Per diet serving: 417 calories, 21 grams protein, 16 grams fat, 48 grams carbohydrate.

BREAKFAST

1 cup cooked iron-enriched farina
  (100)
3 unsweetened prunes (52), mashed
  and spread on 1 slice cracked-
  wheat bread (66)
1 cup skim milk (86)

LUNCH

Canadian BLT: 2 ounces Canadian-
  style bacon, broiled (116); 1 cup
  torn Boston lettuce (8); ½ small
  tomato, sliced (10); 1 slice
  cracked-wheat bread (66)

DINNER

* Swedish Meatballs (250)
* Crisp Red Cabbage (111)
½ cup potato, mashed with milk
  and butter or margarine (93)

TO EAT ANY TIME

2 ounces Swiss cheese (214)
1 whole-grain rye wafer (23)
4 small radishes (5)

Swedish Meatballs

2 slices stale white bread, crusts
  removed
⅓ cup liquid skim milk
1 pound lean ground beef
¾ cup minced, peeled onion
1 teaspoon salt
½ teaspoon ground allspice

⅛ teaspoon black pepper
1 large egg
1 chicken bouillon cube, dissolved
  in ½ cup water
¼ teaspoon allspice
¼ cup plain low-fat yogurt
¼ cup commercial sour cream

Tear the bread into small pieces, put it into a medium-sized bowl, add the milk and let it soak 5 minutes. Add the beef, onion, salt, ½ teaspoon allspice, the pepper and the egg. Mix well with hands, and using 1 tablespoon for each, shape mixture into balls. Heat a large skillet over moderate heat; add meatballs and brown 5 minutes, shaking pan several times to turn meatballs. Remove meatballs to a bowl. Add chicken broth to skillet and heat, stirring to combine brown particles with broth. Add the remaining ¼ teaspoon of allspice, the yogurt and sour cream and mix well. Put meatballs back in skillet and heat over low heat for about 5 minutes, stirring to coat them with the sauce. Do not boil. *Makes 38 to 40 meatballs, or 5 to 6 servings.* For diet serving allow 7 meatballs and ⅙ of the sauce.

Per diet serving: 250 calories, 22 grams protein, 13 grams fat, 9 grams carbohydrate.

Crisp Red Cabbage

4 cups shredded red cabbage
(about ¾ pound)
2 medium-sized tart apples, like
Granny Smiths, cored and cut
into thin wedges
¼ cup red wine vinegar

2 tablespoons light or dark brown
sugar
1 tablespoon lightly salted butter
or margarine
¼ teaspoon ground nutmeg

Place cabbage, apples, vinegar and brown sugar in a large saucepan over moderate heat. Stir to mix, cover and simmer about 10 minutes, until cabbage is crisp-tender. Add butter and nutmeg and toss to mix. *Makes about 4 cups, or 4 servings.* For diet serving allow 1 cup.

Per diet serving: 111 calories, 2 grams protein, 3 grams fat, 21 grams carbohydrate.

BREAKFAST

½ cup unsweetened grapefruit
  juice (51)
1 large egg, hard-cooked (82)
½ toasted English muffin (74),
  spread with 1 teaspoon butter or
  margarine (34)

LUNCH

* Turkish Eggplant Salad (128) on
  ¼ head lettuce, shredded (15),
  sprinkled with 1 ounce shredded
  Swiss cheese (107)
2 whole-grain rye wafers (45)
1½ tablespoons seedless raisins (39)

DINNER

* Flounder Sylvette (177)
1 unpeeled medium steamed or
  boiled potato (104)
6 canned asparagus spears (27)
1 cup fresh or unsweetened frozen
  strawberries (55), sprinkled with
  1 teaspoon sugar (15)

TO EAT ANY TIME

2 cups skim milk (172)
½ medium-sized banana (50)
2 vanilla wafers (28)

Turkish Eggplant Salad

1 small eggplant (about 1¼
  pounds)
¼ teaspoon minced, peeled garlic
½ teaspoon salt
¼ cup minced, peeled onion

1 tablespoon freshly squeezed
  lemon juice
1 tablespoon olive or vegetable
  oil

Wipe eggplant and prick all over with a fork. Place in the oven on a baking sheet. Turn on oven to 500°F. and bake 20 minutes. Turn eggplant over and bake 25 minutes longer. Remove from oven and let cool enough to handle. Meanwhile, in a mixing bowl mash garlic and salt with a wooden spoon. Hold eggplant over the bowl, slit skin and scrape flesh into bowl. Discard eggplant skin. Stir in remaining ingredients, cover salad and refrigerate several hours. *Makes about 1¾ cups.* For diet serving allow ½ the salad.

Per diet serving: 128 calories, 3 grams protein, 7 grams fat, 15 grams carbohydrate.

Flounder Sylvette

¾ cup diced, peeled carrot
⅓ cup thinly sliced celery
½ cup diced, peeled onion
1 cup finely diced, peeled potato
½ cup water

½ teaspoon salt
⅛ teaspoon white pepper
4 large lettuce leaves
1 1-pound block frozen flounder
  fillets, partially thawed

In a medium-sized skillet mix the carrot, celery, onion and potato and then stir in the water, salt and pepper. Cover and bring to a simmer over moderately high heat; reduce heat to moderate and cook 5 minutes. Arrange lettuce leaves over vegetables. Cut block of fish in thirds crosswise and arrange on top of lettuce. Cover and steam over moderate heat 15 to 20 minutes, until fish is white and opaque in the thickest part. *Makes 3 servings.* For diet serving allow ⅓ of fish and vegetables.

Per diet serving: 177 calories, 28 grams protein, 1 gram fat, 13 grams carbohydrate.

BREAKFAST

½ medium-sized grapefruit (40)
¾ cup bran flakes with added
  thiamin and iron (70)
3 tablespoons dark seedless raisins
  (78)
¾ cup skim milk (65)

LUNCH

Sardine Sandwich: 3 ounces sardines
  with skin and bones, drained
  (187); 2 slices sweet onion (6);
  2 slices rye bread (122)
1 small apple (61)
½ cup skim milk (43) with ½ cup
  coffee, served iced or hot

DINNER

* Arroz con Pollo (254)
¾ cup cooked asparagus pieces (23)
2 cups shredded lettuce (20), with
  2 tablespoons Basic Vinaigrette
  Dressing (recipe on page 23, 62)
1 syrup-packed peach half with about
  1½ tablespoons syrup (59),
  sprinkled with 1 tablespoon
  toasted chopped almonds (48)

TO EAT ANY TIME

1 cup tomato juice (46), mixed with
  ½ cup beef broth (15), heated

Arroz con Pollo

1 2½-pound frying chicken,
  cut up
¾ cup chopped, peeled onion
1¼ teaspoons minced, peeled
  garlic
1 cup water
1 chicken bouillon cube
1 16-ounce can plus 1 8-ounce
  can whole peeled tomatoes

1 bay leaf
¾ teaspoon dried oregano leaves
1 cup converted long-grain white
  rice
1 10-ounce package frozen green
  peas
3 pimientos from a can or jar,
  drained and cut in strips

Heat a large skillet over moderate heat. Add chicken pieces, skin side
down, and cook about 10 minutes to brown. Turn chicken and brown
the other side. Remove browned chicken to a 3-quart casserole with a
tight-fitting cover. Heat oven to 350°F. Add onion and garlic to skillet
and cook about 3 minutes, stirring occasionally, until soft. Add water
and bouillon cube; crush cube and stir liquid to dissolve cube and
loosen brown particles from bottom of skillet. Stir in tomatoes, bay
leaf and oregano and bring mixture to a boil. Stir in rice and pour
mixture over chicken in casserole. Cover and bake 35 minutes. Put
peas in a strainer and rinse with water to remove ice. Remove casserole
from oven and stir in peas. Arrange pimientos on top. Cover and bake
10 minutes longer. *Makes 4 to 6 servings.* For diet serving allow 3 ounces
of chicken and ¾ cup of the rice and vegetables.

Per diet serving: 254 calories, 27 grams protein, 4 grams fat, 29 grams carbohydrate.

BREAKFAST

* Coffee Shake (154)
1 slice white bread, toasted (68),
    spread with 1½ teaspoons butter
    or margarine (51)
1 medium egg (72), prepared any
    style, without butter or margarine

LUNCH

Beef on Rye: 3 ounces lean roast
    beef (161); 2 leaves soft lettuce
    (2); 1 slice rye bread (61), spread
    with ½ tablespoon bottled
    Russian dressing (37)

DINNER

* Stuffed Cabbage (189)
½ cup cooked rice (93)
½ cup sliced fresh mushrooms (10),
    cooked with 1 teaspoon oil (40)
    and 1 teaspoon butter or
    margarine (34)
Fall Fruit Compote: 4 dried, pitted
    prunes (66) and 5 dried apricot
    halves (46), cooked without sugar
    and mixed with ¼ cup sliced
    bananas (26)

TO EAT ANY TIME

1 cup skim milk (86)

Coffee Shake

1 cup skim milk
1½ teaspoons granulated sugar
1 tablespoon instant coffee
    granules

1½ tablespoons instant non-fat
    dry milk

Put all ingredients in a blender, cover and blend until smooth and foamy. Serve over ice cubes in a tall glass. *Makes 1 diet serving.*

Per diet serving: 154 calories, 12 grams protein, 0 grams fat, 24 grams carbohydrate.

Stuffed Cabbage

1 2-pound head of green cabbage
Water
1 pound lean ground beef
¾ cup finely chopped, peeled
  onion
½ cup cooked rice (see note)
2 teaspoons salt

¼ teaspoon black pepper
1 1-pound can whole tomatoes
2 tablespoons dark seedless raisins
1½ teaspoons lemon juice
2 tablespoons brown sugar
⅔ cup thinly sliced, peeled onion

Place cabbage in a large saucepot or kettle and add enough water to cover. Cover pot and bring to a boil over high heat. Reduce heat to moderate and cook about 15 minutes, until cabbage is tender. Meanwhile, in a large bowl mix ground beef with chopped onion, rice, 1 teaspoon of the salt and the pepper. When cabbage is tender, drain and let cool until it is comfortable to touch. Core cabbage with a knife and remove leaves one by one. Put 2 tablespoons of meat mixture at the core end of each leaf, wrap end of leaf over meat, fold in sides and roll up. Put tomatoes and their juice in a 5-quart saucepot or Dutch oven and break up tomatoes with a spoon. Add raisins, lemon juice, brown sugar, sliced onion and the remaining 1 teaspoon of salt. Arrange cabbage rolls in pot. Bring to a simmer over moderately high heat. Turn heat to moderately low, cover pot and cook 1 hour. *Makes about 20 cabbage rolls, or 6 servings.* For diet serving allow 3 rolls and 3 tablespoons sauce.

NOTE: Cook extra rice to serve with Stuffed Cabbage.

Per diet serving: 189 calories, 16 grams protein, 7 grams fat, 16 grams carbohydrate.

BREAKFAST

1 medium egg (72), prepared any
  style, without butter or margarine
1 slice cracked-wheat bread,
  toasted (66)
1 cup tomato juice (46)

LUNCH

Toasted Swiss–Ham Sandwich:
  1 ounce Swiss cheese (107),
  melted over 1 ounce ham (66) on
  1 slice rye bread (61)
Spinach–Mushroom Salad: 2 cups
  torn spinach leaves (28); ½ cup
  sliced fresh mushrooms (10); 2
  teaspoons oil (80); 1 tablespoon
  lemon juice (4)
1 cup canned green pea soup, made
  with skim milk (179)

DINNER

* Sauerbraten with Tangy Vegetable
  Sauce (197)
½ cup mashed turnips (27)
1 cup braised turnip greens (29)
2 gingersnaps (59)

TO EAT ANY TIME

1 cup skim milk (86)
3 tablespoons raisins (78)
1 6-inch stalk celery (5)

Sauerbraten with Tangy Vegetable Sauce

1 cup cider vinegar
1½ cups water
2 tablespoons light or dark brown
  sugar
½ teaspoon ground cloves
½ teaspoon ground cinnamon
1 teaspoon salt
½ teaspoon black pepper

4 peppercorns
1 bay leaf
1 cup diced, peeled onion
1½ cups diced, peeled carrot
1⅓ cups diced celery
1 4-pound boneless beef round or
  rump roast, trimmed of all
  visible fat

In a medium-sized saucepan combine all ingredients except meat and stir over moderate heat until mixture is simmering. Remove pan from heat and cool about 30 minutes. Place meat in a large bowl and pour the cooled vinegar marinade over it. Cover and refrigerate 8 to 12 hours, turning meat once or twice in the marinade. Discard peppercorns and bay leaf. Remove meat from marinade and dry with paper towels. Place meat with the fattiest side down in a large, heavy pot over moderately high heat. When some of the fat has cooked out, turn and brown on all sides. Pour marinade into a strainer set over measuring cup. Add vegetables to pot along with ½ cup of the liquid. Cover and cook over moderately low heat for 2 hours, until meat is tender. Remove meat to a serving platter. Pour vegetables and liquid from pot into a blender. Cover and blend a few seconds at medium speed to make a smooth puree. Cut meat into thin slices and serve the pureed vegetable sauce separately. *Makes 8 to 10 servings.* For diet serving allow 3 ounces of meat and ¼ cup of the sauce.

Per diet serving: 197 calories, 25 grams protein, 8 grams fat, 5 grams carbohydrate.

Good Gravy

Gravies and sauces don't have to be off-limits. You can make delicious ones without the addition of flour, cornstarch or other thickeners such as egg yolks, by pureeing the cooked vegetables in stewed or poached meat, fish or poultry with the broth they were cooked in. Delicious examples with beef, Sauerbraten with Tangy Vegetable Sauce, Chapter 7; with fish, Fish with Pureed Vegetable Sauce, Chapter 3; with poultry, Michel Guérard's Chicken Poached in Apple Cider, Chapter 5.

BREAKFAST

½ cup unsweetened grapefruit
   juice (51)
⅔ cup cooked oatmeal (99)
1 cup skim milk (86)

LUNCH

Tuna Salad Plate: 3 ounces water-
   packed tuna, drained (117);
   1 lettuce leaf (1); 1 celery stalk,
   cut into sticks (7); 1 scallion or
   green onion (6); 1 teaspoon
   mayonnaise (34)
1 ½-inch-thick slice French bread
   (2½ x 2 inches, 44)
1 pear (90)

DINNER

½ cup apple juice (59)
* Hungarian Goulash (294)
½ cup cooked noodles (100)
1 large dill pickle (15)
1 cup cooked spinach (41), served
   with a lemon wedge (2)
3 medium-sized, water-packed
   apricot halves and 1¾ tablespoons
   juice (32)

TO EAT ANY TIME

1 cup skim milk (86)
1 small orange (45)

Hungarian Goulash

¾ cup beef bouillon or
   consommé
¾ cup water
¾ cup tomato juice
1½ pounds beef bottom round,
   cut into 1-inch cubes
½ medium-sized green pepper,
   seeded and diced

¾ teaspoon paprika
1 bay leaf
¾ teaspoon salt
⅛ teaspoon black pepper
2 medium-sized potatoes, peeled
   and halved
4 medium-sized carrots, peeled
   and cut into 1½-inch pieces

Early in the day, or the day before, put consommé, water, tomato juice, meat, green pepper, paprika, bay leaf, salt and pepper in a large sauce-pot or Dutch oven. Cover and cook over moderately high heat until mixture comes to a boil; reduce heat to moderately low and cook 1½ to 2 hours, or until meat is almost tender. Remove pot from heat. Cool and chill in refrigerator so that fat will harden on surface. Remove and discard all hardened fat. Place goulash over high heat until liquid boils; reduce heat to moderately low, add potatoes and carrots and cook 20 to 25 minutes, or until vegetables and meat are tender. *Makes 3 or 4 servings.* For diet serving allow ¼ of the sauce, 1 carrot, ½ potato and 3 ounces of meat.

Per diet serving: 294 calories, 13 grams protein, 11 grams fat, 39 grams carbohydrate.

BREAKFAST

¼ cantaloupe (41), served with
a lime wedge
1 cup 4-grain multivitamin-and-iron-
supplement cereal (110)
1 cup skim milk (86)

LUNCH

Peanut Butter Sandwich: 2 tablespoons peanut butter (188); 1
tablespoon raisins (26); 2 slices
whole-wheat bread (112)
1 medium-sized carrot (30)
½ cup skim milk (43)

DINNER

* Persian Meatballs (309)
* Pita Salad Sandwich (108)
2 purple plums (64)

TO EAT ANY TIME

10 seedless grapes (34)
½ cup skim milk (43)

Persian Meatballs

1½ pounds lean ground beef
¾ cup minced, peeled onion
1 teaspoon salt, ¼ teaspoon
reserved
½ teaspoon black pepper
1¼ teaspoons ground coriander
seed, 1 teaspoon reserved

2 cloves garlic, peeled and
cracked open
1 13¾-ounce can beef broth
1 tablespoon lemon juice
1 20-ounce can chick-peas, drained
1 10-ounce package fresh spinach,
washed and thick stems
removed

In a medium-sized bowl mix beef, onion, ¾ teaspoon of the salt, the
pepper and ¼ teaspoon of the coriander until thoroughly combined.
Shape into sixteen 1½-inch-round meatballs, using about 3 tablespoons
meat mixture for each. Sprinkle the remaining ¼ teaspoon salt in the
bottom of a large saucepot or Dutch oven. Heat over moderately high
heat; add meatballs and cook 5 minutes, turning once, until browned.
Cover pot and cook 10 minutes longer, until meatballs are no longer
pink in the center. Set a colander over a bowl and drain meatballs;
return meatballs to pot. Using a metal spoon, skim off and discard fat
from liquid remaining in bowl. Pour liquid over meatballs in pot and
add the remaining 1 teaspoon coriander, the garlic, beef broth and
lemon juice. Cover and cook over moderately low heat 15 minutes.
Discard garlic. Stir in chick-peas and arrange spinach on top. Cover
and cook 5 minutes, until spinach has wilted slightly. *Makes 4 to 6*

servings. For diet serving allow 2 meatballs and ⅙ of the vegetables and broth.

Per diet serving: 309 calories, 26 grams protein, 12 grams fat, 26 grams carbohydrate.

Pita Salad Sandwiches

4 cups crisp, torn lettuce leaves
⅓ cup chopped, seeded green
  pepper

¾ cup Basic Vinaigrette Dressing
  (recipe on page 23)
4 1-ounce pita breads

In a medium-sized bowl toss lettuce and green pepper with dressing until leaves are well coated. Make a slit in the side of each pita bread and fill with 1 cup of the salad mixture. *Makes 4 sandwiches.* For diet serving allow 1 filled pita sandwich.

Per diet serving: 108 calories, 3 grams protein, 4 grams fat, 16 grams carbohydrate.

BREAKFAST

¾ cup bran flakes with added
thiamin and iron (70), sprinkled
with 1 tablespoon toasted wheat
germ (23) and 1 teaspoon
granulated sugar (15)
1 cup skim milk (86)
½ cup orange juice, made from
frozen concentrate (61), or ½
large banana (50)

LUNCH

* Chopped Chicken Livers (185)
on 1 slice whole-wheat or rye
bread (61) with 1 slice sweet
onion (3)
1 cup tomato juice (46)

DINNER

* Noodle Kugel (249)
½ cup cooked green peas (57)
Crisp Cabbage Salad: 1 cup finely
shredded cabbage (22), tossed
with 1 teaspoon oil (40), 1
tablespoon wine vinegar (2), a
pinch of dried dillweed, salt and
pepper
* Cranberry–Peach Betty (139)

TO EAT ANY TIME

1 cup fresh or unsweetened frozen
strawberries (55)
1 cup skim milk (86)

Chopped Chicken Livers

1 pound chicken livers
1 chicken bouillon cube
½ cup water
1 tablespoon vegetable oil

½ cup finely chopped, peeled
onion
½ teaspoon salt
⅛ teaspoon pepper

Rinse livers and remove any bits of fat clinging to them; pat dry with
paper towels. In a small saucepan dissolve bouillon cube in water. Add
livers and bring to a boil over moderately high heat. Reduce heat to
moderate and simmer gently 7 minutes, until livers are just firm. With
a slotted spoon remove livers to a bowl. Reserve cooking liquid. In a
small skillet heat oil over moderately high heat; add onion and cook
about 10 minutes, stirring often, until onion begins to brown. Add
onion and pan juices to livers and then add 2 tablespoons of the reserved
cooking liquid. Chop or mash the livers and onion to a coarse paste.
Mix in salt and pepper. *Makes about 2 cups, or 3 or 4 servings.* For diet
serving allow ½ cup.

Per diet serving: 185 calories, 23 grams protein, 8 grams fat, 5 grams carbohydrate.

Noodle Kugel

1 teaspoon butter or margarine
½ pound fresh mushrooms, sliced
 (3 cups)
½ cup sliced scallions or green
 onions
2 tablespoons plain low-fat yogurt
2 tablespoons commercial sour
 cream

½ pound medium egg noodles,
 cooked according to package
 directions and drained
½ teaspoon salt
⅛ teaspoon black pepper
1 pound cottage cheese
4 large eggs, beaten
2 tablespoons freshly grated
 Parmesan cheese

In a medium-sized skillet melt butter over moderate heat. Add mushrooms and scallions and cook, stirring constantly, until liquid comes
out of mushrooms. Add yogurt and sour cream and stir until mixture
is hot but not boiling. Remove skillet from heat. Heat oven to 350°F.
Put drained, cooked noodles in a 2-quart casserole; add mushroom
mixture, salt, pepper and cottage cheese. Stir thoroughly to blend. Mix
in eggs. Level surface of kugel, sprinkle with Parmesan and bake 1
hour, until hot and browned. *Makes 6 servings.* For diet serving allow
⅛ of the kugel.

NOTE: Kugel may be assembled ahead and refrigerated.

Per diet serving: 249 calories, 16 grams protein, 9 grams fat, 25 grams carbohydrate.

Cranberry–Peach Betty

2 cups fresh or frozen cranberries
2 tablespoons red raspberry
 preserves
1 29-ounce can syrup-packed
 peach slices, drained, rinsed
 and thoroughly drained

4 slices white bread
1 tablespoon softened butter or
 margarine
1 tablespoon granulated sugar
 mixed with ⅛ teaspoon ground
 cinnamon

In an 8-inch square aluminum baking pan place cranberries and preserves and stir to coat cranberries with preserves. Cover pan tightly with
foil and place over moderately high heat about 5 minutes, until cranberries pop their skins. Remove from heat, add peaches and stir to
combine, being careful not to break the fruit. Spread bread with the
butter and cut into small squares. Scatter bread cubes over fruit and
sprinkle with cinnamon sugar. Heat oven to 350°F. Bake 30 to 40
minutes, until bread is browned and crisp. *Makes 4 to 6 servings.* For
diet serving allow ⅙ of the dessert.

Per diet serving: 139 calories, 2 grams protein, 3 grams fat, 27 grams carbohydrate.

BREAKFAST

½ grapefruit (40)
2 ounces broiled kippers (120)
½ bagel (83)

LUNCH

Pumpernickel Sandwich: 2 ounces
farmer's cheese (48); 6 cucumber
slices (4); 2 slices pumpernickel
bread (158)
1 pear (90)

DINNER

* Stewed Chicken with Matzo
Balls (312)
Dried-Fruit Compote: ¼ cup cooked
unsweetened prunes (63) and
¼ cup cooked unsweetened
apricots (53)

TO EAT ANY TIME

1 cup skim milk (86)
1 small apple (61)
½ cup seedless grapes (53)
2 vanilla wafers (28)

Stewed Chicken with Matzo Balls

1 5½-pound fowl, cut up
Boiling water
1 sprig parsley
1 bay leaf
1 small onion, peeled and cut in
half
2 small carrots, peeled and cut
into 1-inch slices

1 stalk celery
½ pound fresh green beans,
trimmed and sliced in 1-inch
pieces
½ pound fresh peas, shelled
2 teaspoons salt
Matzo Balls (recipe on page 234)

Clean and wash fowl. Place the chicken pieces in a large saucepot or
Dutch oven and add boiling water to cover. Add parsley, bay leaf, onion,
carrots and celery. Cover and cook over low heat 2 hours. Add beans,
peas and salt; cover and cook ½ hour longer or until chicken is tender.
Remove from heat. Lift chicken and vegetables onto a platter; keep
warm. Let broth cool.

Meanwhile, make up the Matzo Balls. With a large spoon skim fat
off the cooled broth. Heat broth to boiling; drop balls into boiling soup
and simmer 15 minutes. Remove balls and keep warm. Return chicken
and vegetables to pot and heat. *Makes 4 to 6 servings.* For diet serving
allow 3 ounces chicken, ¼ cup carrots, ¼ cup peas, ½ cup green beans,
2 matzo balls and as much broth as desired.

Per diet serving (including matzo balls): 312 calories, 33 grams protein, 10 grams fat, 22 grams
carbohydrate.

Matzo Balls

1 cup hot chicken broth	1 egg, slightly beaten
1 cup matzo meal	½ teaspoon salt
2 tablespoons vegetable oil	Few grains ground nutmeg

In a small bowl combine matzo meal and hot broth; mix well. Add oil, egg and seasonings; mix until blended. Chill. Form rounded tablespoons of dough into balls. Cook as directed above. *Makes 12 matzo balls.*

Per diet serving: 111 calories, 3 grams protein, 6 grams fat, 11 grams carbohydrate.

Don't Just Say "Cheese"

Many traditional Italian pasta dishes call for whole-milk ricotta cheese (789 calories per pound) or mozzarella (1,276 calories per pound). Choose instead part-skim ricotta for 626 calories or part-skim mozzarella for 1,153 calories per pound. Or replace the ricotta with creamed cottage cheese and slide the caloric count down to 481 calories per pound. Or go to 99%-fat-free cottage cheese and pare on down to 328 calories per pound.

BREAKFAST

1 large egg, prepared any style,
without butter or margarine (82)
½ English muffin (74), spread
with 1 teaspoon butter or
margarine (34)
2 ounces cooked Canadian-style
bacon (116)

LUNCH

Open-Face Sardine Sandwich:
1 3¼-ounce can sardines, drained
(187); 2 slices red onion (6);
2 lettuce leaves (3); 2 radishes,
sliced (1); 1 slice rye bread (61)
¾ cup unsweetened applesauce
(75)

DINNER

* Pasta, Tomatoes and Peas (256)
Tossed Salad: 2 cups torn lettuce
leaves (20); ½ medium-sized
carrot, sliced (15); Basic
Vinaigrette Dressing (recipe on
page 23, 31)
1 ½-inch-thick slice French bread
(about 2½ x 2 inches, 44)

TO EAT ANY TIME

1 cup corn flakes (110)
1 cup skim milk (86)

Pasta, Tomatoes and Peas

½ teaspoon butter or margarine
½ cup chopped, peeled onion
1 28-ounce can whole, peeled
tomatoes, undrained
½ teaspoon dried basil leaves
¼ teaspoon salt

¼ teaspoon ground black pepper
1 10-ounce package (1⅓ cups)
frozen green peas, thawed
6 ounces (about 2 cups) macaroni
twists, cooked according to
package directions and drained

In a large saucepot or Dutch oven melt butter over moderately high heat. Add onions and cook 3 to 5 minutes, stirring frequently, until soft and translucent. Add tomatoes and their liquid; break up tomatoes with a spoon. Stir in basil, salt and pepper. Reduce heat to moderately low and simmer 10 to 12 minutes; add peas and cook 5 minutes longer, until heated through. Just before serving, stir in macaroni. Serve in a bowl and eat with a spoon. *Makes 3 or 4 servings.* For diet serving allow ¼ of the pasta and vegetables.

Per diet serving: 256 calories, 11 grams protein, 1 gram fat, 52 grams carbohydrate.

BREAKFAST

1 frozen waffle (120), with 1
   teaspoon butter or margarine
   (34), and 2 teaspoons blueberry
   preserves (37)
½ cup skim milk (43)

LUNCH

* Polenta Pizza (299)
5 dried apricot halves (55)
1 cup skim milk (86)

DINNER

* Chicken Scallopini with Linguini
   and Mushrooms (398)
Tossed Salad: 1 cup romaine lettuce
   leaves (10); 1 small tomato,
   sliced (20); Basic Vinaigrette
   Dressing (recipe on page 23, 31)
2 syrup-packed purple plums with
   2 tablespoons syrup (74)

Polenta Pizza

1 cup water
½ teaspoon salt
1 cup yellow cornmeal
1 8-ounce can tomato sauce
2 tablespoons tomato paste
⅛ teaspoon garlic powder

½ teaspoon dried basil leaves
8 ounces part-skim mozzarella
   cheese, grated (2 cups)
1 green pepper, seeded and cut
   into rings

Heat oven to 350°F. Grease a 12-inch pizza pan. In a medium-sized
saucepan bring water to a boil. Remove from heat and add salt and
cornmeal; stir until all the water is absorbed and cornmeal is a thick,
moist paste. Using wet fingertips, press cornmeal mixture evenly on the
prepared pizza pan. Bake 20 minutes, until dry and slightly crisp around
the edges. In a small bowl mix tomato sauce, tomato paste, garlic
powder and basil. Sprinkle half the cheese over cornmeal; pour sauce
over cheese and top with remaining cheese. Arrange pepper rings on
top and bake 15 minutes, until cheese has melted. *Makes 1 pizza, 3 or 4
servings.* For diet serving allow ¼ of the pizza.

NOTE: Eat this pizza with a fork.

Per diet serving: 299 calories, 18 grams protein, 10 grams fat, 35 grams carbohydrate.

Chicken Scallopini with Linguini and Mushrooms

¼ cup unseasoned dry bread
  crumbs
¼ teaspoon salt
Few grains of black pepper
2 tablespoons grated Parmesan
  cheese
2 boned, skinless chicken breasts
  (1 pound), cut in half
2 tablespoons butter or margarine
1 teaspoon chicken-flavor instant
  bouillon granules, dissolved in
  ¼ cup hot water

2 tablespoons dry sherry wine
8 ounces fresh mushrooms, sliced
  (2 cups)
1 teaspoon freshly squeezed
  lemon juice
6 ounces linguini, cooked
  according to package directions
  and drained (about 2½ cups
  cooked)
Lemon slices (optional)

On a plate mix bread crumbs, salt, pepper and cheese. Fold back small fillet of meat on underside of each chicken breast half. Place breasts between 2 sheets of wax paper and pound to ⅛-inch thickness. Coat breasts with crumb mixture, shaking off excess. In a 14- to 15-inch skillet melt 1 tablespoon of the butter over moderately high heat. Add chicken and cook 4 to 5 minutes on each side, until golden, adding more of the butter as needed. Transfer cooked chicken to a dish and keep warm. Add bouillon and sherry to skillet and stir briskly to release browned bits from bottom. Lift skillet and swirl frothing liquid around. Return to heat; add mushrooms and lemon juice and cook a few seconds, stirring constantly, until sauce looks syrupy. Quickly arrange linguini on a platter and toss with mushroom sauce. Arrange chicken and lemon slices on top. *Makes 3 or 4 servings.* For diet serving allow ½ chicken breast and ¼ of the linguini and sauce.

Per diet serving: 398 calories, 36 grams protein, 12 grams fat, 37 grams carbohydrate.

BREAKFAST

1 cup bran flakes with added thiamin and iron (105)
¾ cup skim milk (65)
5 dried, pitted prunes (82)

LUNCH

Roast Beef Sandwich: 3 ounces lean roast beef (161); 1 slice rye bread (61), spread with 1 teaspoon prepared mustard (4)
Marinated Broccoli Salad: 1 cup cooked broccoli pieces (40), tossed with 2 teaspoons oil (80), 1 tablespoon lemon juice (4), salt and pepper

DINNER

* Lasagna (326)
2 cups torn Boston lettuce leaves (16), tossed with 2 tablespoons Basic Vinaigrette Dressing (recipe on page 23, 62)
Pineapple–Raspberry Compote: ¼ cup juice-packed pineapple chunks (24); ⅓ cup thawed frozen raspberries (69)

TO EAT ANY TIME

1 cup skim milk (86)
10 thin pretzel sticks (12)

Lasagna

¾ pound lean ground beef
¾ cup finely chopped, peeled onion
½ teaspoon minced, peeled garlic
1 15-ounce can tomato sauce
1 6-ounce can tomato paste
1 teaspoon salt
¼ teaspoon black pepper
½ teaspoon dried oregano leaves

4 ounces lasagna noodles (6 noodles), cooked according to package directions and drained
8 ounces part-skim mozzarella cheese, grated or chopped
1 pound small-curd cottage cheese
2 10-ounce packages frozen spinach, thawed and thoroughly drained

In a large skillet brown meat over moderate heat, stirring with a spoon to break up. Using a slotted spoon, remove meat to a bowl or plate. Pour off all but about 1 teaspoon fat from the skillet; add onion and garlic and cook 3 to 4 minutes, stirring frequently, until softened. Stir in tomato sauce, tomato paste, salt, pepper and oregano. Mix in browned meat. Turn heat to low and simmer for about 15 minutes. Heat oven to 350°F. Place 3 of the noodles in an 11¾-x-7½-x-1¾-inch baking dish. Top with layers of about ⅓ each of the tomato sauce, the mozzarella cheese and the cottage cheese. Spread spinach evenly over cheese. Top spinach with another ⅓ each of the tomato sauce, mozzarella and cottage cheese. Top cheese with remaining noodles and then with remaining ⅓ of tomato sauce, mozzarella and cottage cheese. Bake 30 minutes, until cheese is bubbly. Cut in squares to serve. *Makes 6 to 8 servings*. For diet serving allow ⅛ of the lasagna.

Per diet serving: 326 calories, 30 grams protein, 12 grams fat, 25 grams carbohydrate.

BREAKFAST

1 cup cooked iron-enriched farina
(100), sprinkled with cinnamon
½ cup skim milk (43)

LUNCH

* Fresh Green Pea Soup (83)
3 ounces water-packed tuna (117),
served with 2 teaspoons mayonnaise (68)
2 rye wafers (45)
2 fresh apricots (36)

DINNER

1 cup cooked spaghetti (210), with
*Easy Meat Sauce (207), and
1 tablespoon grated Parmesan
cheese (23)
1 cup cooked, sliced zucchini squash
(22)
Italian-Style Tossed Salad: 1 cup
torn lettuce leaves (10); ¼ cup
chopped celery (5); ¼ cup sliced
cucumber (4); 2 radishes (1);
5 black ripe olives (30); Basic
Vinaigrette Dressing (recipe on
page 23, 31)
1 nectarine (88)

TO EAT ANY TIME

1 cup skim milk (86)

Fresh Green Pea Soup

1 teaspoon vegetable oil
1 cup chopped, peeled onion
4 cups shredded iceberg lettuce
(about ½ head)
2 10-ounce packages frozen green
peas (4 cups)

3 13¾-ounce cans chicken broth
½ teaspoon salt
¼ teaspoon black pepper

In a large saucepot or Dutch oven heat oil over moderate heat. Stir in
onion; cover and cook 5 minutes, until onion is translucent but not
brown. Add remaining ingredients; cover and bring to a boil over
moderately high heat. Reduce heat to moderately low and simmer 5 to
7 minutes, stirring occasionally, until peas are tender. Remove from
heat and put 2 cups of the soup mixture into a blender (see note).
Cover and blend 40 seconds at low speed, until pureed. Pour into a large
bowl and repeat with remaining soup. Pour pureed soup back into pan
and heat over moderately low heat, until hot. Soup freezes well. *Makes 8
cups, or 6 to 8 servings.* For diet serving allow 1 cup soup.

NOTE: For safety, do not puree more than 2 cups soup at one time
in blender.

Per diet serving: 83 calories, 7 grams protein, 1 gram fat, 13 grams carbohydrate.

Easy Meat Sauce

1 pound lean ground beef
½ cup chopped, peeled onion
1 28-ounce can whole peeled
  tomatoes
1 8-ounce can tomato sauce

1 teaspoon dried basil leaves,
  crumbled
½ teaspoon salt
¼ teaspoon black pepper

In a large saucepot or Dutch oven cook meat over moderate heat for 5 to 10 minutes, stirring occasionally to break up large chunks, until meat has lost its pink color. Drain and discard fat; return meat to pot and add remaining ingredients. Cover pot, leaving lid slightly ajar, and cook 45 minutes over moderate heat until flavors are blended. Sauce freezes well. *Makes 5¼ cups.* For diet serving allow 1 cup sauce.

Per diet serving: 207 calories, 19 grams protein, 10 grams fat, 10 grams carbohydrate.

Dieting Alone?

For a lot of reasons, it's easier to diet alone—no tempting snacks being brought into the house by others, no opportunity to snitch some of the extras provided for a family and no unsupportive roommate assuring you that you're just fine the way you are. But, since most of the Wise Woman's Diet meals have purposely been planned as family menus, you'll want to simplify recipes, cut them in halves or fourths and make good use of your freezer storage space. In the Spaghetti and Meat Sauce Dinner, by freezing the extra pea soup and meat sauce you'll be way ahead on cooking time anytime you want to switch back to it for a pasta-dinner day. A tip from people who have dieted alone: Have an assortment of individual-portion refrigerator or freezer containers ready. Spoon the leftovers into them and store them *before* you eat to avoid the temptation to have "just a little more."

BREAKFAST

½ grapefruit (40)
½ cup cooked cornmeal (60)
2 slices crisp, lean bacon (61)
1 cup skim milk (86)

LUNCH

½ cup cubed eggplant (19) stewed
  with fresh large tomato (27)
2 ½-inch-thick slices French bread
  (about 2½ x 2 inches, 88)
½ cantaloupe (82) filled with
  ½ cup creamed cottage cheese
  (119)

DINNER

1 cup canned chicken consommé
  (44)
* Chicken Cacciatore (156)
1 medium peeled potato, boiled
  (80)
½ cup cooked spinach (20)
1 lettuce wedge (¼ head, 14), with
  1 tablespoon bottled low-calorie
  Italian salad dressing (8)
* Orange Whip (68)

TO EAT ANY TIME

1 medium-sized banana (101)
1 small peach (38)
1 cup skim milk (86)

Chicken Cacciatore

1 3-pound broiler-fryer chicken,
  cut up
Salt and black pepper
1 tablespoon vegetable oil
1 8-ounce can tomatoes
1 medium-sized green pepper,
  seeded and sliced thin

2 medium-sized onions, peeled
  and sliced thin
2 teaspoons minced, peeled garlic
¾ teaspoon salt
Few grains of black pepper
1 cup sliced mushrooms

Wash chicken and pat dry with paper towels. Sprinkle chicken lightly
with salt and pepper. In skillet over moderately high heat, heat oil; add
chicken and cook until lightly browned on all sides. In a bowl mix
tomatoes, green pepper, onion, garlic, the ¾ teaspoon salt and the few
grains of pepper; pour over chicken, cover and cook over moderately
low heat 10 minutes. Add mushrooms; cover and cook 20 minutes
longer, or until chicken is fork-tender. *Makes 3 or 4 servings.* For diet
serving allow 3 ounces of chicken and ¼ of the sauce.

Per diet serving: 156 calories, 22 grams protein, 3 grams fat, 9 grams carbohydrate.

Orange Whip

1 3-ounce package orange-flavored
  gelatin
1 cup boiling water
1 teaspoon freshly grated orange
  peel
¼ cup orange juice

1 tablespoon lemon juice
½ cup cold water
2 egg whites, at room temperature
1 pint fresh or unsweetened
  frozen blueberries
Fresh mint sprigs

In a metal bowl or saucepan dissolve gelatin in the boiling water. Stir in orange peel, orange juice, lemon juice and cold water. Chill gelatin until it is slightly thickened. (The bowl of gelatin may be placed over ice cubes and stirred constantly to hasten chilling.) Add egg whites and beat with an electric mixer set at high speed for about 5 minutes, or until gelatin mixture is doubled in bulk and appears creamy. Pour mixture into a 1-quart gelatin mold and chill several hours, until set. Unmold and garnish with blueberries and mint. *Makes 8 servings.* For diet serving allow ½ cup of the gelatin and ¼ cup blueberries.

Per diet serving: 68 calories, 2 grams protein, 0 grams fat, 15 grams carbohydrate.

How to Put Glamour in a Balanced Diet

Dr. George Christakis, writing about his experience in the obesity clinics of the Department of Health of the City of New York, where many of the international menus in this chapter were developed, had this to say about the joys of dieting:

"We had learned from the experiences our patients had had before coming to us that common sense is seldom the factor that makes a diet appeal to an obese person. Gimmick diets, surely unbalanced ones, that promised quick weight loss were glamorous. It was in order to invest *balanced* diets with the kind of glamour our patients found in the diets we regarded as unsound that we devised the variety of ethnic menus that did appeal to so many different groups of people."

BREAKFAST

½ cup unsweetened grapefruit
   juice (51)
1 large egg, poached (82)
1 slice raisin bread, toasted (66)

LUNCH

* Cottage Salad Plate: 1 cup torn
   spinach leaves (14); ½ cup sliced
   fresh mushrooms (10); ½ cup
   creamed cottage cheese (119)
1 slice whole-wheat bread (61)
1 medium-sized banana (101)

DINNER

* Chinese Beef (280)
½ cup cooked rice (93)
1 cup sliced Chinese cabbage (10),
   with Vinaigrette Dressing (recipe
   on page 23, 31)
2 plums (64)

TO EAT ANY TIME

2 cups skim milk (172)
½ cup fresh sweet cherries (41)
1 stalk celery (7)

Chinese Beef

1½ to 2 pounds flank steak,
   trimmed of any visible fat
1 tablespoon vegetable oil
½ cup coarsely chopped, peeled
   onion
1½ cups beef broth
2 tablespoons soy sauce
½ teaspoon ground ginger
1 cup thinly sliced, peeled carrots

Few grains of black pepper
½ cup thinly sliced celery
1 small green pepper, seeded and
   sliced thin
1 16-ounce can bean sprouts,
   drained
1 tablespoon cornstarch
1 tablespoon water

Slice steak on the diagonal into thin slices. In a large skillet over
moderately high heat, heat oil; add sliced steak a few pieces at a
time and cook until slices are just browned and still pink in the middle.
Remove beef and reduce heat to moderately low. Add onion and cook
until tender, stirring occasionally. Return meat to skillet and add beef
broth, soy sauce, ginger, carrots and pepper; cover and cook 5 minutes.
Uncover and add celery, green pepper and bean sprouts; cover and
cook 5 minutes. Mix cornstarch and water in a cup; stir into beef
mixture and cook 2 to 3 minutes, until thickened. *Makes 5 servings.*
For diet serving allow 3 ounces of meat and ½ cup of the vegetables
and sauce.

Per diet serving: 280 calories, 30 grams protein, 12 grams fat, 12 grams carbohydrate.

BREAKFAST
1 medium orange (78)
1 cup 4-grain multivitamin-and-iron-supplement cereal (110)
1 cup skim milk (86)

LUNCH
3 ounces lean broiled hamburger (4 ounces before cooking, 210), on ½ hamburger bun (60)
Tossed Salad: 2 cups torn chicory leaves (28); ¾ cup shredded red cabbage (15); 1 teaspoon vegetable oil (40); 1 teaspoon vinegar
1 small apple (61)

DINNER
1 cup hot clam broth (46)
* Oriental Steamed Flounder (281)
½ cup steamed rice (93)
½ cup juice-packed pineapple chunks (48) with lime wedge

TO EAT ANY TIME
½ medium-sized banana (50)

Oriental Steamed Flounder

2 tablespoons soy sauce
2 tablespoons dry sherry wine
1 tablespoon vegetable oil
1 teaspoon minced, peeled fresh gingerroot or ½ teaspoon ground ginger
2 tablespoons water

1 pound frozen flounder fillets, thawed and separated
3 lemon slices
1 large cucumber, peeled and diced
¼ cup sliced scallion or green onion

In a wok or large skillet bring the soy sauce, sherry, oil, ginger and water to a boil over moderately high heat. Arrange fish in wok, in 2 layers if fillets are very thin, and arrange lemon slices on top. Return liquid to boiling, reduce heat to low, cover and cook 10 minutes. Transfer fish and pan liquid to a serving dish. Surround with cucumber and sprinkle with scallion. *Makes 2 servings.* For diet serving allow ½ the fish, vegetables and sauce.

Per diet serving: 281 calories, 10 grams protein, 9 grams fat, 8 grams carbohydrate.

BREAKFAST

1 cup tomato juice (46)
1 medium egg, poached (72)
1 slice cracked-wheat bread, toasted (66), spread with 1 teaspoon butter or margarine (34)

LUNCH

Cheese Salad Plate: ½ cup creamed cottage cheese (119), on 1 lettuce leaf (1), with ½ small tomato, sliced (10), and ½ medium-sized carrot, cut into sticks (15)
1 slice rye bread (61)
1 small apple (61)

DINNER

Fruit Cup: ½ small orange (23) and ½ medium grapefruit, sectioned (40)
* Classic Stir-Fried Beef and Broccoli (196)
½ cup cooked rice (93)
Cucumber–Radish Salad: 8 slices raw cucumber (8); 5 small radishes, sliced (4); dressed with 1 teaspoon cider vinegar, 1 teaspoon sugar (15), 1 teaspoon soy sauce (4) and 1 teaspoon oil (40)
* Frozen Lemon Creme (69)

TO EAT ANY TIME

2 cups skim milk (172)
½ cup seedless grapes (53)

Stir-Fried Beef with Broccoli

⅓ cup soy sauce
2 tablespoons cider vinegar
¾ teaspoon granulated sugar
1 beef bouillon cube
⅓ cup water
2 teaspoons cornstarch
3 tablespoons vegetable oil
2 large cloves garlic, peeled and halved

¾ pound beef flank steak or top round steak, cut in ⅛-inch diagonal slices
1 large sweet onion, peeled, halved and cut in ¼-inch slices (1½ cups)
1½ cups peeled broccoli stems, cut in ⅛-inch diagonal slices
2½ cups raw broccoli florets
¼ pound fresh mushrooms, cut in ⅛-inch slices

Mix soy sauce, vinegar and sugar in a small bowl or measuring cup. In another bowl mix bouillon cube, water and cornstarch. Assemble remaining ingredients. In a large, heavy skillet or wok heat 1½ tablespoons of the oil over high heat. Add garlic and cook a few seconds to season oil. Add meat and stir-fry 2 minutes, until slices are lightly browned but still slightly pink in the center. Remove meat and any pan juices to a bowl; discard garlic and wipe out skillet. Add 1 tablespoon of the remaining oil and when hot, add onion and broccoli stems; stir-fry

The World of Food: International Favorites **245**

2 minutes, until crisp-tender. Add the remaining ½ tablespoon oil around edge of skillet and add broccoli florets and mushrooms. Stir-fry 2 minutes; pour in meat and juices from the bowl and then the soy-vinegar mixture. Stir, cover and cook 2 minutes. Stir cornstarch mixture (make sure bouillon cube is broken up) and pour into the skillet. Cook, stirring constantly, 2 to 3 minutes, until thickened. *Makes 4 to 6 servings.* For diet serving allow ⅙ of the recipe.

NOTE: Two 10-ounce packages frozen broccoli florets and one 4¾-ounce can mushrooms may be substituted for fresh vegetables. Cook onion and remove. Cook broccoli 3 to 4 minutes, until thawed and separated. Then add mushrooms with meat and soy-vinegar mixture.

Per diet serving: 196 calories, 17 grams protein, 11 grams fat, 11 grams carbohydrate.

Frozen Lemon Creme

1 envelope unflavored gelatin
½ cup granulated sugar
½ cup instant nonfat dry milk
2 cups liquid skim milk

2 teaspoons grated lemon peel
¼ cup lemon juice
2 egg whites

Mix together gelatin, sugar and instant nonfat dry milk in a saucepan. Stir liquid skim milk into dry ingredients and cook over moderately low heat, stirring constantly, for about 5 minutes, or until gelatin is dissolved. Remove gelatin mixture from heat and cool to room temperature. Stir in lemon peel and juice. Pour into a 9-x-5-x-2¾-inch loaf pan and place in freezer until almost firm. While lemon mixture is chilling, place a large mixing bowl and the beaters from an electric mixer in the refrigerator to chill. Turn lemon mixture into the chilled bowl, add egg whites and beat at high speed until smooth and fluffy, and the volume of the mixture is more than doubled. Pour mixture into the loaf pan, cover and freeze several hours. *Makes about 5½ cups, 8 to 10 servings.* For diet serving allow ½ cup creme.

Per diet serving: 69 calories, 4 grams protein, 0 grams fat, 13 grams carbohydrate.

BREAKFAST

* Very Cheesy Toast (214)
1 cup hot apple cider (117)

LUNCH

Open-Face Sardine Sandwich: 3
  ounces boneless and skinless
  sardines (187); 2 tablespoons
  chopped, peeled onion (4); 1
  teaspoon butter or margarine
  (34); 1 slice pumpernickel bread
  (79)
1 cup cocktail vegetable juice (41)

DINNER

* Shrimp Chow Mein (226)
½ cup cooked rice (93)
2 cups fresh spinach leaves (28),
  dressed with 1 teaspoon vegetable
  oil (40), 1 tablespoon cider
  vinegar, 1 teaspoon soy sauce
  (4)
½ cup mandarin orange sections or
  1 medium-sized tangerine (40)

TO EAT ANY TIME

1 cup skim milk (86)

Very Cheesy Toast

1 ounce Swiss cheese, diced fine
2 tablespoons 99%-fat-free cottage
  cheese
Few grains of salt
Few grains of black pepper

1 slice cracked-wheat bread,
  lightly toasted
1 tablespoon grated Parmesan
  cheese

In a small bowl mix Swiss and cottage cheeses, salt and pepper. Spread on toast. Sprinkle grated Parmesan cheese over the top. Place on a baking sheet in broiler 4 inches from heat source (or use a toaster-oven) and broil about 3 minutes, until cheese is melted and lightly browned. Serve at once. *Makes 1 diet serving.*

Per diet serving: 214 calories, 16 grams protein, 10 grams fat, 14 grams carbohydrate.

Shrimp Chow Mein

1 tablespoon vegetable oil
2 pounds raw shrimp, shelled and
  deveined
1 large stalk celery, diagonally
  sliced
½ cup sliced, peeled onion
½ cup green pepper, sliced and
  cut into thin strips
1¼ cups water
2 chicken bouillon cubes
2 tablespoons soy sauce

¼ teaspoon ground ginger
1½ tablespoons cornstarch
¼ cup water
1 1-pound can bean sprouts, well
  drained
2 cups shredded romaine lettuce
  or Chinese cabbage
¼ cup sliced bamboo shoots
3 water chestnuts, sliced
Chow mein noodles
Cooked rice

Assemble all ingredients before starting to cook. In a skillet heat oil over moderate heat. Add shrimp and cook just until they turn pink, stirring frequently. (All of the oil may be absorbed; do not add additional oil.) Remove shrimp. In the same skillet combine celery, onion, green pepper, 1¼ cups of the water, bouillon cubes, soy sauce and ginger. Bring to a boil, stirring to loosen any of the browned bits. Blend together cornstarch and the remaining ¼ cup water; quickly stir into boiling mixture. Boil ½ minute, stirring constantly. Add bean sprouts, lettuce, bamboo shoots, water chestnuts and shrimp. Cover tightly and cook over moderately low heat 3 to 5 minutes, or until lettuce is wilted and mixture is heated to serving temperature. Serve with additional soy sauce, noodles and rice. *Makes 6 servings.* For diet serving allow 1½ cups chow mein, ⅓ cup rice and 2 tablespoons chow mein noodles.

Per diet serving: 226 calories, 38 grams protein, 4 grams fat, 8 grams carbohydrate.

CHAPTER EIGHT

Hold That Line: How to Stay Thin

Congratulations! If you've reached your goal of weighing what you want to weigh, this can be the diet to end all diets. Even a holiday-cookie splurge needn't undo you because you've acquired good eating habits that you can follow for the rest of your life.

But—and it's a big *but*—the transition from a weight-loss diet to a maintenance diet has inherent pitfalls. Most dieters agree that keeping the pounds off is harder than taking them off. Losing weight, you knew, would not be a forever thing; keeping it off, without too many splurges, is forever. You may have to keep reminding yourself that this is a new you—a valuable new you. You are worth every bit of the time and effort it will take now to find your own balancing act: where your own eating should stop if you are to stay as thin as you are!

Before you dip into the menus and recipes in this chapter, read and reread the "Ease on Up" and the "New You Math" advice on the next page. Memorize it if need be.

Ease on Up . . . Slowly

You didn't, by following this diet, crash your weight off. The trick now is not to crash it back on. Ease up, slowly, on your calorie intake and keep watching the scales. Study the "New You Math" (below) to get an approximate idea of the number of calories per day that will keep the pounds off. Age and body type, as well as activity, all help determine the delicate balance between food consumed and energy expended.

For the first week after you've reached your ideal weight, add about 70 calories a day, bringing your daily total to around 1,270. Simply increase portion sizes of your favorite diet menus or try some menus in this Maintenance Diet chapter. In the second week, add another 70 calories per day. If your weight seems to be holding steady, add another 70 calories a day in weeks three, four and five. By then you'll be at 1,480 calories a day. If at the end of the fifth week your weight is still holding steady, start adding 100 calories a day, every two weeks. By the end of the eleventh week, you'll be at about 1,800 calories a day. But don't despair if you don't reach 1,800 without a weight gain. Cut back immediately and know you've found your own personal level at which to eat and be happily slim.

The New You Math

Staying thin is a matter of balancing the calories you take in—eat—with those you expend—breathing, sleeping, walking, swimming and so on. You can estimate the number of calories you can eat each day without gaining weight with this formula: If you live a very sedentary life, multiply your ideal weight by 10. If you lead a moderately active life (not a sitting-down job, some moderate exercise like walking), multiply your ideal weight by 12. (Example: 120 pounds ideal weight times 12 equals 1,440 calories.) If you're very active, multiply your ideal weight by 15. In every case the answer will be the approximate number of calories you can eat each day without gaining weight.

BREAKFAST

1 small apple (61)
* Bacon and Egg Breakfast Bake
  (249)
1 toasted English muffin (148),
  spread with ½ tablespoon butter
  or margarine (51)
1 cup skim milk (86)

LUNCH

* Spanish Tuna Salad (310), on
  4 leaves romaine or Boston lettuce
  (10)
2 ½-inch-thick slices French bread
  (2½ x 2 inches, 88)
1 medium-sized pear (90)

DINNER

1 cup tomato juice (46)
* Pork Chop and Potato Casserole
  (332)
¾ cup cooked green beans (24)
* Apricot Cloud Cake (158)

TO EAT ANY TIME

1 cup skim milk (86)
1 graham cracker (55)

Bacon and Egg Breakfast Bake

4 ounces fully cooked Canadian-
  style bacon or ham, cut in small
  cubes
2 ounces finely chopped
  Muenster, Cheddar or
  Monterey Jack cheese (½ cup)

4 large eggs
1½ cups liquid skim milk
⅛ teaspoon pepper

Heat oven to 450°F. Spread bacon in the bottom of a 9-inch pie plate and sprinkle with the cheese. Beat eggs with the milk and pepper and pour over cheese. Bake 15 minutes. Reduce heat to 350°F. and bake 10 to 15 minutes longer, until browned and puffed and firm in the center. Place pie plate on a wire rack to cool for 10 minutes before cutting in wedges to serve. *Makes 4 large servings.* For maintenance diet serving allow ¼ of the pie.

Per diet serving: 249 calories, 21 grams protein, 16 grams fat, 5 grams carbohydrate.

Spanish Tuna Salad

2 tablespoons olive oil
3 tablespoons red wine vinegar
¼ teaspoon salt
¼ teaspoon black pepper
2 6½-ounce cans chunk-style oil-
  packed tuna, drained
1 cup chopped celery

3 cups cooked elbow macaroni,
  thoroughly drained
1 7½-ounce jar or can roasted red
  sweet peppers or pimientos,
  drained and chopped
½ cup chopped, peeled sweet
  onion

Put oil, vinegar, salt and pepper in a medium-sized serving bowl and beat well with a fork to blend. Add remaining ingredients and toss gently to mix. *Makes about 6 cups, or 4 servings.* For maintenance diet serving allow 1½ cups.

Per diet serving: 310 calories, 30 grams protein, 8 grams fat, 28 grams carbohydrate.

Pork Chop and Potato Casserole

5 ¾-inch-thick loin or shoulder
  pork chops (about 1½ pounds)
½ teaspoon black pepper
½ teaspoon salt
1 tablespoon vegetable oil
4 small cloves garlic, peeled and
  split
4 medium-sized all-purpose
  potatoes (about 1½ pounds),
  peeled and sliced ¼-inch thick
  (or use frozen peeled potatoes)

2 large onions, peeled and sliced
  ¼-inch thick
½ teaspoon salt
3 tablespoons chopped fresh
  parsley
½ cup chicken broth

Sprinkle chops with the pepper and ½ teaspoon salt. In a Dutch oven or rangetop-to-oven casserole heat the oil over moderately high heat. Add chops and garlic and brown chops on both sides in the oil (in 2 batches if necessary); remove chops from pot. Pour off all fat but leave browned bits and garlic in bottom of pot. Heat oven to 300°F. Arrange sliced potatoes in bottom of pot and top with onion slices; sprinkle with the remaining ½ teaspoon salt. Arrange pork chops on top of onions, sprinkle with parsley and pour in the broth. Cover and bake 1 hour, until pork chops are very tender, potatoes a rich-brown color and a small amount of gravy has formed in the bottom of the pot. *Makes 4 servings.* For maintenance diet serving allow 1 chop and ¼ of the vegetables.

Per diet serving: 332 calories, 22 grams protein, 12 grams fat, 34 grams carbohydrate.

Apricot Cloud Cake

1 9-ounce angel food cake
Whites of 2 large eggs, at room
  temperature
⅛ teaspoon salt
¼ teaspoon cream of tartar
¼ cup granulated sugar

¼ cup apricot preserves
2 tablespoons lemon juice
2 tablespoons syrup from canned
  apricots
1 17-ounce can small whole
  apricots, pitted and halved

Cut cake in half horizontally with a serrated knife. Wrap bottom half and reserve for Small Trifles in Menu #7. Cut top part of cake horizontally in half again. In a medium-sized bowl beat egg whites, salt and cream of tartar with an electric or rotary beater. When foamy, beat in sugar, 1 tablespoon at a time, and continue beating until stiff peaks form when beater is lifted. In a small pan heat the preserves and lemon juice over moderately low heat; when liquid, strain into a small bowl. (Both strained solids and liquid will be used.) Heat oven to 500°F. Place bottom portion of cake on a baking sheet; sprinkle with 2 tablespoons of apricot syrup and spread with the strained solids. Arrange 7 apricot halves on the bottom layer. Spread about ¼ of the egg white meringue on the underside of the top portion of cake and place on bottom portion. With a small spatula, spread remaining meringue smoothly over top and sides of cake. (This much can be done up to 1 hour before serving dessert.) Bake cake 2 to 3 minutes, until lightly browned. Remove from oven, arrange remaining apricot halves on top. Spoon strained liquid over apricots to glaze, letting some drip down sides of cake. *Makes 6 servings.* For maintenance diet serving allow ⅙ of the cake.

Per diet serving: 158 calories, 3 grams protein, 0 grams fat, 38 grams carbohydrate.

BREAKFAST

1 cup fresh or unsweetened frozen
strawberries, thawed (55), in
½ cup orange juice (61)
* Bullseye (213)
Café au Lait: 1 cup hot skim milk
with ½ cup coffee (86)

LUNCH

Dried Beef Sandwich: 2 ounces
dried beef (115); ½ tablespoon
mayonnaise (51); 2 slices white
bread (136)
Fresh Vegetable Salad: ½ small
head iceberg lettuce (35);
½ medium-sized carrot, peeled

and grated (15); 2 slices red
onion (6); *Rich Herb Dressing
(73)

DINNER

2 broiled frankfurters (340), with
2 teaspoons mustard (8)
* Hot Potato and Sauerkraut Salad
(147)
* Frozen Mocha (128)

TO EAT ANY TIME

1 cup skim milk (86)
3 whole-grain rye crackers (66),
spread with 2 tablespoons peanut
butter (188)

Bullseye

1 slice white bread
2 teaspoons butter or margarine
1 large egg

Few grains of salt
Few grains of black pepper

Cut out a circle 2 inches in diameter from the center of the bread. In
a heavy skillet melt butter over moderately high heat. Add bread and
"hole" and cook about 45 seconds, until lightly browned on bottom.
Turn over. Break egg into hole in bread slice. Sprinkle lightly with salt
and pepper and cook 1 minute; turn and cook 1 minute longer, until
egg is set. Serve with "hole" over egg. *Makes 1 maintenance diet serving.*

Per diet serving: 213 calories, 9 grams protein, 14 grams fat, 12 grams carbohydrate.

Rich Herb Dressing

½ cup buttermilk or plain yogurt
2 tablespoons mayonnaise
2 tablespoons minced, peeled
onion

½ teaspoon dried dillweed
½ teaspoon dried basil leaves
½ teaspoon salt

Mix ingredients in a small bowl. Covered, sauce will keep several days
in the refrigerator. *Makes about ⅔ cup.* For maintenance diet serving
allow 3 tablespoons.

Per diet serving: 73 calories, 2 grams protein, 6 grams fat, 2 grams carbohydrate.

Hot Potato and Sauerkraut Salad

4 medium-sized potatoes (about
    1½ pounds), peeled and cut in
    ¼-inch slices (or use frozen
    peeled potatoes)
1½ cups drained sauerkraut,
    preferably packaged
½ cup coarsely chopped, peeled
    sweet yellow onion

¼ cup chopped fresh parsley
½ teaspoon minced, peeled garlic
¾ teaspoon salt
2 tablespoons olive or vegetable
    oil
4 tablespoons red wine vinegar
¼ teaspoon pepper

Boil potatoes in salted water until tender but not overcooked. Drain and
place in a large serving bowl; add sauerkraut, onion and parsley. Sprinkle
the garlic with ¼ teaspoon of the salt and mash to a paste with a
knife. Mix with the oil, vinegar, pepper and the remaining ½ teaspoon
salt and pour over the potato mixture. Toss gently but thoroughly to
mix. *Makes about 5½ cups, or 4 to 6 servings.* For maintenance diet
serving allow 1 cup.

Per diet serving: 147 calories, 3 grams protein, 5 grams fat, 23 grams carbohydrate.

Frozen Mocha

5 tablespoons instant coffee
    granules
¼ cup unsweetened cocoa
¼ cup granulated sugar

Few grains of salt
3 cups liquid skim milk
1 teaspoon vanilla extract

In a 2-quart saucepan mix coffee, cocoa, sugar, salt and milk and stir
over moderate heat until coffee and cocoa are dissolved and mixture
is smooth. Remove from heat and stir in vanilla. Pour mixture into a
9-inch square aluminum pan and freeze several hours, until firm. Before
serving, remove from freezer and let soften about 10 minutes. Break up
mixture with a fork and mash to a slush. If mixture melts too much,
return to freezer for a few minutes. Spoon into cups or glasses. *Makes
4 servings.* For maintenance diet serving allow ¼ of mocha.

Per diet serving: 128 calories, 7 grams protein, 1 gram fat, 24 grams carbohydrate.

BREAKFAST

2 1-ounce slices canned luncheon
  meat, broiled (167)
1 English muffin (148), toasted and
  spread with ¼ cup creamed
  cottage cheese (60)
1 cup tomato juice (46)

LUNCH

Mashed Mackerel Sandwich: 2
  slices cracked-wheat bread (132);
  2 slices red onion (6); 2 ounces
  (¼ cup) canned mackerel,
  drained (102), mashed with 1
  tablespoon mayonnaise (102),
  2 teaspoons lemon juice (3), and
  1 teaspoon dried dillweed
½ medium-sized carrot (15)
1 medium-sized apple (77)
2 gingersnaps (58)
1 cup skim milk (86)

DINNER

* Chinese Chicken Livers (183)
½ cup cooked fine egg noodles
  (100)
1¼ cups escarole (50), with 4 slices
  green pepper (11) and
  2 tablespoons Garlic
  Vinaigrette Dressing (recipe on
  page 61, 62)
1 cup vanilla ice milk (180), with
  2 slices juice-packed pineapple
  (116)

TO EAT ANY TIME

1 cup skim milk (86)

Chinese Chicken Livers

1 pound chicken livers
¼ cup soy sauce
2 tablespoons dry sherry wine
  (optional)
½ teaspoon minced, peeled garlic

½ teaspoon ground ginger
2 teaspoons vegetable oil
2 tablespoons minced scallion or
  green onion

Rinse livers, discarding any bits of fat that cling to them, and pat dry with paper towels. Cut each liver in half. Heat broiler. In a shallow, foil-lined broiler pan combine the soy sauce, sherry, garlic, ginger and oil. Add livers and spoon soy mixture over them. Broil 4 inches from heat for 5 minutes. Turn livers and broil 5 minutes longer. Place on a heated platter, spoon pan juices over livers and sprinkle with the scallion. Livers are also delicious cold. *Makes 4 servings.* For maintenance diet serving allow ¼ of the livers.

Per diet serving: 183 calories, 23 grams protein, 7 grams fat, 6 grams carbohydrate.

BREAKFAST

1 cup bran flakes with added
thiamin and iron (105)
½ banana (50)
1 cup skim milk (86)
1 cup orange juice (122)
1 slice white bread, toasted (68),
spread with 2 teaspoons butter or
margarine (68)

LUNCH

1 cup canned cream of asparagus
soup, made with skim milk (111)
Egg Salad Sandwich: 2 slices white
bread (136); 2 large leaves
lettuce (4); 2 large eggs, hard-
cooked (164); 1 tablespoon
mayonnaise (102); 1 tablespoon
pickle relish (21)

DINNER

* Lemon-Broiled Chicken (185)
* Green Rice (179)
* Braised Carrots with Scallions
(47)
1 cup vanilla ice milk (180), with
½ cup warm, unsweetened
applesauce (50)

TO EAT ANY TIME

12 unshelled, roasted peanuts (126)

Lemon-Broiled Chicken

2 2½-pound broiler fryer chickens,
cut into serving pieces
5 tablespoons lightly salted butter
or margarine
⅓ cup freshly squeezed lemon
juice
½ teaspoon salt
¼ teaspoon black pepper

Rinse chicken pieces and pat dry with paper towels. Melt butter in a
small pan and stir in lemon juice. Sprinkle chicken pieces with salt and
pepper. Place, skin side down, on a rack in a broiler pan and brush with
the lemon-butter mixture. Broil 5 to 7 inches from heat source for 20
minutes, brushing once with the lemon-butter mixture. Turn chicken,
brush with lemon-butter mixture and broil about 20 minutes longer,
brushing twice with mixture. Wrap and reserve 1 chicken for sandwiches and diet lunch in Menu #5. For maintenance diet serving allow
¼ of remaining chicken.

Per diet serving: 185 calories, 20 grams protein, 11 grams fat, 0 grams carbohydrate.

Green Rice

1 13¾-ounce can chicken broth
Water
½ teaspoon salt
1 cup uncooked white rice

1 10-ounce package frozen collard
greens
2 teaspoons dried dillweed

Mix broth with enough water to make 2 cups. Pour into a medium-sized saucepan and bring to a boil over moderately high heat. Add salt and rice, and when boiling, reduce heat to moderately low, cover pan and cook 10 minutes. Add greens and dill; cover and cook 10 minutes longer, until rice is tender. Remove from heat and let stand, covered, for about 3 minutes. *Makes about 4½ cups, or 4 servings.* For maintenance diet serving allow 1 cup.

Per diet serving: 179 calories, 6 grams protein, 0 grams fat, 38 grams carbohydrate.

Braised Carrots with Green Onions

1 pound carrots, peeled and sliced
⅛ inch thick (2⅔ cups)
½ cup chicken broth
½ teaspoon salt

⅛ teaspoon black pepper
3 tablespoons thin-sliced scallion
or green onion

Place carrots, broth, salt and pepper in a medium-sized saucepan; cover and bring to a boil over moderately high heat. Reduce heat to moderate and cook 5 to 7 minutes, until carrots are just tender. Uncover pot and increase heat to high; cook about 5 minutes, until most of liquid has evaporated. Stir in scallion. *Makes about 2⅓ cups, 3 or 4 servings.* For maintenance diet serving allow ½ cup.

Per diet serving: 47 calories, 2 grams protein, 0 grams fat, 10 grams carbohydrate.

BREAKFAST

* Blueberry Breakfast Shake (187)
* Melba Cinnamon Crisps (250)

LUNCH

3 ounces Lemon-Broiled Chicken
(reserved from Menu #4, 120)
Asparagus Salad: 1 8-ounce can
asparagus pieces, drained (49);
½ cup cooked green peas (57);
with 2 tablespoons Garlic Vinaigrette Dressing (recipe on page
61, 64)
1 syrup-packed peach half with 1½
tablespoons of the juice (59)
1 cup skim milk (86)

DINNER

Raw Vegetables with Cottage Dip:
½ cup creamed cottage cheese
(119); mixed with 2 tablespoons
buttermilk (11) and ½ teaspoon
caraway seeds; 4 small radishes
(5); ½ green pepper, cut in
strips (8); ½ cup raw cauliflower
florets (14)
* Fish Creole (256)
* Apple Crunch (269)

TO EAT ANY TIME

1 slice whole-wheat bread (61),
spread with 2 tablespoons peanut
butter (188)

Blueberry Breakfast Shake

1 cup buttermilk
1 cup unsweetened frozen
blueberries (not thawed)

½ teaspoon granulated sugar
1 teaspoon vanilla extract

Place all ingredients in a blender; cover and blend at medium speed
about 30 seconds, until thick and well blended. *Makes 1 maintenance
diet serving.*

Per diet serving: 187 calories, 10 grams protein, 1 gram fat, 37 grams carbohydrate.

Melba Cinnamon Crisps

6 oblong Melba toasts
4 teaspoons butter or margarine

1½ teaspoons granulated sugar
¾ teaspoon ground cinnamon

Spread toasts evenly with the butter. In a small cup mix sugar and
cinnamon together. Place toasts on a baking sheet or the baking tray of
a toaster-oven. Sprinkle toasts with cinnamon-sugar. Bake in a 400°F.
oven about 3 minutes or until sugar melts. *Makes 1 diet serving.*

Per diet serving: 250 calories, 6 grams protein, 12 grams fat, 25 grams carbohydrate.

Fish Creole

1½ cups chicken broth
¼ teaspoon salt
⅛ teaspoon black pepper
¾ teaspoon dried basil leaves
1 10-ounce package frozen whole
  baby okra

1 14½-ounce can sliced baby
  tomatoes
1 1-pound block frozen sole or
  flounder fillets, thawed enough
  to separate
2 cups cooked rice

In a medium-size saucepan bring broth, salt, pepper and basil to a boil over moderately high heat. Add okra, reduce heat to moderate, cover and cook about 5 minutes, until just tender and still bright green. Add tomatoes and their juice; then arrange fish fillets on top. Cover and cook 3 to 5 minutes longer, or until fillets are done. To serve, put ½ cup of the rice in the bottom of each of 4 soup bowls and ladle creole over it. *Makes about 5 cups, or 4 servings.* For maintenance diet serving allow 1¼ cups.

Per diet serving: 256 calories, 25 grams protein, 1 gram fat, 36 grams carbohydrate.

Apple Crunch

2 cups unsweetened applesauce
1 cup coarsely chopped, cored
  tart cooking apple, such as
  Granny Smith
4 teaspoons granulated sugar

2 teaspoons ground allspice or
  cinnamon
¾ cup crunchy nutlike cereal
  nuggets
4 tablespoons butter or margarine

Heat oven to 400°F. or use toaster-oven. Mix applesauce and chopped apple and divide equally among 4 medium-sized custard cups. Mash the sugar, allspice, cereal and butter with a small spatula until well mixed and sprinkle an equal amount over each cup. Bake about 15 minutes, until apple mixture is heated and top is well browned. *Makes 4 servings.* For maintenance diet serving allow 1 custard cup.

Per diet serving: 269 calories, 2 grams protein, 12 grams fat, 39 grams carbohydrate.

BREAKFAST

1¼ cups fortified high-protein
  cereal (110)
3 tablespoons raisins (78)
1 cup skim milk (86)
Cinnamon Toast: 1 slice white
  bread, toasted (68); 2 teaspoons
  butter or margarine (68); 1
  teaspoon sugar (24); ¾ teaspoon
  ground cinnamon

LUNCH

1 cup canned baked beans (383)
1 large slice pumpernickel bread
  (79), spread with 2 teaspoons
  butter or margarine (68)
* Coleslaw with Creamy Dill
  Dressing (85)
1 cup skim milk (86)

DINNER

* Meatloaves Marinara (350)
½ cup cooked spaghetti (78)
1½ cups torn romaine leaves (60);
  with 2 tablespoons Garlic Vinaigrette Dressing (recipe on page
  61, 62)
3 syrup-packed purple plums with
  2 tablespoons of the juice (110)

Coleslaw with Creamy Dill Dressing

2 cups green cabbage, thinly sliced
1 carrot, peeled and grated (¼
  cup)
¾ cup plain low-fat yogurt
2 teaspoons minced onion

½ teaspoon dried dillweed
1 teaspoon freshly squeezed
  lemon juice
¼ teaspoon salt
⅛ teaspoon black pepper

In a medium-size bowl mix cabbage and carrot. In a small bowl blend the yogurt, onion, dillweed, lemon juice, salt and pepper. Add the yogurt mixture to the cabbage and toss to mix well. *Makes 2 cups.* For diet serving allow 1 cup.

Per diet serving: 85 calories, 5 grams protein, 2 grams fat, 12 grams carbohydrate.

Meatloaves Marinara

⅓ cup liquid skim milk
1 slice white bread
¼ small peeled onion
1 large clove garlic, peeled
¼ cup fresh parsley sprigs, packed tight to measure
½ teaspoon dried basil leaves
3 tablespoons freshly grated Parmesan cheese
1 teaspoon salt

⅛ teaspoon black pepper
1 large egg
1 pound lean ground beef
⅓ cup plain dry bread crumbs
2 tablespoons olive or vegetable oil
1 cup canned pear-shaped tomatoes, chopped, with their juice

In a blender put the milk, bread, onion, garlic, parsley, basil, cheese, salt, pepper and egg. Cover and blend at high speed about 7 seconds, or just until blended. Place meat in a medium-sized bowl, add blended mixture and mix well. Shape mixture into 4 small meatloaves; coat evenly with the bread crumbs. In a large, heavy skillet heat the oil over moderately high heat. Carefully place loaves in oil and brown evenly all over, about 7 minutes. Pour off as much fat as possible from skillet. Pour chopped tomatoes and juice around loaves; stir in browned bits from bottom of skillet. Reduce heat to moderately low, cover skillet and simmer 25 to 30 minutes, basting meat once or twice with pan juices. If sauce seems too dry, add up to ¼ cup of water. *Makes 4 servings.* For maintenance diet serving allow 1 loaf and ¼ of sauce.

Per diet serving: 350 calories, 29 grams protein, 20 grams fat, 14 grams carbohydrate.

BREAKFAST

2 4-inch whole-wheat pancakes (made with a pancake and waffle mix, 166), spread with 2 teaspoons butter or margarine (68), and ½ cup unsweetened applesauce (50)
1 cup skim milk (86)

LUNCH

1 cup minestrone soup, prepared from canned condensed (105)
1 ½-inch-thick slice French bread (about 2½ x 2 inches, 44)
2 ounces Muenster cheese (184)

DINNER

* Stifado (470)
½ cup cooked noodles (100)
2 cups escarole (80), with Rich Herb Dressing (recipe on page 254, 73)
* Small Trifles (297)

TO EAT ANY TIME

1 cup skim milk (86)

Stifado (Greek Beef Stew)

2 tablespoons olive or vegetable oil
3 pounds boneless top or bottom round or rump of beef, cut in 1½-inch cubes
3 pounds small white onions, peeled
1 cup dry red wine
1 teaspoon chopped, peeled garlic

2 teaspoons salt
1 28-ounce can whole pear-shaped tomatoes, drained
2 tablespoons tomato paste
¼ teaspoon black pepper
5 whole cloves
1 teaspoon ground cinnamon
1 bay leaf (optional)
¼ cup sliced pitted black olives

In a large saucepot or Dutch oven heat oil over moderately high heat. Dry meat on paper towels. Brown about ½ the meat at a time in the pot, turning to brown all over. Remove browned meat to a plate. Brown about half the onions at a time in the same pot, stirring or turning to brown lightly. When browning is completed, put all meat and onions back in pot. Add wine and stir to mix. Using the blade of a knife, mash the garlic and salt to a paste; add to stew with remaining ingredients except olives. Heat oven to 325°F. Cover pot and bring to a boil. Set in heated oven and bake about 1½ hours, until meat is very tender and onions have cooked down to form a thick, rich gravy. Sprinkle with olives. *Makes 7½ to 8 cups, 6 to 8 servings.* For maintenance diet serving allow 1 cup.

Per diet serving: 470 calories, 38 grams protein, 25 grams fat, 21 grams carbohydrate.

Small Trifles

1 3¼-ounce package vanilla
   instant pudding and pie filling
2 cups buttermilk

1 10-ounce package frozen
   raspberries
Angel food cake (reserved from
   Menu #1)

Prepare pudding according to package directions, using buttermilk instead of whole milk. Defrost raspberries. Cut the angel food cake into 8 pieces and toast lightly on both sides. At serving time put ½ cup of the pudding and 2 slices of the cake into each of 4 small serving bowls. Top with equal amounts of the raspberries and juice. *Makes 4 servings.* For maintenance diet serving allow 1 trifle.

Per diet serving: 297 calories, 7 grams protein, 0 grams fat, 68 grams carbohydrate.

A Lifetime Process

"There are two parts to weight reduction: taking it off and keeping it off. The latter is the more difficult to achieve. Losing weight, for most of the fat population, is a short-term situation; maintaining the weight loss is a lifetime process.

"Good taste and good nutrition are entirely compatible, and both can co-exist with weight control. What is essential is that you consider constantly whether the food you are eating is contributing to your health or injuring it. Learning the difference is easily accomplished; practicing it is a commitment; the rewards are self-evident."

—Myron Winick, M.D.
Director, Institute of Human
   Nutrition, Columbia University,
   New York City
Consultant to *Redbook*'s
   Wise Woman's Diet

BREAKFAST

1¼ cups fortified high-protein
cereal (110), sprinkled with 2
tablespoons crunchy nutlike
cereal nuggets (50)
½ banana (50)
1 cup skim milk (86)
1 cup orange juice (122)

LUNCH

1 3-ounce broiled lean hamburger
(4 ounces before cooking, 186),
on 1 hamburger roll (119) with
2 tablespoons catsup (30)
Coleslaw with Creamy Dill Dressing
(recipe on page 261, 85)
1 cup skim milk (86)

DINNER

* Baked Mushroom-Stuffed Fillets
of Sole (283)
½ cup cooked winter squash (65),
with 2 teaspoons butter or
margarine (68)
* Tangy Mustard Beans (103)
Winter Fruit Compote: 4 dried,
pitted prunes (66); 4 dried
apricot halves (36); ½ small
apple, cored and sliced (30);
cooked together in water with
1 stick cinnamon
1 large oatmeal cookie (86)

TO EAT ANY TIME

1 cup hot chocolate, made with
1 cup skim milk, 1 tablespoon
unsweetened cocoa and 2
teaspoons sugar (131)

Baked Mushroom-Stuffed Fillets of Sole

2 1-pound blocks frozen sole or
flounder fillets, thawed enough
to separate
¼ pound mushrooms
coarsely chopped
1 large egg
1 teaspoon salt, divided in two

⅛ teaspoon white pepper
2 tablespoons butter or margarine,
melted and mixed with 2
tablespoons freshly squeezed
lemon juice
¼ cup unseasoned dry bread
crumbs

Heat oven to 425°F. Separate fillets and set aside 8 whole ones or the equivalent. Cut remaining fillets in pieces (about 1 cup, tightly packed down). Put cut-up fillets in a blender with the mushrooms, egg, and ½ teaspoon of the salt. Cover and blend at medium speed until a thick puree is formed. Sprinkle reserved fillets with the remaining salt, the pepper and a little of the lemon-butter. Place a heaping tablespoon of the mushroom mixture near the thinner end of each fillet. Roll up fillet and spear with a wooden toothpick to hold. Place in a baking dish and sprinkle with remaining lemon-butter and then the bread crumbs. Bake about 15 minutes, until fish is done and filling is set. *Makes 4 servings.* For maintenance diet serving allow 2 fish rolls.

Per diet serving: 283 calories, 41 grams protein, 10 grams fat, 7 grams carbohydrate.

Tangy Mustard Beans

2 10-ounce packages Italian green
  beans
¾ cup water
½ teaspoon salt
2 teaspoons Dijon-style or brown
  mustard

2 tablespoons vegetable oil
3 tablespoons cider vinegar
½ teaspoon granulated sugar

Put beans, water and salt in a medium-sized saucepan; cover and bring to a boil over moderately high heat. Reduce heat to moderate and cook about 5 minutes, until beans are hot but still bright green. In a small bowl mix mustard, oil, vinegar and sugar. Add to undrained beans and stir to coat beans completely. *Makes about 4 cups.* For maintenance diet serving allow 1 cup.

NOTE: Leftover beans may be refrigerated and are delicious cold.

Per diet serving: 103 calories, 2 grams protein, 7 grams fat, 10 grams carbohydrate.

BREAKFAST

Toast and Cheese: 1 slice cracked-wheat bread, toasted (66), with 2 ounces Swiss cheese (214)
1 cup hot chocolate, made with 1 cup skim milk (86), 1 tablespoon unsweetened cocoa (14) and 2 teaspoons sugar (31)
1 tangerine (40)

LUNCH

Sardine and Red Onion Sandwich: 3 ounces sardines with skin and bones (187); 2 slices red onion (6); 2 large leaves lettuce (6); 2 slices rye bread (122), spread with 1 tablespoon softened butter or margarine (102)
½ cup unsweetened applesauce (50)
1 gingersnap (29)
¾ cup skim milk (65)

DINNER

* Liver and Onion Potato-Topped Pie (473)
Cabbage Salad: 2 cups finely shredded cabbage (40); 2 tablespoons minced, peeled onion (8); dressed with 1 tablespoon oil (120), 2 tablespoons cider vinegar, 1 teaspoon dried dillweed, salt and pepper
* Chocolate Chiffon Pots (75)

TO EAT ANY TIME

Hot Tomato Bouillon: 1 cup tomato juice (46), mixed with ½ cup beef bouillon (15); lemon slice (2)

Liver and Onion Potato-Topped Pie

2 tablespoons vegetable oil
1½ pounds beef liver, cut in ¼-inch-thick slices
¼ teaspoon black pepper
1 small clove garlic, peeled
1 large onion, peeled and sliced thin

¼ pound mushrooms, sliced ⅛ inch thick
½ cup boiling water
1 beef bouillon cube
1 large egg
3 cups firm mashed potatoes (prepared from instant)

In a 10-inch, rangetop-to-oven skillet or shallow casserole heat oil over moderately high heat. Sprinkle liver with pepper and put in skillet with garlic clove; cook 5 minutes, until browned on bottom; turn and cook 3 minutes longer. Discard garlic; add sliced onion and mushrooms and cook 3 to 4 minutes, stirring frequently, until soft. Remove liver and cut into 2-inch pieces. Return to skillet, add water and beef bouillon cube. Mash beef cube with back of spoon and stir to dissolve. Beat egg into potatoes and spread over liver mixture. Broil 3 inches from heat source about 5 minutes, until slightly browned. *Makes 4 servings.* For maintenance diet serving allow ¼ of pie.

Per diet serving: 473 calories, 42 grams protein, 18 grams fat, 39 grams carbohydrate.

Chocolate Chiffon Pots

1½ cups liquid skim milk
2 envelopes unflavored gelatin
3 tablespoons unsweetened cocoa
2 tablespoons granulated sugar
Few grains of salt

2 teaspoons vanilla extract
1 cup ice cubes (6 to 8)
4 teaspoons semisweet chocolate
    shavings (optional)

Place milk in a medium-sized saucepan and add gelatin, cocoa, sugar and salt. Stir over moderate heat until gelatin is completely dissolved. Remove from heat; add vanilla and stir briskly with a fork or wire whisk to mix ingredients well. Pour into a blender, add ice cubes, cover and blend at medium-high speed until ice cubes dissolve. Uncover, stir once with a rubber spatula and let stand 2 to 3 minutes to jell. Spoon into 4 dessert dishes or parfait glasses and top each serving with 1 teaspoon chocolate shavings. *Makes 4 servings.* For maintenance diet serving allow 1 dish.

Per diet serving: 75 calories, 6 grams protein, 1 gram fat, 11 grams carbohydrate.

BREAKFAST

1 cup tomato juice (46)
1 large egg, boiled (82)
1 slice cracked-wheat bread,
   toasted (66), spread with 2
   teaspoons butter or margarine
   (68)
1 cup skim milk (86)

LUNCH

Swiss on Pumpernickel: 2 ounces
   Swiss cheese (214); 5 medium-
   sized radishes, sliced (4); 2 slices
   pumpernickel bread (158), spread
   with 1 tablespoon butter or
   margarine (102)
1 cup apple juice (117), cold or
   heated with a 1-inch long lemon
   peel, a 1-inch stick cinnamon
   and 2 whole cloves

DINNER

* Lamb Kabobs with Indian Mint
   Sauce (310)
Cool Cucumber Salad: 1 small
   cucumber, pared and sliced (20);
   2 tablespoons thin-sliced scallion
   (10); 2 tablespoons vinegar; salt
½ cup cooked rice (93), mixed
   with ½ cup cooked green peas
   (57)
Oasis Compote: ½ large orange,
   peeled and sliced (43); ½
   banana, sliced (50); 4 sliced,
   pitted dates (88)

TO EAT ANY TIME

1 cup skim milk (86)
10 thin pretzel sticks (12)
1 large oatmeal cookie (86)

Lamb Kabobs with Indian Mint Sauce

1 pound boneless shoulder or leg
   of lamb, cut in 1-inch cubes
½ teaspoon salt
⅛ teaspoon black pepper

1 tablespoon vegetable oil
Indian Mint Sauce (recipe
   on page 270)

Sprinkle meat with salt and pepper and thread on 4 skewers, about 7 cubes to a skewer. Brush with some of the oil; place on a rack over a broiling pan and broil about 3 inches from heat source for 4 minutes. Turn, brush with remaining oil and broil 4 minutes longer. Serve with Indian Mint Sauce. *Makes 4 servings.* For maintenance diet serving allow 1 skewer of meat and ¼ of the sauce.

Per diet serving (including sauce): 310 calories, 21 grams protein, 22 grams fat, 7 grams carbohydrate.

Indian Mint Sauce

1 small green pepper, seeded and
    diced
1 peeled clove of garlic, diced
4 drops Tabasco Sauce

¼ teaspoon salt
1 teaspoon dried mint leaves
About ⅔ cup plain yogurt

Put all ingredients in a blender with ⅓ cup of the yogurt. Cover and blend at medium speed about 20 seconds, until just smooth. Scrape into a small bowl and stir in remaining yogurt. Cover and refrigerate 2 hours or longer to blend flavors. *Makes about 1 cup.* For maintenance diet serving allow ¼ cup.

Per diet serving: 26 calories, 1 gram protein, 1 gram fat, 4 grams carbohydrate.

Shift the Balance

In the 1,200-calorie weight-loss menus, the proportion of daily calories from protein, carbohydrate and fats was 25, 45 and 30% respectively. For long-term maintenance of weight, the balance, *Redbook*'s consultants say, should be a slight shift: 15 to 20% of the daily calories should come from protein, 45 to 50% from carbohydrates and 30 to 40% from fats. This balance, within caloric limits, is your guarantee you can weigh what you want to weigh, always.

BREAKFAST

* Mexican-Style Eggs (327)
1 medium-sized pear (90)
1 cup skim milk (86)

LUNCH

1 cup onion soup (64)
2 cups romaine lettuce leaves (20),
  with 2 tablespoons Parslied
  Vinaigrette Dressing (recipe on
  page 116, 62)
2 ½-inch-thick slices French bread
  (2½ x 2 inches, 88), spread with
  1 teaspoon butter or margarine
  (34)
3 ounces lean boiled ham (183)

DINNER

* Herb-Stuffed Hamburgers with
  Mushroom Sauce (194)
1 cup cooked egg noodles (200)
1 cup cooked green beans (31),
  served with a lemon wedge (2)
1 small tomato, sliced (20), and
  8 thin slices cucumber (4) with
  1 teaspoon mayonnaise (34)
1 cup diced fresh pineapple (96)

TO EAT ANY TIME

1 cup skim milk (86)
2 saltine crackers (24), spread with
  4 teaspoons peanut butter (125)
1 tablespoon raisins (26)

Mexican-Style Eggs

1 corn tortilla
1 teaspoon butter or margarine
2 large eggs
¼ teaspoon salt

¼ cup taco sauce, from a can or
  jar
2 tablespoons grated Cheddar
  cheese

In a medium-sized skillet warm tortilla over moderate heat 2 to 3 minutes; remove to a broiler pan and cover with aluminum foil to keep warm. In the same skillet melt butter over moderately high heat; add eggs and salt and cook about 3 minutes, stirring constantly, until eggs are scrambled and cooked but still soft. Put scrambled eggs on center of tortilla; cover with taco sauce and sprinkle with cheese. Broil 3 to 5 inches from heat source for 2 minutes, until cheese has melted. *Makes 1 maintenance diet serving.*

Per diet serving: 327 calories, 18 grams protein, 21 grams fat, 19 grams carbohydrate.

Herb-Stuffed Hamburgers with Mushroom Sauce

1 pound lean ground beef
2 tablespoons chopped fresh
  parsley
2 tablespoons finely sliced scallion
  or green onion
½ teaspoon salt

½ cup water
4 ounces fresh mushrooms, sliced
  (about 1 cup)
1 teaspoon Worcestershire sauce
⅛ teaspoon black pepper

Divide meat into 8 equal portions; press each portion into a 3-inch patty. Mix parsley and scallion. Put 1 tablespoon of parsley mixture in center of 4 of the patties; top with remaining patties and press firmly around edges to seal. Sprinkle salt into a large skillet and heat over moderately high heat. Add stuffed hamburgers and cook about 3 minutes on each side for medium-rare, 4 minutes for medium well-done. Remove hamburgers to a serving plate and keep warm. Drain and discard any fat from skillet; add water, mushrooms, Worcestershire and pepper and cook over high heat 3 minutes, stirring constantly to dissolve brown bits on bottom of pan. When liquid is reduced to about ¼ cup, pour this sauce over the hamburgers and serve at once. *Makes 4 to 6 servings.* For maintenance diet serving allow 1 hamburger and 1 tablespoon sauce.

Per diet serving: 194 calories, 24 grams protein, 10 grams fat, 1 gram carbohydrate.

BREAKFAST

2 medium eggs, prepared any style, without butter or margarine (144)
1 English muffin (148), spread with 2 teaspoons butter or margarine (68) and 1½ teaspoons orange marmalade (27)
1 cup grapefruit juice (102)

DINNER

* Rice with Cheese and Chilies (461)
2 stalks celery (14)
6 radishes (4)
½ cantaloupe (82), served with lime wedge (2)
5 whole almonds (30)

LUNCH

Chef's Salad: 2 cups torn lettuce leaves (20); 3 ounces water-packed tuna fish, drained (117); 6 cherry tomatoes (20); ½ cup alfalfa sprouts (19); ½ medium-sized carrot, sliced (15); 2 table-spoons Parslied Vinaigrette Dressing (recipe on page 116, 62)
4 whole-grain rye wafers (88)
1 cup skim milk (86)
1 medium apple (77)

TO EAT ANY TIME

1½ cups skim milk (129)
1 large oatmeal cookie (86)

Rice with Cheese and Chilies

1 teaspoon lightly salted butter or margarine
1¼ cups converted long-grain white rice
1 4-ounce can chopped green chilies, drained

3 cups liquid skim milk
2 teaspoons chicken-flavor bouillon granules
6 ounces Cheddar cheese, shredded (about 1½ cups)

In a large saucepan melt butter over moderately high heat. Add rice and chilies and cook 3 to 5 minutes, stirring occasionally, until rice is hot and shiny. Stir in milk and bouillon granules and bring to a boil. Cover pan; reduce heat to moderately low and cook 20 to 25 minutes, until rice is tender and milk has been absorbed. Remove from heat and lightly stir in cheese with a fork; let stand 1 to 2 minutes, until melted. *Makes 4 cups rice.* For maintenance diet serving allow 1 cup. Reserve 1 diet serving for breakfast in Menu #14.

Per diet serving: 461 calories, 21 grams protein, 16 grams fat, 57 grams carbohydrate.

BREAKFAST

1 cup orange juice (122)
2 1½-ounce frozen waffles, heated
(240), spread with 2 teaspoons
butter or margarine (68) and 2
teaspoons strawberry preserves
(33)
1 cup skim milk (86)

LUNCH

Cheese and Sprout Sandwich: 3
ounces Monterey Jack cheese
(315); ½ cup alfalfa sprouts
(19); 1 small tomato, sliced (20);
1 teaspoon mayonnaise (34); 2
slices whole-wheat bread (112)
1 medium-sized carrot (15)
2 stalks celery (14)
1 cup papaya cubes (55), served
with lime wedge

DINNER

* Chinese Pepper Steak (220)
1 cup cooked white rice (186)
¼ cup Chinese noodles, from a
can (55)
* Strawberry Ice Milk (73)

TO EAT ANY TIME

10 seedless grapes (34)
1 cup skim milk (86)
10 thin pretzel sticks (12)

Chinese Pepper Steak

1 pound beef round steak,
  trimmed of visible fat
1 tablespoon cornstarch
3 tablespoons water, divided
2 tablespoons minced fresh
  gingerroot or ½ teaspoon
  ground ginger

4 tablespoons soy sauce, divided
4 teaspoons vegetable oil, divided
3 green peppers, seeded and sliced
  thin (about 2 cups)
6 scallions or green onions, cut
  into thin strips (see note)

Slice steak thinly across the grain; this is easiest if meat is partially
frozen. In a medium-sized bowl mix cornstarch, 1 tablespoon water,
the ginger and 2 tablespoons soy sauce; add sliced steak and toss to
coat. In a wok or large, heavy skillet heat 2 teaspoons oil over moderately high heat; add green peppers and scallions and stir-fry 2
minutes, until peppers are crisp-tender; remove to a bowl. Add the
remaining 2 teaspoons of oil to the wok; when hot, add steak and stir-fry
2 minutes. Return peppers and scallions to wok; add the remaining
2 tablespoons water and 2 tablespoons soy sauce. Cook 30 seconds longer,

stirring constantly, until sauce is boiling and slightly thickened. *Makes 3 or 4 servings.* For maintenance diet serving allow ¼ of the recipe.

NOTE: Cut scallions into 3-inch lengths and then quarter lengthwise.

Per diet serving: 220 calories, 24 grams protein, 9 grams fat, 13 grams carbohydrate.

Strawberry Ice Milk

1 13-ounce can evaporated skim   2 tablespoons granulated sugar
  milk, undiluted   1 teaspoon vanilla extract
3 cups fresh or unsweetened
  frozen strawberries

Put all ingredients in a blender; cover and blend 40 to 50 seconds on low speed, until mixture is smooth. Put blender container in freezer and freeze about 2 hours, until mixture is frozen around edges. Blend 40 to 50 seconds on medium-high speed, stopping once and scraping down sides with a rubber spatula. Freeze about 2 hours longer, until slightly frozen in center; then blend again and pour into a chilled bowl or individual paper cups. Freeze 2 hours or longer, until frozen solid. Remove from freezer about 20 minutes before serving to soften slightly. *Makes about 4 cups ice milk.* For maintenance diet serving allow ½ cup. Reserve 1 diet serving for dinner in Menu #14.

Per diet serving: 73 calories, 4 grams protein, 0 grams fat, 14 grams carbohydrate.

BREAKFAST

Rice with Cheese and Chilies
(reserved from Menu #12, 461)
½ grapefruit (40)

LUNCH

1 cup cranberry juice (164)
Salmon Salad Plate: *Salmon–Dill
Salad (179); 1 large tomato, sliced
(27); 2 large lettuce leaves (2)
7 saltine crackers (94)

DINNER

* Chicken Liver Spread (249)
2 slices white bread (136), spread
with 2 teaspoons butter or
margarine (68)
1 cup raw cauliflower florets (27)
and 1 cup raw broccoli florets
(36), with 2 tablespoons Low-
Calorie Mayonnaise (recipe on
page 158, 40)
Strawberry Ice Milk (reserved from
Menu #13, 73)

TO EAT ANY TIME

20 seedless grapes (68)
1 graham cracker (55)
1 cup skim milk (86)

Salmon–Dill Salad

1 7¾-ounce can salmon, drained
1 hard-cooked egg, peeled and
chopped
2 tablespoons plain low-fat yogurt
¼ teaspoon salt

⅛ teaspoon dried dillweed
⅛ teaspoon black pepper
¼ teaspoon lemon juice
2 tablespoons thin-sliced scallion
or green onion

In a medium-sized bowl mix salmon, egg, yogurt, salt, dillweed, pepper
and lemon juice until well blended. Add scallion just before serving.
Makes about 1½ cups salad, or 2 servings. For maintenance diet serving
allow ¾ cup.

Per diet serving: 179 calories, 26 grams protein, 6 grams fat, 3 grams carbohydrate.

Chicken Liver Spread

1 pound chicken livers
Water
1 teaspoon lightly salted butter or
  margarine
½ cup finely chopped, peeled
  onion
⅓ cup finely chopped, seeded
  green pepper

⅓ cup finely chopped, peeled
  carrot
2 hard-cooked eggs, peeled and
  chopped
1 teaspoon salt
¼ teaspoon black pepper

Rinse livers, discarding any bits of fat that cling to them, and pat dry with paper towel. Put livers into a large skillet; add water to cover and bring to a boil over moderately high heat. Cover skillet; reduce heat to moderate and simmer gently for 7 minutes, until livers are brown on the outside and still slightly pink in the middle. With a slotted spoon remove livers to a bowl; pour cooking liquid into a measuring cup. Wipe out skillet with a paper towel; add butter and heat over moderately high heat. When butter is melted, add onion, green pepper and carrot and cook 4 to 5 minutes, stirring frequently, until onions are soft and translucent; remove from heat. Chop livers fine; add to vegetables with eggs, salt and pepper. Stir in about ¼ cup of the reserved cooking liquid; stir until mixture comes together, adding more liquid if desired. Spread keeps well for several days in the refrigerator. *Makes 3 cups spread.* For maintenance diet serving allow ¾ cup.

Per diet serving: 249 calories, 34 grams protein, 9 grams fat, 7 grams carbohydrate.

BRUNCH

Purple Plum and Grapefruit
Compote: 3 water-packed plums
with 1½ tablespoons juice (44);
½ grapefruit, sectioned (40)
½ cup canned corned beef hash,
pan-fried without fat (229)
1 English muffin (148), spread with
1 tablespoon butter or margarine
(102) and 1 tablespoon jam or
jelly (55)

DINNER

* Braised Chicken with Zucchini
(303)
Buttered Cheese-Noodles: ½ cup
cooked egg noodles (100); 1
teaspoon butter or margarine
(34); 1 tablespoon grated
Parmesan cheese (25)
8 leaves escarole (40), with 2
teaspoons olive oil (84) and
1 tablespoon lemon juice (4)
Raspberry-Peach Parfait: 1 syrup-
packed peach half (39), topped
with ½ cup frozen sweetened
raspberries, partially thawed (121)

TO EAT ANY TIME

Cucumber and Cottage Cheese
Sandwich: ¼ cup cottage cheese
(60); ½ cucumber, peeled and
sliced (15); 4 medium-sized
pimiento-stuffed green olives,
sliced (15); 2 slices cracked-wheat
bread, toasted (132)
Tomato Consommé: 1 cup tomato
juice (46), heated with 1 beef
bouillon cube (7) and ½ cup
water
1 cup skim milk (86)
1 small apple (61)

Braised Chicken with Zucchini

2½ pounds broiler-fryer chicken parts
¼ teaspoon salt
1 8-ounce can whole peeled tomatoes, drained and liquid reserved
Water
1 tablespoon olive or vegetable oil

½ teaspoon minced, peeled garlic
1 chicken-flavored bouillon cube
1 pound zucchini squash, washed and cut into 1-inch chunks (about 3½ cups)
¼ cup chopped fresh parsley

Rinse chicken and pat dry with paper towels. Sprinkle chicken with salt and place, skin side down, on a rack in a broiler pan. Broil 3 to 4 inches from heat source for 10 minutes. Turn pieces and broil 5 minutes longer. Place reserved tomato liquid in a measuring cup and fill to 1 cup with water. In a large skillet heat oil over moderate heat; add garlic and cook 30 seconds. Add tomatoes and cook 3 minutes, breaking up with a spoon and stirring often. Stir in the reserved tomato liquid mixture and the bouillon cube and bring to a boil over high heat. Break up bouillon cube with a spoon to be sure it is dissolved. Place chicken in a single layer in skillet; baste with sauce and return to a boil. Cover, reduce heat to moderate and simmer 20 minutes, turning chicken and basting once. Add zucchini and parsley, cover and cook 5 minutes longer, until zucchini is crisp-tender. *Makes 4 servings.* For maintenance diet serving allow ¼ of the chicken and vegetables.

Per diet serving: 303 calories, 38 grams protein, 13 grams fat, 7 grams carbohydrate.

BREAKFAST

1 medium-sized orange (78)
2 slices cracked-wheat bread (132)
1 ounce Cheddar cheese (114)
Café au Lait: ½ cup hot skim milk
(43) with ½ cup strong coffee

LUNCH

Parisienne Ham Sandwich: 2 ounces
boiled ham (122); 1 tablespoon
butter or margarine (102); 1
teaspoon Dijon-style mustard
(4); 1 large slice French bread
(¼ of an 8-ounce loaf, 164)
1 cup tomato juice (46)
1 medium-sized apple (77)

DINNER

3½ ounces broiled flounder (202),
with *Sauce Verte (75)
* Pear-Creamed Spinach (78)
1 medium-sized unpeeled boiled
potato (105), with 1 teaspoon
butter or margarine (34)
½ cup vanilla ice cream (135) with
2 tablespoons chopped walnuts
(99)

TO EAT ANY TIME

3 whole-grain rye wafers (68),
spread with 1 tablespoon peanut
butter (94)
½ cup skim milk (43)

Sauce Verte

2 tablespoons mayonnaise
2 tablespoons plain low-fat yogurt
2 tablespoons lemon juice
½ teaspoon salt
⅛ teaspoon pepper

½ cup thin-sliced scallion or
green onion
1 cup fresh parsley sprigs, packed
tight to measure

Place ingredients in a blender; cover and blend at medium speed to a green puree, stopping machine if necessary to push down contents. Covered, sauce will keep several days in the refrigerator. *Makes ⅔ cup.* For maintenance diet serving allow 2 tablespoons.

Per diet serving: 75 calories, 1 gram protein, 6 grams fat, 6 grams carbohydrate.

Pear-Creamed Spinach

½ cup water
2 10-ounce packages frozen
  spinach
1 8-ounce can pears, drained

2 tablespoons liquid skim milk
½ teaspoon salt
⅛ teaspoon black pepper
⅛ teaspoon ground nutmeg

Bring water to a boil in a medium-sized saucepan. Add spinach, cover and cook over moderate heat 15 minutes. Drain. Place ½ the pears and 1 tablespoon of the milk in a blender; with a spoon transfer ½ the spinach to the blender. Cover and blend at medium speed to a smooth puree, stopping blender often to push down contents. Remove pureed spinach and repeat with remaining pears, milk and spinach. Return pureed spinach to saucepan with salt, pepper and nutmeg. Place over moderate heat and cook 5 minutes, stirring 2 or 3 times, just until hot. *Makes about 3 cups, or 4 servings.* For maintenance diet serving allow ¾ cup.

Per diet serving: 78 calories, 4 grams protein, 0 grams fat, 17 grams carbohydrate.

BREAKFAST

* Baked Orange Toast (309)
1 cup skim milk (86)

LUNCH

Tuna Salad Sandwich: 3 ounces
    oil-packed tuna, drained (166);
    1 tablespoon mayonnaise (101);
    1 tablespoon plain yogurt (9);
    2 slices rye bread (122)
1 small green pepper, seeded and
    cut in strips (16)
1 medium carrot, peeled and cut
    in strips (20)
1 slice fresh pineapple (58)
3 vanilla wafers (42)

DINNER

* Spiced Beef and Acorn Squash
    (210)
1 cup cooked green peas (114)
1 medium-sized cucumber, peeled
    and sliced (30), with Rich Herb
    Dressing (recipe on page 254, 73)
1 2¾-inch square gingerbread (175)
    with ½ cup unsweetened apple-
    sauce (50)

TO EAT ANY TIME

½ cup vanilla ice cream (135)
1 cup skim milk (86)

Baked Orange Toast

2 slices white bread
2 teaspoons butter or margarine

1 orange, peeled and sliced
2 teaspoons brown sugar

Heat oven to 350°F. Spread bread with butter. Arrange orange slices on bread slices; sprinkle with brown sugar. Bake on a baking sheet in lower third of oven or in a toaster-oven for 15 minutes. *Makes 1 maintenance diet serving.*

Per diet serving: 309 calories, 5 grams protein, 10 grams fat, 50 grams carbohydrate.

Spiced Beef and Acorn Squash

1 tablespoon vegetable oil
2 pounds beef round, cut into
  1-inch cubes
2 cups diced, peeled onion
1 teaspoon minced, peeled garlic
2 tablespoons catsup
1½ cups beef broth

2 3-inch cinnamon sticks
Few grains of crushed red pepper
  flakes
½ teaspoon salt
2 pounds unpeeled acorn squash,
  washed, seeded and cut into
  1½-inch chunks

In a Dutch oven or large saucepot heat oil over high heat; add ½ the meat and cook 5 minutes, stirring often, until well browned. Remove to a plate and repeat with remaining meat. Add onion and garlic to pot and reduce heat to moderate; cover and steam 2 minutes, until soft. Stir in catsup and cook 3 minutes longer, stirring often. Return beef to pot, add broth, cinnamon sticks and red pepper, increase heat and bring to a boil. Cover pot, reduce heat to moderately low and simmer gently 1 hour. Stir in salt, place squash on top of meat, cover and cook 30 minutes longer. *Makes 6 to 8 servings.* For maintenance diet serving allow ⅛ of the stew.

Per diet serving: 210 calories, 24 grams protein, 7 grams fat, 15 grams carbohydrate.

BREAKFAST

Sautéed Sausage and Apples: 2
  ounces bulk sausage (125), fried
  with 1 medium-sized sliced apple
  (77)
1 slice white bread, toasted (68),
  spread with 1 tablespoon butter
  or margarine (102) and 1 tablespoon orange marmalade (54)
1 cup skim milk (86)

LUNCH

Fresh Vegetable Salad: ½ small
  head iceberg lettuce (30); 1 green
  pepper, seeded and diced (16);
  1 medium-sized carrot, peeled
  and grated (30); 2 slices onion
  (6); Rich Herb Dressing (recipe
  on page 254, 73)
1 cup tomato juice (46)
2 whole-grain rye wafers (45)
10 unshelled roasted peanuts (105)
3 tablespoons raisins (80)

DINNER

* Cheese and Bacon Flan (311)
1 ½-inch-thick slice French bread,
  toasted (44)
1 cup brussels sprouts (55)
Mushroom Salad: 2 cups torn
  romaine lettuce leaves (20); 3
  large raw mushrooms, sliced (21);
  1 tablespoon vegetable oil (120);
  1 tablespoon freshly squeezed
  lemon juice (4)
1 medium-sized pear (90)

TO EAT ANY TIME

* Frozen Ricotta Pudding (201)

Cheese and Bacon Flan

4 ounces sliced Canadian-style
  bacon, cut into thin strips
1 large onion, peeled and sliced
  thin
¼ pound fresh mushrooms, sliced
  thin (1½ cups)
4 ounces coarsely grated
  Parmesan cheese (1 cup)

3 eggs
1½ cups liquid skim milk
½ teaspoon salt
¼ teaspoon ground nutmeg
⅛ teaspoon black pepper

Place bacon in a cold skillet over moderate heat until some of the fat
begins to melt; add onion, increase heat to moderately high and cook
5 minutes, stirring often, until onion begins to brown. Add mushrooms
and cook 2 minutes longer, stirring often. Heat oven to 450°F. Spread
bacon-onion mixture in the bottom of a 9-inch pie plate and sprinkle
with the cheese. Beat eggs with the remaining ingredients and pour over
cheese. Bake 15 minutes. Reduce heat to 350°F. and bake 20 minutes

longer, until pie is browned and center is firm. Place pie plate on a wire rack to cool for 10 minutes before cutting. Cut in wedges to serve. *Makes 4 servings.* For maintenance diet serving allow ¼ of the pie.

Per diet serving: 311 calories, 27 grams protein, 19 grams fat, 10 grams carbohydrate.

Frozen Ricotta Pudding

8 ounces ricotta cheese (1 cup)
1 teaspoon finely grated orange
   peel
1 tablespoon granulated sugar
Few grains of salt

1 tablespoon rum
¼ teaspoon vanilla extract
2 tablespoons dark seedless
   raisins

Combine ingredients in small bowl. Spoon into 2 paper cups or custard cups. Cover and freeze 2 hours, or until firm. *Makes 2 servings.* For maintenance diet serving allow 1 pudding.

Per diet serving: 201 calories, 17 grams protein, 5 grams fat, 17 grams carbohydrate.

BREAKFAST

½ grapefruit (40), with 1 teaspoon honey (22)
2 medium-sized eggs, soft-cooked (144)
1 English muffin (148), spread with 1 tablespoon butter or margarine (102)

LUNCH

Chicken Salad Sandwich: 3½ ounces diced, cooked chicken (166); 1 tablespoon mayonnaise (102); 2 tablespoons plain yogurt (18); 2 small stalks celery, diced (10); 2 large lettuce leaves (5); 2 slices pumpernickel bread (158)
4 radishes (5)
4 giant green olives (30)
½ small cucumber (15)
* Chocolate Shake (139)

DINNER

1 3-ounce cooked hamburger (4 ounces before cooking, 186)
Herbed Garlic Bread: 2 ½-inch-thick slices French bread, about 2 x 2½ inches (88), spread with 1 tablespoon butter or margarine (102), sprinkled with minced garlic and dried oregano, and toasted
* October Vegetable Pot (101)
* Honey-Steamed Apples (80), with ½ cup vanilla ice cream (135)

Chocolate Shake

1 cup liquid skim milk
1 tablespoon unsweetened cocoa
2 teaspoons granulated sugar

¼ teaspoon vanilla extract
1 cup ice cubes

Place ingredients in a blender; cover and blend at medium speed 20 seconds, until frothy. *Makes 1 maintenance diet serving.*

Per diet serving: 139 calories, 9 grams protein, 2 grams fat, 23 grams carbohydrate.

October Vegetable Pot

1½ pounds yellow squash, cut into 1-inch chunks (about 6 cups)
1 large green pepper, seeded and cut into thin strips
1 large onion, peeled and sliced thin

1 14½-ounce can sliced tomatoes
1 teaspoon minced, peeled garlic
¾ teaspoon salt
⅛ teaspoon black pepper
1 10-ounce package frozen cut okra, partially thawed

Combine all ingredients except okra in a Dutch oven or large saucepot. Using 2 large spoons, mix vegetables and seasonings. Place over high heat, and when liquid begins to bubble, cover pot, reduce heat to moderate and cook 10 minutes. Stir in okra and cook uncovered 10 minutes longer. *Makes 6 cups or 4 servings.* For maintenance diet serving allow 1½ cups.

Per diet serving: 101 calories, 5 grams protein, 1 gram fat, 22 grams carbohydrate.

Honey-Steamed Apples

4 small McIntosh apples, cored
1 stick cinnamon

½ cup water
4 teaspoons honey

Place apples in a medium-sized saucepan; add cinnamon stick, water and honey and bring to a boil over high heat. Cover, reduce heat to moderate and cook 15 minutes. Remove from heat and let cool slightly. Cover and refrigerate before serving. *Makes 4 servings.* For maintenance diet serving allow 1 apple.

Per diet serving: 80 calories, 0 grams protein, 0 grams fat, 20 grams carbohydrate.

BREAKFAST

1 cup orange juice (122)
1 cup bran flakes with raisins, with
    added thiamin and iron (145)
½ banana (50)
½ cup skim milk (43)
1 toasted corn muffin (130), with
    2 teaspoons butter or margarine
    (68)

LUNCH

1 3-ounce cooked lean hamburger
    (4 ounces before cooking, 186),
    on 1 hamburger roll (119) with
    1 tablespoon catsup (15)
Coleslaw, with Creamy Dill Dressing
    (recipe on page 261, 85)
Fresh Fruit Compote: ¼ grapefruit,
    sectioned (20); ½ medium-sized
    orange, sectioned (35); ¼ apple,
    diced (19); 10 seedless grapes
    (34)

DINNER

* Flounder with Crisp Clam
    Topping (187)
1 cup cooked Italian green beans
    (31), with 2 teaspoons butter or
    margarine (68)
4 large leaves escarole (10) with
    *Tomato Juice Dressing (49)
3 water-packed peach halves with
    4 tablespoons juice (84)
2 macaroons (134)

TO EAT ANY TIME

Raspberry Milk Shake: ½ cup skim
    milk (43), whipped in a blender
    with ½ cup frozen sweetened
    raspberries (121)

Flounder with Crisp Clam Topping

1 1-pound block frozen flounder
    or sole fillets, thawed
1 tablespoon lemon juice
¼ teaspoon salt
1 8-ounce can minced clams,
    drained and liquid reserved
2 slices white bread, crumbled

½ teaspoon minced, peeled garlic
¼ teaspoon dried oregano leaves
¼ cup chopped fresh parsley
2 tablespoons grated Parmesan
    cheese
1 egg

Separate fish fillets; rinse and pat dry. Arrange fillets in a single layer
in a shallow 6-x-9-inch baking dish; sprinkle with lemon juice and salt.
Place remaining ingredients, except clam liquid, in a bowl and blend
with a fork. Spread clam mixture evenly over fish and sprinkle with
¼ cup of the reserved clam liquid. Place in an unheated oven, turn
oven on to 400°F. and bake 20 to 25 minutes, until topping is lightly
browned and crisp. *Makes 4 servings.* For maintenance diet serving
allow ¼ of fish and topping.

Per diet serving: 187 calories, 26 grams protein, 5 grams fat, 8 grams carbohydrate.

Tomato Juice Dressing

1 cup tomato juice
2 tablespoons olive or vegetable
  oil
1 tablespoon wine vinegar

¼ teaspoon minced, peeled garlic
½ teaspoon dried basil leaves
¼ teaspoon salt
⅛ teaspoon black pepper

Combine ingredients in a small screw-top jar and shake to blend. Dressing will keep several days in the refrigerator. *Makes about 1¼ cups.* For maintenance diet serving allow 3 tablespoons.

Per diet serving: 49 calories, 0 grams protein, 5 grams fat, 2 grams carbohydrate.

To Binge or Not to Binge

"Actually, the best assurance of healthful eating for the rest of your life is the acceptance of the fact that you are at all times responsible for what you are eating. When you know that having a "mile-high" hamburger with French fries for lunch means you'll be able to eat only a plate of carrots for dinner, you may think twice about the size of the hamburger and the choice of French fries; it's *your* decision.

—Myron Winick, M.D.
Director, Institute of Human
  Nutrition, Columbia University,
  New York City
Consultant to *Redbook's*
  Wise Woman's Diet

BRUNCH

1 bagel (165), spread with 1 tablespoon butter or margarine (102)
Sardine Plate: 3 ounces sardines,
drained (187); ½ cup cherry
tomatoes (33); ¼ red onion,
peeled and sliced (10)
Prune and Apricot Compote: ⅓ cup
each unsweetened cooked dried
prunes (98) and apricots (160)

TO EAT ANY TIME

2 whole-grain rye wafers (45), spread
with 1 tablespoon peanut butter
(94)
½ small banana (50)
1 cup skim milk (86)

DINNER

* Swedish Lamb Stew (293)
1 cup cooked cracked-wheat pilaf or
bulgur (245)
Carrot Salad: 2 medium-sized
carrots, peeled and sliced (60);
1 scallion, sliced (9); 1½ tablespoon raisins (40); 2 tablespoons
plain yogurt (18)
* Grapefruit Ice (99)

Swedish Lamb Stew

4 pounds lamb neck, cut into
2-inch pieces
4 cups water
1 teaspoon salt
1 onion, peeled and quartered
4 whole cloves
½ teaspoon black peppercorns

2 tablespoons butter or margarine
3 tablespoons flour
2 egg yolks
2 tablespoons lemon juice
½ cup chopped fresh parsley
(optional)

In a large saucepot or Dutch oven bring lamb, water, salt, onion, cloves
and peppercorns to a boil over high heat. Reduce heat to moderate,
cover pot and simmer 1¼ hours, until meat is tender. Cover and refrigerate overnight or up to 3 days. About 30 minutes before serving,
remove saucepot from refrigerator and with a spoon lift off and discard
hard, white fat from jellied broth. Heat lamb in broth over moderate
heat until broth has melted. Place a colander or strainer over a large
bowl and strain meat and broth. With fingers separate the layers of
meat from the fat and bones. You will have about 4 cups of meat.
Discard fat, bones, onions and spices in strainer and reserve broth.

In the original saucepot melt butter over moderate heat; sprinkle with flour and cook, stirring constantly, until mixture is smooth and thick. Add lamb broth and bring to a boil, stirring constantly; simmer 5 minutes, until broth is smooth and thickened. In a small bowl beat egg yolks with lemon juice. Mix in about 3 tablespoons of the hot broth and then whisk this mixture into the remaining hot broth. Do not boil. Return boned meat to sauce for about 3 minutes, just until heated through. Remove pot from heat and serve stew very hot, sprinkled with parsley if desired. *Makes 6 servings.* For maintenance diet serving allow ⅙ of the stew.

Per diet serving: 293 calories, 29 grams protein, 17 grams fat, 4 grams carbohydrate.

Grapefruit Ice

1 6-ounce can unsweetened frozen   3 juice cans water
   grapefruit juice concentrate   2 tablespoons granulated sugar

Place ingredients in a blender; cover and blend at medium speed 20 seconds. Pour into a 9-inch square metal pan; cover and freeze several hours, until firm. Remove ice from freezer 15 minutes before serving. *Makes about 2 cups.* For maintenance diet serving allow ¾ cup.

Per diet serving: 99 calories, 1 gram protein, 0 grams fat, 23 grams carbohydrate.

Quality Control

Once you've reached your ideal weight and plan to keep it that way for life, it doesn't mean you can't ever go back to having some of your old favorites. Dr. Winick relates this story about a patient of his:

"I know a woman who limits the occasions she indulges in her fattening favorites by promising herself the very best available of that food. If she wants cheesecake, she will wait for a trip to a bakery that provides the absolutely quintessential cheesecake. And she will wait for the juiciest sirloin, the bluest Roquefort, the cheesiest pizza, the creamiest fudge. For her, quality is the great reward."

BRUNCH

* Strawberry–Orange Juice (118)
French Toast: 3 ½-inch-thick slices
   French bread, about 2 x 2½
   inches (132); rolled in 1 egg (82)
   beaten with ¼ cup skim milk
   (23); fried in 1 tablespoon butter
   or margarine (102) and sprinkled
   with 1 teaspoon sugar (15)

TO EAT ANY TIME

Salami Sandwich: 3 ounces salami
   (390); 2 slices rye bread (122)
1 large dill pickle (15)
¼ cup sweet and sour red cabbage,
   from a jar (31)
1 medium-sized apple (77)
½ cup skim milk (43)

DINNER

* Oven-Fried Chicken Legs (246)
* Turnips Rémoulade (110)
1 cup canned stewed tomatoes (60)
1 2-inch square corn bread (93)
½ cup vanilla ice cream (135)

Strawberry–Orange Juice

1 6-ounce can frozen orange
   juice concentrate
3 juice cans water

2 cups unsweetened frozen
   strawberries

Place ingredients in a blender; cover and blend at high speed 15 seconds, until smooth and foamy. *Makes about 4 cups.* For maintenance diet serving allow 1 cup.

Per diet serving: 118 calories, 2 grams protein, 0 grams fat, 28 grams carbohydrate.

Oven-Fried Chicken Legs

2 pounds chicken legs (about
  8 legs)
2 tablespoons butter or margarine
2 tablespoons lemon juice
1 teaspoon minced, peeled garlic

½ teaspoon salt
⅛ teaspoon black pepper
About ½ cup unseasoned dry
  bread crumbs

Heat oven to 375°F. Rinse chicken legs and pat dry with paper towels. In a small skillet melt butter over moderate heat. Mix in lemon juice, garlic, salt and pepper. Place bread crumbs on a plate. Dip each chicken leg in butter mixture and then roll in bread crumbs until evenly coated. Place on a lightly greased baking sheet and bake 1 hour, until brown and crisp. *Makes 4 servings.* For maintenance diet serving allow 2 legs. Wrap 1 leg and store in refrigerator for Monday lunch, Menu #23.

Per diet serving: 246 calories, 27 grams protein, 12 grams fat, 7 grams carbohydrate.

Turnips Rémoulade

3 tablespoons mayonnaise
3 tablespoons plain yogurt
1 tablespoon Dijon-style mustard
2 teaspoons lemon juice
½ teaspoon salt

⅛ teaspoon black pepper
1 pound white turnips, peeled and
  cut into matchstick pieces
  (about 4½ cups)

Combine all ingredients except turnips in a bowl. Add turnips and toss to mix. Serve at once or cover and refrigerate 2 to 3 hours. *Makes 4 servings.* For maintenance diet serving allow 1 cup.

Per diet serving: 110 calories, 1 gram protein, 9 grams fat, 7 grams carbohydrate.

BREAKFAST

1¼ cups fortified high-protein
cereal (107)
1 cup skim milk (86)
1 cup unsweetened frozen strawberries, thawed (55)
1 slice packaged date-nut cake (94),
with 1 1-inch cube cream cheese
(60) and 1 tablespoon apple
butter (37)

LUNCH

1 Oven-Fried Chicken Leg (reserved
from Menu #22, 123)
1 cup canned asparagus pieces (45)
1 clover leaf roll (83), with 1
tablespoon butter or margarine
(102)
1 cup tomato juice (46)
1 medium-sized pear (90)

DINNER

* Sole with White Wine and
Mushrooms (199)
1 cup cooked white rice (186)
Chilled Broccoli Salad: 2 large
spears cooked broccoli (90);
1 tablespoon vegetable oil (120);
1 tablespoon vinegar; ¼ hard-
cooked egg, chopped (20)
½ cup lemon sherbet (130)

TO EAT ANY TIME

10 seedless grapes (34)
1 cup skim milk (86)

Sole with White Wine and Mushrooms

1 1-pound block frozen sole or
flounder fillets, partially thawed
½ pound fresh mushrooms, left
whole if small, halved if large;
or 1 8-ounce can mushrooms,
drained
1 8-ounce bottle clam juice
¼ cup dry white wine

1 tablespoon butter or margarine
¼ cup minced scallion or green
onion
3 tablespoons flour
1 cup liquid skim milk
¼ teaspoon salt
⅛ teaspoon white pepper
½ teaspoon lemon juice

Cut fish into 1½-inch chunks; place in a 2-quart saucepot with the
mushrooms, clam juice and wine and bring to a boil over moderately
high heat. Reduce heat to moderate, cover and simmer gently 5
minutes. With a slotted spoon transfer fish and mushrooms to a plate.
Bring cooking liquid to a boil and boil fast until just 1 cup remains.

Meanwhile, in a small saucepan melt butter over moderate heat. Add
scallion and cook 5 minutes, stirring often, until soft; sprinkle with flour
and continue stirring 1 minute longer, until smooth. Whisk in the
reduced cooking liquid and bring to a boil over high heat, whisking
constantly until sauce is smooth and thick. Add milk, salt, pepper and

lemon juice and return to boiling. Boil sauce 4 minutes, whisking often. Carefully lift cooked fish and mushrooms into the sauce and heat 1 minute. Serve with rice. *Makes 3 servings.* For maintenance diet serving allow ¼ of the fish and sauce.

Per diet serving (rice not included): 199 calories, 25 grams protein, 4 grams fat, 9 grams carbohydrate.

Does Exercise = Eating More?

Doing nothing physically while dieting is simply not going to lead to a good weight loss. It's helping to hoard calories rather than burn them off. Dr. Jules Hirsch, one of *Redbook*'s Wise Woman's Diet consultants, says:

"The occasional dip in a neighbor's pool followed by a quick rubdown with a Turkish towel probably increases the appetite. But those who have incorporated more regular physical activity into their lives do not develop bigger appetites. Quite the reverse. They seem to be more able to cope with any adverse feelings there may be when on a diet. Exercise tends to elevate body temperature and heart rate, give a feeling of warmth and promote the expenditure of calories long after the exercise ends."

Hold That Line: How to Stay Thin 295

BREAKFAST

Pineapple-Grapefruit Juice: combine ½ cup each unsweetened pineapple juice (68) and unsweetened grapefruit juice (51)
Cheddar and Banana Sandwich: 1 ounce sharp Cheddar cheese (114); ½ banana, sliced (50); 1 tablespoon butter or margarine (102); 1 hard roll (155)

LUNCH

* "Deli" Chopped Liver (271)
4 whole-grain rye wafers (90)
¾ cup sauerkraut (31)
1 small tomato (20)
1 medium apple (77)

DINNER

* Quick Chicken Almondine (378)
½ cup cooked egg noodles (100)
½ cup green peas (57)
* Orange Freeze (141)

TO EAT ANY TIME

5 dried apricot halves (55)
½ cup skim milk (43)

"Deli" Chopped Liver

1 pound chicken livers
1 cup water
2 tablespoons vegetable oil
¾ cup diced, peeled onion

2 hard-cooked eggs, peeled and coarsely chopped
½ teaspoon salt
⅛ teaspoon black pepper

Rinse livers discarding any bits of fat that cling to them, and pat dry with paper towels. In a small saucepan bring livers and water to a boil over moderately high heat. Reduce heat to moderate and simmer gently 7 minutes, until livers are firm. With a slotted spoon remove livers to a bowl and reserve cooking liquid. In a small skillet heat oil over moderately high heat; add onion and cook about 10 minutes, stirring often, until onion begins to brown. Add onion and pan juices to livers and then add the hard-cooked eggs and ¼ cup of the reserved cooking liquid. Chop or mash the livers, onion and egg to a coarse paste. Mix in salt and pepper. *Makes 2 cups.* For maintenance diet serving allow ½ cup.

Per diet serving: 271 calories, 26 grams protein, 15 grams fat, 4 grams carbohydrate.

Quick Chicken Almondine

4 teaspoons soy sauce
2 teaspoons dry sherry wine
2 teaspoons cornstarch
1 1-pound boneless, skinless
  chicken breast, cut into ½-inch
  chunks
2 teaspoons vegetable oil

½ cup blanched slivered almonds
2 tablespoons vegetable oil
1 head iceberg lettuce, cut into
  ½-inch-wide strips (about 8
  cups)
1 teaspoon salt

Mix soy sauce, sherry and cornstarch in a small bowl; add chicken pieces and stir to coat. In a wok or large skillet heat the 2 teaspoons oil over moderately high heat; add almonds and stir-fry about 1 minute, until golden. Remove nuts to plate. Heat the 2 tablespoons of oil in the wok; add chicken and stir-fry 2 minutes. Add the lettuce and salt and toss gently for about 30 seconds longer, just until lettuce begins to wilt. Stir in almonds and serve from wok or skillet. *Makes 4 servings.* For maintenance diet serving allow ¼ of the chicken and vegetables.

Per diet serving: 378 calories, 36 grams protein, 22 grams fat, 8 grams carbohydrate.

Orange Freeze

1 6-ounce can frozen orange
  juice concentrate

3 juice cans liquid skim milk

Place orange juice concentrate and milk in a blender; cover and blend at medium speed about 10 seconds, until smooth. Pour into four 8-ounce paper cups, cover with foil and freeze several hours or overnight, until firm. To serve, tear cup away from frozen mixture and invert mold onto a serving plate. *Makes 4 servings.* For maintenance diet serving allow 1 Orange Freeze.

Per diet serving: 141 calories, 6 grams protein, 0 grams fat, 28 grams carbohydrate.

BREAKFAST

½ cup juice-packed pineapple
chunks (48)
1 cup cooked oatmeal (132), with
2 teaspoons butter or margarine
(68) and 2 teaspoons brown sugar
(34)
1 slice raisin bread, toasted (66),
with 1 tablespoon apple butter
(37)

LUNCH

Salmon Sandwich: 3 ounces canned
salmon, drained (188); ½ green
pepper, seeded and sliced (8); 1
tablespoon mayonnaise (102); 2
slices cracked-wheat bread (132)
½ cucumber, peeled and sliced (7)
1 cup cocktail vegetable juice (41)
½ cup unsweetened applesauce (50)

DINNER

* Chinese Spareribs (390)
* Succotash Salad (212)
1 cup cooked kale (44)
1 cup sliced fresh peaches (65)

TO EAT ANY TIME

10 unshelled roasted peanuts (105)
3 tablespoons raisins (78)

Chinese Spareribs

**3 pounds pork loin country-style
ribs**
Water

2 tablespoons honey
¼ cup soy sauce

With a sharp knife cut racks of ribs into individual ribs and remove any
visible fat around meat. Place ribs in a Dutch oven, cover with water,
add salt and bring to a boil over high heat; reduce heat to moderate,
cover and simmer 45 minutes, until ribs are tender when pierced with a
fork. Heat oven to 450°F. Drain ribs (discard cooking liquid) and pat
dry with paper towels. Arrange ribs on a foil-lined baking pan. In a small
bowl mix honey with soy sauce. Brush ribs with ½ the honey-soy sauce;
bake 15 minutes. Turn ribs, brush with the remaining sauce and bake
15 minutes longer, until ribs are brown and crisp. *Makes 6 servings.* For
maintenance diet serving allow ⅙ of the ribs.

Per diet serving: 390 calories, 20 grams protein, 31 grams fat, 6 grams carbohydrate.

Succotash Salad

1 10-ounce package frozen lima
 beans
2 tablespoons vegetable oil
2 tablespoons cider vinegar
¼ teaspoon salt
⅛ teaspoon black pepper

1 16-ounce can whole kernel corn,
 drained
1 large green pepper, seeded and
 diced
¼ cup diced, peeled red onion

Cook lima beans according to package directions, being careful not to overcook them. Meanwhile, combine oil, vinegar, salt and pepper in a mixing bowl. Add drained beans and remaining ingredients and toss gently to mix. Cover and refrigerate 1 hour or longer. Toss again before serving. *Makes 4 cups, or 4 servings.* For maintenance diet serving allow 1 cup.

Per diet serving: 212 calories, 7 grams protein, 8 grams fat, 32 grams carbohydrate.

BREAKFAST

1 cup plain low-fat yogurt (127),
    topped with 1 medium-sized pear
    (90) peeled and diced and 1
    tablespoon maple syrup (50)
1 bran muffin, toasted (120), with
    1 tablespoon butter or margarine
    (102)

LUNCH

3 ounces roast beef (161); 1 table-
    spoon sour cream (25); 1
    teaspoon horseradish
2 cups raw cauliflower florets (54),
    with Rich Herb Dressing (recipe
    on page 254, 73)
1 cup water-packed sour cherries
    (105)

DINNER

* Macaroni and Cheese with
    Tomatoes (374)
1 cup cooked green beans (31), with
    1 tablespoon butter or margarine
    (102)
Pickled Beets: 1 cup sliced cooked
    beets (55); 2 tablespoons cider
    vinegar; 1 tablespoon sugar (46)
½ cup mint-chocolate-chip ice
    cream (150)

TO EAT ANY TIME

½ cup skim milk (43)
3 gingersnaps (88)

Macaroni and Cheese with Tomatoes

1 16-ounce can whole peeled
    tomatoes, drained and diced,
    liquid reserved
Liquid skim milk
1 tablespoon butter or margarine
¼ cup flour
½ teaspoon dry mustard

¾ teaspoon salt
⅛ teaspoon black pepper
8 ounces sharp Cheddar cheese,
    coarsely grated (2 cups)
6 cups cooked macaroni (about
    3 cups uncooked)

Pour the reserved tomato liquid into a 1-quart measuring cup and add
enough skim milk to make 3 cups liquid. In a 2-quart rangetop-to-oven
casserole or Dutch oven melt butter over moderate heat; sprinkle with
flour and stir with a wooden spoon about 1 minute, until butter and
flour mixture is thickened. Stir in tomato-milk mixture, increase heat
and bring to a boil, whisking constantly, until thickened and smooth.
Add dry mustard, salt and pepper and simmer 4 minutes, whisking
often. Remove pan from heat, stir in 1½ cups of the cheese and continue stirring until cheese is melted and sauce is smooth. Add tomatoes
and macaroni and gently stir with 2 wooden spoons, taking care not
to mash macaroni. Sprinkle top with the remaining cheese. Heat oven
to 400°F. Place casserole in oven and bake 30 minutes, until top is
browned and bubbly. *Makes 4 servings.* For maintenance diet serving
allow 1½ cups.

Per diet serving: 374 calories, 19 grams protein, 13 grams fat, 45 grams carbohydrate.

BREAKFAST

½ cup orange juice (61)
1¼ cups fortified high-protein cereal (107)
1 cup skim milk (86)
1 English muffin (148), with 2 teaspoons butter or margarine (68)

LUNCH

Toasted Swiss Cheese Sandwich: 1 slice white bread, toasted (68); 1 ounce Swiss cheese (105)
½ cup canned vegetarian beans in tomato sauce (150)
1 cup watercress (19)
1 cup hot apple juice (117)

DINNER

* Crisp Oven-Fried Fish (192) with *Calorie-Cut Tartar Sauce (128)
Wilted Cabbage Salad: 1 tablespoon vegetable oil (120), heated with 1 tablespoon vinegar and salt and pepper; poured over 2 cups shredded cabbage (60)
1 cup canned pumpkin (81), heated with 2 teaspoons margarine (68)
* Cranberry Quartz (124)

TO EAT ANY TIME

1 square graham cracker (28)
¾ cup skim milk (65)

Crisp Oven-Fried Fish

1 1-pound block frozen fish fillets (such as cod, flounder or sole), partially thawed
1 egg
Salt
Few grains of white pepper

2 tablespoons flour
½ cup dry bread crumbs
¼ teaspoon salt
1 tablespoon vegetable oil
Calorie-Cut Tartar Sauce (recipe on page 302)

Heat oven to 500°F. With a cleaver or large knife cut block of fish into four 2-x-3-inch pieces. In a shallow bowl beat egg with ¼ teaspoon salt and the pepper. Coat fish with flour and tap off any excess. Dip fish into beaten egg and then in bread crumbs, turning to coat evenly on all sides. Sprinkle coated fish with a few grains of salt and place pieces 3 inches apart on a rack in a baking pan. Drizzle oil over each piece and bake 15 to 20 minutes, until crust is crisp and golden. Serve with Calorie-Cut Tartar Sauce. *Makes 3 or 4 servings.* For maintenance diet serving allow 1 piece of fish and 3 tablespoons sauce.

Per diet serving (without sauce): 192 calories, 21 grams protein, 6 grams fat, 10 grams carbohydrate.

Calorie-Cut Tartar Sauce

¼ cup mayonnaise
½ cup plain low-fat yogurt
2 tablespoons minced, peeled
  onion

2 tablespoons sweet pickle relish
¼ teaspoon salt

Combine ingredients in a small bowl. Covered, sauce will keep several days in the refrigerator. *Makes ¾ cup.* For maintenance diet serving allow 3 tablespoons sauce.

Per diet serving: 128 calories, 1 gram protein, 11 grams fat, 5 grams carbohydrate.

Cranberry Quartz

3 cups cranberry juice cocktail

Pour juice into an 8-inch square metal pan; cover with foil and freeze several hours until firm. Remove ice from freezer 15 minutes before serving to soften slightly before scraping into serving dishes. *Makes 4 servings.* For maintenance diet serving allow ¾ cup.

Per diet serving: 124 calories, 0 grams protein, 0 grams fat, 31 grams carbohydrate.

BRUNCH

English Compote: ½ medium
orange, sectioned (39); 3 canned
figs and 2 tablespoons syrup (84)
1 large egg, soft-cooked (82)
1 3 x 2 x ½ inch slice pork butt
(¼ pound, raw), broiled (164)
1 baking powder biscuit (129), with
2 teaspoons butter or margarine
(68)

TO EAT ANY TIME

1 cup canned split pea soup,
prepared with water (136)
1 slice pumpernickel bread (79),
spread with 2 tablespoons peanut
butter (188)
1 medium-sized pear (90)
1 cup skim milk (86)

DINNER

* Scalloped Beef and Potatoes (345)
Braised Celery with Mushrooms:
1 cup sliced celery (15); 4 large
fresh mushrooms, sliced (28);
braised in 2 tablespoons water
and ½ tablespoon butter or
margarine (51)
Spinach, Orange and Red Onion
Salad: 1 cup fresh spinach leaves
(14); ½ medium-sized orange,
sectioned (39); 2 slices red onion
(6); Tomato Juice Dressing
(recipe on page 289, 49)
* Black Bottom Pudding (114)

Scalloped Beef and Potatoes

1 tablespoon butter or margarine
1 cup chopped, peeled onion
½ teaspoon minced, peeled garlic
1 pound lean ground beef
½ teaspoon salt
⅛ teaspoon black pepper

1 pound unpeeled potatoes,
washed, dried and cut into ⅛-
inch-thick slices
1 cup beef broth
1 tablespoon butter or margarine

In a 2-quart rangetop-to-oven casserole heat 1 tablespoon butter over
moderate heat; add onion and garlic and cook 5 minutes, stirring often,
until onion is soft. Add beef, salt and pepper, increase heat to
moderately high and cook 5 minutes longer, stirring often, until meat
loses most of its pink color. Remove meat to a plate. Heat oven to
425°F. Arrange ⅓ of the potatoes in an even layer in the bottom of the
casserole and top with ½ the meat. Repeat with remaining potatoes and

meat, ending with a layer of potatoes on top. Pour broth over potatoes, dot with remaining tablespoon of butter and bring to a boil over high heat. When liquid in casserole begins to bubble, place in upper third of oven and bake 45 minutes, until potatoes are tender. *Makes 4 servings.* For maintenance diet serving allow ¼ of the casserole.

Per diet serving: 345 calories, 27 grams protein, 17 grams fat, 20 grams carbohydrate.

Black Bottom Pudding

1 package unflavored gelatin	2 tablespoons granulated sugar
2 cups liquid skim milk	½ teaspoon vanilla extract
2 tablespoons unsweetened cocoa	Few grains of salt

Sprinkle gelatin over ¼ cup milk in a small saucepan; stir over moderate heat about 5 minutes, until gelatin dissolves. Pour gelatin mixture into a blender; add cocoa, sugar, vanilla and salt. Cover and blend at medium speed about 10 seconds to mix. Add remaining milk and blend again until smooth. Pour into 3 small custard cups, cover and refrigerate until set. Pudding may be eaten from cup or turned out onto individual serving plates. *Makes 3 servings.* For maintenance diet serving allow 1 pudding.

Per diet serving: 114 calories, 3 grams protein, 2 grams fat, 18 grams carbohydrate.

CHAPTER NINE

Choose How You Lose: How to Personalize Redbook's Wise Woman's Diet

Because any successful diet, whether it's for weight loss or maintenance, should never deprive anyone of the sheer enjoyment of food, we've included this chapter on how to tailor the diet to your time, tastes and cooking interests.

As you will see, freedom to choose your own foods, make your own menus and perfect your own great balancing act does take time, know-how and responsibility. But in time, making the right choices will be second nature and you will be on your way to being truly knowledgeable about food.

If you have a real interest in food selection, like being a creative cook and want to learn how to make your own menus for weight loss or weight maintenance, know that it's challenging. At first you'll have to use the sample diet pattern on page 309 and do a little searching through the Nutrient-Source charts in this chapter. But once you've spent some time planning balanced diets that please your tastes, it will become easier. You'll be in charge of your eating habits, your weight control and your good health. We won't promise you that it's easy, but we will promise you that it's enormously rewarding.

Learning the Language

You may well know what a macronutrient is, what thiamin is, what a balanced menu means. If so, skip on to the next section. If you've doubts, skim these definitions:

Balanced Diet—A diet that includes a proper proportion of all the basic food groups: meat, fish, poultry and eggs; fruits; enriched or whole-grain breads and cereals; milk and milk products; fats and oils. These foods provide proteins, carbohydrates and fats as well as the vitamins and minerals necessary for good health.

Calorie—A measure of the energy (or heat) a food will give. Every food has a specific energy value, a caloric quantity.

Gram—A metric weight measure applied to protein, carbohydrate and fat. A gram of protein has 4 calories; a gram of carbohydrate, 4 calories; a gram of fat, 9 calories.

Macronutrients—Protein, carbohydrate and fat are the macronutrients; they carry in them the micronutrients, or vitamins and minerals. Few foods are all protein or all carbohydrate or all fat; most are a combination of two or all three.

Micronutrients—These are the vitamins—such as A, D, E, C, K, thiamin, riboflavin and niacin—and minerals—including calcium, iron, phosphorus, magnesium and a group called the trace minerals. The micronutrients provide no calories; they are found in the macronutrients and in leafy vegetables, which contain very little carbohydrate, protein or fat.

U.S. RDA's—United States Recommended Daily Allowances, published by the U.S. Food and Drug Administration. A panel of nutritionists, doctors and scientists working continually with nutrition research through the National Academy of Sciences has established recommended amounts for protein and a selected group of vitamins and minerals necessary for good health. The amounts of these nutrients in food are expressed in percentages of U.S. RDA's. (Turn to the Vitamin C Sources list on page 313 to see how these are shown.)

Understanding the Great Balancing Act

Our weight-loss diets of 1,200 calories were "balanced" according to these proportions recommended by our consultants:

Protein—25% of the daily calories, or 75 grams of protein
Carbohydrates—45% to 50% of the daily calories, or about 135 grams of carbohydrate
Fat—25% to 30% of the daily calories, or about 40 grams of fat

On a 1,200-calorie diet, getting 100% of the RDA's for the micronutrients can be difficult, particularly for iron and thiamin. To understand how the balancing works, turn back to one of your favorite diet menus and check the protein, carbohydrate and fat totals as well as the vitamin and mineral percentages in the Nutrient-Source charts that begin on page 310.

To understand how the balancing act works, turn back to the first week of diet menus in Chapter 1. In the Sunday menu you'll find that the mainly protein foods are eggs, bacon, milk and chicken; the mainly carbohydrate foods are the muffin, roll and cereal and the fat is largely from the butter-margarine allowance. The vitamin food sources are strawberries, orange juice, tomato; riboflavin sources, milk and chicken; niacin source, chicken; calcium source, milk; iron source, cereal. Notice that there is no good source of vitamin A on this day. This vitamin, along with vitamin D, is fat-soluble and can be stored in the body so you can backlog a healthy supply. On Monday's menu both the spinach and the broccoli give you that supply. Iron, the elusive mineral, is used by the body in proportion to its need; that's why it is good insurance to have some extra intake once a week and why you'll find liver on the menus. It's a remarkable source of both iron and vitamin A. So the balancing act doesn't go on just day-by-day but rather on a long-term basis.

When you're designing your own diet, it fortunately isn't necessary to calculate the amount of every vitamin and mineral. By choosing a wide variety of foods you can be reasonably sure of covering your needs adequately, if you don't ignore the foods that are good sources of essential nutrients.

If you've achieved your ideal weight and are now planning a weight-maintenance diet of 1,800 calories, be aware that the balance of macro-nutrients changes slightly:

Protein—15% to 20% of the daily calories, or 68 to 90 grams per day
Carbohydrate—40% to 50% of the daily calories, or 180 to 225 grams per day
Fat—35% to 40% of the daily calories, or 70 to 80 grams per day

You should continue to keep an eye on the listed vitamins and minerals in the Nutrient-Source charts to be sure you're getting as close to 100% of the RDA's as possible.

Variety--More Than the Spice of Life

You've heard of—maybe even tried—diets that call for the use of only certain food elements, such as protein. Such diets are not healthy because they do not provide the body with all the different nutrients it needs. If you take time to browse through the Nutrient-Source charts starting on page 310, you'll see for instance that there is no protein-rich source that is a good source of vitamin C, and that only cheeses of the protein foods are a good source of calcium. Only by selecting a variety of foods from all of the food groups is it possible to achieve a good healthy diet.

Start with a Pattern

The sample diet pattern that follows may look a little stark and uninteresting, but it's the easy way to plan a diet menu. Put it side by side with any of the diet menus in any of the previous chapters of this book and you'll discover how elements have been combined; for example, take the pot cheese serving from lunch, combine it with a high-vitamin-C fruit (tomato), substitute pasta for the bread serving and end up with lasagna for dinner. Make use of the Food Substitution List (starting on page 7). Using it in combination with the Sample Diet Pattern, make a game of seeing how many daily menus you can make that would taste good to you and suit the way you like to eat. That's exactly the way *Redbook*'s Food and Nutrition editors planned and tested and tasted the diet menus in this book. They juggled and borrowed and combined foods from the Sample Meal Pattern to balance out the protein-carbohydrate-fat ratio and checked to see that needed vitamins and minerals were adequately supplied. You should use the pattern only as a starting checklist, never as a curb to your creativity.

Dieting As You Like It

"If you plan your own diet on sound principles of nutrition and design your own menus according to your own food preferences, you will be starting with familiar eating patterns that will be easy to maintain after you've lost weight. Since diet patterns often involve profound psychological and sociocultural factors, a change of food habits may be resisted. A restricted diet pattern often results in boredom, which is a major stumbling block, as is the increased sense of deprivation and isolation the dieter may feel when she has to sit at the table and eat a food different from her family's. With careful planning this is not necessary on *Redbook*'s Wise Woman's Diet."

—George Christakis, M.D.
Chief of Nutrition Division, Dept.
of Epidemiology and Public
Health, University of Miami
School of Medicine
Consultant to *Redbook*'s
Wise Woman's Diet

A Sample Diet Pattern (for **1,200 Calories***)

BREAKFAST

Protein food; choose 1:
1 cup skim milk
1 egg (no more than 4 per week)
½ cup cottage cheese
2 ounces cooked or canned fish
Bread or cereal; choose 1:
1 slice bread
½ to ¾ cup cooked cereal
1 ounce (about ⅔ cup) ready-to-eat cereal
Fruit, preferably a fruit high in vitamin C (see Nutrient-Source List, page 313). Choose ½ cup juice or fruit or a normal portion, such as 1 small orange.

LUNCH

Protein food; choose 1:
3 ounces cooked fish, poultry or lean meat (about 4 ounces boneless raw)
4 ounces cottage or pot cheese
2 ounces hard cheese, such as Cheddar or Swiss (not more than twice a week)
Bread, enriched or whole grain: Choose 2 slices of any variety.
Vegetables: Choose 1 cup raw vegetable in the form of salad or about ½ cup any cooked vegetable. Use low-calorie dressing or lemon juice on salads.
Fruit, any kind: Choose ½ cup or a normal portion, such as 1 apple. Use fresh fruit, or frozen or canned packed in juice or water without added sugar.

DINNER

Protein food: Choose 3 ounces lean meat, poultry or fish.
Vegetables, raw or cooked: choose 2, using 1 cup raw or ½ cup cooked for a portion:
1 vegetable high in vitamin A (see Nutrient-Source List, page 313)
1 other vegetable
Bread or Potato or substitute: Choose 1 serving.
Fruit, any kind: Choose ½ cup or a normal portion, such as 1 small apple or other fresh fruit; or canned or frozen fruit packed in water or juice without added sugar.

TO EAT ANY TIME

Choose 2 cups skim milk, dried fruits, raw vegetables, a small peanut butter sandwich, according to calorie total.

ADDITIONAL

One tablespoon or 2 half-tablespoons vegetable oil or mayonnaise or butter or margarine to be used as desired.

---

* For an 1,800 calorie diet you can increase portions, have 3 tablespoons of the oil, mayonnaise or butter but the selection from groups remains the same.

Nutrient-Source Charts

The following charts give a variety of food sources for protein, carbo-hydrate and fat and the best sources for specific vitamins and minerals. The charts are, of course, to be used to provide a frequent check on exactly what percentage of the vitamins and minerals you're getting in your diet and just how many grams of protein or carbohydrate or fat you'll be eating in common foods. But, more than that, you might find some surprising good sources of nutrients that you never were aware of before. If, for example, you always thought of orange juice as *the* source of vitamin C, you'll find that strawberries, raw green pepper or a cup of brussels sprouts are equal or better. These charts are meant not to curb your food choices but to expand them.

PROTEINS

Protein-rich foods include both animal and some vegetable foods. The relatively small amount of protein in breads, cereals, pasta and other grain products is important since we eat these foods in relatively large amounts. Most vegetable sources of protein are best eaten in conjunction with an animal source, so that the proteins complement each other. For example, meat with rice or pasta, cereal with milk, or cooked dried beans with cheese. Select variety from these protein sources:

PROTEIN SOURCES	CALORIES	GRAMS OF PROTEIN
Meat		
Beef, cooked lean only, 3 ounces		
Ground round	186	23
Rib roast	205	24
Round roast	161	27
Sirloin steak	176	27
Flank steak	167	26
Lamb, cooked, 3 ounces		
Leg, lean only	158	24
Liver, cooked, 3 ounces	187–222	22–25
Pork, fresh, cooked, 3 ounces		
Roast, lean only	216	25
Veal, cooked, 2½ ounces		
Loin chop, lean only	199	22
Fish, cooked, 3 ounces		
Cod	89	20
Flounder	90	19
Haddock	90	21

PROTEIN SOURCES	CALORIES	GRAMS OF PROTEIN
Mackerel	180	25
Salmon, canned, drained	118	18
Sardines, canned, drained	187	22
Shrimp	99	21
Tuna, canned, drained, water-packed	117	26
Poultry, cooked, 3 ounces, boneless, no skin		
Chicken	115	20
Turkey	150	28
Cheese		
Cheddar, 1 ounce	113	7
Cottage, creamed, ¾ cup	179	23
Cottage, 99%-fat-free, ¾ cup	123	21
Parmesan, 1 ounce	132	12
Swiss, 1 ounce	105	8
Dried peas and beans; nuts		
Great Northern beans, cooked, drained, 1 cup	212	14
Red kidney beans, cooked, drained, 1 cup	218	14
Peanut butter, 2 tablespoons	188	8
Split peas, cooked, 1 cup	230	20
Eggs, 2 large	164	13
Milk		
Buttermilk, 1 cup	88	9
Liquid skim, 1 cup	86	9
Whole, 1 cup	160	9
Yogurt, low-fat, plain, 1 cup	144	12

CARBOHYDRATES

Carbohydrate foods—breads, cereals, grains, starchy vegetables such as potatoes and corn—are used by the body as a source of energy. Foods containing starches should not be omitted from a weight-loss diet, because they carry important vitamins, especially B vitamins, that are not found in great quantity in other foods. But limit sugar, a carbohydrate that supplies calories and little else. Get your sweetenings from fruits and naturally sweet foods that also supply nutrients. Plan to include three or four servings of carbohydrate foods in your diet menus and make sure that all grain products (breads, pasta, ready-to-eat or hot cereals) are either whole-grain (such as oatmeal or whole-wheat bread), made with enriched flour or fortified with B vitamins and iron. Since it is hard to get enough iron on a 1,200-calorie diet, you may want to use ready-to-eat cereals that are fortified with 45% to 100% of the U.S. RDA for iron and certain other vitamins.

CARBOHYDRATE SOURCES	CALORIES	GRAMS OF CARBOHYDRATE
Breads		
1 slice white, whole-wheat, cracked-wheat, rye, pumpernickel, French, Italian, raisin, one 6-inch corn tortilla	44–83	11–17
Cereals and grains		
Cereal, ready-to-eat, unsweetened, 1 ounce (1 cup)	105–110	18–24
Cornmeal or grits, cooked, ½ cup	62	13
Egg noodles, cooked, ½ cup	100	19
Farina, cooked, 1 cup	100	22
Macaroni or spaghetti, cooked, ½ cup	78	16
Oatmeal, cooked, ½ cup	66	11
Pancake, plain, wheat or buttermilk, 4-inch cake	61	9
Rice, cooked, ½ cup	93	20
Rye wafers, whole-grain, 2	45	10
Starchy vegetables		
Beans, peas or lentils, dried, cooked, 1 cup	212–230	14–20
Corn, cooked, ½ cup kernels	87	21
Green peas, cooked, ¾ cup	86	15
Lima beans, cooked, ½ cup	95	17
Plantain, 3 inches	78	21
Potato, baked, 4 inches long	145	33
Sweet potato or yam, 1 medium	161	37

FATS AND OILS

Fats and oils are the most concentrated sources of calories, and therefore of energy. They should not be eliminated from a weight-reduction diet—indeed, that would be almost impossible, since many animal protein foods such as meat contain fat. To help keep the cholesterol and saturated-fat content of the diet at a reasonably low level, choose salad oils that are high in polyunsaturates; these include safflower, sunflower and corn oil. You also may wish to select a highly polyunsaturated margarine; look for a label on which liquid corn, sunflower or safflower oil is listed first.

SOURCES OF FATS AND OILS	CALORIES	GRAMS OF FAT
Butter, margarine (fortified with vitamin A), mayonnaise, 1 tablespoon	100	12
Cream cheese, 1 ounce	106	10
Salad dressing, bottled, 1 tablespoon	65–100	6–11
Vegetable oil, 1 tablespoon	120	14

VITAMIN C

Vitamin C is not stored in the body, so it is important to try to include one or two good sources in your diet each day. Fortunately, many of the good sources are relatively low in calories.

VITAMIN C SOURCES	CALORIES	PERCENT OF U.S. RDA
Fruits		
Cantaloupe, ¼ medium	41	75
Grapefruit, ½	40	62
Grapefruit juice, unsweetened, from concentrate, ½ cup	51	78
Orange, 1 medium	78	110
Orange juice, from concentrate, ½ cup	61	100
Papaya, raw, cubed, 1 cup	55	170
Strawberries, hulled, 1 cup	55	147
Vegetables		
Broccoli, cooked, cut in ½-inch pieces, 1 cup	40	233
Brussels sprouts, cooked, 7 or 8, 1 cup	56	225
Cabbage, shredded, raw, 1 cup	17	55
Cauliflower, cooked, 1 cup florets	28	115
Collards, cooked, 1 cup	60	240
Kale, cooked, 1 cup	43	170
Peppers, green, raw, 1 medium	16	156
Spinach, cooked, 1 cup	41	83
Tomato, 1 small	20	70
Tomato juice, 1 cup	46	65

VITAMIN A

Vitamin A can be stored in the body, so it is not necessary to include it in the diet every day; try to use one of the vitamin-A-rich vegetables once a week.

VITAMIN A SOURCES	CALORIES	PERCENT OF U.S. RDA
Fruits		
Cantaloupe, ¼ medium	41	77
Papaya, raw, cubed, 1 cup	55	64
Vegetables		
Broccoli, cooked, cut in ½-inch pieces, 1 cup	40	78
Carrot, 1 medium	30	140
Collards, cooked, 1 cup	60	296
Kale, cooked, 1 cup	43	183
Mustard greens, cooked, 1 cup	32	162

VITAMIN A SOURCES	CALORIES	PERCENT OF U.S. RDA
Pumpkin, mashed, ½ cup	40	146
Spinach, cooked, 1 cup	41	292
Squash, winter, mashed, 1 cup	130	172
Sweet potato, 1 medium	161	185
Turnip greens, cooked, 1 cup	29	183
Other foods		
Eggs, 2 large	164	23
Liver, cooked, 3 ounces		
Beef	195	995
Calves'	222	510
Chicken	187	274

THIAMIN

Thiamin, a B vitamin, is somewhat hard to get in the proper quantity on a 1,200-calorie diet. Here the fortified cereals are a big help; so is pork.

THIAMIN SOURCES	CALORIES	PERCENT OF U.S. RDA
Meat		
Beef, cooked, lean only, 3 ounces		
Ground round	186	5
Flank steak	167	8
Lamb, cooked, 3 ounces		
Leg, lean only	158	21
Liver, cooked, 3 ounces	187–222	15
Pork, fresh, cooked, 3 ounces		
Roast, lean only	216	61
Cereals and grains		
Bread, whole-wheat or enriched white, 1 slice	61–76	4
Four-grain multivitamin-and-iron-supplement cereal, 1 ounce (1 cup)	110	100
Rice, enriched, cooked, ½ cup	93	6
Starchy vegetables		
Great Northern beans, cooked, drained, 1 cup	212	14
Potato, 1 baked, 4 inches long	145	10

RIBOFLAVIN

Riboflavin, another of the B vitamins, usually is not too difficult to get in amounts of sufficient quantity if you use milk and milk products. Here, as with so many of the micronutrients, liver is the glorious source.

RIBOFLAVIN SOURCES	CALORIES	PERCENT OF U.S. RDA
Meat		
Liver, cooked, 3 ounces	187–222	222
Poultry		
Chicken, cooked, 3 ounces, boneless, no skin	115	10
Milk		
Liquid skim, 1 cup	86	26
Cheese		
Cottage, 99%-fat-free, ¾ cup	123	33
Swiss, 1 ounce	105	6
Vegetables		
Greens, such as turnip, cooked, 1 cup	30–43	12
Mushrooms, raw, 1 cup	20	19

NIACIN

Niacin, also a B vitamin, is one of the reasons we use pork once a week in Wise Woman's Diet menus. (Pork is also a good thiamin source.)

NIACIN SOURCES	CALORIES	PERCENT OF U.S. RDA
Meat		
Beef, cooked, lean only, 3 ounces		
Ground round	186	19
Flank steak	167	20
Lamb, cooked, 3 ounces		
Leg, lean only	158	27
Pork, fresh, cooked, 3 ounces		
Roast, lean only	216	28
Poultry		
Chicken, cooked, 3 ounces, boneless, no skin	115	58
Vegetables		
Mushrooms, 1 cup, raw	20	15

CALCIUM

Calcium is important for maintaining healthy bones in adults. It's present in generous amounts in milk, milk products (but not butter) and cheese, which are also rich in phosphorus.

CALCIUM SOURCES	CALORIES	PERCENT OF U.S. RDA
Cheese		
American, 1 ounce	105	16
Cheddar, 1 ounce	113	21
Cottage, 99%-fat-free, ¾ cup	123	14
Parmesan, 1 ounce, grated	132	39
Swiss, 1 ounce	105	27
Milk		
Buttermilk, 1 cup	88	30
Liquid skim, 1 cup	88	30
Nonfat dry, ⅓ cup	87	30
Yogurt, low-fat, plain, 1 cup	144	29
Other foods		
Greens, such as turnip, cooked, 1 cup	30–43	20
Sardines, with skin and bones, canned, drained, 3 ounces	174	37

IRON

Iron is not naturally present in any significant quantity in many foods except liver. It is an essential part of hemoglobin, the protein substance that enables red blood cells to carry oxygen throughout the body, and is a nutrient needed especially by women of childbearing age.

IRON SOURCES	CALORIES	PERCENT OF U.S. RDA
Meat		
Beef, cooked, lean only, 3 ounces		
Ground round	186	16
Round roast	161	18
Liver, cooked, 3 ounces		
Beef, calves', chicken	187–222	41–67
Pork	205	137
Pork, fresh, cooked, lean only		
Roast, 3 ounces	216	18
Cereals and grains		
Bread, whole-wheat or enriched white, 1 slice	61–76	9
Bran flakes, with added thiamin and iron, 1 cup	106	68
Fortified farina, cooked, 1 cup	100	45

IRON SOURCES	CALORIES	PERCENT OF U.S. RDA
Fortified high-protein cereal, 1 ounce (1¼ cups)	107	25
Four-grain multivitamin-and-iron-supplement cereal, 1 ounce (1 cup)	110	100
Oatmeal, cooked, 1 cup	132	8
Rice, enriched, cooked, ½ cup	112	5
Eggs, 2 large	165	14
Fruits		
Apricots, dried, 5 halves	46	7
Prunes, dried, 4	66	9
Prune juice, ¼ cup	49	14
Raisins, ¼ cup	105	7
Vegetables		
Greens, such as turnip, cooked, 1 cup	30–43	10
Tomato juice, 1 cup	46	12

GOOD ALL-AROUND FRUITS AND VEGETABLES

The following fruits and vegetables are not extremely high in any specific vitamin or mineral, but they are relatively low in calories (check them on the Up-to-Date Calorie Counter that starts on page 319), and they provide a variety of needed nutrients: apples, artichokes, asparagus, bananas, beets, celery, cucumber, eggplant, green beans, lettuce, okra, peaches, pears, pineapple, plums, radishes, sauerkraut, summer or zucchini squash, turnips, wax beans. For relatively little calorie cost they can provide variety in satisfying quantities in your menus.

WATER

Although it is not a nutrient as such, water is essential to good health. Water carries the nutrients to the body cells and helps carry away waste products. Try to include five or six cups or glasses of liquid a day. These can be in the form of plain water, tea, coffee, club soda or bouillon. Your milk allowance counts as liquid too.

Also, you can toast your own newfound freedom with an adequate amount of water in some delightful drink recipes designed to get you over the hurdle of the cocktail hour. At zero calories, water is the lowest calorie drink of all and you can flavor it lightly with little cost in calories.

Diet Drinks for the Cocktail Hour

Raspberry Shrub

1 10-ounce package frozen
   raspberries, partially thawed
¼ cup white vinegar

¾ cup cold water
3 or 4 ice cubes

Put raspberries and vinegar in a blender; cover and blend at low speed 20 seconds. Strain to remove seeds. To serve, measure 3 tablespoons raspberry mixture into a tall glass, add water and ice cubes, and stir. *Makes enough raspberry syrup for about 5 drinks.* In a covered container syrup keeps well for a week in the refrigerator. (51 calories per drink)

Golden Apple

Ice cubes
½ cup unsweetened apple juice

½ cup club soda
Lemon slice

Fill stemmed wine glass with ice cubes. Add apple juice and club soda; drop in lemon slice and stir. *Makes 1 serving.* (60 calories per serving)

Lemon Bouillon

Ice cubes
½ cup canned condensed beef
   bouillon, undiluted

½ cup water
1 tablespoon lemon juice

Fill an Old-Fashioned glass with ice cubes. Add remaining ingredients and stir. *Makes 1 serving.* (28 calories per serving)

Ironade

Ice cubes
¼ cup unsweetened prune juice

¾ cup cold water
Large lemon wedge

Fill a stemmed wine glass with ice. Add prune juice and water. Squeeze juice from lemon wedge into glass, drop in wedge and stir. *Makes 1 serving.* (50 calories per serving and 14% of your daily iron requirement)

Sparkling Lime

Lime slice
2 ice cubes

Chilled club soda

Wipe lime slice around the inside of a stemmed wine glass. Drop in lime slice, add ice cubes and fill glass with club soda. *Makes 1 serving.* (0 calories)

Redbook's Up-to-Date Calorie Counter

A calorie counter is really the only way to keep a check on just exactly how many calories you're eating each day, but it also can serve another equally important purpose—making you aware of which foods have a high calorie count and which are surprisingly low. You may discover to your surprise that orange sherbet has more calories than chocolate ice milk, that alcoholic beverages do indeed have calories and that 1 cup of cooked broccoli has 40 calories but 1 cup of frozen broccoli in hollandaise sauce has nearly 200! Even if you just browse through these pages, you'll be raising your calorie consciousness and begin to weigh the worth of your food choices.

Most of the calorie figures in this chart are taken from Handbook #456, *Nutritive Values of American Foods*, published by the United States Department of Agriculture. It's a good idea to remember that the USDA figures are arrived at by taking averages (of many kinds of apple pie or doughnuts, of vegetables at different times of the year or meats from several sources, for example). A slice of devil's food cake may be more or less than 235 calories—it depends on the recipe.

The best source of calorie information on packaged foods and beverages is the label. Most breads and cereals carry nutrition labeling that tells you the calorie content per serving. These foods can vary widely; check the labels to make comparisons between brands and kinds and styles of breads, cereals, crackers and mixes. If you don't find calorie information on the label of your favorite products, write to the manufacturer and ask him to supply it.

*BEVERAGES

Ale, 8 fluid ounces	98
Beer, 12 fluid ounces	156
Brandy, 1 fluid ounce	73
Cider, sweet, 12 fluid ounces	174
Club soda, unsweetened	0

* All cup measures refer to standard measuring cups.

Cola-type carbonated beverage, 12 fluid ounces 144
Cocoa made with whole milk, 1 cup 257
Coffee, no cream or sugar, 1 cup 2
Fruit-flavored sodas and Tom Collins mix, 12 fluid ouces 163
Gin, rum, vodka, whiskey
    80 proof, 1½ fluid ounces 97
    90 proof, 1½ fluid ounces 110
    100 proof, 1½ fluid ounces 124
Ginger ale, 12 fluid ounces 113
Lemonade, 1 cup 107
Limeade, 1 cup 102
Root beer, 12 fluid ounces 152
Tea, no cream or sugar, 1 cup 1
Tonic or quinine water, 12 fluid ounces 113
Wines, dessert, 3½ fluid ounces 141
Wines, table, 3½ fluid ounces 87

BREADS AND CRACKERS

Bagel, 3-inch diameter 165
Biscuit, from mix, 2-inch diameter 91
Boston brown bread, ½ inch slice, 3 inches in diameter 95
Bread crumbs, dry, 1 cup 392
Butter cracker, 1 small round 15
Cloverleaf or pan roll (commercial), 1 average 84
Corn muffin, from mix, 2⅜-inch diameter 130
Cracked-wheat bread, 18 slices per pound, 1 slice 66
Date nut bread, canned, ½-inch slice 70
Doughnut, plain cake type, 2 ounces 227
English muffin, 1 average 148
Frankfurter or hamburger roll 119
French or Vienna bread, 4 ounces 329
French bread, ½-inch slice, 2 x 2½ inches 44
Graham cracker, 2½-inch square 28
Hard roll, 1 average 156
Italian bread, 4 ounces 313
Melba toast, plain, 1 rectangle 15
Melba toast, plain, 1 round 9
Muffin, 3-inch diameter 118
Pita bread, 4-inch diameter 80
Protein bread, 1 slice 45
Pumpernickel bread, 16 slices per pound, 1 slice 79
Raisin bread, 18 slices per pound, 1 slice 66
Rye bread, 18 slices per pound, 1 slice 61
Rye wafers, 2 45
Saltine, 2-inch square 12
Sprouted-rye bread, 18 slices per pound, 1 slice 65
Sprouted-wheat bread, 18 slices per pound, 1 slice 65
Tortilla, corn, 6-inch 63
Tortilla, flour, 8-inch 112
White bread, firm crumb, 20 slices per pound, 1 slice 63
White bread, soft crumb, 24 slices per pound, 1 slice 76
Whole-wheat bread, firm crumb, 20 slices per pound, 1 slice 61
Whole-wheat bread, soft crumb, 16 slices per pound, 1 slice 67

Roll, hoagie or submarine, 4½ ounces   392
Oyster cracker, 1 small   3

CEREALS AND GRAIN PRODUCTS

Barley, pearled, uncooked, 1 cup	697
Bran flakes, 1 cup	106
Bran flakes with raisins, 1 cup	144
Buckwheat groats, uncooked, 1 cup	317
Bulgur, uncooked, 1 cup	602
Corn flakes, 1 cup	110
Corn flakes, presweetened, 1 cup	154
Corn grits, cooked, 1 cup	125
Cornmeal, cooked, 1 cup	120
Cornmeal, uncooked, 1 cup	502
Corn, puffed, presweetened, 1 cup	115
Farina, cooked, 1 cup	100
Farina, uncooked, 1 cup	668
Granola, ½ cup	253–295
Macaroni, cooked, 1 cup	192
Macaroni, uncooked, 1 pound	1,674
Millet, uncooked, 1 cup	586
Noodles, cooked, 1 cup	200
Noodles, uncooked, 1 pound	1,760
Oatmeal or rolled oats, cooked, 1 cup	132
Oatmeal, uncooked, 1 cup	312
Oats, puffed, presweetened, 1 cup	139
Pancakes, 1 cake, 4-inch diameter	61
Pancakes, whole-wheat from mix, 1 cake, 4-inch diameter	83
Rice, brown, cooked, 1 cup	232
Rice, brown, uncooked, 1 cup	666
Rice, instant, cooked, 1 cup	180
Rice, puffed, 1 cup	60
Rice, converted white, cooked, 1 cup	186
Rice, converted white, uncooked, 1 cup	672
Rye flour, unsifted, 1 cup	364
Spaghetti, cooked, 1 cup	192
Spaghetti, uncooked, 1 pound	1,674
Waffle, 7-inch diameter	206
Wheat flakes, 1 cup	106
Wheat flour, cake, sifted, 1 cup	349
Wheat (white) flour, all-purpose, sifted, 1 cup	419
Wheat (white) flour, all-purpose, unsifted, 1 tablespoon	28
Wheat germ, toasted, ¼ cup	110
Wheat germ, toasted with honey, ¼ cup	110
Wheat, puffed, 1 cup	54
Wheat, shredded, plain, 1 large oblong biscuit	89
Whole-wheat flour, 1 cup	400
Wild rice, uncooked, 1 cup	565

CAKES, CANDY, COOKIES, ICE CREAM, PIES

Cakes

Angel food, from mix, 1/12 of 10-inch-diameter cake	161
Cupcakes, from mix, with chocolate icing, 2½-inch diameter	125

Devil's food, marble or yellow, from mix, without icing, 1/12 of
13-x-9-x-2-inch cake | 250–330
   with icing | 320–490
Gingerbread, from mix, 1/9 of 9-inch-square cake | 371
Pound cake, homemade, ½-inch slice | 142
Sponge cake, homemade, 1/12 of 10-inch-diameter cake | 196

Candy

Caramel candies, 1 ounce | 113
Chocolate, sweet milk, 1 ounce | 150
Chocolate, sweet milk, dietetic, 1 ounce | 168
Chocolate-coated peanuts, 1 ounce | 159
Fondant, uncoated mints, candy corn, 1 ounce | 103
Fudge, plain or chocolate, 1 ounce | 113
Gumdrops, 1 ounce | 98
Hard candy, 1 ounce | 109
Jelly beans, 1 ounce, about 10 small | 28
Marshmallows, 1 ounce | 90

Cookies

Brownies, with nuts, 1 1¾-inch square | 97
Chocolate chip, 1 cookie, 1¾-inch diameter | 25
Gingersnap, 1 cookie, 2-inch diameter | 29
Oatmeal, with raisins, 1 cookie, 2⅝-inch diameter | 59
Vanilla wafer, 1 cookie, 1¾-inch diameter | 18

Frozen desserts

Chocolate ice cream, ½ cup | 150
Ice milk, chocolate, ½ cup | 95
Ice milk, vanilla, ½ cup | 90
Low-fat frozen yogurt, vanilla, ½ cup | 90–120
Sherbet, orange, ½ cup | 135
Strawberry ice cream, ½ cup | 132
Vanilla ice cream, ½ cup | 135
Water ice, lime, ½ cup | 124

Pies (all portions are ⅛ of 9-inch pie)

Apple (2-crust) | 302
Blueberry (2-crust) | 286
Butterscotch (1-crust) | 304
Cherry (2-crust) | 308
Custard (1-crust) | 249
Lemon meringue (1-crust) | 268
Mincemeat (2-crust) | 320
Pecan (1-crust) | 431
Pumpkin (1-crust) | 241
Turnover, frozen, apple | 315

Puddings

Chocolate, ½ cup | 193
Custard, baked, 1 cup | 305
Gelatin dessert, sweetened, 1 cup | 142
Vanilla, ½ cup | 141

FATS, OILS AND SALAD DRESSINGS

Blue-cheese dressings, 1 tablespoon	76
Butter, regular, 1 tablespoon	102
Butter, whipped, 1 tablespoon	67
French dressing, low-fat, with artificial sweeteners, 1 tablespoon	15
French dressing, regular, 1 tablespoon	66
Lard, 1 tablespoon	117
Margarine, regular, 1 tablespoon	102
Margarine, soft in tub, 1 tablespoon	102
Margarine, whipped, 1 tablespoon	68
Mayonnaise, 1 tablespoon	102
Salad dressing, mayonnaise-type, 1 tablespoon	65
Thousand Island, 1 tablespoon	80
Vegetable shortening, 1 tablespoon	111
Vegetable oils: corn, cottonseed, olive, peanut, safflower, soybean, 1 tablespoon	120

FISH AND SHELLFISH

Cooked or canned

Bluefish, baked or broiled, 3 ounces	135
Clams, canned, solids and liquid, 7½–8 ounces	114
Clams, breaded and fried, 3½ ounces	179
Crab, cooked, meat only, 1 pound	422
Crabmeat, canned, flaked, ½ cup	86
Fish sticks, 4	200
Haddock, fried, 3 ounces	140
Mackerel, broiled, with butter or margarine, 3 ounces	201
Ocean perch, breaded, fried, 3 ounces	271
Salmon, canned, drained, 3 ounces	188
Sardines, drained, 3 ounces	187
Shad, baked, 3 ounces	171
Shrimp, breaded, fried, 3 ounces	192
Shrimp, canned, drained, ½ cup	74
Swordfish, broiled, with butter or margarine, 3 ounces	138
Tuna, oil-packed, drained, 3 ounces	166
Tuna, water-packed, undrained, 3 ounces	117

Uncooked

Bass, striped, flesh only, 1 pound	476
Bass, striped, whole, 1 pound	205
Bluefish, flesh only, 1 pound	531
Bluefish, whole, 1 pound	271
Clams, hard, meat only, 1 pound	363
Clams, soft, meat only, 1 pound	372
Cod, flesh only, 1 pound	354
Flatfish (flounder, sole), flesh only, 1 pound	358
Flatfish (flounder, sole) whole, 1 pound	118
Haddock, flesh only, 1 pound	358
Halibut, flesh only, 1 pound	454
Lobster, meat only, 1 pound	413
Lobster, whole, 1 pound	107
Mackerel, Atlantic, flesh only, 1 pound	866

Mackerel, Pacific, flesh only, 1 pound 721
Ocean perch, flesh only, 1 pound 399
Oysters, meat only, ½ cup 79
Oysters, meat only, 1 pound 299
Perch, white, flesh only, 1 pound 535
Perch, yellow, flesh only, 1 pound 413
Salmon, steak, with bone, 1 pound 886
Scallops, bay and sea, 1 pound 508
Shad, flesh only, 1 pound 912
Shrimp, flesh only, 1 pound 526
Shrimp, flesh only, 4 ounces 103
Shrimp, in shell, 1 pound 285
Trout, brook, whole, 1 pound 224

FRUITS AND FRUIT JUICES

Apple, dried rings, ½ cup 117
Apple, raw, 1 medium 77
Apple, raw, 1 small 61
Apple juice, fresh or canned, 1 cup 117
Applesauce, sweetened, 1 cup 232
Applesauce, unsweetened, 1 cup 143
Apricot nectar, 1 cup 144
Apricots, canned in heavy syrup, halves and syrup, ½ cup 111
Apricots, dried, cooked, unsweetened, 1 cup 213
Apricots, dried, uncooked, 10 small halves 91
Apricots, raw, 3 55
Avocado, mashed, ¼ cup 76
Avocado, ½ medium 132
Banana, 1 medium 101
Blackberries, raw, 1 cup 85
Blueberries, raw, 1 cup 41
Cantaloupe, ¼, medium 82
Cherries, red sour, water-packed, 1 cup 105
Cherries, sweet, raw, 1 cup 82
Cherries, sweet, raw, 1 pound 286
Cherries, sweet, water-packed, 1 cup 119
Cranberries, raw, 1 pound 200
Cranberry juice cocktail, 1 cup 164
Cranberry sauce, sweetened, 2 tablespoons 41
Dates, dried, pitted, cut up, ¼ cup 122
Figs, fresh, 3 small 96
Figs, fresh, 1 pound 360
Figs, dried, 1 medium 58
Fruit cocktail, canned in heavy syrup, 1 cup 194
Grapefruit, canned in heavy syrup, 1 cup 178
Grapefruit, pink or red, raw, ½ medium 40
Grapefruit, water-packed, 1 cup 73
Grapefruit juice, canned, sweetened, 1 cup 117
Grapefruit juice, canned, unsweetened or frozen, diluted, 1 cup 102
Grapefruit juice, fresh, 1 cup 98
Grape juice, bottled, 1 cup 167
Grape juice, frozen, diluted, 1 cup 133
Grapes, raw, 1 cup 89

Grapes, raw, slip skin, 1 pound	207
Grapes, raw, adherent skin, 1 pound	304
Honeydew, 1/10 of 7-inch melon	49
Kiwi fruit, 1 medium	52
Lemon juice, 1 tablespoon	3
Lime juice, fresh and canned, 1 tablespoon	4
Mango, 1 medium	152
Orange-flavored instant breakfast drink, diluted, 1 cup	110
Orange juice, canned, unsweetened or frozen, diluted, 1 cup	122
Orange juice, fresh, 1 cup	112
Orange, 1 medium	78
Papaya, ½ medium	60
Peach, raw, 1 medium	38
Peaches, canned in heavy syrup, 1 cup	200
Peaches, frozen, sweetened, 1 cup	220
Peaches, raw, sliced, 1 cup	65
Peaches, water-packed, 1 cup	76
Pear, raw, 1 medium	90
Pears, canned in heavy syrup, 1 cup	194
Pears, water-packed, 1 cup	78
Pineapple, canned in heavy syrup, crushed, 1 cup	189
Pineapple, canned in heavy syrup, sliced, 1 large or 2 small slices	78
Pineapple, canned in pineapple juice, chunks, 1 cup	96
Pineapple, raw, diced, 1 cup	81
Pineapple juice, canned, 1 cup	138
Plantain, raw, 3 inches	78
Plum, raw, 1 medium	32
Plums, canned in heavy syrup, 1 cup	214
Prune juice, canned, 1 cup	197
Prunes, dried, cooked, unsweetened, 1 cup	253
Prunes, dried, uncooked, 4 medium	66
Raisins, ¼ cup	105
Raspberries, frozen, sweetened, ½ cup	123
Raspberries, red, raw, 1 cup	70
Rhubarb, cooked with sugar, ½ cup	190
Strawberries, frozen, whole, sweetened, ½ cup	117
Strawberries, raw, unsweetened, 1 cup	55
Tangerine, 1 medium	40
Watermelon, slice, 10-inch diameter, 1 inch thick	111

MEATS

Beef, cooked

Corned, canned, 3 ounces	184
Corned beef hash, 3 ounces	154
Dried beef, 2 ounces	116
Hamburger patty, lean ground round, 3 ounces	186
Hamburger patty, regular ground beef, 3 ounces	235
Potpie, frozen, 8 ounces	558
Roast beef, with a relatively large amount of fat, such as rib, 3 ounces	379
Roast beef, with a relatively small amount of fat, such as heel of round, 3 ounces	161
Round roast, lean only, 3 ounces	161

Rump roast, lean and fat, 3 ounces	295
Rump roast, lean only, 3 ounces	177
Steak, broiled, flank, 3 ounces	167
Steak, broiled, round, lean and fat, 3 ounces	222
Steak, broiled, sirloin, lean and fat, 3 ounces	329
Steak, broiled, sirloin, lean only, 3 ounces	176
Tongue, boiled, 3 ounces	208

Beef, uncooked

Beef, chuck, good grade, lean and fat, 1 pound (with bone)	905
Beef, chuck, lean only, 1 pound	717
Club steak, good grade, lean and fat, 1 pound (with bone)	1,443
Club steak, lean, 1 pound	717
Corned, medium fat, 1 pound	1,329
Flank, lean, 1 pound	653
Hamburger, lean, 1 pound	812
Hamburger, regular, 1 pound	1,216
Porterhouse, choice grade, lean and fat, 1 pound (with bone)	1,603
Rib, choice grade, lean and fat, 1 pound (with bone)	1,673
Round, lean, 1 pound	612
Round, choice grade, lean and fat, 1 pound (with bone)	863
Rump, lean, 1 pound	640
Rump, good grade, lean and fat, 1 pound (with bone)	1,037
Sirloin, choice grade, lean and fat, 1 pound (with bone)	1,316
Tongue, canned, pickled, 1 pound	1,216
Tongue, whole, medium fat, 1 pound	714
T-bone, choice grade, lean and fat, 1 pound (with bone)	1,596

Kidneys

Beef, raw, 1 pound	588
Calf, raw, 1 pound	512
Lamb, raw, 1 pound	476

Lamb, cooked

Chop, lean and fat, 1 thick chop (cut 3 per pound)	341
Roast leg, lean and fat, 3 ounces	237
Roast leg, lean only, 3 ounces	158
Shoulder, roast or braised, fat and lean, 3 ounces	287

Lamb, uncooked

Leg, choice, 1 pound (with bone)	845
Leg, choice, 1 pound (without bone)	1,007
Loin, choice, 1 pound (with bone)	1,146
Rib, choice, 1 pound (with bone)	1,229
Shoulder, choice, 1 pound (with bone)	1,082
Shoulder, choice, 1 pound (without bone)	1,275

Liver

Beef, fried, 3 ounces	195
Beef and calves', uncooked, 1 pound	635
Calves', fried, 3 ounces	222

Pork, cooked

Bacon, broiled or fried, 2 slices	90
Bacon, Canadian-style, broiled or fried, 1 ounce	58

Chops, lean and fat, 1 3-ounce chop	216
Fresh roast, lean and fat, 3 ounces	308
Ham, boiled and sliced, 2 ounces	122
Ham, smoked, baked, 3 ounces	246
Liver, 3 ounces	205
Luncheon meat, canned, 2 ounces	167

Pork, uncooked

Bacon, sliced, 1 pound	3,016
Ham, lean only, 1 pound	984
Ham, 1 pound (with bone and skin)	1,188
Pork, Boston butt, lean and fat, 1 pound (with bone)	1,220
Pork, lean and fat, 1 pound	1,397
Pork, lean, 1 pound	789
Pork loin, 1 pound (with bone)	1,065
Pork, picnic, 1 pound (with bone)	1,083
Pork, spareribs, medium fat, 1 pound (with bone)	976

Pork, cured

Ham, Boston butt, 1 pound (no bone or skin)	1,320
Ham, Boston butt, medium fat, 1 pound (with bone)	1,227
Ham, lean, 1 pound	848
Ham, picnic, medium fat, 1 pound (with bone)	1,060
Ham, canned, 1 pound	875
Pork, salt, 1 pound (with skin)	3,410

Rabbit, cooked, lean and fat, 3 ounces	345

Sausages

Bologna, 4-inch diameter, 2 slices	134
Braunschweiger, 2-inch diameter 2 ¼-inch thick slices	64
Deviled ham, canned, 1 tablespoon	46
Frankfurter, cooked, 8 per pound, 1 frankfurter	176
Frankfurters, 1 pound	1,402
Pork links, cooked, 20 per pound, 2 links	144
Salami, cooked, 1 ounce	88
Salami, dry, 1 ounce	128
Vienna sausage, canned, 1	38

Veal, cooked

Cutlet, broiled, 3 ounces	185
Loin chop, lean only, 3 ounces	199
Roast, 3 ounces	229

Veal, uncooked

Chuck, 1 pound (without bone)	785
Loin, medium fat, 1 pound (with bone)	681
Round and rump, medium fat, 1 pound (with bone)	573
Round and rump, 1 pound (without bone)	744
Sweetbreads, calf, 3 ounces	143

MILK, EGGS AND CHEESE

Brie, 1 ounce	95
Buttermilk, 1% fat, 1 cup	88

Camembert, 1 ounce	85
Cheddar, 1 ounce	114
Cheddar, shredded, 1 cup	450
Cottage cheese, creamed, 1 ounce	30
Cottage cheese, creamed, 1 cup	217
Cottage cheese, uncreamed, 1 ounce	24
Cottage cheese, uncreamed, 1 cup	123
Cottage cheese, 99%-fat-free, 1 cup	164
Cream, dairy half-and-half, 1 tablespoon	20
Cream, heavy or whipping, 1 tablespoon	53
Cream, light or coffee, 1 tablespoon	29
Creamer, imitation, powdered, 1 teaspoon	11
Cream cheese, 1 ounce	106
Cream cheese, imitation, 1 ounce	50
Eggs, 1 egg white	19
Eggs, 1 egg yolk	63
Eggs, fried or scrambled with fat, 1 large	99
Eggs, raw, soft-cooked or poached, 1 large	82
Eggs, 1 medium	72
Feta cheese, 1 ounce	75
Gruyere cheese, 1 ounce	115
Milk, 1% fat, 1 cup	102
Milk, skim, 1 cup	86
Milk, nonfat dry, 1/3 cup	81
Milk, sweetened condensed, 1 tablespoon	61
Milk, undiluted evaporated, 1 tablespoon	21
Milk, undiluted evaporated, skim, 1 tablespoon	12
Milk, whole, 1 cup	157
Monterey Jack, 1 ounce	106
Mozzarella, 1 ounce	80
Mozzarella, part skim, 1 ounce	72
Muenster, 1 ounce	92
Parmesan, grated, 1 tablespoon	25
Process American cheese, 1 ounce	105
Process cheese food, 1 tablespoon	45
Process cheese spread, 1 ounce	82
Process Swiss cheese, 1 ounce	101
Roquefort or blue, 1 ounce	111
Sour cream, 1 tablespoon	26
Swiss, 1 ounce	107
Whipped topping, frozen, 1 tablespoon	14
Whipped topping, in pressurized can, 1 tablespoon	11
Yogurt, from whole milk, plain, 1 cup	139
Yogurt, plain, low-fat, 1 cup	144
Yogurt, low-fat, fruit-flavored, 1 cup	194–260

NUTS, SEEDS

Almonds, shelled, 1/4 cup	212
Brazil nuts, shelled and broken, 1/4 cup	229
Cashew nuts, 1/4 cup	196
Coconut, fresh, shredded, 1/4 cup	69
Coconut, dried, shredded, unsweetened, 1/4 cup	152
Coconut, dried, shredded, sweetened, 1/4 cup	126

Filberts, 10	87
Peanuts, unshelled, roasted, 4	42
Peanut butter, 1 tablespoon	94
Pecans, shelled, halves, ¼ cup	185
Pignolias (pine nuts), ¼ cup	168
Pistachios, shelled, 30 nuts	88
Pumpkin seeds, hulled, ¼ cup	194
Sesame seeds, hulled, ¼ cup	218
Sunflower seeds, hulled, ¼ cup	203
Walnuts, English, shelled, ¼ cup	196

POULTRY

Cooked

Chicken, ½ breast, fried	161
Chicken, broiled, meat only, 3 ounces	115
Chicken, canned, boneless, 3 ounces	140
Chicken, leg, fried	88
Chicken potpie, frozen, 8 ounces	533
Duck, roasted, meat only, 3 ounces	310
Turkey, roasted, light meat only, 3 ounces	150
Turkey, roasted, dark meat only, 3 ounces	173

Uncooked

Capon, ready to cook, 1 pound	937
Chicken, breasts, ready to cook, 1 pound	394
Chicken, drumsticks, ready to cook, 1 pound	313
Chicken, fryer, ready to cook, 1 pound	382
Chicken, hen, ready to cook, 1 pound	987
Chicken livers, 1 pound	585
Chicken, roaster, ready to cook, 1 pound	791
Chicken thighs, ready to cook, 1 pound	435
Chicken wings, ready to cook, 1 pound	325
Turkey, ready to cook, 1 pound	722

SAUCES

Barbecue sauce, ¼ cup	57
Beef gravy, canned, ¼ cup	44
Cheese sauce, ¼ cup	130
Chicken gravy, canned, ¼ cup	51
Hollandaise sauce, 1 tablespoon	45
Mushroom gravy, canned, ¼ cup	27
Soy sauce, 1 tablespoon	12
Tartar sauce, 1 tablespoon	74
Tomato sauce, ¼ cup	79
White sauce, medium, ¼ cup	107

*SOUPS (canned, condensed, ready to serve)

Bean soup with pork, 1 cup	168
Beef bouillon, broth and consommé, 1 cup	30
Beef-noodle soup, 1 cup	67

* Prepared with water, except where noted.

Borscht, 1 cup	72
Chicken-noodle soup, 1 cup	62
Clam chowder, 1 cup	81
Cream of chicken soup, prepared with milk, 1 cup	179
Cream of chicken soup, 1 cup	94
Cream of mushroom soup, prepared with milk, 1 cup	216
Cream of mushroom soup, 1 cup	134
Minestrone, 1 cup	105
Split-pea soup, 1 cup	145
Tomato soup, prepared with milk, 1 cup	173
Tomato soup, 1 cup	88
Turkey-noodle soup, 1 cup	79
Vegetable-beef soup, 1 cup	78
Vegetarian vegetable soup, 1 cup	78

SPREADS AND SUGARS

Chocolate syrup, thin, 1 fluid ounce	92
Honey, strained, 1 tablespoon	65
Jams, marmalades, preserves, 1 tablespoon	54
Jellies, 1 tablespoon	59
Molasses, 1 tablespoon	50
Syrup, maple, 1 tablespoon	50
Syrup, table blends, 1 tablespoon	59
Brown sugar, 1 tablespoon, packed to measure	51
Confectioners' sugar, 1 tablespoon	31
Granulated sugar, 1 tablespoon	46

*VEGETABLES AND VEGETABLE JUICES

Alfalfa sprouts, 2 ounces	23
Artichoke, globe, cooked, 1 large	44
Asparagus, canned, 1 cup	44
Asparagus, cooked, 4 medium spears	12
Asparagus, raw spears, 1 pound	118
Baked beans, canned, with pork, 1 cup	294
Bean sprouts, mung, uncooked, 1 cup	37
Bean sprouts, soy, cooked, 1 cup	48
Beets, canned, 1 cup	84
Beets, cooked, diced or sliced, 1 cup	54
Broccoli, chopped, yield from 10-ounce frozen package	82
Broccoli, cooked, 1 cup	40
Broccoli, raw stalks, 1 pound	145
Broccoli, stalks, frozen in hollandaise sauce, 1 cup	200
Brussels sprouts, cooked, 1 cup	56
Brussels sprouts, raw, 1 pound	204
Cabbage, green, cooked, 1 cup	30
Cabbage, green and savoy, raw, coarsely shredded, 1 cup	17
Cabbage, green, raw, 1 pound	109
Cabbage, red, raw, coarsely shredded, 1 cup	22
Cabbage, red, raw, 1 pound	141
Carrot, raw, 1 medium	30

* Except where noted, vegetable caloric counts do not include added butter or dressing of any kind.

Carrots, cooked, sliced, 1 cup	48
Carrots, raw, grated, 1 cup	46
Carrots, raw, 1 pound, without tops	212
Cauliflower, cooked, 1 cup	28
Cauliflower, raw, trimmed, 1 pound	122
Celery, raw, diced, 1 cup	20
Celery, raw, 8-inch stalk	7
Chard, Swiss, raw, 1 pound	113
Chinese cabbage, cooked, 1 cup	16
Chinese cabbage, raw, 1 cup	10
Chinese cabbage, raw, 1 pound	64
Collards, cooked, 1 cup	60
Corn, canned, 1 cup	174
Corn, canned, cream-style, 1 cup	210
Corn, 5-inch ear, cooked	70
Cucumber, raw, 6 slices	4
Cucumber, raw, pared, 1 medium	35
Dandelion greens, cooked, 1 cup	60
Dandelion greens, raw, trimmed, 1 pound	204
Eggplant, cooked, drained, diced, ½ cup	19
Eggplant, raw, 1 pound	92
Endive, raw, 1 cup	10
Endive, raw, 1 pound	91
Escarole, raw, 1 pound	91
Garlic clove	4
Green beans, raw, 1 pound	145
Green beans and wax beans, canned, 1 cup	45
Green beans and wax beans, cooked, 1 cup	31
Green beans, frozen, with toasted almonds, 1 cup	44
Kale, cooked, 1 cup	44
Kale, raw, leaves without stems and midribs, 1 pound	240
Kohlrabi, raw, diced, 1 cup	41
Leeks, raw, 1 pound	123
Lettuce, Boston, raw, 1 head	23
Lettuce, iceberg, raw, 2 large leaves	6
Lettuce, iceberg, ¼ head, wedge	14
Lima beans, cooked, 1 cup	189
Mushrooms, canned, 1 cup	20
Mushrooms, raw, sliced, 1 cup	20
Mushrooms, raw, whole, 1 pound	127
Mustard greens, cooked, 1 cup	32
Mustard greens, raw, 1 pound	141
Okra cooked, 10 pods	31
Okra, raw, 1 pound	163
Onion, dehydrated flakes, 1 tablespoon	15
Onion, raw, 1 medium	40
Onion, raw, chopped, 1 cup	65
Onion, raw, large, 1 slice	3
Onion rings, French-fried, frozen, 2 ounces	166
Onions, cooked, 1 cup	61
Onions, frozen in cream-style sauce, 1 cup	254
Onions, green, raw, 1 cup	36
Parsley, raw, chopped, 1 tablespoon	2
Parsnips, cooked, diced, 1 cup	102

Parsnips, raw, 1 pound	293
Peas, green, canned, 1 cup	164
Peas, green, cooked, 1 cup	114
Peas, green, frozen with sautéed mushrooms, 1 cup	134
Peas, green, raw, in pod, 1 pound	145
Pepper, sweet green, raw or cooked, 1 medium	16
Peppers, green, raw, 1 pound	100
Peppers, red, raw, 1 pound	141
Pimiento, canned, 1 medium	11
Potato, baked, 4 inches long	145
Potato, peeled, boiled, 1 medium	104
Potatoes, raw, with skins, 1 pound	259
Potatoes, French-fried, frozen, 10 3½-inch pieces	111
Potatoes, mashed with milk, ½ cup	68
Potatoes, mashed with milk and butter, ½ cup	98
Pumpkin, canned, 1 cup	81
Radishes, raw, 10 small	8
Sauerkraut, canned, drained, 1 cup	42
Spinach, cooked, 1 cup	41
Spinach, raw, packaged, 1 pound	118
Spinach, raw, untrimmed, 1 pound	85
Squash, summer, cooked, 1 cup	27
Squash, summer varieties, raw, 1 pound	86
Squash, winter, cooked, 1 cup	130
Squash, winter varieties, raw, 1 pound	180
Sweet potato, baked or boiled, unpeeled, 1 medium (5 ounces)	161
Sweet potato, candied, 4 ounces	190
Sweet potatoes, canned, 1 cup	216
Sweet potatoes, raw, 1 pound	375
Tomato, raw, 1 medium	20
Tomato juice, canned, 1 cup	46
Tomatoes, canned or cooked, 1 cup	63
Tomatoes, raw, 1 pound	91
Turnip greens, cooked, 1 cup	29
Turnip greens, raw, untrimmed, 1 pound	127
Turnips, cooked, 1 cup	36
Turnips, raw, 1 pound	117
Vegetable juice, canned, 1 cup	41
Water chestnuts, 4	20
Watercress, 10 sprigs	7
Yams, raw, 1 pound	394

DRIED VEGETABLES

Chick-peas, cooked, 1 cup	272
Chick-peas, uncooked, 1 pound	1,633
Great Northern beans, cooked, 1 cup	212
Kidney beans, cooked, 1 cup	218
Kidney beans, uncooked, 1 pound	1,556
Lentils, cooked, 1 cup	212
Lentils, uncooked, 1 pound	1,542
Lima beans, cooked, 1 cup	189
Lima beans, uncooked, 1 pound	1,565
Navy (pea) beans, cooked, 1 cup	224

Navy beans, uncooked, 1 pound	1,542
Soybeans, cooked, 1 cup	234
Soybeans, uncooked, 1 pound	1,828
Soy flour, defatted, 1 cup (5 ounces)	326
Soy flour, full-fat, 1 cup (2½ ounces)	295
Split peas, cooked, 1 cup	230
Split peas, uncooked, 1 pound	1,579

MISCELLANEOUS

Arrowroot, 1 tablespoon	29
Bouillon cube	5
Carob flour, 1 tablespoon	14
Catsup, tomato, 1 tablespoon	15
Chili sauce, 1 tablespoon	16
Chocolate, semisweet, small pieces, 1 cup	862
Chocolate, unsweetened, 1 ounce	143
Cocoa, unsweetened, 1 tablespoon	14
Corn chips, 1 ounce	161
Cornstarch, 1 tablespoon	29
Enchilada, 1 frozen	130–371
Gelatin, plain, 1 envelope	23
Miso paste, 4 ounces	194
Mustard, prepared, 1 teaspoon	4
Olives, green, 4 medium	13
Olives, ripe black, 3 small	18
Pickle relish, 1 tablespoon	21
Pickles, dill, 1 large	15
Pickles, sweet, 1 small	20
Pizza, with cheese, ⅛ of 14-inch pie	153
Popcorn, popped, with oil and salt, 1 cup	41
Potato chips, 10 medium	114
Pretzels, small sticks, 10	12
Pretzels, thin twist, 1	23
Rice flour, 1 tablespoon	30
Tofu, 2½ x 2¾ x 1 inch	86
Vinegar, 1 tablespoon	trace
Worcestershire sauce, 1 teaspoon	4

Index

with per-serving calorie counts

Pita (*continued*)
  Salad Sandwiches, 230 (108 cal.)
Pizza
  Pita, 209 (336 cal.)
  Polenta, 236 (299 cal.)
Poached Pears in Red Wine, 99 (54 cal.)
Polenta Pizza, 236 (299 cal.)
Pork
  and Broccoli Stir-Fry, 81 (314 cal.)
  caloric value of, 326–27
  -Chop and Potato Casserole, 252 (332 cal.)
  Ham and Rice Salad, 94 (405 cal.)
  Loin Roast Teriyaki, 171 (270 cal.)
  Pan-Broiled Pork Chops, 200 (151 cal.)
  Skillet Pork Chops with Apricot Sauce, 72 (248 cal.)
  Stroganoff, 43 (221 cal.)
  See also Bacon; Ribs
Portuguese Baked Fish, 82 (151 cal.)
Pot Roast in Wine, 49 (255 cal.)
Potato(es)
  Brown-Baked, 197 (132 cal.)
  Creamy Potato Salad, 185 (182 cal.)
  Hot Potato and Sauerkraut Salad, 255 (147 cal.)
  Liver and Onion Potato-Topped Pie, 267 (473 cal.)
  New Potatoes Vinaigrette, 35 (132 cal.)
  Pork Chop and Potato Casserole, 252 (332 cal.)
  Sardines with Potatoes Vinaigrette to Go, 117 (286 cal.)
  Scalloped Beef and, 303 (345 cal.)
  substitutes for, 7
  See also "French fries"
Poultry
  caloric value of, 329

Roast Stuffed Capon, 156 (404 cal.)
Roast Turkey Drumsticks, 97 (220 cal.)
Tarragon Baked Cornish Game Hens, 86 (196 cal.)
See also Chicken
Proteins
  chart on sources of, 310–11
  in weight-maintenance diet, 307
Prunes, Spiced, 47 (105 cal.)
Pudding
  Black Bottom, 304 (114 cal.)
  Breakfast Bread, 170 (201 cal.)
  caloric value of, 322
  Chocolate, 64 (110 cal.)
  Creamy Peach, 131 (72 cal.)
  Frozen Ricotta, 285 (201 cal.)
  Snow, 165 (120 cal.)

Quick Chicken Almondine, 297 (378 cal.)
Quick Clam-Vegetable Chowder, 104 (140 cal.)
Quick Shrimp Creole, 110 (138 cal.)

Raspberry(ies)
  Christiana Sutor's Steamed Pears with Raspberry Sauce, 158 (131 cal.)
  Rhubarb, 196 (133 cal.)
  Sauce, 129 (15 cal.)
  Shrub, 318 (51 cal.)
Ratatouille, 30 (66 cal.)
Recipe use, tips on, 5–6
Red Cabbage
  Crisp, 220 (111 cal.)
  German-Style, 50 (39 cal.)
Relatively Russian Dressing, 121 (86 cal.)
Rhubarb
  Orange-Rhubarb Dessert, 110 (128 cal.)
  Raspberry, 196 (133 cal.)
Riboflavin, chart on sources of, 315
Ribs
  Barbecued, 184 (248 cal.)

Salad Dressing(s) (continued)
  Low-Calorie Tomato, 179 (12
    cal.)
  Piquant, 50 (11 cal.)
  Relatively Russian, 121 (86
    cal.)
  Rich Herb, 254 (73 cal.)
  Tomato Juice, 289 (49 cal.)
  White Wine, 68 (36 cal.)
  See also Vinaigrette
Salmon
  -Dill Salad, 276 (179 cal.)
  Steamed Eggs with, 126 (179
    cal.)
Salsa, Mexican, 70 (12 cal.)
Sample diet pattern, 309
Sandwich(es)
  Antipasto Salad, 134 (277 cal.)
  Chili-Beef Tacos, 217 (231 cal.)
  Crispy Salad Tortillas, 138 (410
    cal.)
  Double Cheese Toast, 28 (190
    cal.)
  Garden Grill Open, 65 (371
    cal.)
  Hot Tomato-Cheese Rolls, 196
    (319 cal.)
  Pita Pizza, 209 (336 cal.)
  Pita Salad, 230 (108 cal.)
  Very Cheesy Toast, 247 (214
    cal.)
  See also individual menus
    throughout this book
Sardine(s)
  with Potatoes Vinaigrette to
    Go, 117 (286 cal.)
  Spread, 214 (116 cal.)
Sauce(s)
  caloric value of, 329
  Calorie-Cut Tartar, 302 (128
    cal.)
  Chocolate, 161 (29 cal.)
  Cool Cucumber, 25 (61 cal.)
  Custard, 165 (42 cal.)
  Easy Meat, 240 (207 cal.)
  Indian Mint, 270 (26 cal.)
  Mexican Salsa, 70 (12 cal.)
  Minted Cucumber, 154 (49 cal.)
  Mock Hollandaise, 38 (21 cal.)

  Orange, 73 (16 cal.)
  Raspberry, 129 (15 cal.)
  Verte, 280 (75 cal.)
Sauerbraten with Tangy Vegetable
  Sauce, 226 (197 cal.)
Sautéed Mushrooms, 160 (66 cal.)
Saving tips, 93
Savory Braised Beef, 88 (297 cal.)
Scalloped Beef and Potatoes, 303
  (345 cal.)
Scrambled Eggs with Green
  Pepper, 184 (277 cal.)
Seasoup, 176 (282 cal.)
Seeds, see Nuts and seeds
Self-knowledge and behavior
  modification, 54
Senegalese Soup, 150 (87 cal.)
Shake(s)
  Berry-Buttermilk, 40 (145 cal.)
  Blueberry Breakfast, 259 (187
    cal.)
  Chocolate, 286 (139 cal.)
  Chocolate-Banana, 101 (124
    cal.)
  Coffee, 224 (154 cal.)
  Fruit Salad, 188 (259 cal.)
  Icy Chocolate Milk, 139 (117
    cal.)
  Peachy Buttermilk, 197 (160
    cal.)
  Strawberry, 202 (156)
  Strawberry-Pear, 69 (136 cal.)
Shellfish, caloric value of, 323–24
Sherbet, Tangerine-Buttermilk,
  155 (139 cal.)
Sherried Chicken Livers, 124 (285
    cal.)
Shrimp
  Chow Mein, 248 (226 cal.)
  Egg Foo Young, 17 (373 cal.)
  and Poached Fish Salad, 29
    (250 cal.)
  Quick Shrimp Creole, 110 (138
    cal.)
  Salad, 136 (224 cal.)
Skewered Chicken Livers, 40 (274
    cal.)
Skillet Pork Chops with Apricot
  Sauce, 72 (248 cal.)